Anne Hamet

Using

Microsoft Excel 97

Using Microsoft Excel 97

Josh Nossiter

Using Microsoft Excel 97

Library of Congress Catalog No.: 96-70776

ISBN: 0-7897-0955-4

98 97 96 6 5 4 3 2 1

Interpretation of the printing code: the rightmost double-digit number is the year of the book's printing; the rightmost single-digit number, the number of the book's printing. For example, a printing code of 96-1 shows that the first printing of the book occurred in 1996.

Screen reproductions in this book were created using Collage Plus from Inner Media, Inc., Hollis, NH.

Composed in *ITC Century*, *ITC Highlander*, and *MCPdigital* by Que Corporation.

Credits

President
Roland Elgey

Publishing Director
Lynn E. Zingraf

Editorial Services Director
Elizabeth Keaffaber

Managing Editor
Michael Cunningham

Director of Marketing
Lynn E. Zingraf

Acquisitions Editor
Martha O'Sullivan

Product Development Specialist
Lorna Gentry

Production Editor
Theresa Mathias

Assistant Product Marketing Manager
Christy M. Miller

Strategic Marketing Manager
Barry Pruett

Technical Editor
Cynthia A. O'Brien

Technical Support Specialist
Nadeem Muhammed

Software Relations Coordinator
Patty Brooks

Editorial Assistant
Ginny Stoller

Book Designer
Barbara Kordesh

Cover Designer
Dan Armstrong

Production Team
Jason Carr
DiMonique Ford
Jessica Ford
Brad Lenser
Steph Mineart
Darlena Murray
Paul Wilson

Indexer
Debra Myers

For Jason, an excellent fellow in every way.

About the Author

Joshua C. Nossiter received a B.A. in English from Dartmouth College and an M.B.A. in Finance from Columbia University. He has worked in broadcasting in California, and in public finance on Wall Street. His interest in computers dates back to the 1970s, when he first began using the Dartmouth mainframe system. Josh now lives in San Francisco with his two children, where he writes about software, among other things.

Acknowledgments

A book like this is a collaborative effort, and many skilled hands contribute to its design and content. Criticisms can be laid at the author's door, but all praise is due to the team responsible for *Using Microsoft Excel 97.* Among the praiseworthy:

Martha O'Sullivan, Acquisitions Editor, uses two secret weapons to ensure that her impossible deadlines are always met: sheer kindness and timely encouragement. They're infallible.

Lorna Gentry, Product Development Specialist, transformed what was a mass (not to say mess) of bits and bytes into the useful object now before you, and she did it with unfailing enthusiasm and good humor.

Theresa Mathias, Production Editor, was both tireless and thorough in her insistence on clear prose and lucid explanations.

Cynthia O'Brien, Technical Editor, helped ensure accuracy and made valuable suggestions.

We'd Like to Hear from You!

As part of our continuing effort to produce books of the highest possible quality, Que would like to hear your comments. To stay competitive, we *really* want you, as a computer book reader and user, to let us know what you like or dislike most about this book or other Que products.

You can mail comments, ideas, or suggestions for improving future editions to the address below, or send us a fax at (317) 581-4663. For the online inclined, Macmillan Computer Publishing has a forum on CompuServe (type **GO QUEBOOKS** at any prompt) through which our staff and authors are available for questions and comments. The address of our Internet site is **http://www.mcp.com/que** (World Wide Web).

In addition to exploring our forum, please feel free to contact me personally to discuss your opinions of this book: I'm **75703,3251** on CompuServe, and I'm **lgentry@que.mcp.com** on the Internet.

Thanks in advance—your comments will help us to continue publishing the best books available on computer topics in today's market.

Lorna Gentry
Product Development Specialist
Que Corporation
201 W. 103rd Street
Indianapolis, Indiana 46290
USA

Contents at a Glance

Table of Contents

Introduction

Part I: Getting Acquainted with Excel

1 First Things First: Worksheet Basics

3 Help Is But a Click (or Two) Away

Part II: Excel Essentials: Editing, Formatting, and More

4 Let's Make Some Changes Around Here

10 Functions You'll Use Often

Part IV: Working with Charts

11 Charts Explained (in English)

Part V: Serious Number Crunching

13 Analyzing Data in Tables

14 More Analyzing, and Auditing Too

Part VII: Beyond the Basics: Your Workbooks, the Office, and the World

17 Linking and Sharing Workbooks

18 Data Maps and Templates, for Data that Fits a Mold

Introduction

Software surprises have always been more like practical jokes; not very funny, and not at all practical. Sometimes a program won't do what we want it to do. Occasionally it grinds to a halt and doesn't do anything at all. But now that our computers, bristling with crisp color, stereo sound, and CD-ROMs, have gotten more sophisticated, software has grown up as well.

Excel's newest version is a case in point. Excel 97 is still good for a surprise or two, but the surprises will be entirely pleasant.

Along with the calculating you might expect, you'll find animated paint brushes, contortionist paper clips, 3-D lighting effects, and cameo appearances by a Shakespeare stand-in and an Einstein-like genius. There's also a direct connection to the world of information and entertainment on the Internet, and to your colleagues' computers on a local intranet. While these new Excel gadgets are not strictly necessary for calculating tables of numbers, they are useful—and a lot of fun. The result is an edition of Excel that lets its hair down just a little.

Few of us, of course, are paid to have fun. We still need Excel to help us crunch numbers, analyze data, and produce charts. We also want to do all those things in time to be home for dinner. That's where *Using Excel 97* comes in. It's written and designed to show you exactly how to do what you need to do, clearly and simply, no matter how complex the task at hand. *Using Excel 97* will help you get through your work with ease, for results that will surprise you—pleasantly.

What makes this book different?

Between the covers, there are plenty of Tips to speed your work, Cautions to help you avoid trouble, and Q&As to solve mysteries. For operations that involve more than a click or two, numbered steps take you from start to finish, with no unwanted complications. What's more, *Using Excel 97* is written in plain English, so you'll never have to scratch your head and ask "What the heck does that mean?" Where jargon is completely unavoidable, unfamiliar terms are carefully explained.

If you're new to Excel, you'll find that learning the program is easy. Experienced Excel users will discover faster and better ways to do things, as well as useful features you might not have come across before.

What's new in Excel 97?

Anyone familiar with recent versions of Excel will feel right at home with the program's latest incarnation. The basic workings will be familiar, but there are some new features that might get you out of the office a little faster.

There's a world of data on the World Wide Web

Digging up facts and figures from dusty volumes and crowded tables still has its place. But with the Internet software included with Excel, and an account with an Internet service provider (like the Microsoft Network), you can do all your digging with the mouse. Excel is plugged into the vast global network of computers that makes up the World Wide Web. A click or two takes you to millions of pages of information. You can check the stock market, read the news and weather, study Etruscan art, or listen to a baseball game. It's like having a giant multimedia library inside your computer. Turn your worksheet into a Web page with Excel's Internet publishing tools, and add your own work to the mix, right from Excel. With easy-to-insert Hyperlinks, send your worksheet readers anywhere in the world, or anywhere in the company network, with a single click.

The Office Assistant, for help that thinks like you do

Online Help is supposed to provide answers, but too often the information you get just leads to more questions. Wouldn't it be great if you could type in your query in your own words, and get the answers you're really looking for? You can. The Office Assistant gives you clear answers to questions in plain English. The Assistant watches over your shoulder as you work, suggesting better ways to get the job done. When you try an Excel feature, the Office Assistant pops up to offer step-by-step instructions. And if you don't like the way the Office Assistant turned up for work, send it home and choose another. Take your pick, from an Einstein look-alike, to a hovering robot, to Mother Nature herself.

Easier-to-edit charts, and more of them

The idea behind a chart is simple: to make numbers clearer and more dramatic. Getting those results is easier than ever in Excel 97. There are arresting new cone, pyramid, cylinder, and bubble charts, and a collection of preformatted custom charts that are bound to save you time. If you're formatting your own chart, Excel tells you exactly what part of the chart you're selecting and editing.

AutoCalculate gives you all kinds of results, instantly

You have a column of figures to total. Do you write a formula, or call up a function? No need to do either. Just drag through the numbers with the mouse, then glance at the bottom of the screen. AutoCalculate is already displaying the total for you. You can also display averages and item and number counts; and find the highest and lowest values in a column of figures.

You'll like these other improvements too

Formatting text and numbers is simplified in Excel 97. So is printing and file management. New gadgets help you write flawless formulas. And if you have a Microsoft IntelliMouse, even scrolling has been made easier.

You'll find Excel 97 an improved edition of a program that was pretty good to begin with.

How do I use this book?

Most of the time, you'll probably want fast help with a specific chore. The Table of Contents is a good place to start. It's very detailed, and chances are your job will be listed among the topics there. If it isn't, check the Index in the back of the book.

When you have some spare time, try browsing. Each chapter of *Using Excel 97* begins with a list of the topics covered in that chapter. You can scan the list to see what lies ahead in the chapter, or to zero in on a topic that interests you.

Each chapter is divided into sections. Look through the section headings in each chapter, and you might discover Excel features you didn't know about. You'll also get ideas about using Excel to tackle your work in new ways.

Of course, there's nothing to stop you from sitting down and reading a chapter through from beginning to end. To really master an Excel feature, that's the way to go. I can't promise you the excitement of a thriller, but I've tried to keep things lively.

How this book is put together

When you have a big project to do, you probably break it up into smaller parts and tackle them one at a time. Excel is a big program, so that's how this book is set up too. There are seven parts.

Part I: Getting Acquainted with Excel

Whether you plan on occasional get-togethers or extended daily visits, here's the place to find out what you're getting into. You'll learn how Excel works, the basics of building a worksheet, and how to get help fast, whenever you need it.

Part II: Excel Essentials: Editing, Formatting, and More

These are the things you'll do when you fire up Excel every day. From vast columns of numbers to a few simple calculations, Excel can handle whatever you throw at it. Staring at columns and rows of numbers can be pretty dull, but not when you add borders and patterns, change fonts, and splash on some color. With an amazing feature called AutoFill, parts of your worksheets are filled in for you. If you make a mistake, or need to make changes of any kind, you'll find that editing data is easy and quick. Organizing your work in worksheets and workbooks is just like using an accordion file.

Part III: Formulas and Functions

Data is the flesh on the bones of an Excel worksheet. Formulas and functions are the muscles. Write a formula from scratch, use the dozens of built-in functions, or get creative and do both together. From summing up columns and rows to financial and statistical analysis, there's a push-button solution to every problem. Excel's Office Assistant guides you step by step through the building of powerful worksheet functions.

Part IV: Working with Charts

You might know them as graphs. Excel calls them charts. By whatever name, they give you a colorful snapshot of your data. By summarizing and clarifying, a single chart can include more than a thousand numbers. You get a big choice of charts to use, and you can alter them any way you like. With the Chart Wizard to guide you step by step, turning your data into a dazzling picture is as easy as finger painting.

Part V: Serious Number Crunching

Put your numbers on a conveyor belt and send them through a function one by one, then have the results appear neatly alongside. That's what a data table does, automatically. Or maybe you have a solution in search of a problem. Excel has the tools to find it. As your worksheets get more complex, tracking down errors gets trickier. Excel has a built-in detective to find them for you. Auditing is the painless way to find mistakes and fix them fast.

Part VI: Using Excel as a Database

You might think of Excel as a great tool for handling numbers, and it is. Maybe you didn't know that it's just as good at coping with databases. From a list of sales contacts to a vast collection of invoices, Excel can store them, sort them, and report on them any way you like. Follow a few simple guidelines, and Excel gives you powerful tools to find and analyze any amount of stored information. It even creates a form for you to enter your data quickly and accurately. All you do is point and click.

Part VII: Beyond the Basics: Your Workbooks, the Office, and the World

No matter what you're looking for, from financial market data, to the price of tea in China, to the latest memo from the boss, it's on the World Wide Web or your local intranet. Excel connects you to either one with a couple of clicks. And for worksheets that deserve an audience, Excel's Internet publishing tools turn your work into Web pages ready for posting on the networks.

How about setting up a system of workbooks that automatically update each other? Or taking chunks of raw data and turning them into a powerful Excel list? Pour your data into a map for a dramatic graphical display, or into a template to create practical worksheets you'll really use. You can even build your own toolbars and get Excel to do your typing for you. There are plenty of amazing features in Excel, and this is the place to check them out.

Special book elements

Using Excel 97 has a number of special elements and conventions to help you find information quickly.

Tips point out information often overlooked in the documenta-tion. Some tips are shortcuts that help you use Excel more efficiently; others help you solve or avoid problems.

Cautions alert you to possible software dangers, especially when the result might be the loss of your hard work!

What are Q&A notes?

Cast in the form of questions and answers, Q&As suggest ways to avoid common problems. They also provide quick fixes for problems you might have already run into.

Plain English, please!

When technical terms and jargon are unavoidable, these notes explain what it all means in plain English. ”

Sidebars are interesting nuggets of information

Sidebars are nonessential but relevant reading, side trips you can take when you're not at the computer or when you just want some light relief. You'll often find technical details, or interesting background information.

Throughout the book, we'll use a comma to separate the parts of a pull-down menu command. For example, to start a new workbook, you might choose File, New. That means "Pull down the File menu, and choose New from the list."

And if you see two keys separated by a plus sign, such as Ctrl+X, that means to press and hold the first key, press the second key, then release both keys.

Right-click means clicking the right mouse button.

And when we talk about dragging, we mean holding down the left mouse button and moving the mouse pointer.

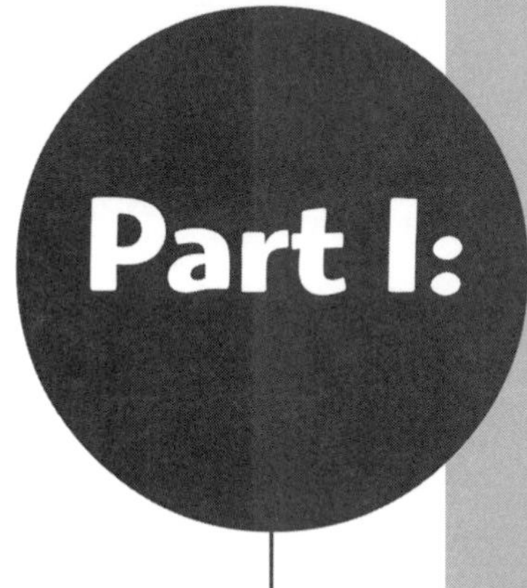

Part I: Getting Acquainted with Excel

1

First Things First: Worksheet Basics

In this chapter:

- **What am I looking at?**
- **Workbooks? Worksheets? Explain, please!**
- **Getting around in Excel is an easy commute**
- **I need to see different parts of my sheet at the same time**
- **What do all these buttons do?**

If you're in a foreign city, a map and a phrase book can save you a lot of trouble. Similar tools come in handy when you explore Excel . . . .

Remember being late for school? The days when a discussion was already in full swing were the worst. A room full of people talking; no clue as to what they were talking about. Days like that always gave me a headache.

I get that same feeling sometimes when I read about software. The discussion always sounds knowledgeable and assured, but if the terms are unfamiliar, all I can do is gape.

Let's take a look at how Excel is organized and learn some key terms. That'll save a few headaches down the road.

Why do I need Excel?

You might think of Excel as an immensely powerful, yet easy-to-use calculator. Or as an electronic financial guru. It's also a private publishing house, a personal statistician, a graphics artist, and a bottomless card file. Oh yes, and an unfailing organizer and filer too.

Excel takes chunks of disorderly data, organizes it, analyzes it, and presents it neatly and attractively. It solves problems unerringly and without complaint. And Excel is organized in such a way that it's impossible to get lost.

Excel does a much better job of organizing than you could possibly do yourself. You not only have more time to go over your data, you also see it more clearly. A clean, uncluttered view can make your thinking a lot more insightful.

Excel's orderliness might take a little getting used to, but it's remarkably helpful.

The whole is greater than the sum of its parts

Using Excel is a little like having dinner at a fancy French restaurant. At first glance, the menu looks incomprehensible. What on earth is "Poulet à la crème au sauce Champagne"? Then you take a closer look. Below the flowery script are tiny English translations: "chicken in a cream of champagne sauce." That makes a little more sense. It also sounds good. From all those no-longer-indecipherable menu choices, you assemble a delicious meal.

By the time you finish, you realize that not only was every dish terrific, but each complemented the other. The meal has been completely harmonious.

There *are* a lot of components to Excel, and at first glance they might seem a little inscrutable. But everything is clearly labeled. Better still, everything works together seamlessly. You exploit different facets of the program without even being aware of it. As you build your worksheets, you pick a function here, a format there, and probably add a chart to sum it all up. By the time you're done, you've put Excel through its paces without any effort on your part.

You can concentrate on getting the results you want, without having to figure out how the program makes it all work. Like a master chef preparing a menu, Excel does that part of the job for you. What's more, there's no check to pay.

Where do I start?

After you install Excel, you'll want to go right to work. Running Excel is straightforward:

1. Click the Start button and choose Programs. The Programs menu will cascade across the screen.

Microsoft Excel

2. On the Programs menu, click Microsoft Excel.
3. You'll see the Excel title screen appear as the program loads, and in a moment or two Excel is up and running.

You're ready to explore the orderly world of worksheets. No need for a seat belt; this is going to be a smooth ride.

Where's my Excel directory?

Users of DOS and older versions of Windows may be accustomed to keeping their files and programs in directories and subdirectories. That's the basic setup in Windows 95 too, but the directories and subdirectories are called **folders**. They look like little file folders on the screen, so the new nomenclature is at least descriptive. You probably don't stick one folder inside another in your office filing cabinet (I don't either), but that's exactly what Windows does. If you go poking around in the Windows Explorer, you'll see that Excel was installed in a folder called Excel, within a folder called Microsoft Office.

Can't I put the Excel icon on my desktop?

If you like the old Windows double-click, and you plan on using Excel every day, you can put the Excel icon right on your desktop. That lets you bypass the Start, Programs menu and run Excel with a double-click of the icon.

To put the Excel icon on your Windows desktop:

1 Close Excel and minimize any programs you have running.

If you have two or more programs running, here's a quick way to minimize the program windows and return to the desktop: right-click the taskbar background and choose Minimize All Windows from the shortcut menu.

2 Right-click the Start button and choose Open from the shortcut menu.

3 In the Start Menu window that pops up, double-click the Programs folder.

4 That gets you the Start Menu\Programs window; right-click the Microsoft Excel icon and choose Copy from the shortcut menu (see Figure 1.1).

5 Close the open windows. Right-click the Desktop background and choose Paste Shortcut. The Microsoft Excel icon appears on the desktop, and it's back to work.

Now when you want to run Excel, just double-click the Excel icon on the Desktop. You can perform this maneuver for any frequently used programs.

If you change your mind, you can get rid of any shortcut icon, fast. Just drag the icon to the Recycle Bin on the desktop.

Creating a shortcut to a program doesn't remove it from the Start, Programs menu, and deleting the shortcut icon doesn't affect the program itself in any way.

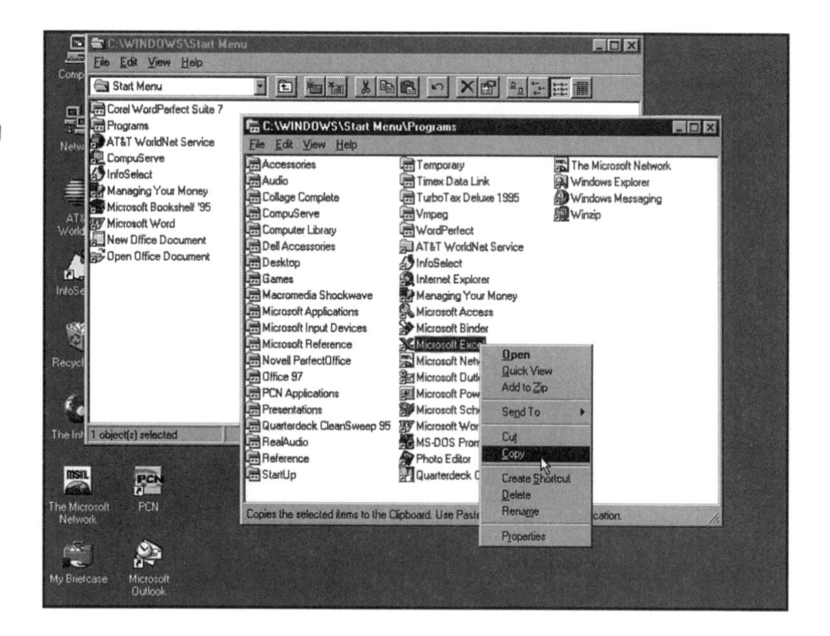

Fig. 1.1
There are lots of ways to copy and paste in Windows 95, but I find the right-click menu method the handiest.

Spreadsheets versus worksheets versus workbooks

If your car breaks down in England, you might tell the mechanic that the tools are in the trunk. If you do, you're in for a long afternoon at the garage. In England, the trunk of a car is called the "boot," and a "trunk" is something you pack for a long trip. Like a little knowledge of "English" in England, learning some of Excel's terms can help you avoid a lot of confusion.

Coming to terms with Excel terms

In Excel, a spreadhseet is called **worksheet**, or just a **sheet**. They both mean the same thing. A worksheet is like a blank sheet of paper where you do your work. One Excel file holds a stack of worksheets in a **workbook**.

Think of a ring binder filled with sheets of graph paper. The binder itself is your workbook, and each sheet of paper in the binder is a worksheet. When you first start Excel, it's as though you opened your binder at the first blank page.

Excel automatically gives a new workbook the file name Book 1, which you'll see at the top of the screen.

As soon as you give your workbook a real name, the name Book 1 disappears—at least until you run the program again. If you open another new workbook in that session, Excel calls it Book 2 until you give it a better name. Imaginative? No. Logical? Yes.

A new workbook starts out with three worksheets, labeled Sheet1, Sheet2, and Sheet3. Their labels are on **tabs** down at the bottom of the screen. You can flip from sheet to sheet, just like in a ring binder. You can tear sheets out and put more in. You can trim down your workbook to a single sheet, or fatten it up with as many sheets as you like. It's a flexible setup, just like your old ring binder.

Pick a sheet, any sheet

We'll have more to say about workbooks and worksheets later. For now, just to get an idea of what's going on, let's play with it a little. Move your pointer to the bottom of the screen and click Sheet2. You just turned a page in your workbook. Click Sheet3—another page gone by. As you can see, the sheets look a lot alike, at least until you put something on them.

A sheet by any other name

Let's do one more simple trick to help get a handle on Excel's organizing scheme. Just as you wouldn't stick your files into unlabeled file folders, you don't want to do your work on unnamed worksheets. Sheet1 doesn't tell you much, so we'll change it to something more descriptive.

1 Double-click the Sheet1 tab; that highlights the name `Sheet1`.

2 Now type in your own name for the sheet. The old name is overwritten as soon as you start typing (see Figure 1.2).

Fig. 1.2
A worksheet has to start somewhere, so why not with a name?

3 When you're finished typing, press Enter to save the new sheet name.

You can call your sheets whatever you want, and you get 31 characters, including spaces, to do it with. Excel won't accept the following characters in sheet names: / ? * : [ ]. If you type an illegal character, it simply won't appear on the screen.

The worksheet at a glance

Excel files are called workbooks. The file name, FINANCIAL CONDITION, is also the workbook name.

Letters in the column headings identify each column

The formula bar is where you edit your formulas and data. You can also edit right in the cell

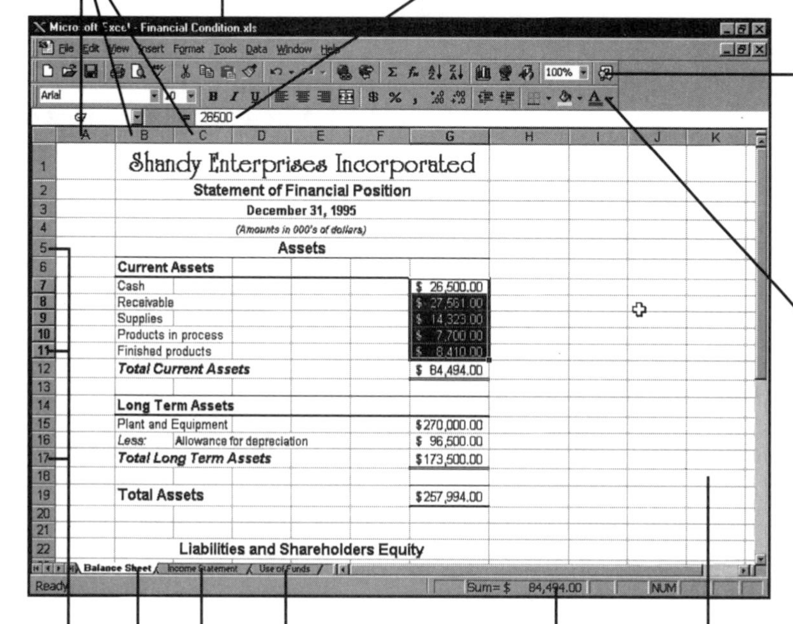

The Standard toolbar has buttons for what you'll do most often. One click opens files, saves, prints, cuts, copies and pastes, sums, and sorts

The Formatting toolbar has buttons to select fonts; add bolding, italics, and underlining; change alignment; format numbers; and add borders and color

Worksheet tabs identify each worksheet in the workbook. Just like file folder tabs, you give them your own names. Click the tab to flip from sheet to sheet

AutoCalculate gives you a running count, average, total, or the minimum and maximum values of selected cells; right-click to flip from Count to Average to Sum

A cell is where you enter numbers, text, dates, formulas...any data at all. Cells expand to fit the size of whatever you type in

Row headings are numbers identifying each row

Congratulations! You're well launched on the first stage of a successful workbook building project. Now let's learn more about the parts of the worksheet and how they work.

East side, west side, all around the worksheet

New Yorkers walk fast; they know where they want to go, they know how to get there, and they're always in a big hurry. San Franciscans go more slowly, partly because San Francisco streets do odd things. They cut across town or end after two blocks. They disappear over crests, turn into staircases, or twist into crazy shapes. You need a map to get around, to say nothing of a pair of well-developed calves.

In New York, a glance at a street sign instantly orients you. Grasp that avenues run north and south and streets go east and west, and you can always find your way (at least until you get to Greenwich Village). It's set up like a grid—no map needed.

Rows and columns

Excel is just as logical as the streets of New York. Its layout consists of **columns** that go up and down and **rows** that go from side to side. Columns are lettered and rows are numbered. **Column headings** start with column A; **row headings** with row 1. What could be simpler?

Plain English, please!

In New York, the grid is defined by streets and avenues. In Excel, they're called **grid lines**. You can make them disappear, but don't do it yet. New Yorkers should be so lucky.

Rendezvous at the cell

All the real estate on the Excel grid has an address, so you always know where to find things. In New York, streets meet at easily identified intersections, such as "33rd and 3rd." In Excel, the intersection of each column and row is a little box called a **cell**.

Every cell has an address derived from its column and row. The intersection of column C and row 3, for example, is cell C3. The cell's address is called the **cell reference**.

When you click a cell, it becomes the **active cell**. That's where you enter or edit your data or formula, and it's identified by a heavy border.

If you happen to glance out the window for a moment and lose track of where you are, take a look at the upper-left corner of the screen. The last cell you selected is displayed in the **name box**. Click a cell and try it. You'll also notice that the column and row headings for the active cell are raised and in boldface.

Figure 1.3 shows all of these things.

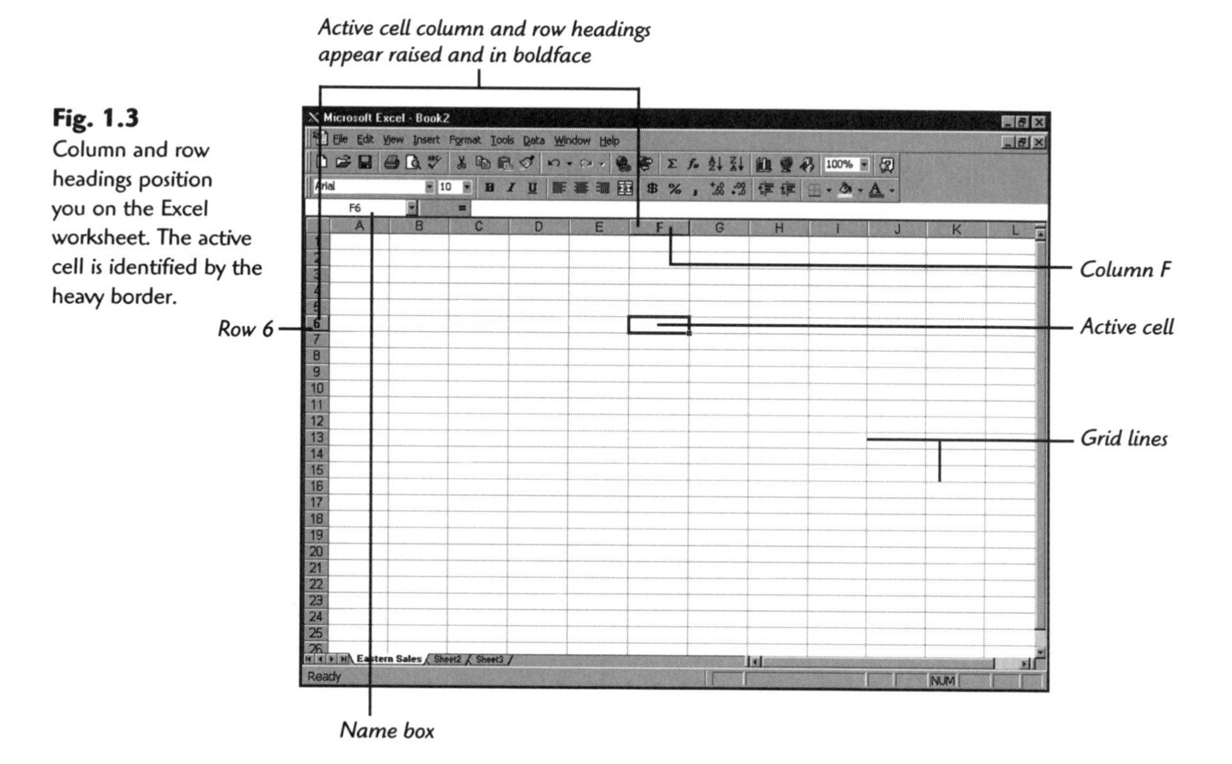

Fig. 1.3
Column and row headings position you on the Excel worksheet. The active cell is identified by the heavy border.

Moving around a worksheet

If you filled every available cell in an Excel worksheet and printed it out (don't try this at home), you'd need a strip of paper wider than all the guards and tackles on an offensive line and as long as the entire football field. Chances are, even a really big spreadsheet will only occupy a small corner of the whole Excel worksheet. Even so, you may have to cover a lot of ground.

You get around in Excel with the mouse or the keyboard, depending on what you want to do and how you want to move.

There are two kinds of movement, just to make life interesting. You can **scroll** through a worksheet, exposing a screen full of cells to view with each move. Or you can move within the worksheet, shifting cells or ranges to different locations on the sheet. Let's deal with scrolling first.

Scrolling along

Ever see the Compact Edition of the *Oxford English Dictionary*? The regular edition runs more than 20 volumes. The Compact Edition squeezes everything into just two volumes by reducing the type. The type is so tiny that you need a magnifying glass (thoughtfully provided by the publisher) to read it. You lay the dictionary open on your desk and move the magnifying glass over the page.

That's exactly what happens when you scroll through an Excel worksheet. It's as though the sheet itself, that football field-sized strip, remains stationary, while you slide a magnifying glass over it.

You do that with the scroll bars and buttons on the side and bottom of the worksheet. They're just like scroll bars and buttons in any Windows window.

Figure 1.4 shows you the Excel scrolling options.

TIP **As you scroll up, down, or sideways, the scroll box grows or shrinks** to let you know how much worksheet you have left to cover.

Smarter than the average mouse: IntelliMouse

Just when you thought the language had acquired all the compound words with multiple-capitalization that it could handle, along comes Microsoft's IntelliMouse and the accompanying IntelliPoint software. Although the new gadget complicates our usage of upper- and lowercase letters, the IntelliMouse greatly simplifies scrolling in Excel.

If you have the IntelliMouse, and you've installed the IntelliPoint software, you can forget about the vertical and horizontal scroll bars. Turn the IntelliMouse wheel one notch down or up, and your worksheet scrolls three rows down or up.

Fig. 1.4
You have plenty of ways to get around in Excel. A worksheet is a big place, but commuting is easy.

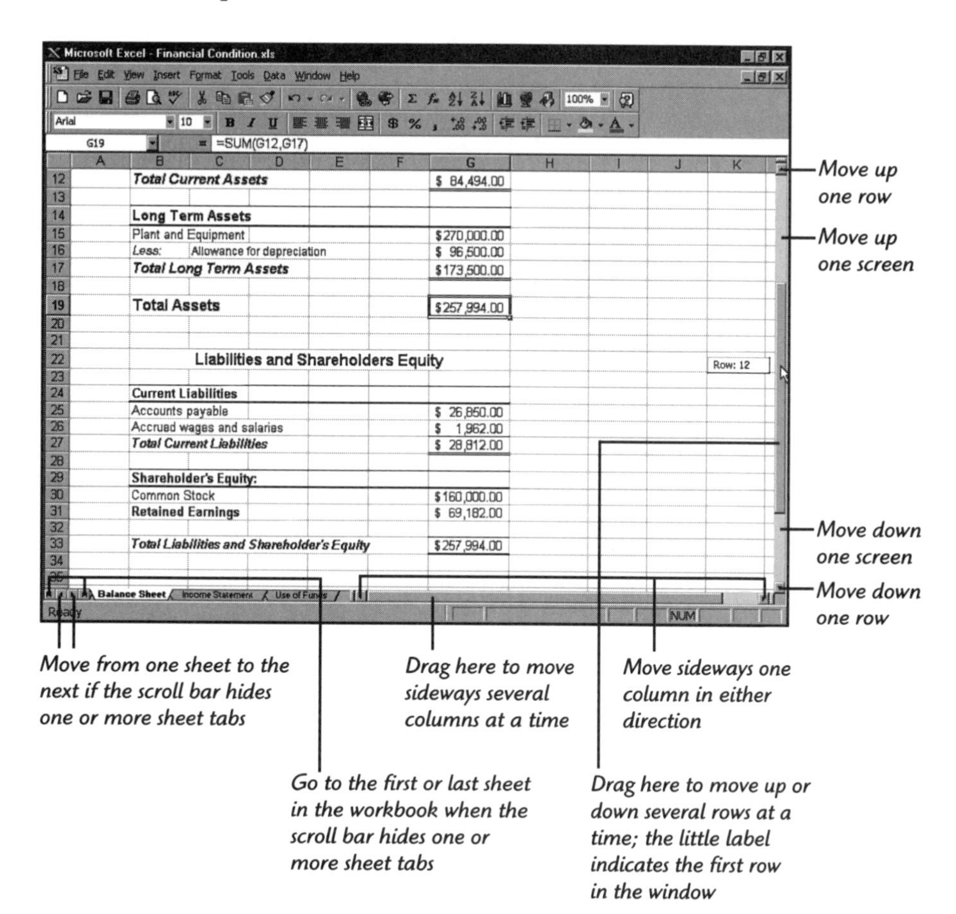

TIP **To adjust the number of rows you scroll with a turn of the** IntelliMouse wheel, double-click the mouse icon on the taskbar. If you don't see the mouse icon, click Start, Settings, Control Panel, and double-click the Control Panel Mouse icon. Either way, you'll pop up the Mouse Properties dialog box. Click the Wheel tab and choose Wheel Settings. In the Settings for Wheel dialog box, enter a new value in the Scroll text box. Or choose Scroll One "Page" at a Time; that makes a one-notch turn of the wheel scroll an entire window at a time. Click OK in both the Settings for Wheel dialog box and the Mouse Properties dialog box to save your changes. Figure 1.5 shows the Settings for Wheel dialog box.

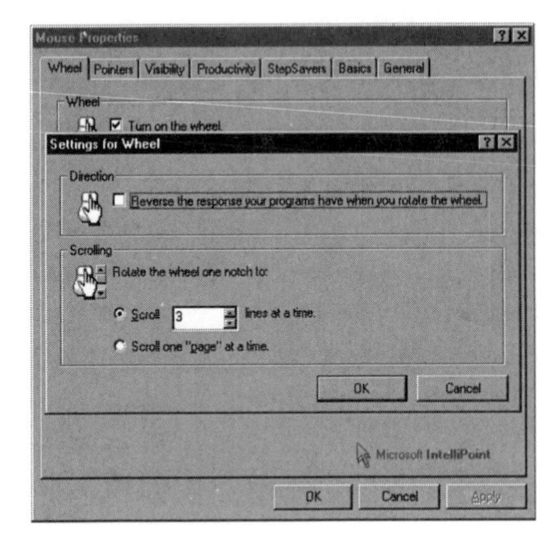

Fig. 1.5
The IntelliMouse wheel is handy right out of the box. That you can adjust it makes the wheel handier still.

To scroll variable distances, press the wheel and move your mouse up, down, or to either side. As if by magic, the worksheet scrolls before your eyes. The farther you move the mouse in any direction while pressing the wheel, the faster you scroll. Scrolling with the IntelliMouse is so easy that it's easy to get carried away; I wound up around row 4241 when I first tried it. If something similar happens to you, press Ctrl+Home to go back to the first cell in the worksheet.

The IntelliMouse has one other trick up its sleeve. To zoom the Excel window, press Ctrl and roll the mouse wheel forward or backward one notch. That increases or decreases the screen magnification by 10% with each turn of the wheel.

How do I keep my column titles from scrolling off the screen?

Here's a minor scrolling nuisance that can be a major pain: your column titles scroll out of sight as you scroll down the worksheet. You want to see the titles though, especially as you add more data to each column.

Excel's programmers thought of everything. You can freeze one section of the window while you scroll down the rest of the sheet.

To freeze a portion of the Excel window:

1. Click the row heading one row below the row you want to freeze.
2. Click Window, Freeze Panes.

3 The section of the worksheet above the selected row is "frozen" in place, even if you scroll all the way to the bottom of the worksheet. Figure 1.6 gives you the idea.

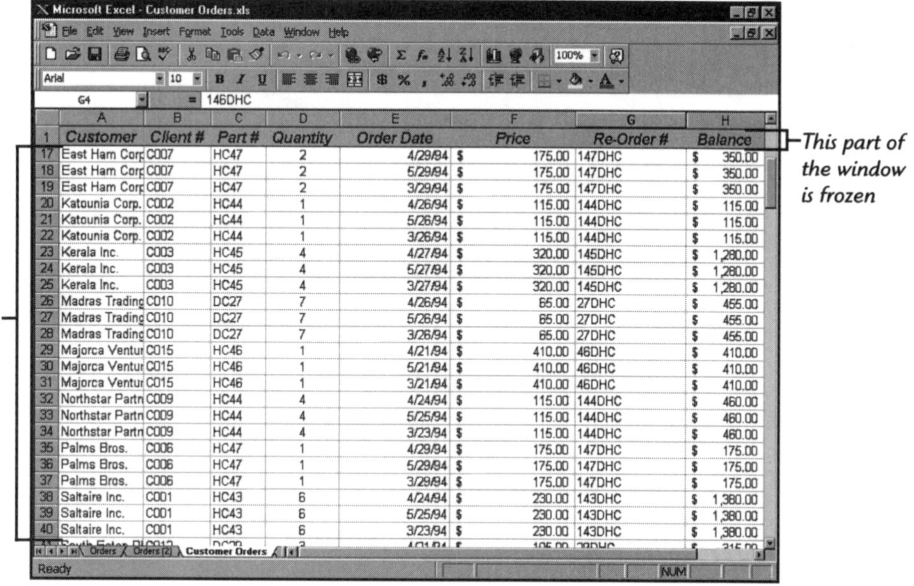

	Customer	Client #	Part #	Quantity	Order Date	Price	Re-Order #	Balance
17	East Ham Corp	C007	HC47	2	4/29/94	$ 175.00	147DHC	$ 350.00
18	East Ham Corp	C007	HC47	2	5/29/94	$ 175.00	147DHC	$ 350.00
19	East Ham Corp	C007	HC47	2	3/29/94	$ 175.00	147DHC	$ 350.00
20	Katounia Corp.	C002	HC44	1	4/26/94	$ 115.00	144DHC	$ 115.00
21	Katounia Corp.	C002	HC44	1	5/26/94	$ 115.00	144DHC	$ 115.00
22	Katounia Corp.	C002	HC44	1	3/26/94	$ 115.00	144DHC	$ 115.00
23	Kerala Inc.	C003	HC45	4	4/27/94	$ 320.00	145DHC	$ 1,280.00
24	Kerala Inc.	C003	HC45	4	5/27/94	$ 320.00	145DHC	$ 1,280.00
25	Kerala Inc.	C003	HC45	4	3/27/94	$ 320.00	145DHC	$ 1,280.00
26	Madras Trading	C010	DC27	7	4/26/94	$ 65.00	27DHC	$ 455.00
27	Madras Trading	C010	DC27	7	5/26/94	$ 65.00	27DHC	$ 455.00
28	Madras Trading	C010	DC27	7	3/26/94	$ 65.00	27DHC	$ 455.00
29	Majorca Ventur	C015	HC46	1	4/21/94	$ 410.00	46DHC	$ 410.00
30	Majorca Ventur	C015	HC46	1	5/21/94	$ 410.00	46DHC	$ 410.00
31	Majorca Ventur	C015	HC46	1	3/21/94	$ 410.00	46DHC	$ 410.00
32	Northstar Partn	C009	HC44	4	4/24/94	$ 115.00	144DHC	$ 460.00
33	Northstar Partn	C009	HC44	4	5/25/94	$ 115.00	144DHC	$ 460.00
34	Northstar Partn	C009	HC44	4	3/23/94	$ 115.00	144DHC	$ 460.00
35	Palms Bros.	C006	HC47	1	4/29/94	$ 175.00	147DHC	$ 175.00
36	Palms Bros.	C006	HC47	1	5/29/94	$ 175.00	147DHC	$ 175.00
37	Palms Bros.	C006	HC47	1	3/29/94	$ 175.00	147DHC	$ 175.00
38	Saltaire Inc.	C001	HC43	6	4/24/94	$ 230.00	143DHC	$ 1,380.00
39	Saltaire Inc.	C001	HC43	6	5/25/94	$ 230.00	143DHC	$ 1,380.00
40	Saltaire Inc.	C001	HC43	6	3/23/94	$ 230.00	143DHC	$ 1,380.00

Fig. 1.6
Freezing your column titles prevents them from slipping out of sight as you scroll down the worksheet.

The frozen section of window remains in sight as you scroll down the worksheet

To freeze a column, select the column to the right of the one you want to freeze, then click Window, Freeze Panes. To unfreeze your window, click Window, Unfreeze Panes.

Make your window do the splits

Freezing panes is handy, but sometimes you'll want to scroll two or more sections of a window independently. If that's the case, split the screen. Drag the vertical and horizontal split bars shown in Figure 1.7 to split the screen vertically, horizontally, or both.

TIP **If you don't see the split bars on the screen, click Window, Split to** make them appear.

To get rid of a split, just double-click the split bar.

Fig. 1.7
Drag the split bars to divide the window into sections you can scroll independently.

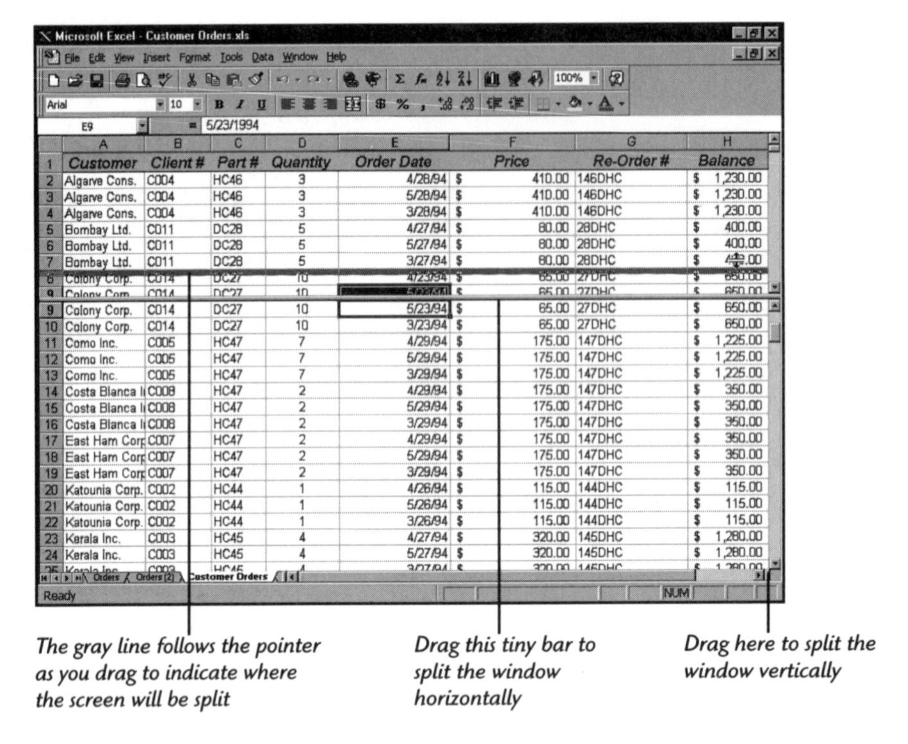

Keyboard moves

For leaps across large worksheets, using the keyboard works best. The following table lists the keyboard options.

Press	To move here
Home	Beginning of row
Page Up/Page Down	Up/down one window
Ctrl+Home	Beginning of worksheet
Ctrl+End	Lower-right corner of occupied cells
Crtl+Page Down	Next sheet
Ctrl+Page Up	Previous sheet
F5	Specified cell or range

The Home key takes you to the beginning of a row, but the End key doesn't take you to the row's end—at least not directly. End turns on **End mode**, which gives you a few other navigational choices. Press End, then Enter (press one key after the other). That *does* take you to the end of the row. Press End, then the Arrow key to move to the next cell with something in it in any direction. Press End, then Home to go to the last cell in the sheet with something in it, just like Ctrl+End.

Paintbrushes, scissors, and globes: the Excel screen

I bet that a lot of people like me, raised on those old DOS programs, must have had the same reaction when they first saw a graphical screen: all those little pictures look great, but what do they mean? Nobody misses those old programs, but there was something to be said for commands described in words. No matter how clever those little icons are, some of them can be pretty cryptic.

At least until Excel came along. Now, the pictures speak! Aim your pointer at an Excel button (don't click, just point), and a little label appears to tell you what that button does. These labels are called **ToolTips**.

Figure 1.8 shows a ToolTip and some of the main features of the Excel screen.

If you're not sure what a button or a menu command does, press Shift+F1, and then click the button or the menu command. That pops up a Help window explaining the function of the button or command.

The **status bar** is easy to overlook, but it displays a lot of useful information. The status bar lets you know what's going on when you copy or save or do other Excel operations. It also tells you if Caps Lock, Num Lock, or Scroll Lock is turned on.

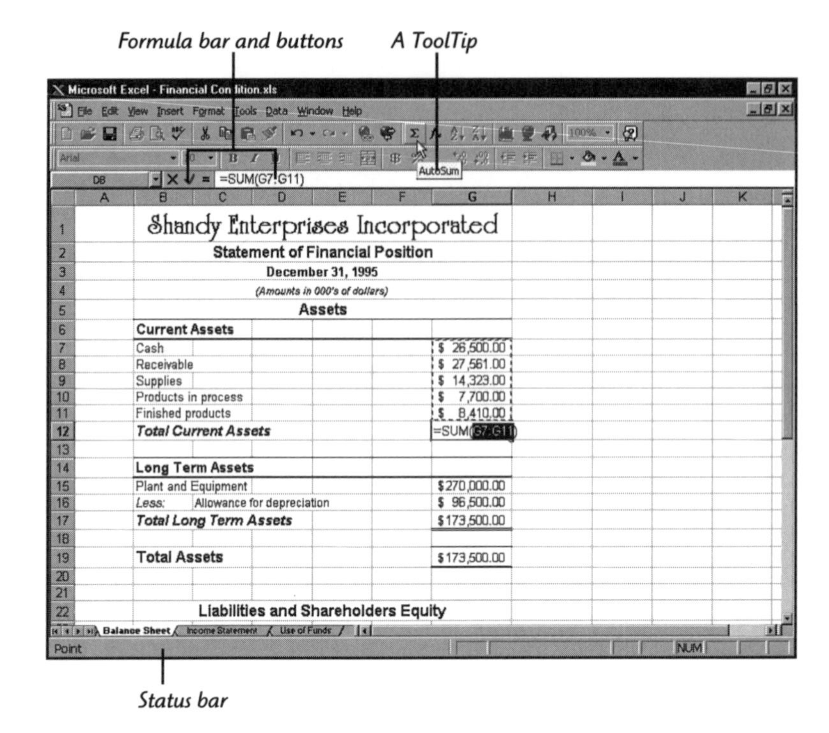

Fig. 1.8
Point at a button to see the ToolTip with the button's name.

Barhopping in Excel

There are a lot of bars in Excel. Between toolbars, scroll bars, and the formula and status bars, you'll never go thirsty—at least for information.

> ***Plain English, please!***
>
> A **button** is a little picture that looks raised when you point at it, like the ones at the top of the screen. Clicking a button is just like giving a command—you get instant action. **Icons** are the little flat pictures that represent programs. They're what you see on the Windows desktop. Buttons are called icons too—but icons are never called buttons. Quirky, but you just have to ride with it. A **toolbar** is a collection of buttons, like a graphical menu. It's called a toolbar because what I call buttons are officially called **tools**.

Bring your tools with you

All the toolbars **float**, which means you can move them. By clicking and dragging their title bars, you can drag them around the screen like a dialog box, shoving them out of the way if they block your work. You can change the shape of the toolbars by dragging their borders, making them longer or taller (though you can't resize them). You can also **dock** toolbars, parking them at the bottom, top, or on either side of the screen where they won't get in the way.

Let's take the Drawing toolbar for a little ride. Any of the other toolbars on the menu can be selected, moved, and reshaped in the same way:

1. Click the Drawing button on the Standard toolbar; the Drawing toolbar appears on the screen.
2. Drag the Drawing toolbar's title bar to another location.
3. Now double-click the Drawing toolbar title bar. That docks it out of the way at the bottom of the screen. Once a toolbar is docked, you can drag or double-click the toolbar handle at its left edge to make it "float" once again. Figure 1.9 shows a toolbar handle.
4. To get rid of it again, click the Drawing button on the Standard toolbar.

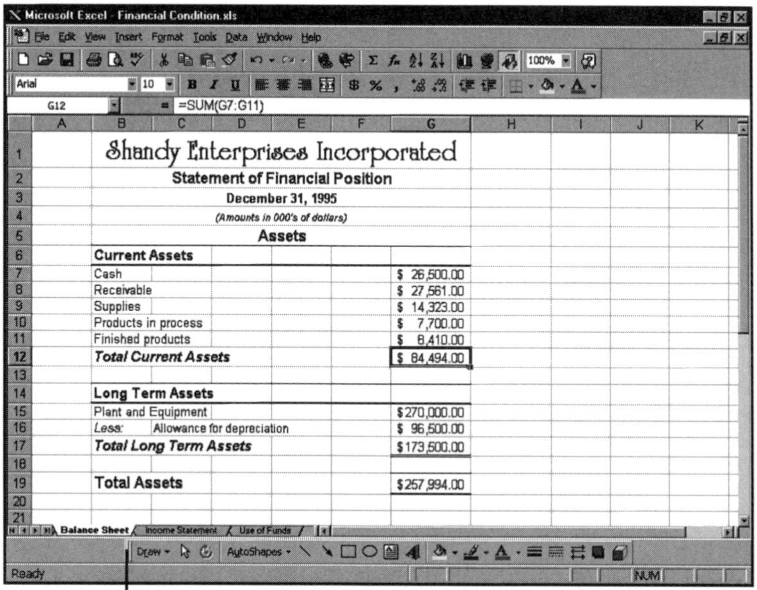

Fig. 1.9
Toolbars are most convenient when they're docked out of the way of your work.

Drag or double-click any docked toolbar handle to make the toolbar float on the screen

The buttons on the Standard toolbar

What are you likely to do most often as you work? The Standard toolbar provides one-stop shopping for your most frequent actions. One click of a button and you're done. Microsoft Word users will be familiar with many of the items on the Excel Standard toolbar. Here's what they do:

Button	Name	What does it do?
	New Workbook	It opens, naturally enough, a new workbook.
	Open	Lets you retrieve an existing workbook.
	Save	Saves your workbook. Get in the habit of using this often—it can also save your life.
	Print	Gets it all on paper. (Why does it look like a dot matrix printer when nobody uses them anymore?)
	Print Preview	Lets you see what the printout looks like before you let 'er rip. A big paper-saver.
	Spelling	Spell checks your work. My crutch.
	Cut	Cuts text, numbers, or formulas out of your worksheet and copies them to the Clipboard.
	Copy	Copies text, numbers, or formulas to the Clipboard.
	Paste	Dumps whatever's in the Clipboard back into your worksheet.
	Format Painter	Grabs the format from selected cells and lays it over a new selection of cells.

Button	Name	What does it do?
	Undo	Cancels your last action if you make a mistake.
	Redo	Clones your last action.
	Insert Hyperlink	Lets you link a cell to any file on your disk or any page on the World Wide Web.
	Web Toolbar	Lets you access the Web, right from Excel.
 Σ	AutoSum	Adds up the numbers in a range. If you haven't selected a range, it'll suggest one.
 fx	Paste Function	Guides you through the process of writing a function, then dumps it in the active cell. Worth the price of admission by itself.
	Sort Ascending	Sorts a range from lowest to highest. Works alphabetically for text.
	Sort Descending	Like Sort Ascending, but it orders the range from highest to lowest.
	Chart Wizard	Another show stopper. Lets you put a chart anywhere you want one, then leads you through the chart-making options and creates a chart for your selected data.
	Map	Inserts a nifty map into the worksheet, giving you an instant eye-grabbing illustration for geographic data.
	Drawing	Pops up the Drawing toolbar, which is loaded with tools to help create worksheet art.
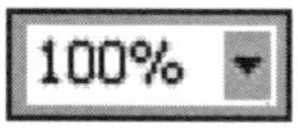 100%	Zoom	Shrinks or blows up your view of the worksheet.
	Office Assistant	Summons an animated helper to guide you through Excel's many features. It's what used to be called Help.

Ranges and references

Cells hold numbers, text, and formulas. You can work in a single cell at a time, or select several cells and work with them simultaneously. When you select several cells, it's called a **range**. Just as you'd refer to a block in New York as, say, the fifteen hundred block of Third Avenue, a range has a reference too. Instead of typing "the cells from A1 to A9," you use a kind of shorthand and call the range A1:A9. A **range reference** is always the first and last cells of the range separated by a colon.

Selecting a range

There are lots of ways to pick a range. Click a column heading; you just selected that entire column as your range. It'll look like Figure 1.10. Selecting a row works the same way.

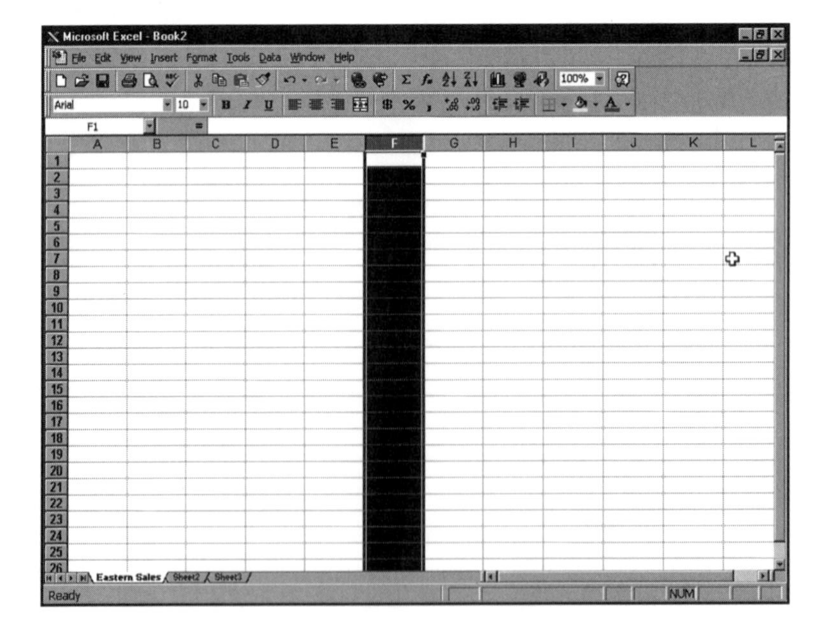

Fig. 1.10
Clicking a column heading selects the entire column.

Now try this: select cell B2, hold the mouse button, and drag across the row to cell E2. Your range is B2:E2, and it should look like Figure 1.11. If you prefer the keyboard to the mouse, press Shift+arrow key to select ranges of cells. Say you selected a range with the mouse, but now you want to extend the selection. Use the Shift+arrow key combination to add adjacent cells to the selected range.

You can also select an entire worksheet by clicking the Select All button. It's unmarked, but you'll find it at the top-left intersection of the column and row headings.

The Select All button

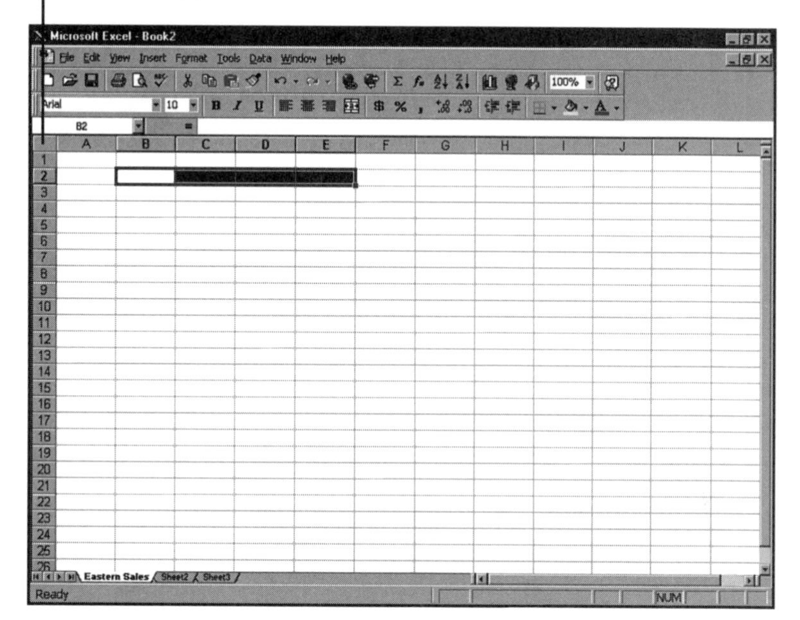

Fig. 1.11
Selecting a cell and dragging across the row selects a range of adjacent horizontal cells.

Selecting an entire worksheet can be dangerous. If you format the worksheet with AutoFormat, for example, don't use the Select All button. Excel will attempt to format every single cell on the sheet, blank or filled. All you're likely to get out of it is an error message from Windows.

I want to work inside one cell of my selected range. When I click it, all the highlighting disappears. How do I pick a cell in a range without deselecting the whole thing?

To move around inside a range, press Tab to move to the right one cell at a time, and Shift+Tab to move left one cell at a time. Pressing Enter moves down one cell at a time; Shift+Enter moves up one cell at a time. Using the arrow keys or the mouse to select a cell inside a range deselects the range.

What if the cells I want aren't next to each other?

Sometimes you'll want to work on data that doesn't happen to be conveniently parked side by side. No problem—you can select **nonadjacent ranges** very easily.

1. Drag through the first part of your nonadjacent range.
2. Move the mouse pointer to the beginning of the next part of the range.
3. Hold down the Ctrl key and click the first cell in the range, then Ctrl+drag through to the last cell.
4. Repeat the Ctrl+drag combination to select additional nonadjacent ranges.

You now have two separate ranges highlighted. Add other nonadjacent ranges if you like. Just be sure to press and hold down the Ctrl key while selecting each range or cell. When you release the mouse button, all of your selected ranges stay highlighted, as shown in Figure 1.12.

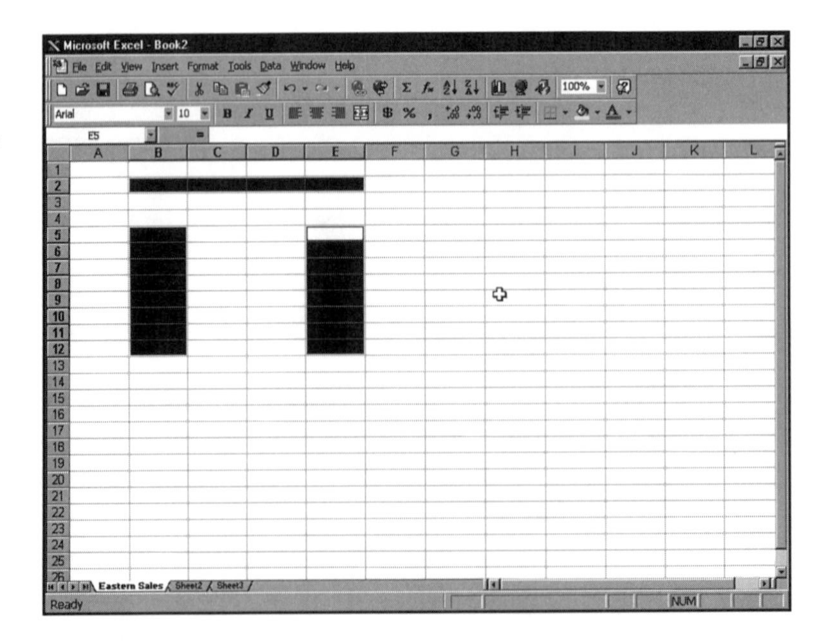

Fig. 1.12
Once selected, you can work with non-adjacent ranges just as you work with ranges that are side by side.

If you get tired of mousing around with your ranges, you can select a range by typing its reference in the name box (refer to Figure 1.10). Click the name box, type **B3:G3** (or whatever range you want), and hit Enter. You can do the same thing for nonadjacent ranges. Just separate your range references with a comma and no spaces: **B3:G3,E2:F2**.

Arranging the windows on the screen

Usually, one screen full of information is about all I can take in at a time. But there are times, even for me, when it's useful to see more than one worksheet or workbook on the screen at the same time. Say you have a chart in one worksheet and your data in another. You make a change in the data, and you want to see how it affects the chart. Here's how to put them both on the screen at once:

1. Click Window, New Window. Another view of your worksheet pops up. If you started in a Workbook called CONSOLIDATED SHIPPING, the new view is labeled CONSOLIDATED SHIPPING:2. If you open a third window, it would be CONSOLIDATED SHIPPING:3, and so on. Not exactly poetry, but handy for keeping track of your windows.
2. Click another sheet tab in the new window if you want two worksheets on the screen at once.
3. Click Window, Arrange. In the Arrange Windows dialog box, choose to tile or cascade your windows, or display them vertically or horizontally, as shown in Figure 1.13.

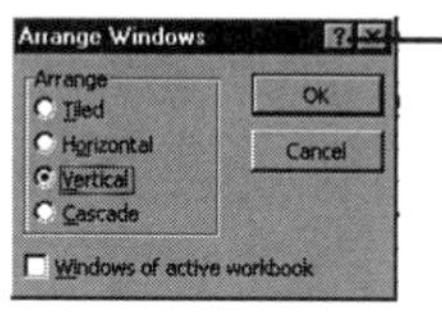

Fig. 1.13
Let the shape of your data determine your window arrangement; narrow tables work better in vertical windows, for example.

Plain English, please!

A **dialog box** is Excel's way of saying "I'm going to execute your command, but I need more information first." Dialog boxes pop up automatically when you give any command that requires more input. Sometimes you type information into dialog boxes; other times you make menu selections or click buttons.

Some dialog boxes hold so many options that they're collected on separate tabs. Click a tab to go to it, just like a worksheet tab. Boxes where you type in information are called **text boxes**. Click the mouse or use the Tab key to move the cursor from one text box to the next.

TIP **If a dialog box gets in the way of what's on the screen, just drag** the dialog box out of the way by its title bar.

4 When you click from window to window, the title bar's color is restored, letting you know which window you're in.

Once selected, a window behaves just like the ordinary Excel screen. You can enter, edit, and work with data just as you always do. Figures 1.14 and 1.15 show two different worksheet views.

TIP **The same techniques apply to viewing more than one workbook** at the same time. Just open the next workbook and use the Window menu to arrange your views.

Sizing and moving

Just as in any Windows program, you can move and size Excel windows by dragging the borders. You can spend a lot of time playing around with stuff like this, and sometimes it's even useful.

TIP **Double-click the Excel title bar to put Excel in a smaller window.** Double-click the title bar again to pop it back to full-screen view. This trick works for any Windows window.

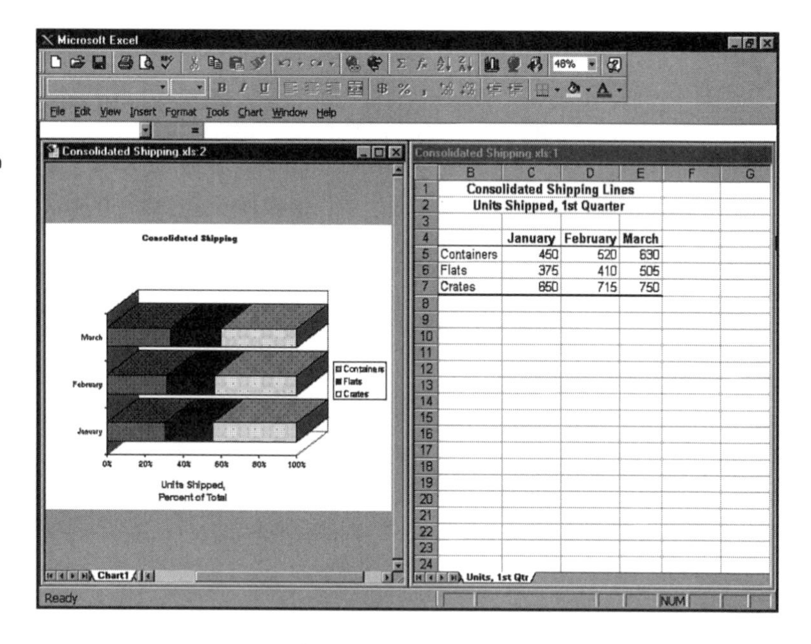

Fig. 1.14
Two different worksheets on the screen at the same time makes working on multiple worksheets much easier. For this view, choose Window, Arrange, Tiled, OK.

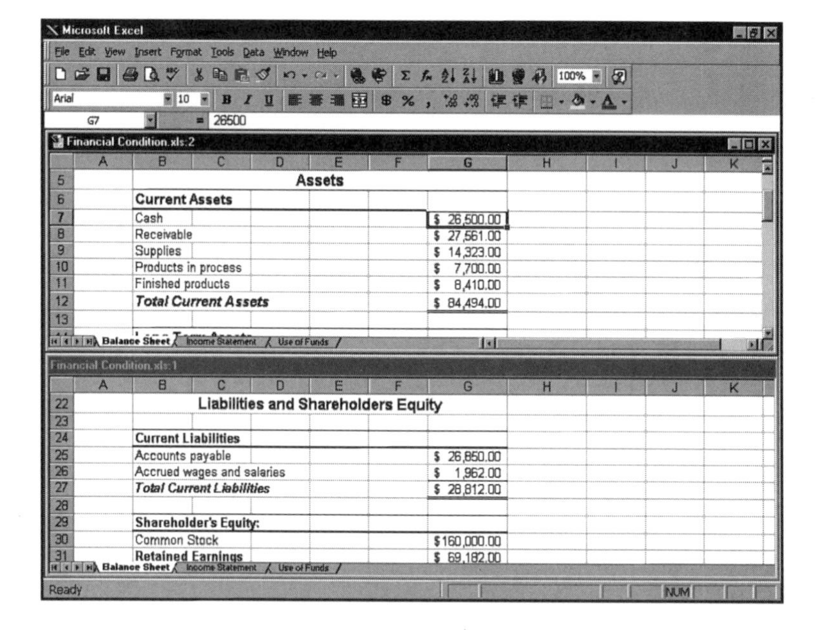

Fig. 1.15
Two views of different parts of the same worksheet. For big sheets, it's a handy feature. For this view, choose Window, Arrange, Horizontal, OK.

2

Building a Worksheet

In this chapter:

- **How do I enter text and numbers?**
- **Hate typing? Let Excel do it for you**
- **What does ###### mean?**
- **Now I'm really done. File this, please**

You can read all the books about tennis ever written, but to learn the game, you have to play it. Excel is no different. To learn it, use it!

Let's face it. For all its analytical prowess and technical wizardry, Excel is nothing without something to work with. It's just like those impressive espresso machines you see in Italian cafes, loaded with knobs and dials and spouts and buttons. Without coffee and water, they might as well be boat anchors. But add those essential ingredients, and aaah…heaven!

For Excel, the "coffee and water" are text and numbers. Without them, you might as well load a screen saver. With them, a world of possibilities opens up.

Make Excel do the dirty work

Entering data isn't much fun. There's no getting around the fact that it involves typing and a certain amount of thinking too. Both activities are things I tend not to do unless forced to. You might be the same way.

Excel can relieve much of the tedium of data entry. There are shortcuts and special features to make the job a little, or even a lot, less burdensome.

Alphabet soup: entering text

Most worksheets start with text. We humans tend to think in terms of descriptions and labels, because they help us make sense of the chaos around us. By labeling things, we impose a little order on them.

Because Excel pretty much forces you to think of your data in terms of workbooks, worksheets, columns, rows, and cells, a certain amount of order is already imposed. Labeling at least some of those elements before you start entering your numbers helps you think about what should go where.

Label rows and columns

Pick a cell near the top of the worksheet to start typing your column and row names. Where exactly? It doesn't really matter, although you may hear a lot of office debate on the subject.

You generally want to start your worksheet near the top of the sheet because that'll save you a lot of scrolling. Just leave a blank row or two at the top to make room for a title. But because you can move everything around anyway, it doesn't really matter where you start typing.

With that in mind, we'll start in cell C4. Select the cell by clicking it. Now type **1st Quarter** and press Enter.

What happened? I typed what I was supposed to type and it spilled over into the next cell. Now what do I do?

You don't *have* to do anything. A cell in Excel is like one of those magician's boxes, stuffed with two rabbits, a violin, a kitchen sink, and whatever else was handy. Similarly, a cell looks small, but it's expandable. If your text doesn't fit, it only *looks* like it's spilling into the next cell. But it really isn't. The other cell is still blank as far as Excel is concerned.

So how do I adjust the size of these columns and rows?

Because you want neat and readable worksheets, not unsightly messes, you'll want to fit the worksheet cells to your data.

To adjust the column width, move the pointer to the border line between columns. In Figure 2.1, that's the line between column heading C and column heading D. Notice how the pointer changes shape. Now double-click. Double-clicking the right border of a column heading automatically widens the column to fit the data.

You can also drag the double-headed arrow in either direction to widen or narrow columns. Figure 2.1 shows you how to adjust column widths.

Don't forget to rename your worksheets. Just double-click the worksheet tab and type in the new name.

I typed my label, I'm pointing at the right column border, but my pointer's a white cross, not a double-headed arrow. What gives?

Type your text, press Enter, *then* point at the right column border. Until you press Enter (or one of the arrow keys), Excel doesn't know that you've finished typing and can't figure out how wide to make the column.

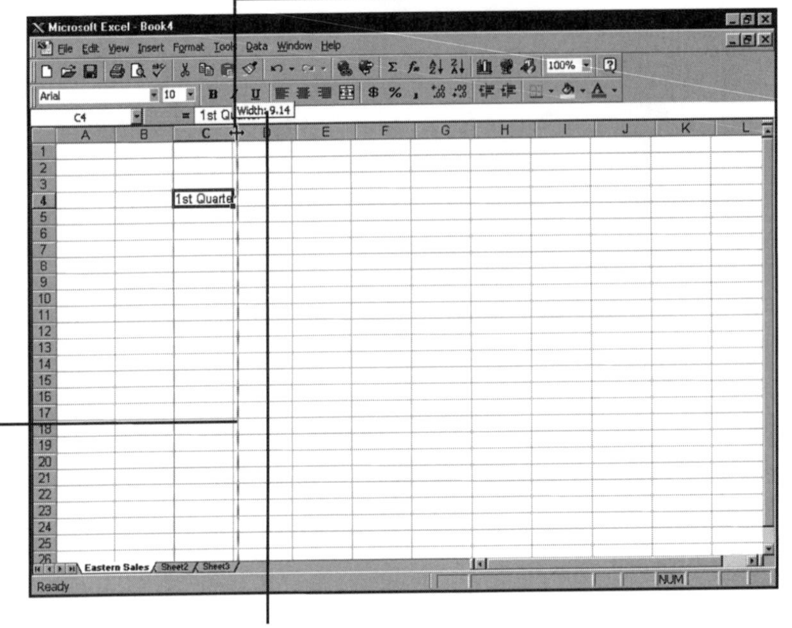

Fig. 2.1
Pointing between column headings and then double-clicking widens the column to fit the widest data in that column.

TIP **As you drag to adjust column width, the width value displayed in** the status box is expressed in terms of the number of characters that will fit in the column. The standard width is 8.43 characters.

To adjust row height and column width for several rows or columns at once, use the menu. Select the cells, then click Format, Row, AutoFit Selection or Format, Column, AutoFit Selection.

The formula bar

You might have noticed something else happening as you typed. Your column title appeared in the cell; it also appeared in the **formula bar** just above the column headings.

You can use the formula bar to edit cell entries—text, numbers, or formulas. Mostly you'll use it for the latter. Figure 2.2 shows you where to find the formula bar.

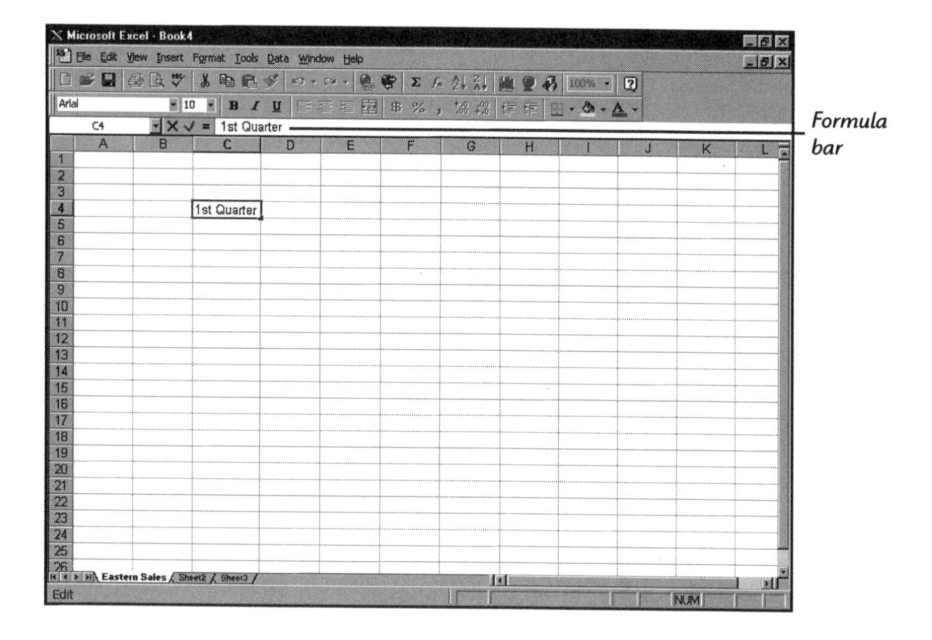

Fig. 2.2
Edit cell entries in the formula bar.

When you started typing, two extra buttons joined the Edit Formula button on the formula bar:

- Click the Edit Formula button to write a formula.

- You can click the Enter button to enter your data in the cell instead of using the Enter key.

If you don't like the look of what you've done, click the Cancel button. It gets rid of what you just typed. If there was anything in the cell before you started, it restores that too.

After you press Enter or move to a new cell, the buttons disappear.

AutoComplete does your typing for you

Typing is always a chore, but repetitive typing adds insult to injury. Ever typed a repetitive list and said to yourself "I can't believe I'm typing this same name *again?*"

Here's some good news: when you type a repetitive entry in an Excel worksheet, you only have to type it once. A nifty Excel gadget called

AutoComplete looks over your shoulder as you type. After you type a couple of letters of the same entry, AutoComplete fills in the rest of the entry for you. Figure 2.3 gives you the idea.

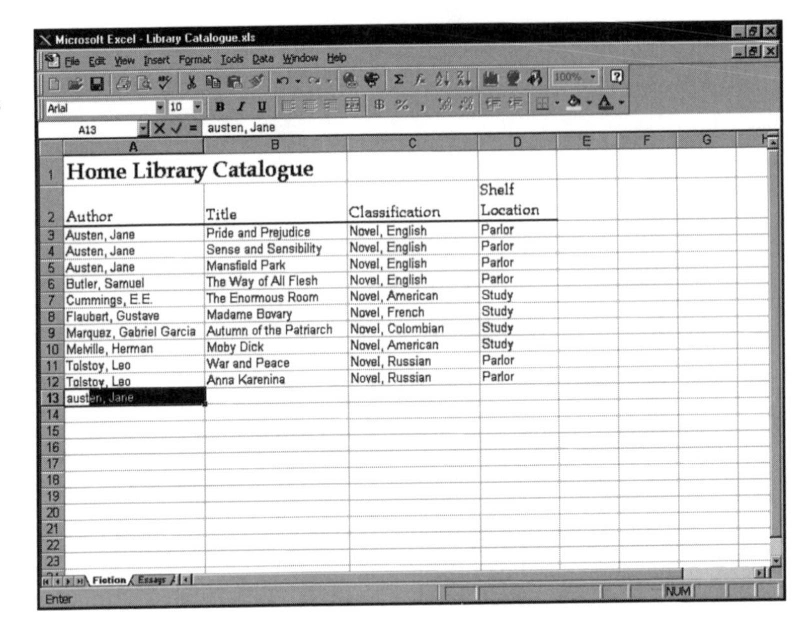

Fig. 2.3
Type **aus** in cell A13, and AutoComplete fills in the highlighted portion of Jane Austen's name.

You don't even have to worry about capitalization. In the example in Figure 2.3, AutoComplete capitalizes Austen's first and last name as soon as you press Enter or an arrow key, exactly as the name appears earlier on the list.

If you type the first few letters of a different listing but AutoComplete fills in the cell anyway, just keep typing—the AutoComplete entry will be overwritten. For example, if I start to type **Austria** in column A, AutoComplete mindlessly fills in Austen, Jane after the first three letters. But as soon as I hit the **r** in Austria, Jane gets obliterated.

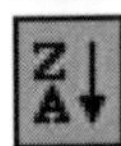

Adding an entry to an Excel list like the one in Figure 2.3 only temporarily disrupts the neat alphabetical order. To re-sort a list in either ascending or descending order, select the list and click the Sort Ascending or Sort Descending buttons on the toolbar. See Chapters 15 and 16 for complete details on creating and managing lists in Excel.

Pick an entry from the AutoComplete list

AutoComplete is a great convenience for repetitive typing jobs. But what if you have entries like the ones in column C of Figure 2.3? Those are identical through the first word and a comma, after which they vary. For AutoComplete to get those kinds of entries right, you'd have to type half the listing before it caught on.

Except that you don't. AutoComplete builds a list of all the entries in a column, and you can fill in a cell by picking from the list.

Select a cell in the column and right-click for the shortcut menu (the pointer has to be the white cross for this to work). Click Pick From List on the shortcut menu, and the AutoComplete list pops up, as shown in Figure 2.4.

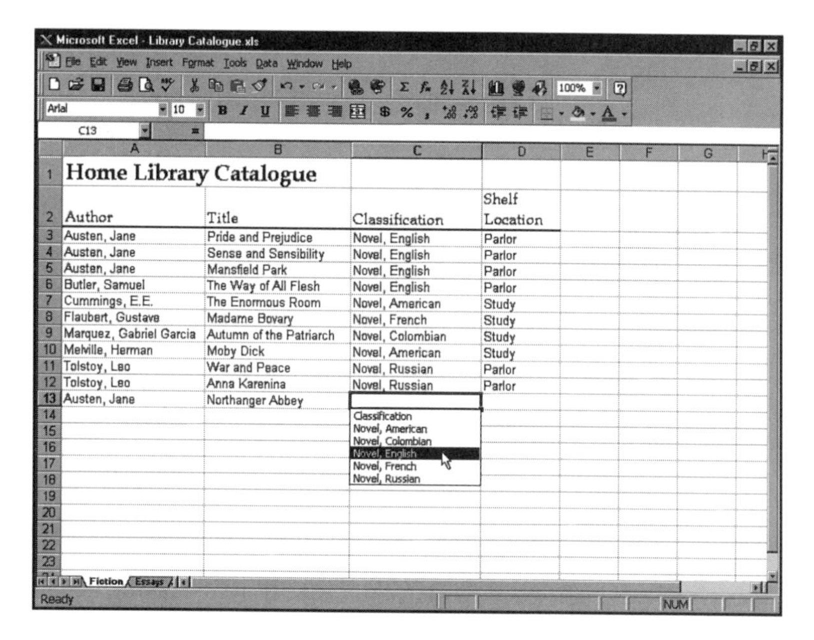

Fig. 2.4
Take your pick from the AutoComplete list, and the value is popped into the selected cell.

Just click a listing on the AutoComplete list and move to the next cell.

How do I turn off AutoComplete!?

If you type a lot of data quickly, you probably won't even notice AutoComplete's efforts to spare your typing fingers. Because AutoComplete's entries are overwritten the second you type something other than the value on the list, it works pretty unobtrusively. But if you really find AutoComplete more annoyance than convenience, just turn it off. Click Tools, Options, and click the Edit tab. Click the Enable AutoComplete for Cell Values check box to remove the check mark, and click OK.

AutoFill also lightens your typing chores

There's an old-fashioned hardware store near my home, run by a guy who's been in the business for 40 years. Although I've seen him do it many times, I can never get over the uncanny way he knows what his customers want, even when they're not sure themselves.

Somebody will wander in and say, "I need a gizmo to hook up a—oh, what's-it-called to a, um, thingie, so that, you know, the sink…" The store owner will interrupt and say, "Sink? Oh, sure. You need a number five double headbolt with a ratchet attachment, a Larsen's wrench, and six one-inch threaded sprockets." Give him one coherent clue, and he gets it right every time.

AutoFill does more or less the same thing. All you do is type in the first value or values in a series, either numbers or text. AutoFill then completes the series for you. How does it do that? You'd have to ask my hardware store owner.

Let's get back to that worksheet we're creating. We've got `1st Quarter` typed into cell C4. Select C4. Now that it's the active cell, it's got a heavy border around it. Notice the lower-right corner of the border. It's a little square and it's called the **fill handle**, as shown in Figure 2.5. It's shown with Zoom Control at 200% so you can see it better.

Aim at the fill handle. The pointer turns into a black cross. Now drag the fill handle through cell F4. Each cell in the range is faintly outlined, and a status box displays each item in the series as you drag. It should look like Figure 2.6.

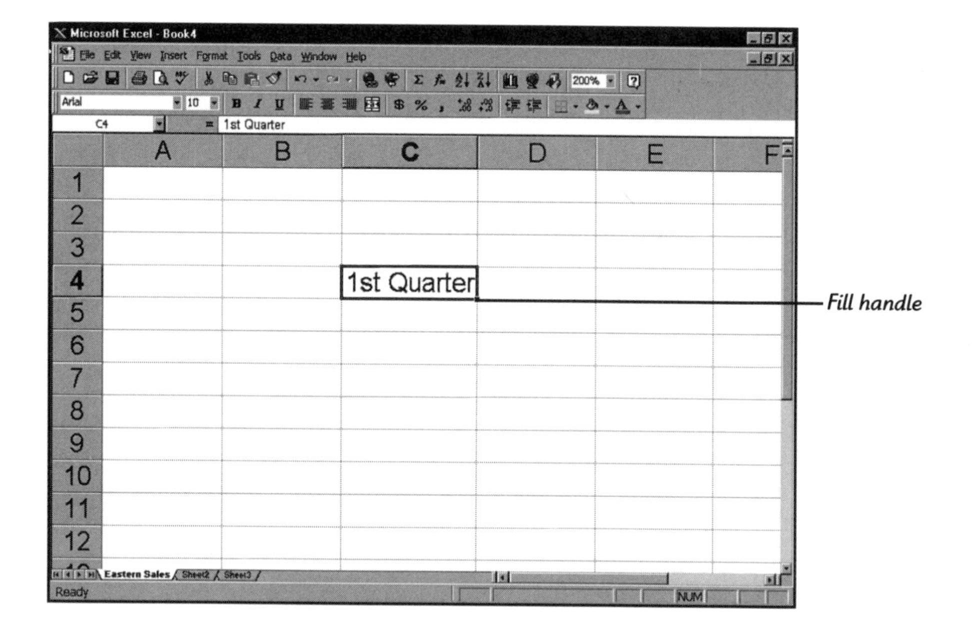

Fig. 2.5
Get to know the fill handle, an amazingly useful Excel feature.

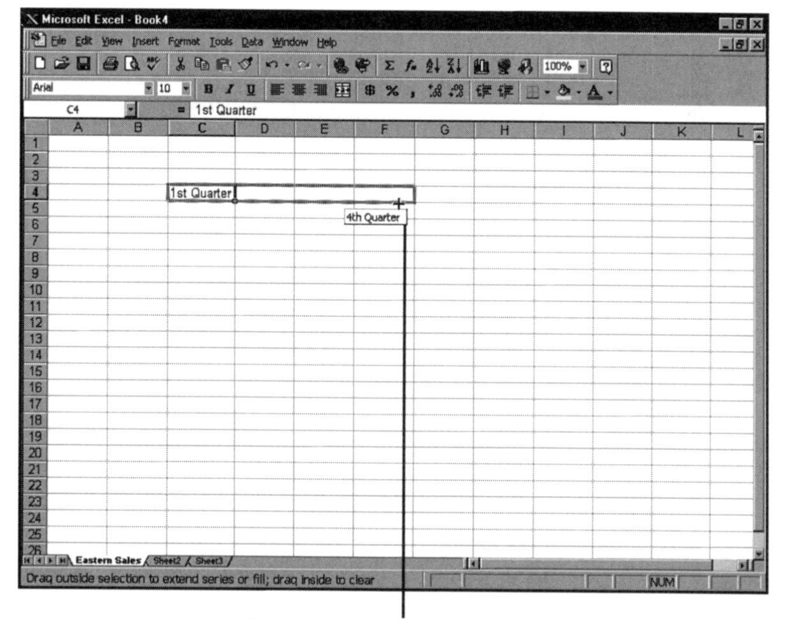

Fig. 2.6
The pointer changes to a black cross when you place it over the fill handle, and cells are outlined as you drag through a range.

Release the mouse button, and—how about that! Your column headings are filled in, as shown in Figure 2.7.

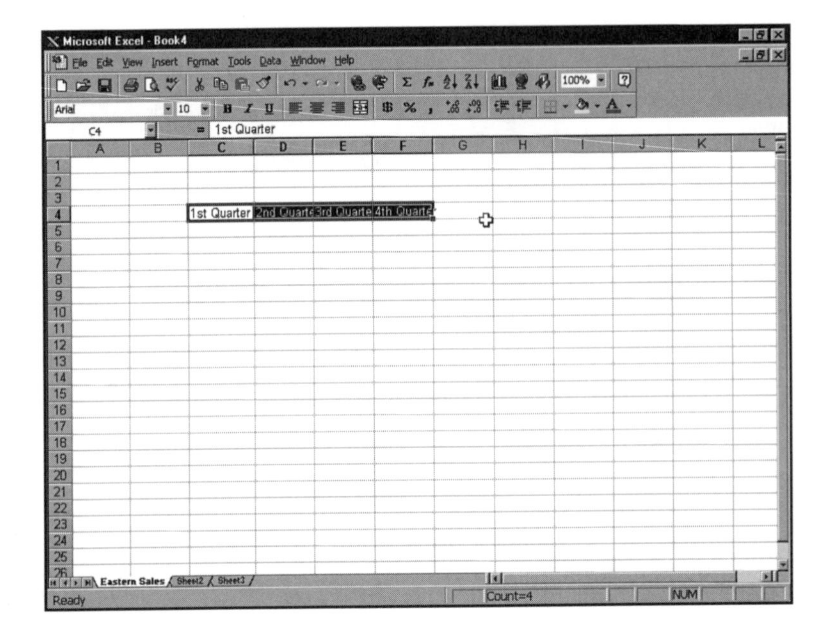

Fig. 2.7
AutoFill looks at the first cell and guesses what you want in the next three.

Q&A ***I've got the fill handle, my pointer is a black cross, but when I start to drag, nothing happens. What gives?***

Keep on dragging. Those faint cell borders that tell you you're filling in a range with AutoFill don't appear until you get about halfway through the first cell.

Handy AutoFill uses

You can do a lot with AutoFill. Use it to repeat values, continue a series, or extend a list. It works with numbers, days of the week, months, and dates. All you do is type in the first value, drag, and release.

If you overshoot your mark, it's no big deal. Just drag the fill handle back to the cell you want to stop at. AutoFill erases the unwanted data and leaves the cell blank.

AutoFill is smart as well as handy. What it puts in the range depends on what you have in the first cell. If you type **Sun** and drag the fill handle, AutoFill obediently continues with `Mon`, `Tue`, and so on. Likewise, a date: type in **1/5/96**, drag the fill handle, and you'll get `1/6/96`, `1/7/96`, and so on. Same with January (or Jan), February, March, and so on.

Plain English, please!

What are these constant references to **values**? Here we leave the realm of computer jargon and enter the older world of mathematical jargon. When we speak of values of the kind that AutoFill repeats or extends, we're using shorthand. Technically, they're **constant values**; so-called because they don't change until we change them. The number 5 is a value, and so is Sunday. Anything like that typed into a cell is a constant value, which we abbreviate to just plain "value."

There are other kinds of values. **Logical values** are True and False, for example. If you write a formula that doesn't make sense, Excel won't solve it for you; instead you'll get an **error value**.

But if you type **Expenses** and drag with the fill handle, you'll just repeat Expenses through the range. That's because AutoFill only recognizes certain words, and "Expenses" isn't one of them. Yet. You can teach AutoFill any words you like, which is exactly what we'll do next.

To see what AutoFill recognizes right now, select Tools, Options, Custom Lists. The lists you'll see there don't include series like 1st Quarter, 2nd Quarter… or Product 1, Product 2…. AutoFill automatically increments numbered series like those if you type the first entry.

This is all fine and dandy, but suppose I enter something that AutoFill thinks I want repeated, like 4,000, but what I want in the next cells is 4,001, 4,002, and so on.

No problem. Press Ctrl as you drag the fill handle. The cross of the fill pointer acquires a little plus sign, and AutoFill extends the series. The Ctlr+AutoFill combination tells Excel to take the value in the starting cell and increment it.

Great. But suppose I enter a value like Sunday that I want to copy across a range? How do I prevent Excel from filling in the series Sunday, Monday, and so on?

Ctrl again. Pressing Ctrl while you drag the fill handle also stops Excel from incrementing values that it normally would.

CAUTION **Dragging the fill handle through cells that have data in them** overwrites the data.

TIP **You might get confused about what AutoFill does with what data.** Even saying it is confusing. But there's an easy way to sort it out.

Drag the fill handle with the *right* mouse button. The pointer turns back into an arrow, and the AutoFill shortcut menu pops up when you release the mouse button (see Figure 2.8). Then you can take your pick of actions from the list.

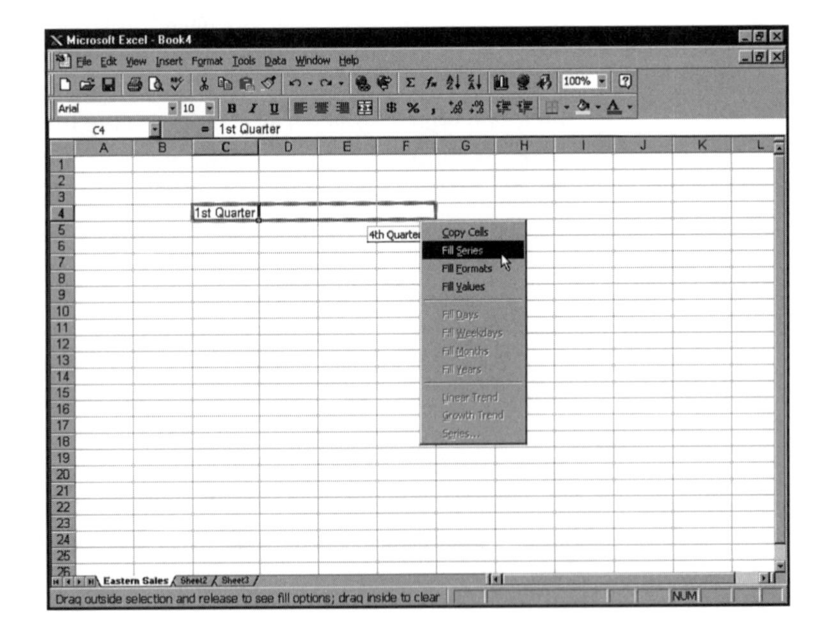

Fig. 2.8
Dragging the fill handle with the right mouse button gets you the shortcut menu, the easy way of keeping AutoFill options straight.

Make your own AutoFill lists

Suppose you use certain column or row headings all the time, but they don't happen to be recognized by AutoFill. Does that mean you have to retype those headings whenever you want them? Not at all. Teach AutoFill to type them in for you!

Let's go back to the spreadsheet we're building. So far we've got a sheet name from Chapter 1 and four column titles. Now let's put in the row titles.

Select cell B5, type **Sales**, and press the down arrow.

After you type data in a cell, the arrow keys have the same effect as pressing Enter, with the advantage that they move the active cell where you want it. If you're filling rows, use the down arrow key; columns, the right or left arrow keys.

In cell B6, type **COGS** (for Cost of Goods Sold). Press the down arrow to cell B7, and type **Selling Expenses**. In B8, enter **Misc. Expenses**; in B9, **Total Expenses**; and in B10, **Net Sales**. Don't forget to double-click the heading border line between columns B and C to fit in your row titles.

Now select column B by clicking the column heading, and let's take AutoFill to school.

1 Click Tools, Options.

2 Click the Custom Lists tab (see Figure 2.9).

3 The range we've selected, column B, appears in the Import List from Cells box. Click Import.

4 There's our list. Click OK and we're done.

The next time your worksheet calls for the row titles (Sales, COGS, Selling Expenses, Misc. Expenses, Total Expenses, and Net Sales), just type in **Sales** and drag the fill handle through the range where you want the rest of the row labels. AutoFill types them in for you when you release the mouse button. Try it!

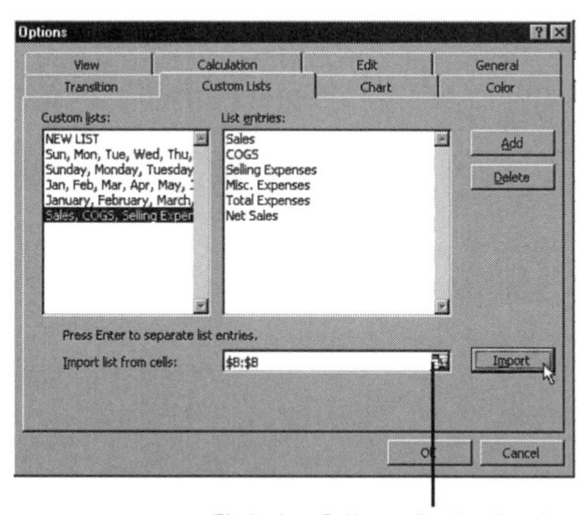

Click the Collapse Dialog Box button to minimize the dialog box if it gets in the way; click the button again to maximize the dialog box

Fig. 2.9
Enter custom lists for AutoFill directly in the Custom Lists tab, or select the list from the worksheet and import it.

Figure 2.10 shows the way our worksheet looks with the rows labeled.

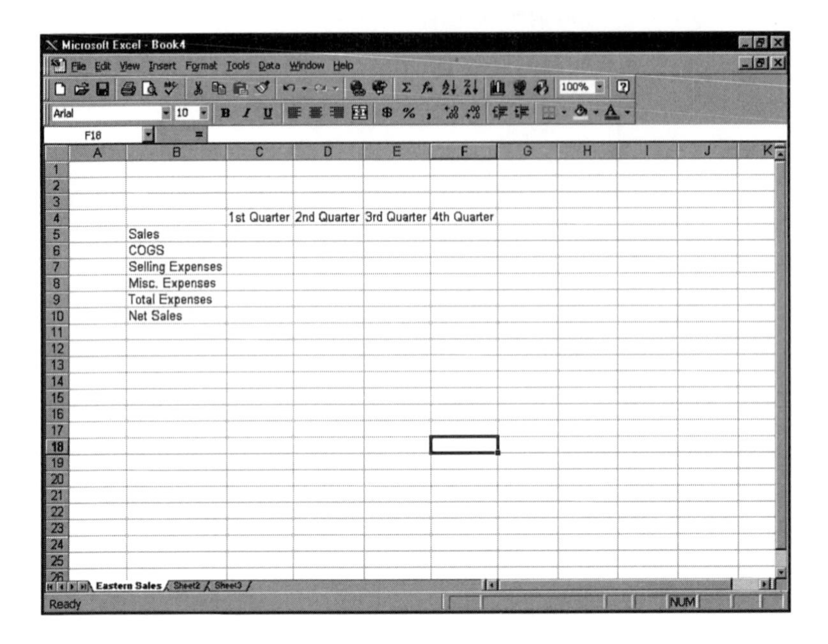

Fig. 2.10
Now that these labels are on an AutoFill list, we'll never have to type them again.

Your number's up: entering numbers

Excel is a program designed to handle numbers, so entering them ought to be pretty straightforward. It is—just select a cell and start typing. That's about all there is to it!

Taking up our worksheet again, select cell C5 and type **2,567,000,498**. Click the Enter button on the formula bar or press the Enter key, whatever's easier.

This number doesn't fit!

Something's wrong. Instead of the number, we see ######. Not a problem. It's just Excel's way of saying, "Your number's too long for that cell, and if I can't display the whole thing, I won't display any of it. So there."

We can widen our columns by double-clicking the right column heading border. Or we can just decide that the worksheet is displaying numbers in thousands. Enter your numbers rounded to the nearest thousand, add a notation on the worksheet to that effect, and go back to work.

Excel can also display numbers too long to fit in cells in scientific notation. If the cell was formatted that way, 2,567,000,498 would look like this: `3.E+09`. That's another way of saying, "Take 3 and multiply it by 10 multiplied by itself 9 times." I tend not to think in those terms either, so I just widen the column or use shorter numbers.

Massaging the numbers

Excel gives you plenty of options for formatting numbers. Adjusting the number of decimal places the program displays and applying preset comma, percentage, and currency styles can all be accomplished with the buttons on the Formatting toolbar (see Figure 2.11). See Chapter 7 for an in-depth look at the Formatting toolbar, and for details on formatting in general, including fancier effects.

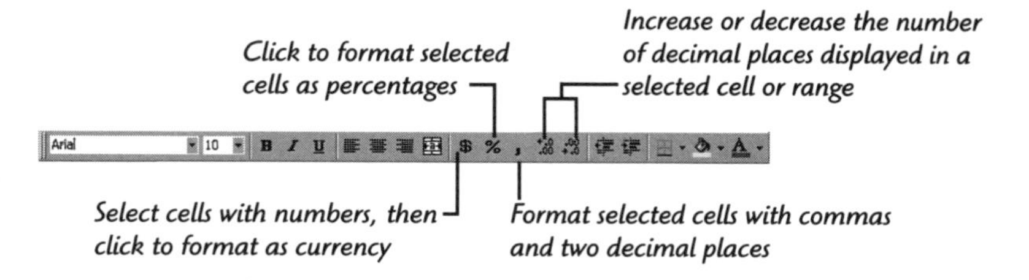

Fig. 2.11
The Formatting toolbar provides quick fixes for formatting numbers.

Meanwhile, back to work. Type the numbers into the worksheet so that it looks like Figure 2.12. If you make a typing mistake, just use Backspace or Delete.

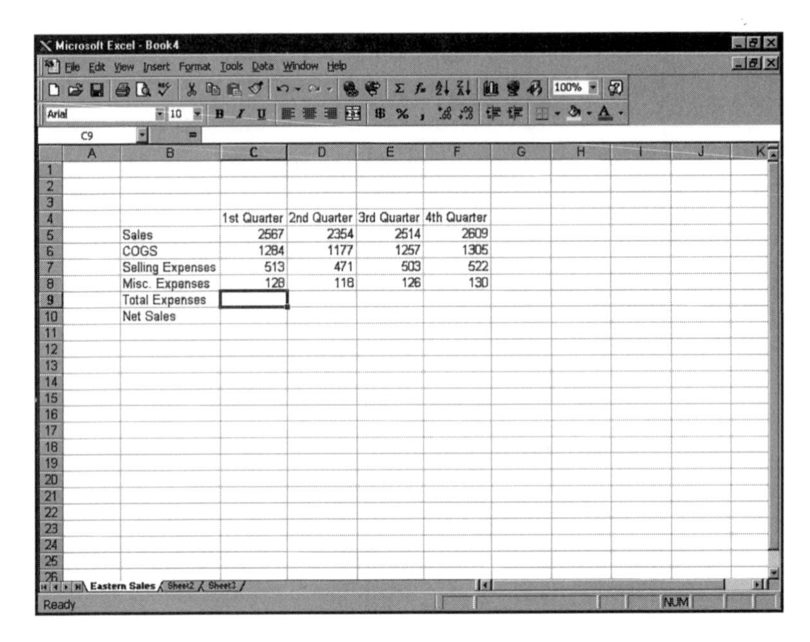

Fig. 2.12
This is what your worksheet should look like so far.

AutoCalculate, for results on-the-fly

We have our data entered. Now all we have to do is sum it up. First, we'll total our expenses. Click C6 and drag through C8 to select the range. Not the fill handle—this time we're highlighting a range. The pointer should be the fat white cross.

Once the range is selected, take a look at the right side of the status bar down at the bottom of the screen. AutoCalculate gives us a running summary of our selected data.

To change the type of running calculation AutoCalculate displays, point at the status bar and right-click for the shortcut menu shown in Figure 2.13.

You get a choice of functions for AutoCalculate to display:

- Average displays the mean of the values in a selected range.
- Count gives you a count of the number of occupied cells in a selected range. Count counts cells with numbers or text; blank cells are ignored.
- Count Nums counts the number of cells containing numbers in a selected range. Cells with non-numeric data and blank cells aren't counted.

- Max and Min display the highest or lowest values in a selected range.
- Sum totals the values in a selected range.

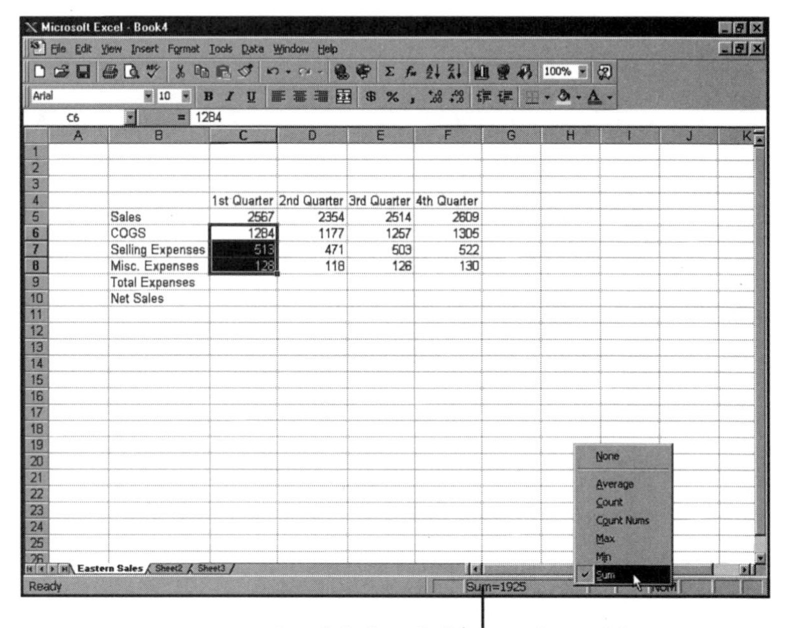

AutoCalculate displays your choice of functions

Fig. 2.13
Right-click anywhere on the status bar to make the AutoCalculate shortcut menu appear.

Summing up with AutoSum

Use AutoCalculate for a quick read on your numbers. It's especially useful when you're testing the effects of changing values, but you don't want to actually insert the totals in the worksheet.

In the case of our worksheet, we do want a total inserted in column C. We still have our expenses in column C selected, C6:C8 (refer to Figure 2.13).

To insert a total for the selected range, click the AutoSum button on the toolbar. Cells C6:C8 are automatically totaled, and the result is dumped in the next cell in the column, C9.

We could repeat this procedure for all our columns, but we won't. We hate typing, remember? And we like to keep our mousing to a minimum as well.

Instead, use that handy fill handle. Select C9, Total Expenses. Notice the formula in the formula bar. AutoSum has produced that for us, and we'll copy it across Row 9 with the fill handle. As we do so, the range automatically adjusts to reflect the cells in each column. It's a neat trick, and it's another reason why spreadsheets have it all over the calculator.

Point at the fill handle in C9 and drag through F9. Figure 2.14 shows you how to do it.

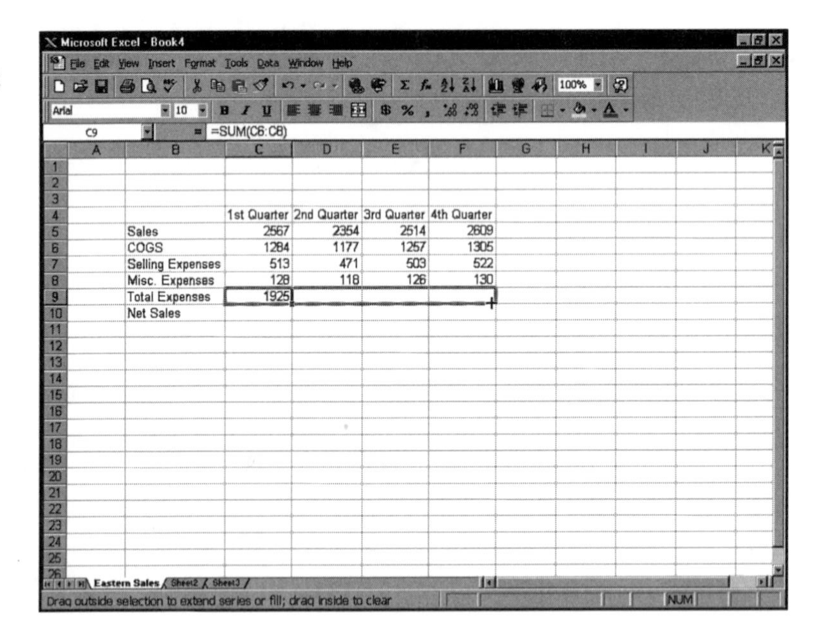

Fig. 2.14
We're actually copying the SUM function across a range of cells.

AutoSum is pretty smart. We selected the range for AutoSum to add, but we didn't have to. Instead of selecting a range, just select the cell in which you want the total to appear. Click the AutoSum button and AutoSum guesses the range you want to sum, putting a moving border (like a movie theater marquee) around the range. If the guess is right, press Enter. If AutoSum guesses wrong, drag through the range you want summed. The moving border moves with you. When it encloses the correct range, press Enter.

The third "R": doing 'rithmetic with Excel

Excel is a genius at arithmetic. It adds, subtracts, multiplies, and divides in the blink of an eye. But like any genius, it has a quirk. Arithmetic operations, or any sort of formula, always start with the = sign. Always. If you leave it out, Excel thinks you're entering a column title, a label, or anything but a formula. Because Excel begins formulas with an = sign automatically, forgetfulness need not be a problem.

Plain English, please!

What is a **formula**? 2+2=4 is a fine example. A formula is just a series of steps, like a recipe. This one says: take the number 2, add 2 to it, and get the number 4. We write it in shorthand as 2+2=4. And in Excel, we write it as =2+2. The answer, 4, gets dumped in the cell where we put the formula. (You can learn more about formulas in Chapter 8.) 

We've got our costs totaled in row 9. If we want to know our Net Sales (Sales minus Expenses), all we need to do is subtract Total Expenses from Sales. Our Sales are in C5, and our Total Expenses are in C9. We know we have to start the formula with an = sign. The formula we'll enter in C10 is **=C5–C9**.

All we need to do is type the formula. The good news? Most of the formula doesn't even have to be typed! Here's the fast way to write an Excel formula:

1. Select the cell where you want to put the formula (here, it's C10) and click the Edit Formula button on the formula bar.
2. Click the first cell we need to put in the formula, C5. You see C5 appear in both the cell and the formula bar, right after the = sign. A moving border called a **marquee** appears around C5 at the same time.
3. Type the – sign, then click C9 to stick the cell in the formula, as shown in Figure 2.15.
4. Press Enter, and the formula is complete. Excel makes the calculation and sticks the answer in C10.

Whenever you need to insert cell references in a formula or a dialog box, just click the cells or drag through a range. The references are inserted at the insertion point.

Entering cell references with the mouse not only saves your time and typing fingers, it also cuts down on reference errors.

Begin any new formula with a click of the Edit Formula button

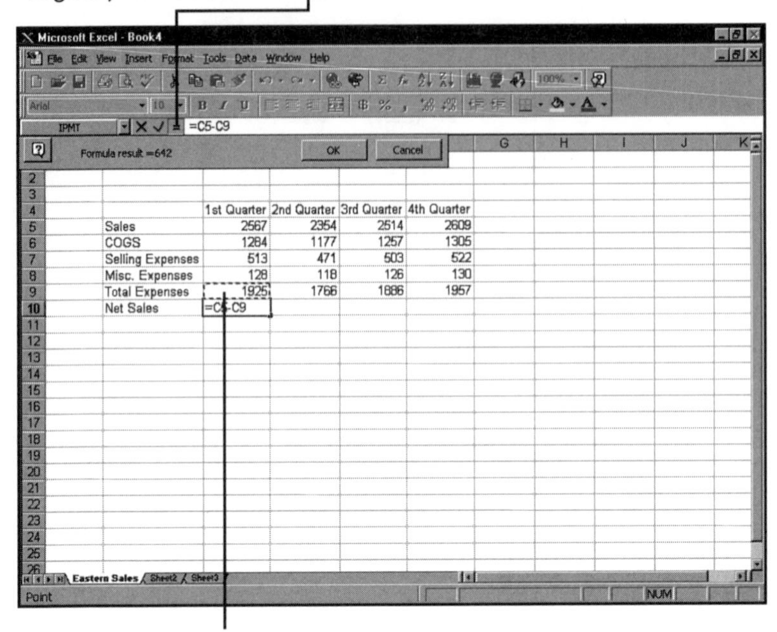

Click the cell you want in the formula; the cell reference appears at the insertion point

Fig. 2.15
Selecting a cell or range with the mouse is the fast way to insert cell references in Excel formulas.

I did what I was supposed to do, but I don't see my formula in C10. All I see is the answer. What's wrong?

The formula *is* in C10. So is the result. Remember that magician's box? There's more to cells than meets the eye.

Your formulas are always visible in the formula bar. When you click a cell with a formula in it, the formula appears up in the formula bar, and the result appears in the cell. To edit a formula you've already entered, just select the cell, and click the part of the formula you want to edit in the formula bar.

We're nearly done. One more turn of the fill handle will see us home. Select C10, and drag the fill handle through F10. Our new formula is copied across the row, with the results neatly dumped into the cells.

Whew! Your first worksheet is done (see Figure 2.16). You'll be able to do the next one in your sleep.

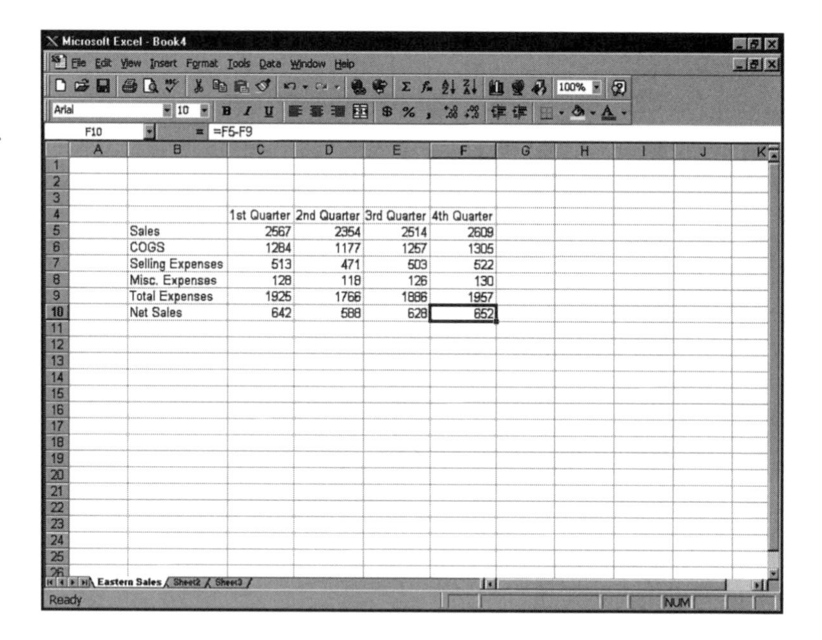

	1st Quarter	2nd Quarter	3rd Quarter	4th Quarter
Sales	2567	2354	2514	2609
COGS	1284	1177	1257	1305
Selling Expenses	513	471	503	522
Misc. Expenses	128	118	126	130
Total Expenses	1925	1766	1886	1957
Net Sales	642	588	628	652

Fig. 2.16
The finished product? Maybe not quite. This table lacks eye appeal.

Make it look good, and fast!

We had a new front staircase put on our house. It's solid, well built, and a lot safer than the rickety thing it replaced. But it badly needs a paint job. Those new stairs look pretty naked without that final touch.

The worksheet we've just created reminds me of my stairs. The numbers all check out, but it looks a little forlorn.

A title might help. In B3, type **XYZ Corporation.** That's better, but we can improve on it. We'll use AutoFormat to give our work a finished look.

1. Click any cell in the table.
2. Click Format, AutoFormat.
3. From the list of formats, select Accounting 3. Take a look at the other formats while you're here. If you prefer a different style, go ahead and pick it.
4. Click OK to instantly format your table in the selected style. If you don't like the way your AutoFormat choice looks, just click any cell within the table and choose another AutoFormat style.

As you can see from Figure 2.17, those quick formatting changes give us a dramatically different look for our table.

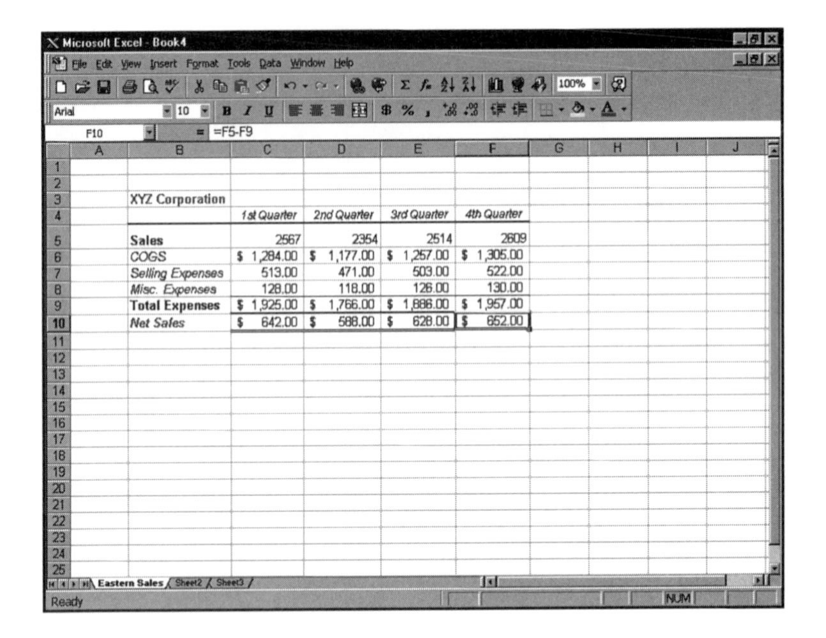

Fig. 2.17
Thanks to a little help from AutoFormat, our worksheet is presentable.

File this, please

I save my important papers in a file cabinet filled with labeled file folders. You probably do the same. Excel workbooks should be stored that way too. Naming the workbook with a name that means something to you months from now is a smart thing to do. It makes your files accessible when you need them again. It can also organize your hard work in a useful way.

You can name your workbooks whatever you want. In Windows 95, you can use up to 255 characters for file names, including spaces. Those obscure old DOS file names are a thing of the past.

Saving a workbook with a helpful name is easy to do. Click the Save button on the toolbar. That pops up the Save As dialog box. Type your workbook name in the File Name text box and click Save. By default, the workbook is saved to the My Documents folder.

Opening and closing workbooks

Once your workbook is named and saved, you can close it, or just exit the program. To reopen saved workbooks, click the Open button on the toolbar.

If you use the File menu to open workbooks, the last four workbooks you've used are displayed. Click a file name to open it.

Help Is But a Click (or Two) Away

In this chapter:

- **An assistant who helps out without being asked? That's helpful!**
- **How do I find help for *my* question?**
- **Is there a better way to do this?**
- **Excel can show me exactly what to do?**
- **This dialog box needs some explaining!**
- **There's a world-wide network of help on the other side of my modem**

Even Excel experts run into occasional dead ends. The quick way out, for experts and nonexperts alike, is through Excel's built-in Help. . . . .

We might take it for granted, but we all need help from time to time. And whether it's that handy call box by the side of the road or that alarming red button in an elevator, help is all around us.

Ordinarily, you just have to know where to look for it. With Excel's new Office Assistant, you don't have to look at all. Help comes to you unprompted and unasked, even when you think you don't need it.

There's plenty of help in Excel, and it's all easy to find. Whatever your problem—from guidance for a new feature, to a thorny worksheet error, to a simple query—Excel Help provides fast answers and practical solutions.

Your new assistant is always on the job

The ideal office worker labors 24 hours a day, knows more about the task at hand than you do, vanishes at the click of a button, has a personality that can be radically changed whenever it becomes annoying—and doesn't exist. Until now, at any rate. Excel's new Office Assistant greets you when you first run the program, sticks around until you dismiss it, then reappears when you try another Excel feature. The Office Assistant is stuffed with helpful tips to improve your efficiency. The Assistant also provides step-by-step guidance through Excel's features if you want it.

Best of all, if you don't like the way the Office Assistant shows up for work, you can give it a complete makeover. A paper clip that bats its eyes might not be your cup of tea. If so, give the creature a complete change of personality and call up the Office Assistant in another incarnation.

To change the Office Assistant character:

1 Insert your Excel or Microsoft Office CD-ROM.

2 If the Assistant and its balloon isn't already visible, click the Office Assistant button on the Standard toolbar. If you have the Assistant window on the screen but no balloon, just click the Assistant (see Figure 3.1).

3 Click Options in the Office Assistant balloon. In the Office Assistant dialog box that appears, click the Gallery tab.

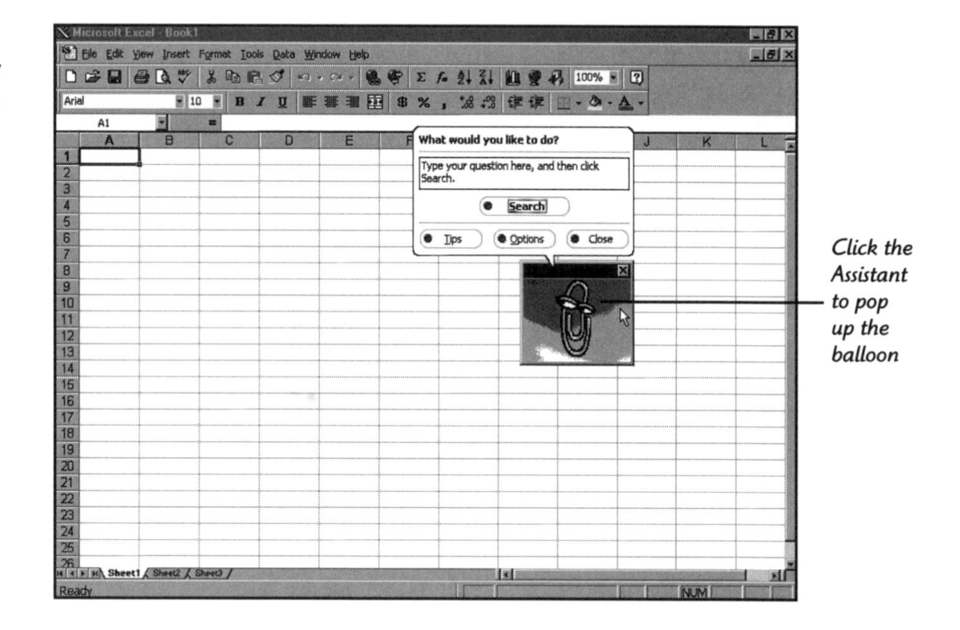

Fig. 3.1
If the appeal of a coy paper clip wears thin, give it a personality transplant.

4 Click Next and Back to cycle through the Office Assistant's various personalities. Among others, you'll find a smiling blob called The Dot, an Einstein look-alike (who immodestly requires about 4M of hard disk space!), a dog, a cat, a robot, and the Bard himself (see Figure 3.2).

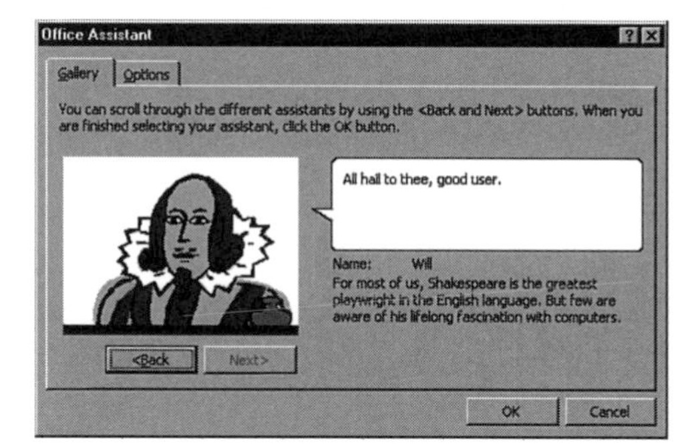

Fig. 3.2
"A man of sovereign parts he is esteem'd," though William Shakespeare might have seen his appearance here as "Like a fair house, built on another man's ground."

5 Make your choice on the Gallery tab, then click the Options tab. Here's the place to turn off sound effects if you don't want them, and to adjust the way the Office Assistant interacts with the program (see Figure 3.3).

6 After you select your choice of Assistant and its options, click OK in the Office Assistant dialog box to save your changes.

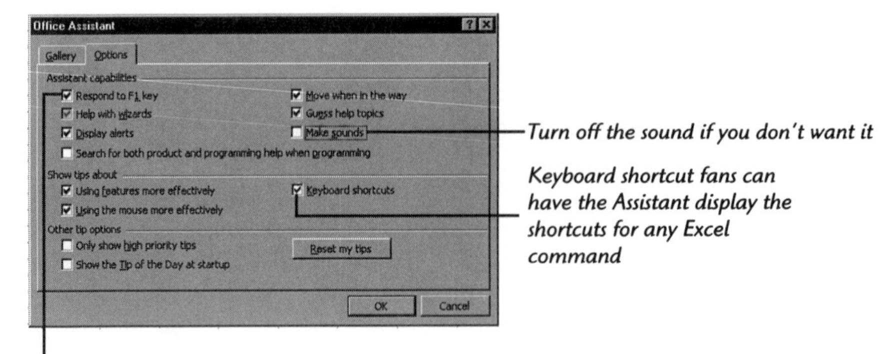

Fig. 3.3
Change the way the Office Assistant behaves to make it more helpful, less intrusive.

TIP **Want to wake up the Office Assistant? Right-click the Office** Assistant window and choose Animate from the shortcut menu.

How do I use the Office Assistant?

If you're learning your way around Excel, you might find it helpful to leave the Office Assistant on the screen, at least at first. Drag the Office Assistant window to an inconspicuous corner of the screen, and carry on with your work. From time to time you'll see a lightbulb appear in the Office Assistant window; click the lightbulb for a tip on how to do what you're doing better.

Try it. With the Office Assistant window displayed, type **Sunday**, press Enter, then type **Monday.** Now click the Office Assistant lightbulb, and you'll get a helpful hint, as shown in Figure 3.4.

Even if the Office Assistant window is closed, you'll find it popping back up when you try a major Excel feature. Click the Paste Function button, for example, and the Assistant appears with an offer of help. Choose Yes, Please Provide Help in the Office Assistant balloon, and you'll get help directly related to what you're trying to accomplish. If you need a function in your calculations and you're not sure which function to use, the Office Assistant is particularly helpful (see Figure 3.5).

The Office Assistant tries to guess what help to offer, based on the Excel commands you give and the features you use. It's not always on the mark; some of the tips will be unrelated to what you're doing. But even when it's not strictly relevant, the Office Assistant still makes a terrific Excel tutor.

Fig. 3.4
Some tips are more helpful than others; this is a good one.

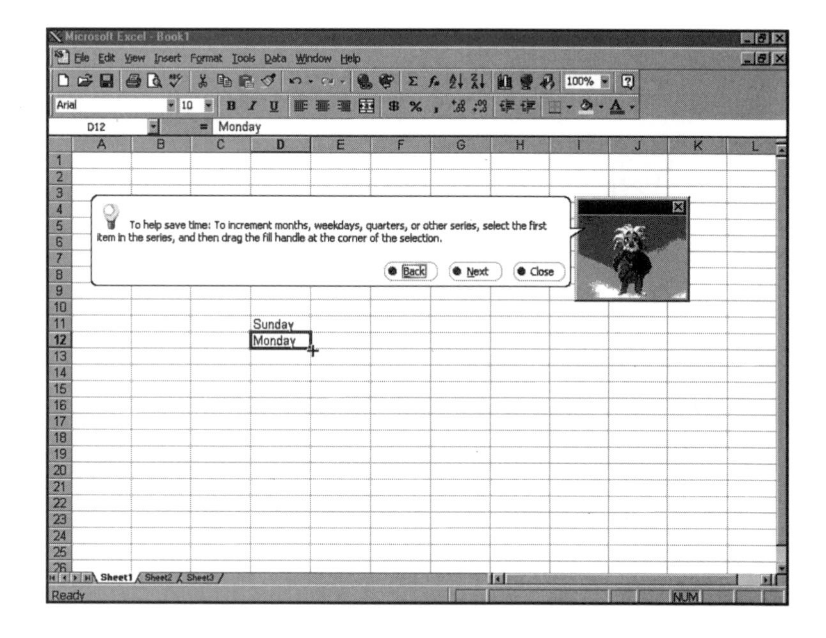

Fig. 3.5
The Office Assistant automatically provides help related to the task at hand.

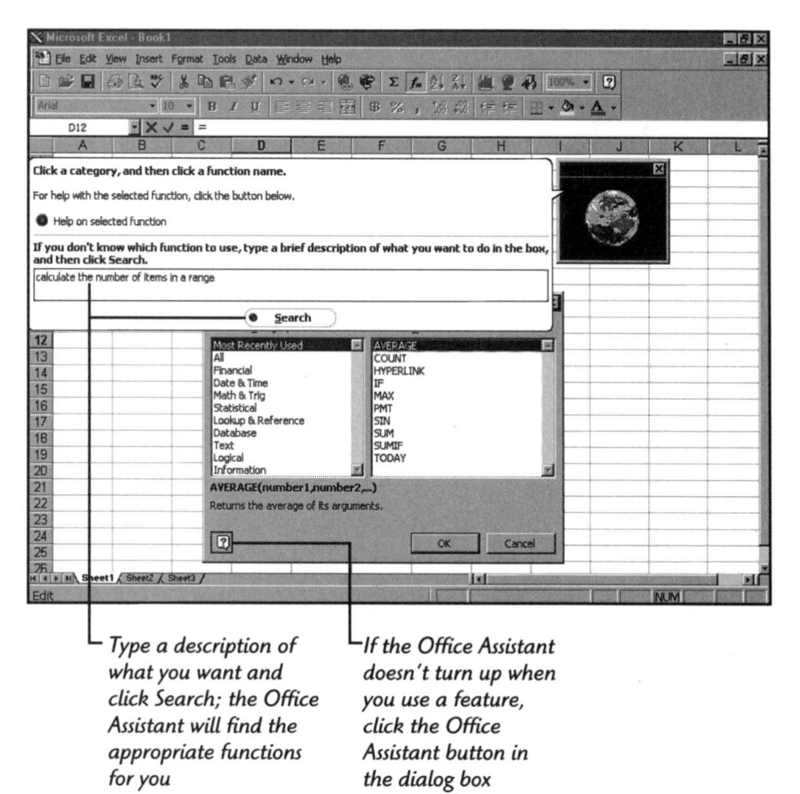

TIP **If the Office Assistant tips don't seem to be responding as you** work, try resetting them. Click the Office Assistant button, and choose Options in the balloon. In the Office Assistant dialog box, select the Options tab, click Reset my tips, and click OK. You may get tips you've seen already, but at least you'll know all is well with the Assistant.

Help you bring with you

You can grab Excel Help and take it with you. Press Shift+F1, and your pointer is joined by the What's This question mark.

Point the question mark at any toolbar button or menu item, and click to see the Help discussion of what it does. Click screen gadgets, like the row or column headings or the formula bar, and you'll get an explanation of what they're all about.

I find that little question mark most useful in explaining cryptic menu commands. If you click Format, Sheet, for example, and wonder what Background does, just grab the question mark with Shift+F1. Point at the command, and the Help explanation pops up. Figure 3.6 shows the What's This question mark in action.

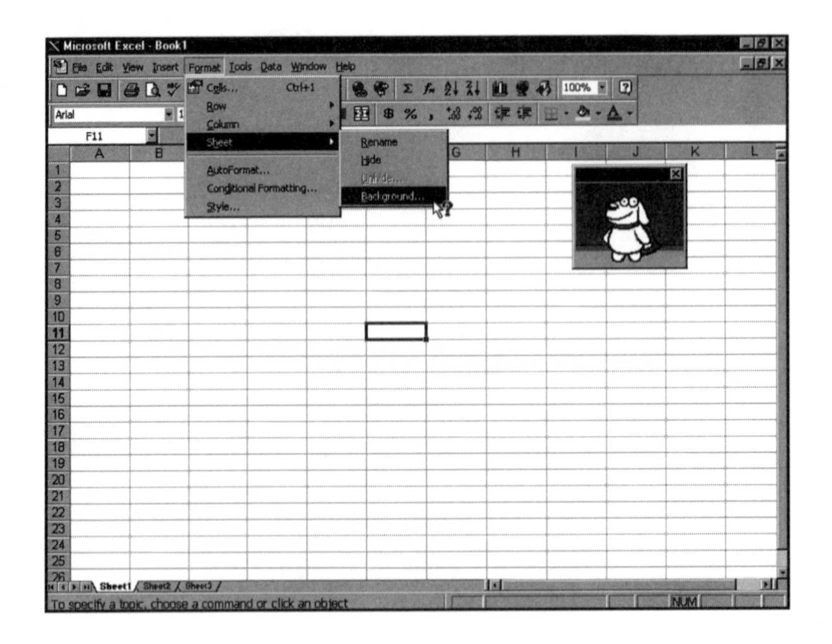

Fig. 3.6
The What's This question mark follows your pointer around like a faithful pup. Click anything on the screen for the associated ScreenTip.

Finding help

The Office Assistant and the What's This question mark are nifty tools, but if you prefer to get help the old-fashioned way, you can. Suppose, for example, that you have to print your worksheet, but your printer isn't printing.

First try the Office Assistant window: type your question in the balloon, and click Search. That'll give you help topics that the Assistant deems most relevant. For something more comprehensive, click Help, Contents and Index. That takes you straight to the Help Topics dialog box. To search for information about a topic, click the Find tab.

Find searches through all the Excel Help topics, looking for matches with any word or phrase you type. Before it can do that, Find has to build a list of the words in Excel's Help topics. That's why the Find Setup Wizard appears, shown in Figure 3.7, the first time you use Find.

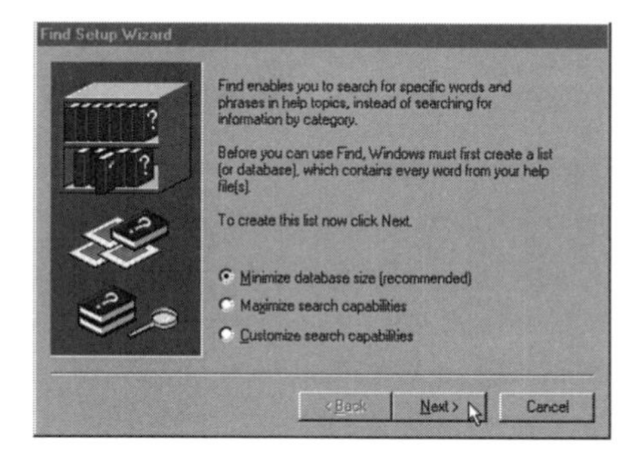

Fig. 3.7
The default choice of database size should work fine; if you have plenty of memory, maximize the database for faster searching.

Putting Find to work is a quick, three-step job:

1. Type a key word in the step 1 text box. Any word that has something to do with your topic will work, but the more specific, the better. If you're having trouble with your printer, for example, type **printer**.
2. Find looks through all the Excel Help files for matches of the word you typed, and displays them in the list in step 2. The Help files in which the words were found are listed in step 3, as shown in Figure 3.8.
3. Take your pick from the list of Help topics in step 3, then click Display. That pops up the Help window you're after (see Figure 3.9).

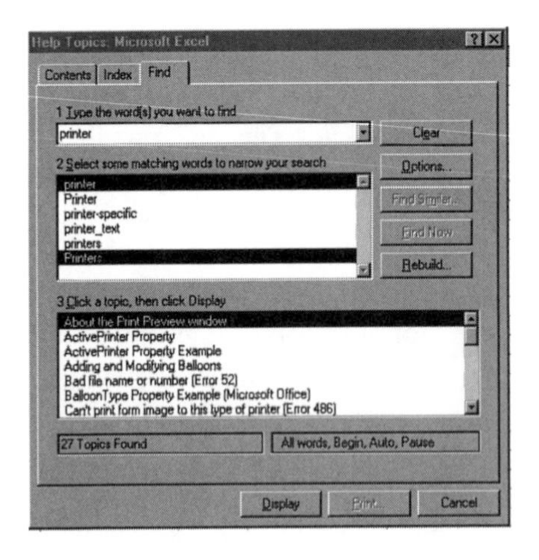

Fig. 3.8
Click one (or Ctrl+click several) word(s) in step 2 if you want to narrow the list of Help files in step 3.

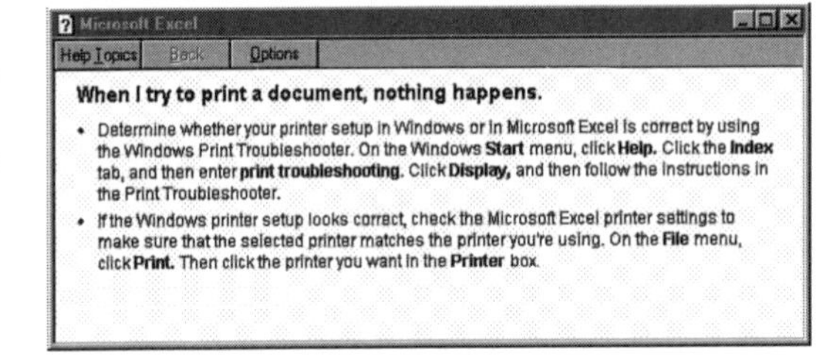

Fig. 3.9
If this is not exactly the help you want, click the Help Topics button and select another topic.

TIP **By default, any Help topic you pop up stays on the worksheet as** you work. If you don't like having Help hanging around like that, click the Options button. Select Keep Help On Top and choose Not On Top.

I just want to browse

You'll discover plenty of useful information by browsing in the Help Topics Contents window. Choose Help, Contents and Index to open the Help Topics dialog box, then click the Contents tab.

All the Excel Help files are organized by topic in those little books displayed in the Contents tab. Double-click any one of them, and the book's contents spill out, as shown in Figure 3.10.

Some help topics give you a kind of electronic brochure, a visual guide to a major feature in Excel 97. If your selected Help topic turns out to be one of these electronic brochures, click any of the topics on display for an explanation of the feature, as shown in Figure 3.11.

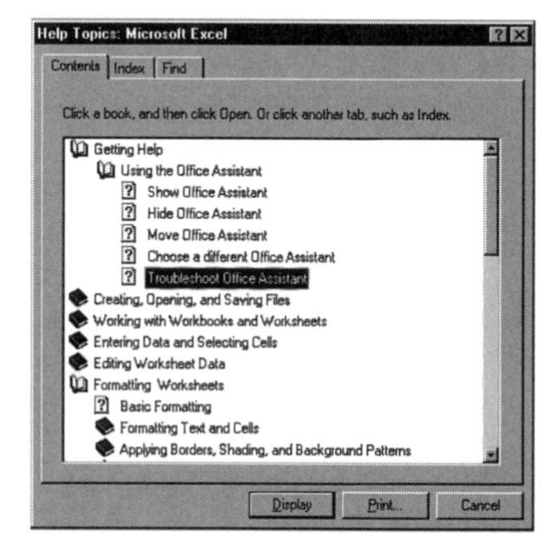

Fig. 3.10
You'll learn a lot about Excel by browsing in the Contents tab.

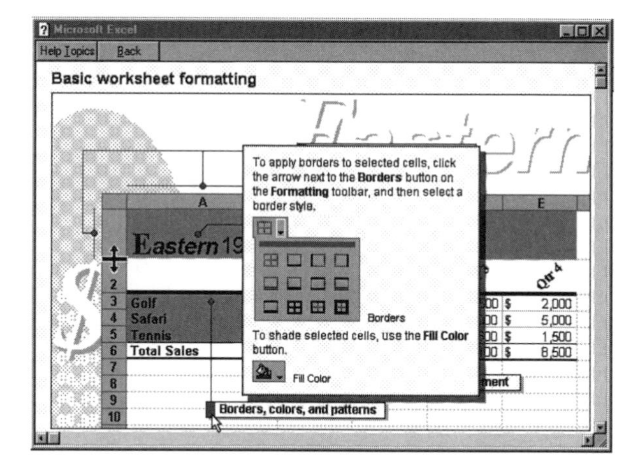

Fig. 3.11
Click a topic with the pointing hand and you'll get an explanation of the feature illustrated in the brochure.

Sometimes help comes in layers

Some Help topics lead to step-by-step explanations of a procedure or feature. Figure 3.12 shows a Help topic with a list of "What do you need help with?" topics and buttons. Click a button to get step-by-step instructions for the selected topic.

If the Help window gets in the way of your work, point at the window's title bar and drag it aside.

Fig. 3.12
Some help leads to more help. These small cross-reference buttons are especially useful.

Clicking one of these little buttons shunts you to further explanations and instructions

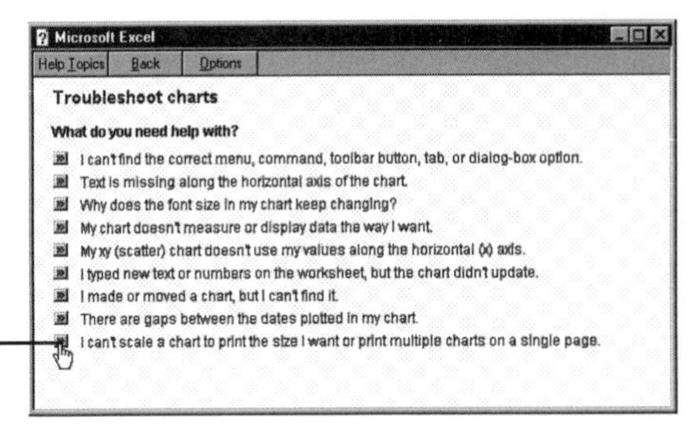

The Index is Help's laundry list

If none of these approaches gets you what you need, try the Index. Just click the Index tab in the Help Topics dialog box, type the first few letters of the topic you're looking for, and the list of topics scrolls automatically to the topic. Double-click any topic on the list to go straight to your help.

Definitions, for those otherwise-obscure Excel terms

When you finally do get to your information, you may want to investigate Help's definitions. **Definitions** are available for words displayed in a different color and marked by a broken underline. Click one of those words, and a little box pops up with an explanation of the term, as shown in Figure 3.13.

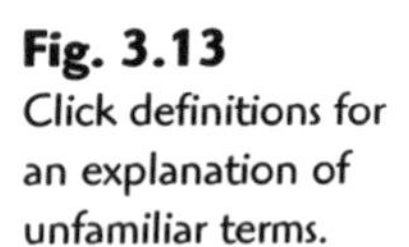

Fig. 3.13
Click definitions for an explanation of unfamiliar terms.

Definitions are available for words marked by a broken underline

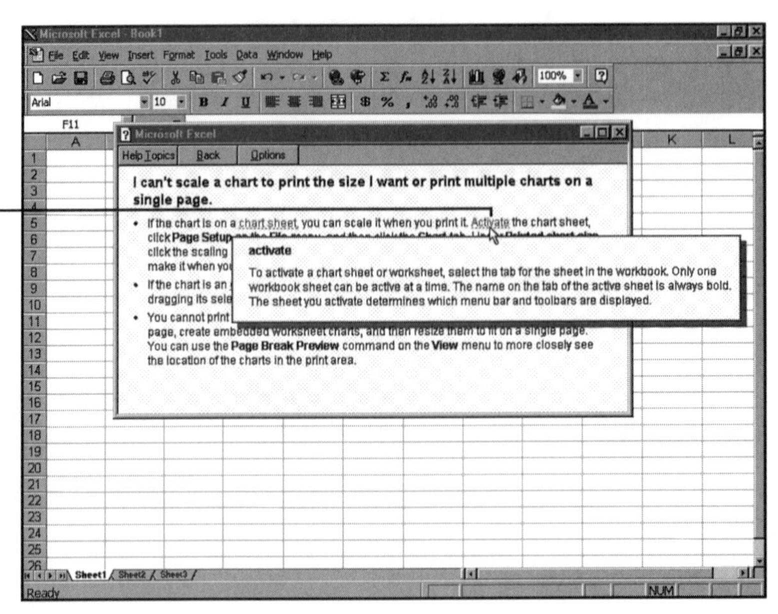

Getting help where you need it

Dialog boxes in Excel have their own What's This buttons—those little question marks in the upper-right corner of the title bar. Click the question mark, and it accompanies your pointer, as shown in Figure 3.14.

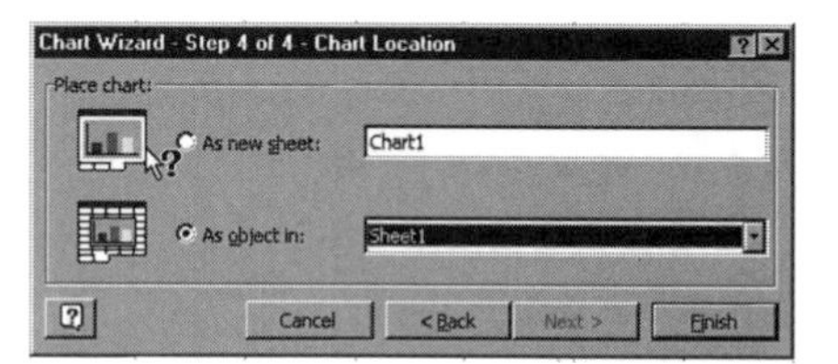

Fig. 3.14
When a dialog box choice seems mysterious, click it with the dialog box's What's This question mark for an explanation.

Click a dialog box option with your pointer and question mark duo, and an explanation of the option pops up. It's especially useful when you've worked your way though a series of dialog boxes, and you want to avoid ruining your work with the wrong choice in the last box. Check the option with the What's This question mark first, and you'll spare yourself a few gray hairs.

TIP **If you right-click a dialog box option and click the What's This box** that pops up, you get exactly the same explanation that you get with the question mark+pointer left-click. Why two different ways of accomplishing the same thing? Excel tries to cater to every taste, left- and right-clickers alike.

Double-clicking the dialog box question mark, on the other hand, just adds the question mark to your pointer. It doesn't call up Help, as you might expect. For general help on the dialog box, click the Office Assistant button inside the dialog box.

There's a world of help on the World Wide Web—Excel Online Support is here!

Excel's built-in help system is like having a combined office helper and reference shelf at hand when you're at work. Terrific resources though they are, you might paint yourself in a particularly tight corner where they're no help.

When that happens, pay a visit to the public library. There's no need to leave your chair, because this library is right on the other side of your modem. If you installed the Internet Explorer 3.0 or Netscape Navigator, and you have a working Internet account, you can visit the giant library that is the World Wide Web without even leaving Excel.

Select Help, Microsoft on the Web, Online Support. Click Connect in your Internet service provider's Connect To dialog box, and you travel across cyberspace directly to the Microsoft Excel Support Wizard Web page. If you get an Excel error message, or if an Excel feature doesn't seem to work properly, put the Support Wizard to work:

1. On the Microsoft Excel Support Wizard Web page, choose Troubleshooting a Problem and click Next.
2. Select the Microsoft Excel Workbook Troubleshooter and click Next. The Microsoft Excel Troubleshooter pops up with a list of potential problems (see Figure 3.15).

Fig. 3.15
If you don't see your particular problem on the list here, Excel online support has plenty of other resources.

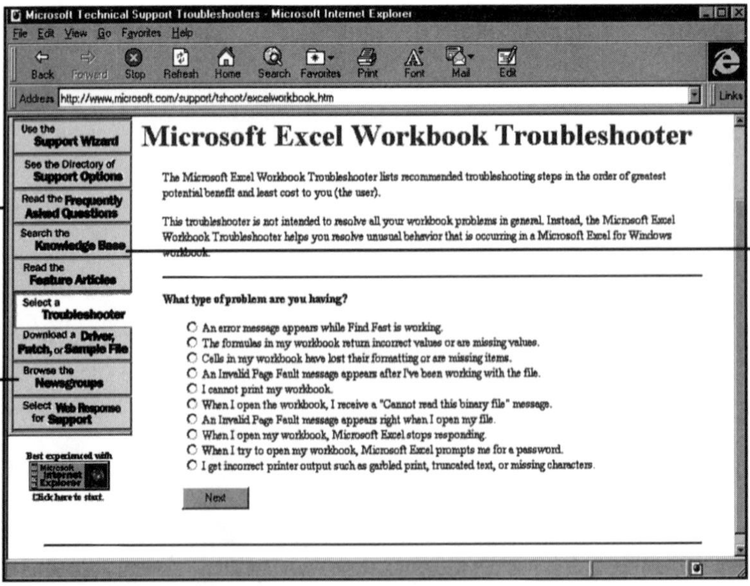

Read the Frequently Asked Questions for Microsoft's solutions to common Excel problems

Browse the Newsgroups to read the questions and answers of other Excel users

Search the Knowledge Base for hundreds of articles on Microsoft software related topics

3. Choose from the list of Excel problems, click Next, and work your way through the question and answer pages that follow. Chances are, you'll get your solution in the end.

The Support Wizard can't answer every Excel question, but you can find many other resources on the Excel Support Web site:

- Click Browse the Newsgroups to read the concerns and suggestions of other Excel users. Newsgroups are discussion groups that focus on specific topics, and there are several newsgroups devoted to Excel. Jump into the discussions yourself by posting your own messages. Many newsgroup participants who begin by asking questions, soon find themselves answering queries.
- Frequently Asked Questions, also called FAQs, are collections of common questions that are answered by experts. If your Excel question is among those in a FAQ, you're assured of an authoritative answer.
- The Microsoft Knowledge Base is a huge collection of articles and papers about Microsoft software. Many of the articles are technical; they might tell you more than you really want to know. On the other hand, the Knowledge Base is enormous and easy to search; with a little persistence, you might find exactly the nugget of information you need.

Ralph Waldo Emerson once wrote, "The aid we can give each other is only incidental, lateral, and sympathetic." Coming from a firm believer in self-reliance, that's not too surprising. Still, Emerson might have approved of Excel Help. It comes to your rescue when you need it, but using Help is a great way to help yourself!

Part II: Excel Essentials: Editing, Formatting, and More

Let's Make Some Changes Around Here

In this chapter:

- **Typing text in a cell gives me claustrophobia!**
- **Text is text and numbers are numbers, except when they're not**
- **How do I get rid of these columns and rows?**
- **Oops! How do I get them back?**
- **Moving data around in a worksheet**
- **AutoCorrect fixes typos on-the-fly!**

A sculptor has to be very, very careful—one slip of the chisel, and it's back to the quarry. But in Excel, nothing is carved in stone . . . .

Writing is rewriting, says an old saw. That's also true of worksheets. Business conditions shift like sand on a beach. Prices rise and fall, supply and demand expand and contract. The only constant is change. To keep up with it, your worksheets need revising all the time.

Like an electronic scoreboard, Excel can track this fast-moving game. It's loaded with powerful editing features that let you adjust your data to changing conditions.

And if you make a mistake, there are plenty of ways to fix it. We may not be carving a public monument, but the keyboard and mouse have a few advantages over the hammer and chisel.

Excel adapts to your writing style

Everyone has a different way of jotting down information. You might start with a fresh piece of note paper, date it, number it, title it, and start writing. I tend to grab whatever scrap of paper happens to be lying around, scribble madly, and then go back later to try to make sense of it. Excel adapts to both styles.

The formula bar

Entering data directly in a cell is convenient if you know pretty much what you're entering. But if you need to eyeball your entry and fiddle with it a bit before pressing Enter, the formula bar might suit you better. It gives you room to spread out, for one thing.

How fast can Excel adjust to changes?

One Excel user I know supervises a global network of PCs for a major international bank. Data pours in from news and quotes services and exchanges around the world. The bank's traders, from Hong Kong to Zurich, hit a button for, say, the price of dollars in francs. Price information starts to appear and gets dumped into an Excel workbook. As the trader makes her trades, she can track her positions in the workbook as prices rise and fall. The Excel workbook keeps a running tally of how she's doing. When tens of millions of dollars are changing hands every moment, keeping score is no game.

If you're typing text or data, the formula bar is just a convenient place to type. Once you click the Edit Formula button to write a formula, the formula bar springs to life, putting some handy tools right at your fingertips, as shown in Figure 4.1.

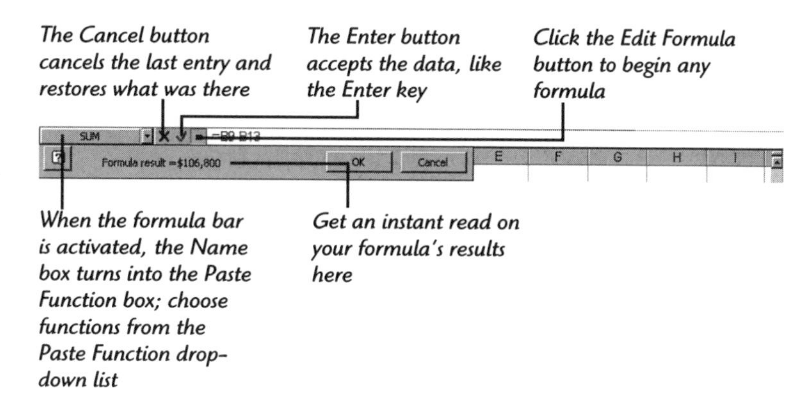

Fig. 4.1
This is the formula bar. Editing here gives you more room to work than the confines of the cell.

To edit in the formula bar, click a cell, then click the formula bar. The cursor (the flashing vertical line) appears inside the bar. Just start typing. Use Backspace and Delete to make corrections.

Fix it in the cell

Don't want to bother with the formula bar at all? Just double-click a cell. That puts the cursor back in the cell, and you can knock out or add characters or numbers at will.

To enable or disable editing in cells, click Tools, Options. Click the Edit tab, and click the Edit Directly In Cell option.

TIP **Press F2 to put the cursor directly in the active cell.**

This cell is all wrong: Clear and Delete

If you don't like what you see in the active cell, you have several options, depending on what you need to do:

- Start typing. You'll type over what's already there.
- Press the Delete key. That wipes out the cell contents.

- Click Edit, Clear. Selecting All clears out everything—formats, formulas, data, or comments that you've attached to the cell. (Selecting Contents Del does the same thing but leaves your formatting and comments alone.) Figure 4.2 shows the Clear options on the Edit menu.

Fig. 4.2
Choose from the options on the Clear submenu to get rid of what's in a cell.

Plain English, please!

In Excel, Clear and Delete do different things. A cell is like an easel that holds a canvas:

Clearing takes a sponge and wipes all or some of the canvas clean. Press the Delete key, type over what's in the cell, or choose Edit, Clear.

Deleting is like taking the easel and throwing it out the window, then rearranging all the furniture in the room to fill the spot where the easel used to be. Selecting Edit, Delete gets rid of the cell (or range of cells), and then rearranges all the surrounding cells to fill the gap. If there are formulas in those cells, the cell references will change too.

Q&A *Wait a minute! My keyboard says Delete. Delete doesn't Delete?*

The Delete key *clears* what's in the cell. The Delete option on the Edit menu takes whole cells out of the worksheet, then pushes surrounding cells around to take their place.

Deleting the delete: Undo

You've just constructed an elaborate formula. The phone rings. Distracted, you accidentally hit the Delete key. Good-bye, formula.

Before you pick up the phone and throw it across the room, click the Undo button. That cancels your last action and replaces whatever you wiped out of the cell.

Although they look similar, don't confuse the Undo button with the Redo button. Redo clones your last command. If you just deleted something you didn't mean to, it's the last thing you want!

If you want to see exactly what you're *undoing*, click the Undo drop-down arrow on the Standard toolbar. Your last actions are displayed on the drop-down menu, with the most recent action listed first. Clicking the Undo button "undoes" that last action. To undo your last several actions, select them on the Undo button drop-down list, as shown in Figure 4.3.

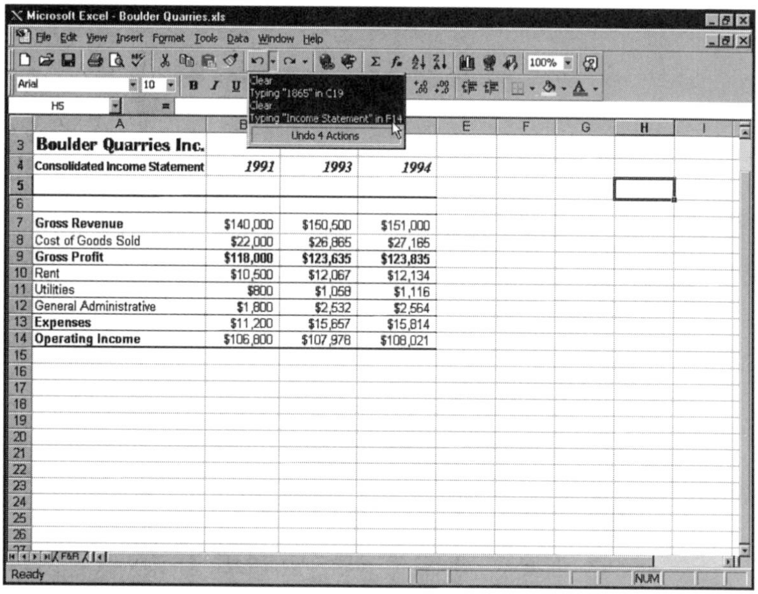

Fig. 4.3
The Undo drop-down list shows your last several actions, in the order you performed them.

	A	B	C	D
3	**Boulder Quarries Inc.**			
4	**Consolidated Income Statement**	*1991*	*1993*	*1994*
7	**Gross Revenue**	$140,000	$150,500	$151,000
8	Cost of Goods Sold	$22,000	$26,865	$27,165
9	**Gross Profit**	**$118,000**	**$123,635**	**$123,835**
10	Rent	$10,500	$12,067	$12,134
11	Utilities	$800	$1,058	$1,116
12	General Administrative	$1,800	$2,532	$2,564
13	**Expenses**	$11,200	$15,657	$15,814
14	**Operating Income**	$106,800	$107,978	$108,021

You can't undo actions out of sequence. For example, if you wanted to undo something you did four actions before, you can undo that fourth action only if you undo the three actions that followed it.

The Redo drop-down list works just like the Undo drop-down list, and allows you to repeat the last several things you did. If you haven't done anything undoable or redoable, the Undo and Redo buttons will be grayed-out.

If I mix up the Undo and Redo buttons more than once in an Excel session, I shove the mouse aside and press Ctrl+Z. That's the keyboard shortcut for Undo.

Editing text

Before laptop computers and modems changed the way reporters worked, hard-working scribes dictated their stories over the telephone. An editing team at the rewrite desk took the reporter's account and crafted a news story out of it. That's why you see reporters in old movies frantically shouting "Get me Rewrite!" when they're on a big story.

Excel has its own rewrite team, but you won't need to shout. Just point.

If you need to add special currency symbols, like yen (¥) or pounds sterling (£), check out the last section of this chapter.

Text is text, even when it's numbers

Excel is pretty discriminating about your typed entries. The program recognizes words as text, and aligns them to the left inside the cell. Numbers are aligned to the right. When you select commands that logically apply only to numbers, the program is smart enough to ignore any text that might be in the way. For example, if you select an entire column and use AutoSum, Excel ignores the column title and just adds the numbers.

My column title is $000, but I don't want Excel to treat it like a number and use it in calculations. What do I do?

Enter the number as text. Type an apostrophe (') before your title, like this: **'$000**, and Excel will think it's text.

If you've got a column or row title that you want in one cell but on two or more lines, wrap it. That flows text from one line to the next automatically, as soon as you run out of room on one line. To wrap text in a cell, right-click the cell and choose Format Cells from the shortcut menu. In the Format Cells dialog box that pops up, click the Alignment tab and select Wrap Text.

Text wrapping is old hat for anyone who's used a word processor. Maybe you're looking for a different angle on your text? Here's something the average word processing program can't do: in the Format Cells dialog box, drag the Orientation "clock hand" up or down to angle your text across the cell, as shown in Figure 4.4.

Fig. 4.4
Excel can wrap text, angle it, or display it vertically for some nifty effects.

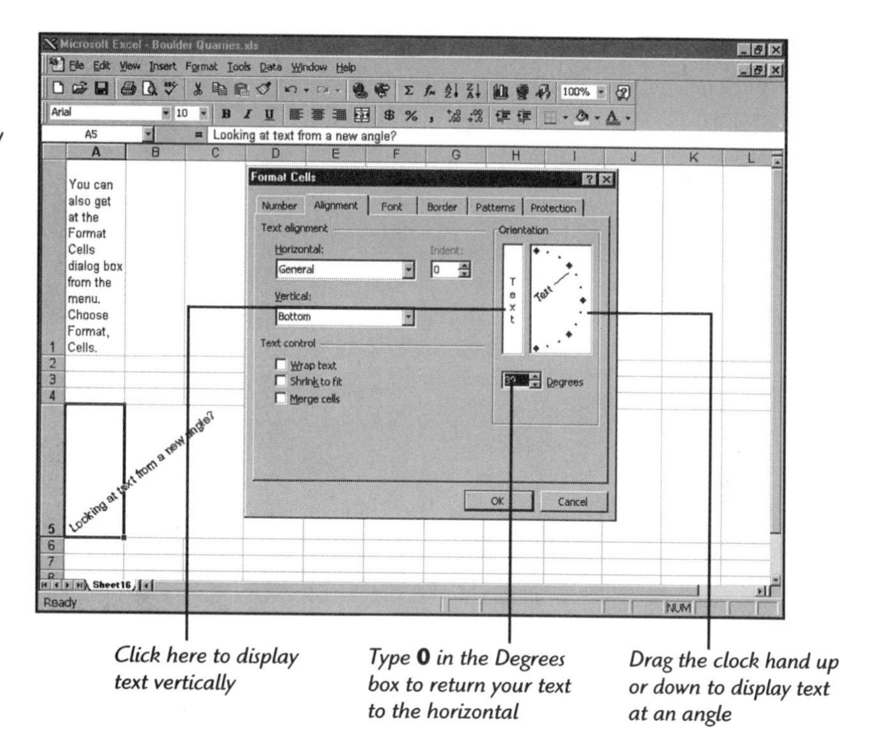

If you experiment with these effects only to find that your text has taken an unacceptable bent, right-click the cell and choose Format Cells. On the Alignment tab of the Format Cells dialog box, type **0** in the Degrees text box to return text to its normal angle. Decided against vertical text after all? Just click the vertical text option again. That clears the highlighting in the option box and, when you click OK in the dialog box, sends text back to the horizontal plane.

TIP **To insert a hard return at the end of a line of text within a cell,** press Alt+Enter. For a tab space, press Ctrl+Alt+Tab.

The numbers game

Excel gives you two basic choices when it comes to editing numbers: the easy way and the hard way. The hard way is fiddling with your signs as you put the number in. You can, if you really want to, type 60%, or $500.00, or 1,000,000, make typos, edit the cell to get it right, and give yourself a few gray hairs.

I like the easy way. Using the Formatting toolbar for numbers gives you the format you want without tears. The following table shows you how.

When you want this...	type this...	and click this
60%	.6	%
1,000,000.00	1000000	,
$500.00	500	$

What's your (decimal) point?

You might be extremely precise, and want your calculations shown out to seven decimal places. Or perhaps your work requires that degree of precision. Maybe you don't care about decimal places at all.

Either way, you can increase or decrease the decimal places shown by your numbers with these two handy buttons on the Formatting toolbar.

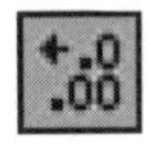

Keep clicking the Increase Decimal button if you want to go from 5, to 5.0, to 5.00.

And just click the Decrease Decimal button if you want to go back from 5.00, to 5.0, to 5 again.

Excel knows it's a date

Excel is pretty smart. If you type **1/18/95**, for example, Excel knows it's a date and treats it accordingly. Likewise 1-18-95, 18-Jan-95, or even 1/18—Excel supplies the current year unasked, although it won't show it.

But if you type **January 18 1995**, Excel treats it as text, not a date. Why does it matter? Excel has built-in functions that use recognized dates in calculations. The program will calculate the number of days between two dates, for example, but it has to recognize your entries as dates before it can use them.

If you don't want the day to show, type Jan-95.

To save yourself some typing, enter your date in the simplest form—6-10-96, for example—and then use Excel's date formats to alter it any way you like.

1 Right-click the cell with the date and choose Format Cells from the shortcut menu.

2 The Format Cells dialog box pops up with the Number tab and Date category already selected. Choose the date format you want from the Type list.

3 Click OK to save your choice and format the date.

I don't want a date—I want 1/18 to be a fraction! How can I tell Excel I don't mean the eighteenth of January?

Well, it does look like a date, doesn't it? You can enter fractions, but they have to be preceded by an integer and a space for Excel to distinguish them from dates. Type **2 1/4** and Excel interprets it as 2 1/4. To enter one eighteenth, type **0 1/18**.

Time on your hands

Excel is just as smart about times. Type **5 PM** or **17:00**, and Excel knows they're times. Remember to put a space and the AM or PM after a twelve-hour clock time.

Is there a quick way to enter the current date and time?

Sure! Pick your cell and hit Ctrl+; for today's date. To enter the current time, press Ctrl+:.

Express editing: using Find and Replace

Ogden Nash once wrote, "I think that I shall never see, a billboard lovely as a tree." That line sometimes comes to mind as I motor down the highways of our fair nation. Wouldn't it be great if you could just press a button and replace all those billboards with trees?

You can't fix the world that way, but it works in Excel worksheets. The Find and Replace command seeks out worksheet problems and replaces them with something better, all with a click or two of the mouse.

First find it...

Click Edit, Find. The Find dialog box pops up, as shown in Figure 4.5. You're prompted to enter whatever you're looking for. Type in text, formulas, or parts of formulas; Find can find just about anything.

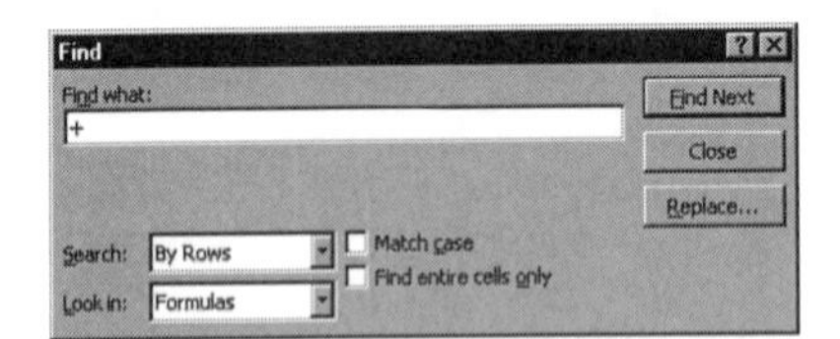

Fig. 4.5
Find is a powerful Excel editing tool.

When does this come in handy? Suppose you were working late and copied a formula all over your worksheet. You look over the worksheet the next morning, and the numbers seem wrong. You suspect your late-night formula is the culprit. Click Edit, Find. Enter whatever you remember of the formula in the Find What text box. You copied it across a bunch of rows, so Search By Rows. You're looking for a formula, so you want Find to Look In Formulas.

Click Find Next, and the first cell containing your buggy formula becomes the active cell.

...then fix it

To change the offending formula, select Replace. In the Replace dialog box that appears, type the correction in the Replace With text box, then click Replace All (see Figure 4.6).

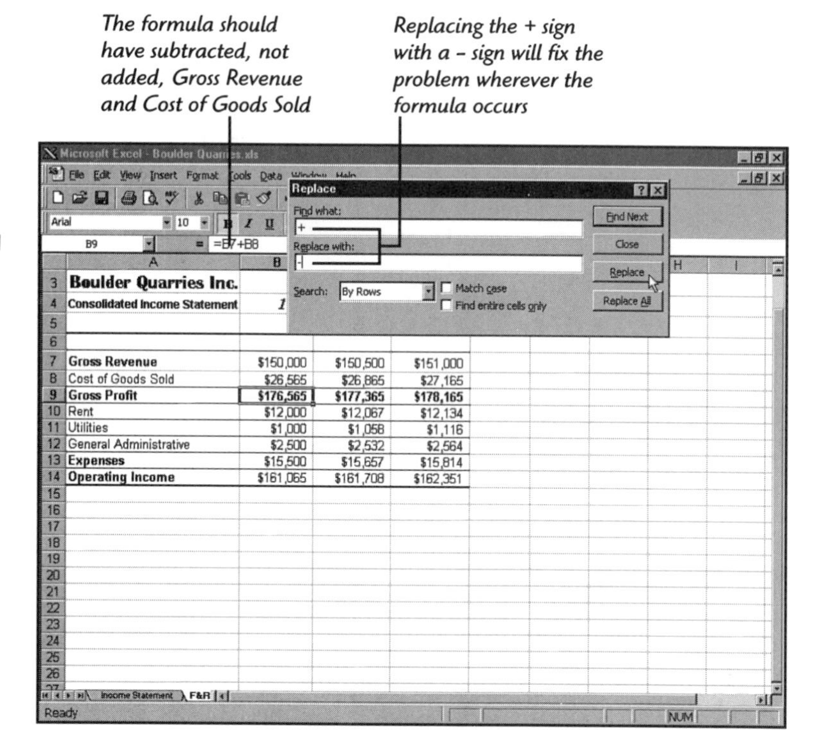

Fig. 4.6
Find and Replace in Excel work a lot like similar features in word processors.

Every instance of the buggy formula is replaced by the corrected version. You might even leave the office on time tonight.

It's a drag: moving things around

Excel usually gives you a choice of how to do things: write your own formulas or paste a function, move around by scroll bar, mouse wheel, or keyboard command, and so on. How you do it depends on your work habits and preferences.

When it comes to moving, cutting, and pasting, you also have a few options. To my mind, the choice is a no-brainer—the easiest and fastest way of moving things from A to B is with the mouse.

Cells on the move

Figure 4.7 shows Boulder Quarries' three-year income statement. Let's move the column titles down one row to make it easier on the eyes.

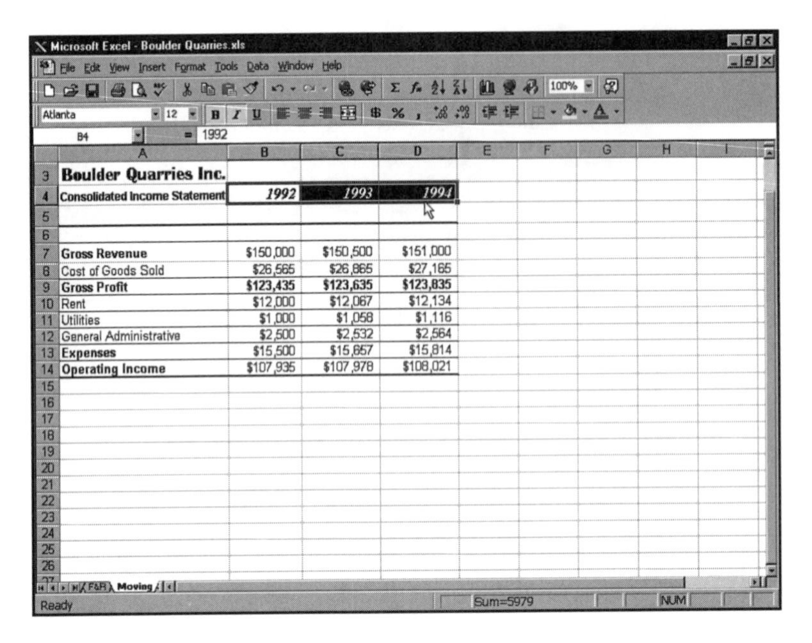

Fig. 4.7
Rearranging worksheet layouts and moving cell contents is easy with the mouse.

1 Select the cell or range you want to move.

2 Point at the dark border of the selection. The pointer should be a white arrow.

3 Click and drag the selection to the new location. A broken gray border moves with the pointer (see Figure 4.8). The size and shape of the cells you're moving is mimicked in the size and shape of the border.

4 Release the mouse button, and the selection slips into the new spot.

Copy that cell

Copying cells works the same way. Just press Ctrl when you point at the gray cell border. The white arrow sprouts a little plus sign.

As you move the copied cell or range, the broken gray border follows the pointer around. Release the mouse button to drop the copy into place.

TIP **I sometimes forget what I'm doing in the middle of one of these** moves or copies. That's why I rely on the right mouse button when I drag a selection. Dragging with the right mouse button pops up the shortcut menu when you get to your destination. That jogs my memory and I take my pick of copying or moving from the menu. Figure 4.9 shows the shortcut menu.

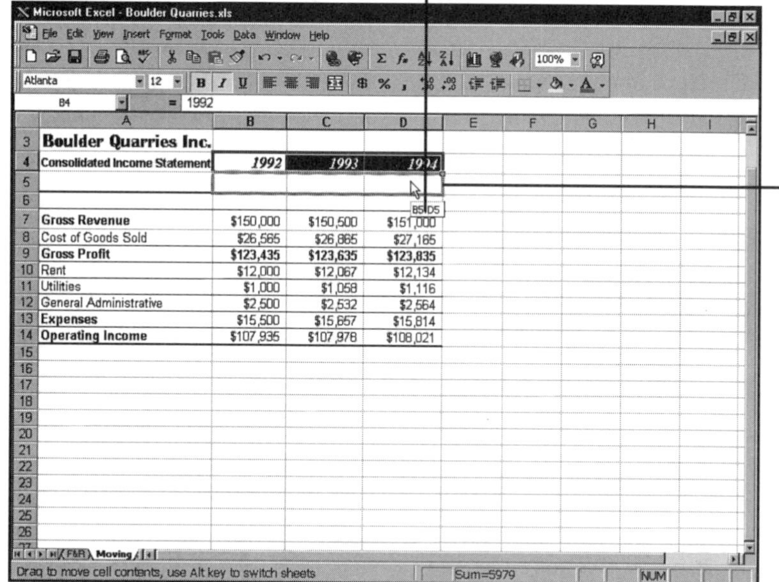

Fig. 4.8
The size and shape of the area to which you move cells is the same size and shape as the moved cells.

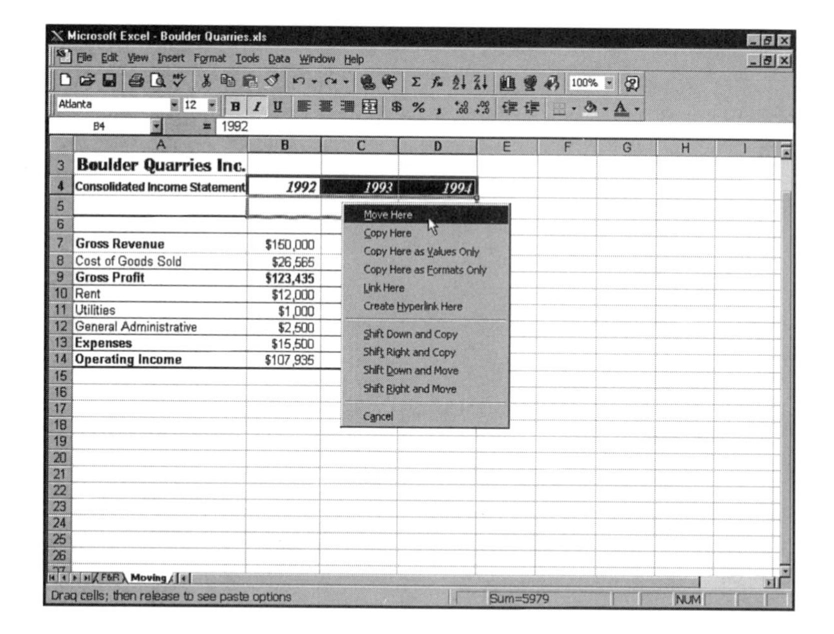

Fig. 4.9
Drag with the right mouse button for a shortcut menu for moves and copies.

Cut here, paste there

We could have moved those column titles by cutting them out of their old range and pasting them into a new range. Cutting and pasting is even easier than moving, because you don't have to worry about positioning that broken gray border in the right spot. Just click the cell that's the upper-left border of where you want your pasted range, click the Paste button, and you're there.

To cut and paste a range:

1 Select the cell or range.

2 Click the Cut button. The selection's border becomes a moving broken gray line, or **marquee** in Windows-speak.

3 Click the cell at the upper-left of the range where you want your cut selection to be pasted, as shown in Figure 4.10.

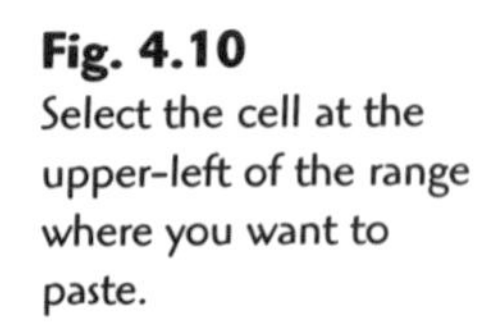

Fig. 4.10
Select the cell at the upper-left of the range where you want to paste.

This is the upper-left cell of the paste area

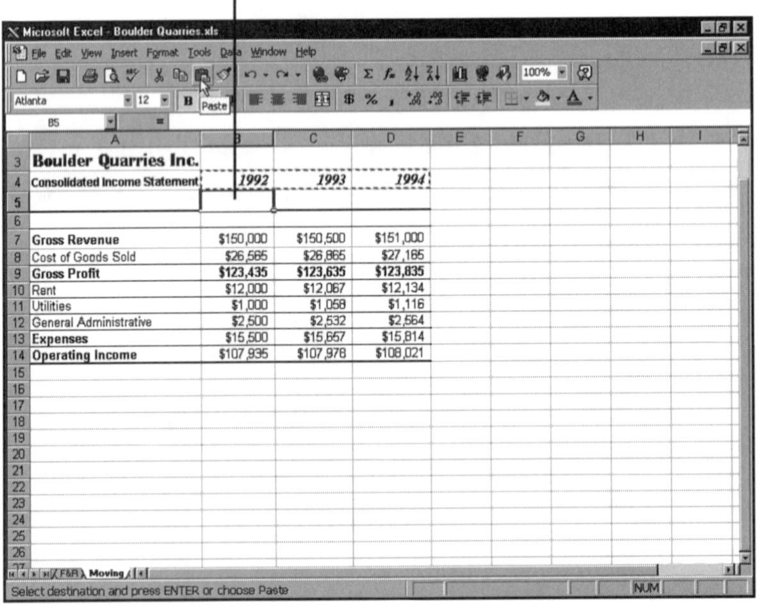

4 Click the Paste button, and the selection is pasted into place.

When should I drag and drop, and when should I cut and paste?

Both methods have more or less the same effect, but you use them for different things. Moving cells works for short distances in a worksheet. Cutting and pasting is handy for moving things across big worksheets, or from worksheet to worksheet or workbook to workbook. Moving cells just doesn't cut it for those latter two applications.

Now copy it

When you cut a selection, you can only paste it once. If you need to repeat a cell or range in a worksheet or across several worksheets or workbooks, follow the same steps you took for cutting and pasting, but click the Copy button instead of Cut. Then you can keep pasting in a selection as many times as needed.

You can copy, cut, and paste formulas as easily as text. Range and cell references in formulas will adjust automatically.

Copying, moving, and pasting to cells that are already occupied overwrites whatever's there. Excel does warn about overwriting, but only during moves. To do any of this without disturbing existing data, choose Insert, Copied Cells.

Don't forget about the Windows cut, copy, and paste keyboard commands, because they work in Excel perfectly well. Press Ctrl+X to cut; Ctrl+C to copy; and Ctrl+V to paste.

I don't want to cut, copy, or move after all!

If you change your mind after moving, cutting, or pasting cells, click the Undo button on the toolbar to reverse the action.

Hey, make room for me! Inserting rows and columns

You've just created a worksheet, totaled everything, and your mind shifts from Excel to lunch. Then you take a second look. Darn. A whole column of data got left out. Now what?

Just insert it. Here's how:

1. Click the column heading to select the column after the one you want to insert. (If you need to insert more than one, select multiple columns.)

2. Click Insert, Columns, as shown in Figure 4.11. In the figure, we're going to insert a blank column to accommodate data from 1992.

3. A new blank column is shoved into place. All your formula references adjust themselves. Figure 4.12 shows how it looks.

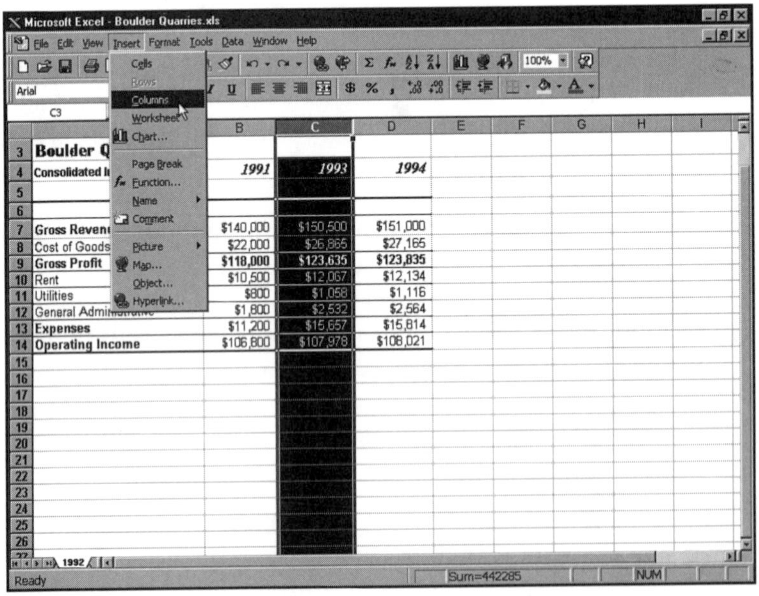

Fig. 4.11
Insert rows and columns at will from the Insert menu.

Do the same thing for rows if you need to insert one of those. Select the row below the one you want to insert, and choose Insert, Rows.

I need to insert cells

A scene in *A Night in Casablanca* puts the Marx Brothers in charge of a packed nightclub. Every inch of floor space is jammed. Table for two? Not a hope. But when a newcomer shows up at the door waving a wad of cash, the brothers seat him immediately. Harpo and Chico just knock aside a few tables (their outraged occupants are in the middle of dinner) and plop a new table down in the space they've made.

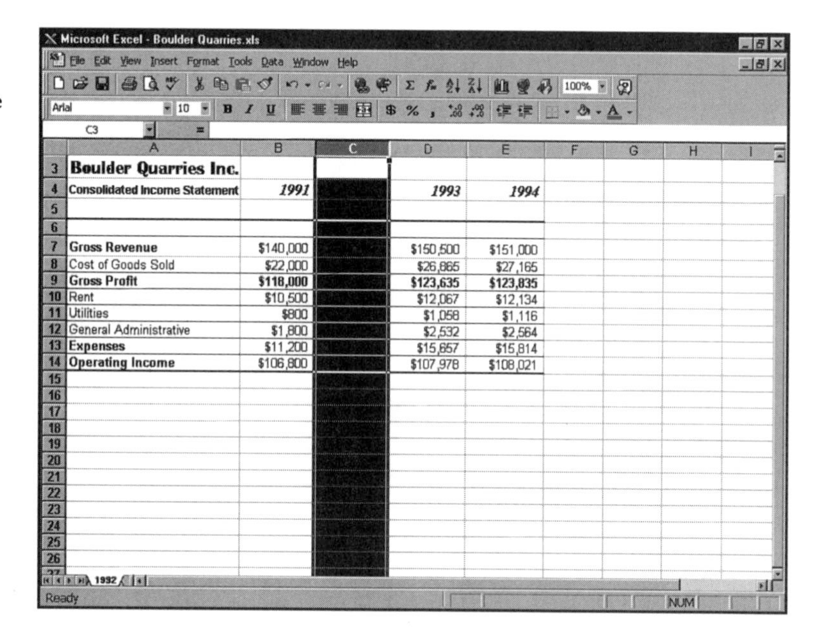

Fig. 4.12
The newly inserted column slips into place before the selected column.

Inserting cells works on the Marx Brothers principle. Grab the cells you want to insert, pick the spot where you want them to be, and the inserted cells will push the existing cells aside.

Inserting blank cells

Insert blank cells with the Insert menu:

1. Select the cell either below or to the right of where you want the blank.
2. Click Insert, Cells. The Insert dialog box appears (see Figure 4.13).
3. Select Shift Cells Right or Shift Cells Down.
4. Click OK.

To insert more than one cell, start the process with a range instead of a single cell. However many cells you select in the range, the same number of blank cells are inserted.

Inserting cells changes cell references in formulas that get moved. If a formula behaves oddly after doing this, go in and change the references.

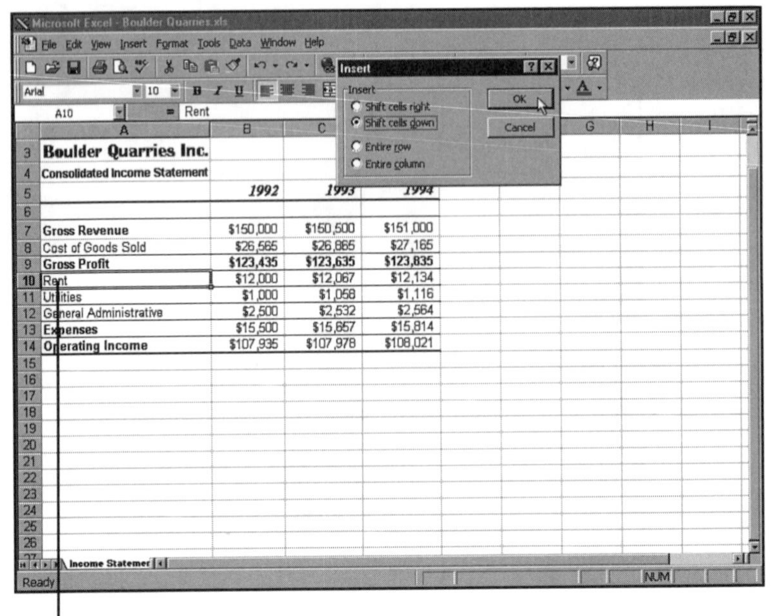

Fig. 4.13
Select a cell, then insert blank cells with the Insert dialog box.

Either Shift Cells Down or Shift Cells Right would put the blank cell here

Unwanted cells? Lose them fast

Remember Clear versus Delete? To get rid of unwanted columns, rows, or cells, click Edit, Delete. In the Delete dialog box, choose Rows or Columns, decide if you want to Shift Cells Left or Up, and then click OK.

Inserting cells that contain data

You can also insert cells or entire rows and columns that already have data in them. This is handy if, for example, you want to shuffle the row or column order in a worksheet.

Let's move the Utilities row and insert it above the Expenses row in Figure 4.14.

1. Select the row, column, or cells to insert.

2. Point at the border of the range. The pointer should be the white arrow.
3. Press Shift, then drag with the left mouse button.
4. A broken gray I-beam follows the pointer around. Position it between the rows, columns, or cells where you want to make the insertion.
5. Release the mouse button and the selection drops into place, pushing the existing rows, cells, or columns aside, à la Marx Brothers. Figures 4.14 and 4.15 show how to shift rows.

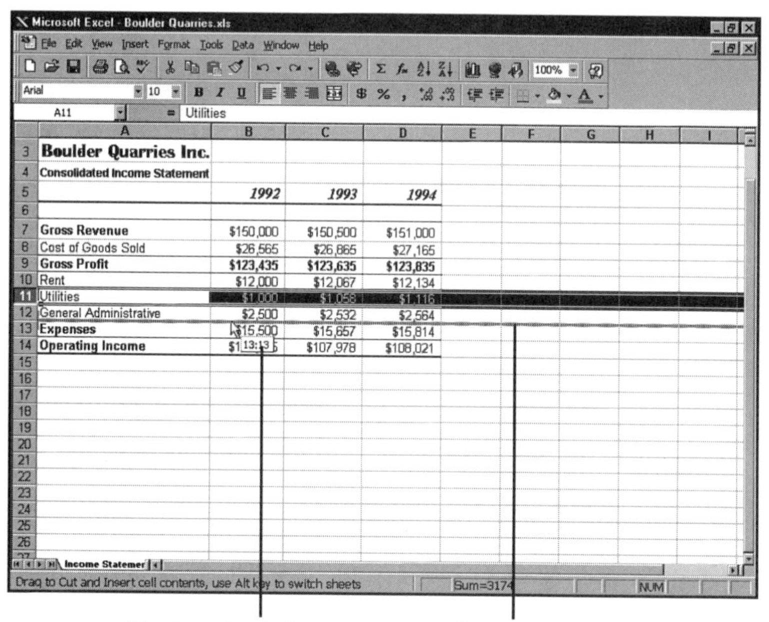

Fig. 4.14
The Shift+drag combination gives you a broken gray I-beam. Position it between the rows where you want the insertion.

TIP **You can also use the shortcut menu for this. Just drag with the** right mouse button and take your choice from the menu. (The menu pops up when you release the mouse button.)

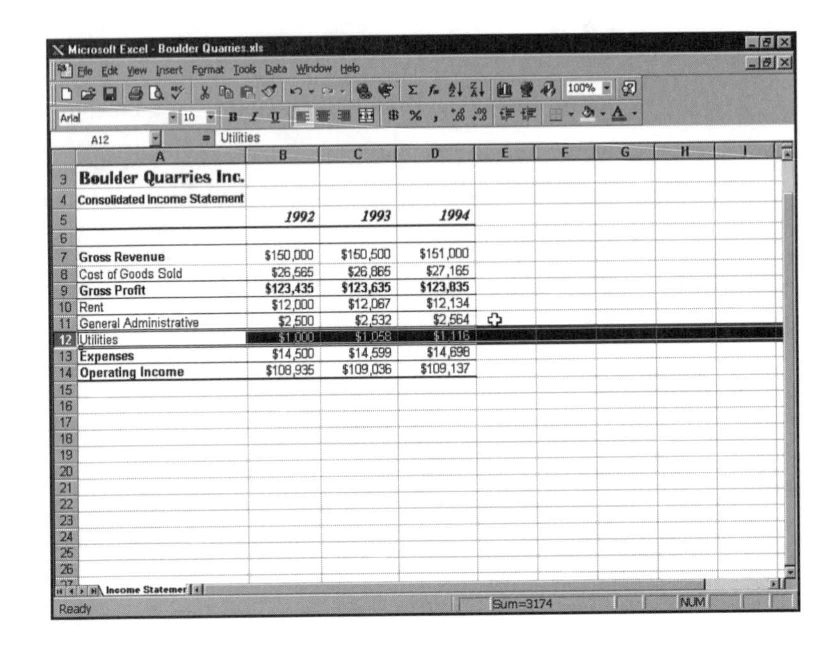

Fig. 4.15
Release the mouse button, and the inserted row drops into place.

Mind your ABCs: spell checking

I couldn't spell as a kid, and I still can't as an adult. Spell checking in word processors gave me a new lease on orthography, and Excel has the same tool for worksheets.

Click the Spelling button to spell check an entire worksheet. Or select a range and spell check that. As in a word processor, you can add words that Excel doesn't recognize, change the misspelled word at Excel's suggestion, or ignore the change. Spell checking is a great way to avoid embarrassing errors. I should know.

AutoCorrect cleans up your typing mistakes

Even world champion spellers aren't necessarily champion typists. For them, Excel has a nifty gadget called AutoCorrect.

I often type **SUnday** or **sunday** when I don't mean to. Maybe you do the same kind of thing. AutoCorrect fixes entries with two initial capitals. It also corrects lowercase letters at the beginning of the names of days. Try it—just type **SUnday** or **sunday**, then press Enter to see AutoCorrect in action.

You can even train AutoCorrect to correct your own common typos. Click Tools, AutoCorrect to open the AutoCorrect dialog box shown in Figure 4.16.

Enter your typo in the Replace text box and type the correction in the With text box. Click Add and OK, and whenever you make the typo, AutoCorrect will quietly replace it with the correction.

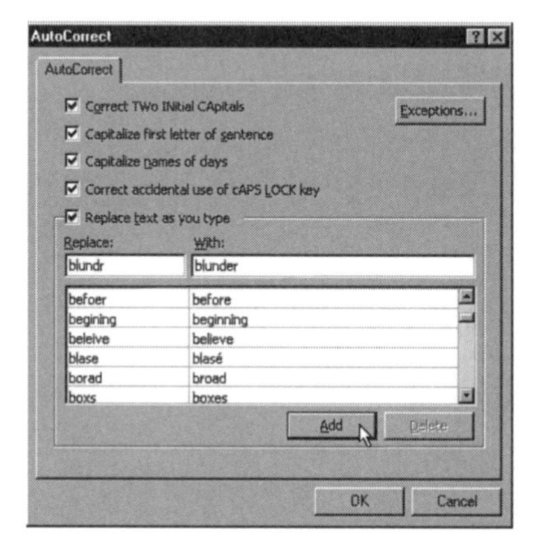

Fig. 4.16
If you're prone to making typos, type them in the AutoCorrect dialog box and they'll be fixed on-the-fly.

If you find AutoCorrect more annoying than helpful, just click the Replace Text As You Type check box to get rid of the check mark. AutoCorrect will cease and desist until you reselect the check box.

TIP **You can also use AutoCorrect to cut down on typing chores. Type** an abbreviation like **exp** in the Replace edit box, and the full word **Expense** in the With text box. Click Add and OK in the AutoCorrect dialog box, and whenever you type **exp**, AutoCorrect will automatically expand it to **Expense**.

Using special characters: I want ¥ and £, not $!

Computer age markets really are global, but you'd never know it from your computer keyboard. You might do plenty of business in England or Japan or France, but how do you stick characters like £ or ¥ or even É in your worksheets?

Those characters and others, along with symbols like bullets and paragraph marks, are part of the **ANSI character set**. ANSI (pronounced *AN-see*) stands for American National Standards Institute, an organization originally formed to set standards for representing things like screw threads in engineering drawings. The ANSI character set includes all the letters, numbers, and symbols that appear on your keyboard, as well as lots of special characters that don't. The ANSI character set is included with Windows.

There are two ways to insert special characters in Excel worksheets. The first is to use the Windows Character Map:

1. Click the Start button and choose Programs, Accessories, Character Map. That pops the Character Map dialog box right over your worksheet (see Figure 4.17).

2. Select a font from the Font list. The System font has most of the currency symbols you'll need; Symbol has Greek letters, playing-card suits, and other interesting items. Most fonts have a mix-and-match set of letters, numbers, and other symbols.

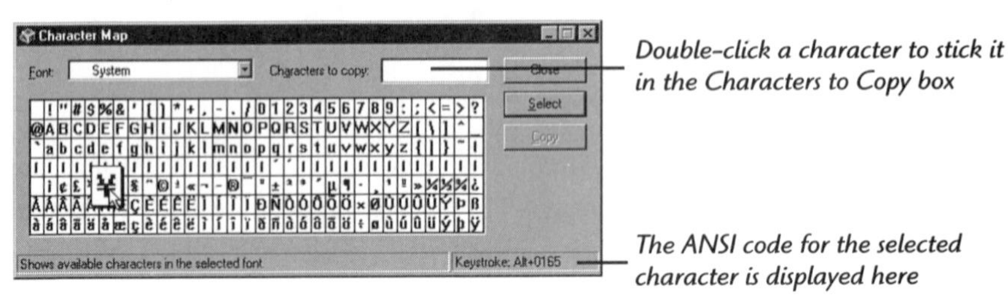

Fig. 4.17
Click and hold down the mouse button for an enlarged view of the Character Map characters.

3. Click any of the characters. The selected character acquires a box around it. If you hold down the mouse button as you click, Windows enlarges the character so you can see it better (refer to Figure 4.17).

4. Double-click the character. Windows puts the selected character in the Characters to Copy text box. Select more than one if you like.

5. Click Copy to copy the character(s) to the Windows Clipboard. Flip back to Excel and click the Paste button on the toolbar. The selected character is pasted into the active cell.

You can also insert special characters in Excel worksheets by typing the character's ANSI code. In the lower-right corner of the Character Map dialog box, you'll notice a little box labeled Keystroke.

There's a numeric code associated with every ANSI character. When you click a character in the Character Map dialog box, the numeric code for the character is displayed in the Keystroke box. To insert a character at the insertion point in Excel, hold down the Alt key and type the character's code on the keyboard number pad. When you release the Alt key, the character is popped right into the worksheet. To insert the Yen symbol, for example, hold down the Alt key and type **0165** on the number pad. The ¥ character is inserted when you release Alt.

This maneuver only works with the number pad numbers, and only when Num Lock is on.

This trick also works in Write, Notepad, Cardfile, and other Windows accessories, and in application programs like Word for Windows.

Putting It All on Paper: Printing Worksheets and Workbooks

In this chapter:

- **Six steps to easy printing**
- **Why can't I just click the Print button?**
- **My little worksheet only fills one corner of a big page**
- **My BIG worksheet won't fit on that dinky page!**
- **Cell Comments make handy, and printable, worksheet reminders**
- **This print job's going up the line. How about something fancier?**

Your worksheet might be small, medium, or large, but your printer is strictly one-size-fits-all. Even so, Excel can custom-tailor attractive printouts. . . . .

Printing pages with a word processor is a cinch. Write a page, click the Print button, go to lunch. Word processors deal with life one page at a time. They're made that way. And because that's how printers see things too, the combination makes for a perfect marriage.

Spreadsheets have a more expansive world view. Their universe is a giant grid the length of a football field. That's great for coping with odd-sized chunks of numbers and text, but try to get your printer to see it that way. It wants to reduce everything to uniform 8 1/2 by 11-inch pages.

Irreconcilable differences? Read on.

All or some of the parts

There are big paintings, and then there are really big paintings. Four hundred years ago, the painter Tintoretto covered a palace wall in Venice with a giant painting called *Paradise.* Art lovers who've never been near Venice marvel at it to this day. How do you view a ballroom-sized painting when you're not in the ballroom? Art books, with page after page of color plates, each showing a small piece of Tintoretto's colossal picture. There might also be a single plate showing a reduction of the whole painting.

Printing a big spreadsheet in Excel works just like that art book. You can print pages with sections of your worksheet on each page. Or you can print a reduction of the whole worksheet. You may not impress any art lovers, but hey—a lot of people in Tintoretto's day thought he couldn't paint for beans. And where are they now?

Choose your weapon: selecting a printer

If you're using Excel, you're also using Windows. And because you're using Windows, you surely installed a printer during Windows setup. The only possible complication is that you might have more than one printer hooked up to your system (or even a fax modem, which Windows considers a printer in its own right).

Just make sure you're about to use the printer you want. Click File, Print. The default printer is listed in the Print dialog box (see Figure 5.1).

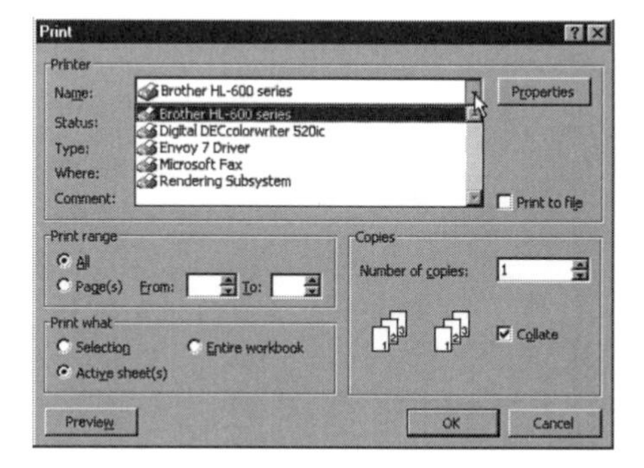

Fig. 5.1
Pop up the Print dialog box to make sure you're using the printer you want.

If the listed printer isn't the one you want, click the Printer drop-down arrow and take your pick.

Easy printing

Maybe you've got a minor masterpiece on your hands and you just want a quick hard copy. For small worksheets, you can get a nice-looking printout with a minimum of fussing. Here's how to do it:

1. When you're ready to print, click the Print Preview button on the toolbar. That gives you a full-page view of your worksheet and some handy buttons and tools, as shown in Figure 5.2.
2. Notice how the data is bunched up at the top of the page in Figure 5.2? Click the Setup button on the toolbar to pop up the Page Setup dialog box, then click the Margins tab (see Figure 5.3).
3. On the Margins tab of the Page Setup dialog box, click the Center on Page Horizontally and Vertically check boxes. That'll center the data instead of cramming it at the upper-left of the page.
4. You probably don't want to print the worksheet grid lines—they just clutter up the printed page. Click the Sheet tab of the Page Setup dialog box and make sure the Print Gridlines check box is deselected. If it's not, click it.
5. Click OK in the Page Setup dialog box and, as you see in Figure 5.4, these quick fixes improved the look of our print preview.

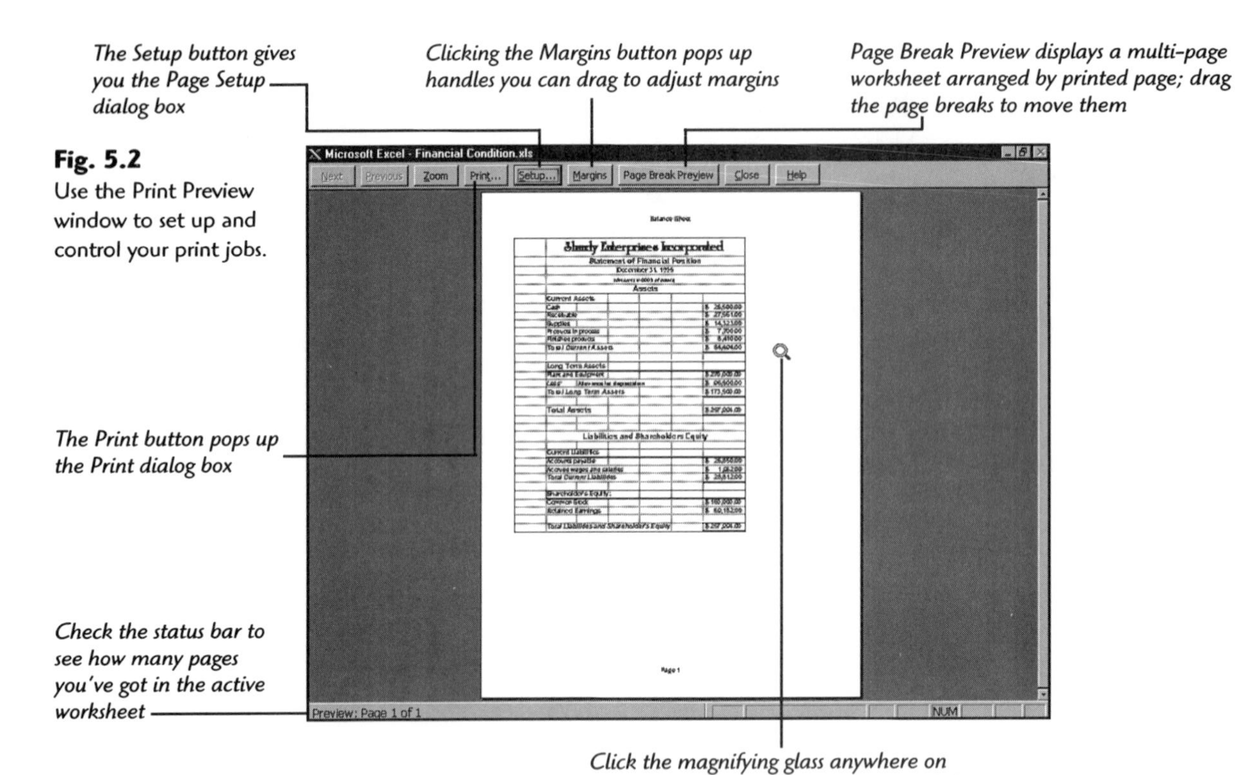

Fig. 5.2
Use the Print Preview window to set up and control your print jobs.

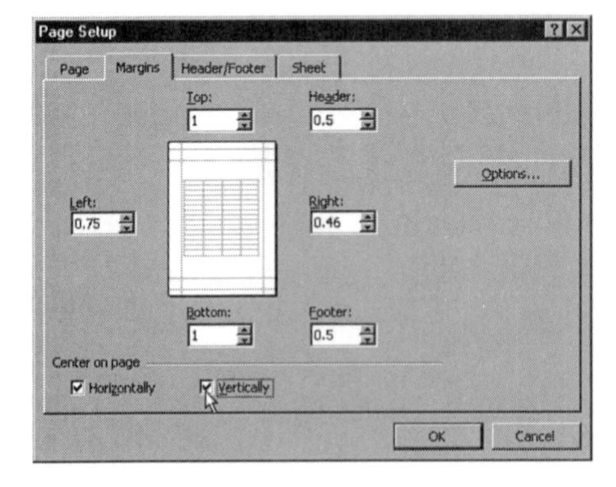

Fig. 5.3
Unless you like to tinker, the default margins are probably fine.

6 Click the Print button on the toolbar to pop up the Print dialog box. If you want one copy of the current worksheet, just click OK. You'll get a respectable-looking printout in moments.

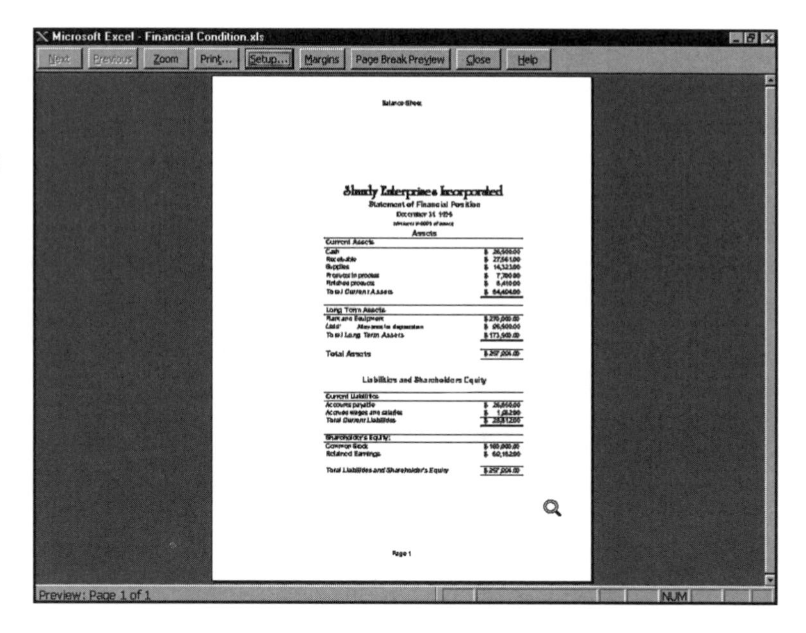

Fig. 5.4
Centering data on the page and skipping the printing of grid lines result in better-looking printouts.

Excel automatically supplies the worksheet name as a header and the page number as a footer. If your worksheet runs to several pages, or if you don't want the default header and footer, read on.

Plain English, Please!

What's a **header**? Look at the top of the pages in this book. There's a header on every page, with the chapter title, page number, and so on. A **footer** would offer the same sort of repeated information at the bottom of every page. On a printed Excel worksheet, the header and footer are printed automatically on every page; the header is the sheet name and the footer is the page number. We'll look at how you can change, add, or delete headers and footers later on in this chapter.

Why do all this for a quick printout? Can't I use the Print button?

You *can* just click the Print button, but you may get some unpredictable results. Excel and your printer have different world views, remember? The Print button prints whatever's in the current window, immediately, no questions asked. If your data fits on one page, and you don't care about where on the page it winds up, fine. Otherwise, align and preview first. It'll save you paper, and hassles.

When you click the Print button, Excel prints everything between the first cell with something in it, all the way to the last cell with something in it. If you put something in cell Z545, forgot it, and then clicked Print, you'd wind up printing a lot of blank pages. It's safer to select a range to print. Or take the extra few seconds and use Print Preview. Check the status bar shown in Figure 5.2 to see how many pages you *really* have. If it shows Page 1 of 200 instead of Page 1 of 1, you'll be spitting out a lot of blank pieces of paper (unless you have a Tintoretto-sized worksheet, of course).

I only want to print some of my worksheet

Maybe you

just want to hand marketing a selection of numbers from your worksheet, instead of confusing them with the whole thing.

Just select the part of the worksheet you want to print and click File, Print to open the Print dialog box. Click Selection under Print What, and then click OK.

Where the selected range ends up on the printed page depends on your settings on the Margins tab of the Page Setup dialog box. Click the Print Preview button after you select the range to see exactly what you'll get in the printout.

TIP

You're probably more dexterous than I am, but I have a heck of a time selecting ranges with the mouse. I go too far and then have to backtrack, or I don't go far enough and then have to start over again. That's why I prefer to select ranges with the keyboard, especially if they're bigger than the size of one window. Pressing Shift+arrow key (left, right, down, or up) does the same thing as dragging with the mouse.

The shape of things to come: Print Preview tools

Before you launch a new product, you study the market to see what you're getting into. Print Preview does the same thing. It gives you a glimpse of the printout before you dip into your paper supply. And if you don't like what you see, Print Preview gives you plenty of tools to make adjustments.

Click the Print Preview button now if you're not already there.

Zoom in for a closer look

Move the pointer over the page in Print Preview and it turns into the little magnifying glass you saw back in Figure 5.2. Click anywhere on the page to zoom in on an area of detail. Click again to go back to normal view. Clicking the Zoom button at the top of the window toggles the same views.

It's a setup (page setup, that is)

Most of the tools you need are in the Page Setup dialog box (refer to Figure 5.3). You get to it either by clicking File, Page Setup, or by clicking Setup from the Print Preview window.

How do I set the margins?

Click the Margins tab to adjust where your printout appears on the page. Refer to Figure 5.3 to see the Margins tab.

- Top and Bottom adjust how far from the top and bottom of the page the print job will start and end. Some printers don't print on the first and last quarter-inch of a page, so setting these to zero won't print from the top edge to the bottom edge.
- Left and Right, for a lot of printers, might have the same limitation. Anyway, you want some white space, don't you?
- Header and Footer position the headers and footers from the top and bottom edges of the page. The default header is the sheet name (it'll be Sheet1 for an unnamed sheet), and the default footer is the page number.
- Center on Page centers the printout for you, from side to side, top to bottom, or both if you select Horizontally and Vertically.

Centering makes your page look balanced, but beware—the more stuff you cram on a page, the smaller your margins will get.

Can I choose which elements of the worksheet to print?

After you fix the margins, decide what to include on the printout. The Sheet tab of the Page Setup dialog box lets you get rid of the row and column headings and prevent any Comments you've attached to the sheet from printing. Or include both in the printout—it's your choice.

Spectacular Technicolor worksheets might look great on the screen, but those good looks may not translate well to print. Lots of shading, patterns, and colors can make worksheets hard to read on a black-and-white printout. If your masterpiece doesn't read well in print, try this quick fix: click the Black and White check box on the Sheet tab of the Page Setup dialog box.

If you want your row and column titles to repeat on every page, click the Rows To Repeat At Top and the Columns To Repeat At Left text boxes on the Sheet tab.

After you click one of those boxes, select the ranges containing your row and column titles. Click anywhere within the ranges, and the range references appear in the boxes. Adjust the range references if you need to (see Figure 5.5).

If you leave the boxes blank, the row and column titles just print on the first page.

Don't confuse row and column *headings* with row and column *titles*. Headings are supplied by Excel: A, B, C, 1, 2, 3, and so on. Titles are what you've typed into the worksheet to label rows and columns.

If the Print dialog box gets in your way while you're selecting ranges, click the Collapse Dialog Box button in the text box you're working in. That leaves the text box on the screen and puts the rest of the dialog box out of sight. Click the Collapse Dialog button again to restore the dialog box to view.

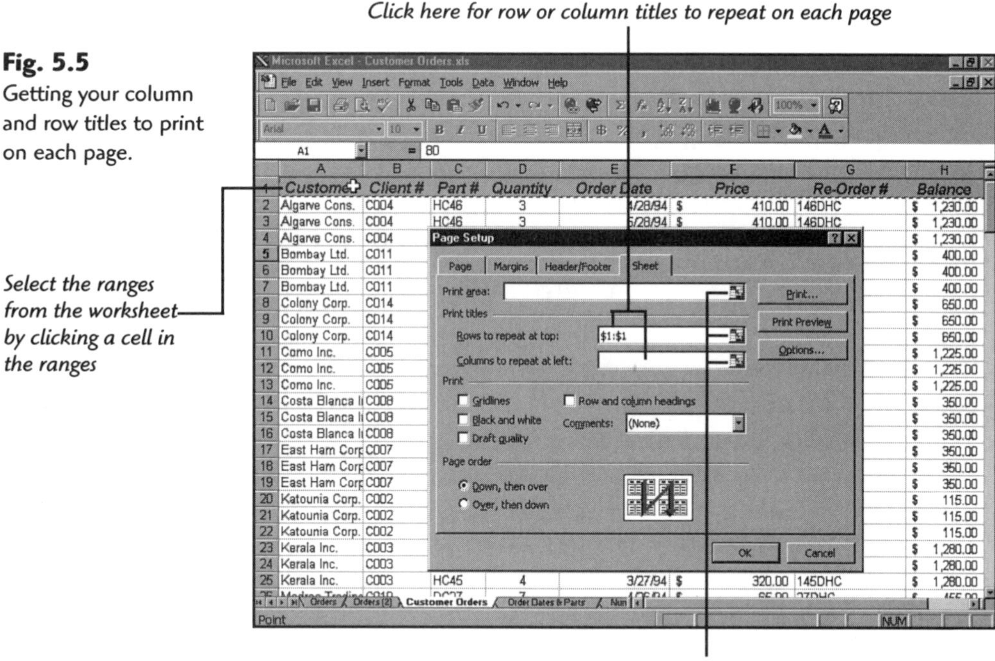

Fig. 5.5
Getting your column and row titles to print on each page.

If you want to print the same area of the worksheet every time, use the Print Area text box in the Sheet tab of the Page Setup dialog box (for this maneuver, you have to select Page Setup from the File menu instead of Setup from the Print Preview window). Type in the range reference for the range you want to print, or click the Print Area text box and select the range with the mouse. You may have to drag the Page Setup dialog box out of the way to do this. If you later want to print a different area, go back in and change this first.

I have several pages of data to print, but all I get out of my printer is one little chunk of my worksheet. What gives?

Chances are, you did what I sometimes do: put a range to print in the Print Area text box, then forgot to blank it out when you wanted to print something else.

Just what is a Comment, anyway?

Those **Comments** that you can choose to print or not in the Sheet tab of the Print dialog box are messages, or annotations, for yourself or others that you attach to a cell on the worksheet. Annotated cells display a little red triangle in the upper-right corner. The Comment itself stays out of sight.

To create new Comments, select the cell and choose Insert, Comment. That pops up a text box with an arrow pointing to the selected cell. Type your comment, and click the cell when you're done to save the annotation.

A Comment Indicator, a tiny red triangle, appears in the annotated cell. Move the pointer over the cell (you don't have to click) and your Comment is displayed, as shown in Figure 5.6.

A Comment displays when you move the pointer over the cell to which it's attached

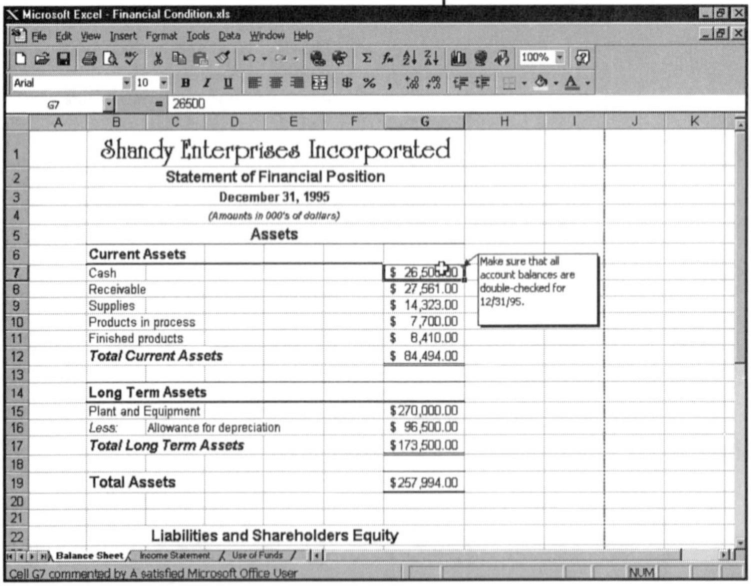

Fig. 5.6
Comments are handy as reminders, or to add extra information to worksheets.

If you want your Comments to display even when you're not pointing at the cell to which they're attached, click Tools, Options and select the View tab. Choose Comments & Indicator and click OK. To hide both the Comments and the Comment Indicators, choose None on the View tab of the Options dialog box.

Once inserted, you can edit or delete Comments. Right-click the cell with the Comment and choose Edit Comment or Delete Comment from the shortcut menu.

TIP **To print your Comments at the bottom of each worksheet page,** click File, Page Setup. On the Sheet tab of the Page Setup dialog box, click the Comment drop-down arrow and choose At End Of Sheet.

Orderly printing

When your worksheet data won't fit on a single page, print several. You just have to decide the order in which the data gets printed.

Say you're laying down new tiles on the bathroom floor. You have two choices: you can work your way across the floor, tile by tile, then go down to the next row and across again, or you can lay tiles one below the other until you get to the wall, then go back and start another column.

Same thing here. Your data gets broken up into tile-like pages. When you print, you choose how to lay them down. The Down, Then Over option on the Sheet tab of the Page Setup dialog box prints your data page by page down the worksheet. After you get to the last row of data, printing starts from the top again, one page to the right. The Over, Then Down option prints data page by page across the width of the worksheet. When the last column of data is reached, printing starts again from the first column, one page down. Look at Figures 5.7 and 5.8 to get the idea.

Fig. 5.7
Print pages of data starting at the top row, working down to the bottom row, then one page over and down again.

Fig. 5.8
Or print starting at the first column, working your way across the columns page by page, then down one page and repeat.

Being spatially impaired, I can never get this straight. In most cases, you'll want to print Down, Then Over. For worksheets with long rows, you may want Over, Then Down. If in doubt, check out both options first in the Print Preview window.

Fine-tuning the print job

Remember that art book on old Tintoretto's *Paradise*? In one plate, you got the whole painting. You just wouldn't see much detail because it was shrunk to fit on the page.

You can do that with your worksheet, too. Click the Page tab in the Page Setup dialog box. Choose Fit to Page(s), then click OK. Cramming your print job onto one page (or several pages) this way makes the scale shrink. To see by how much, click File, Page Setup, then click the Page tab again. The Adjust To % Normal Size text box in the Scaling area shows you how much smaller your printout will appear (see Figure 5.9).

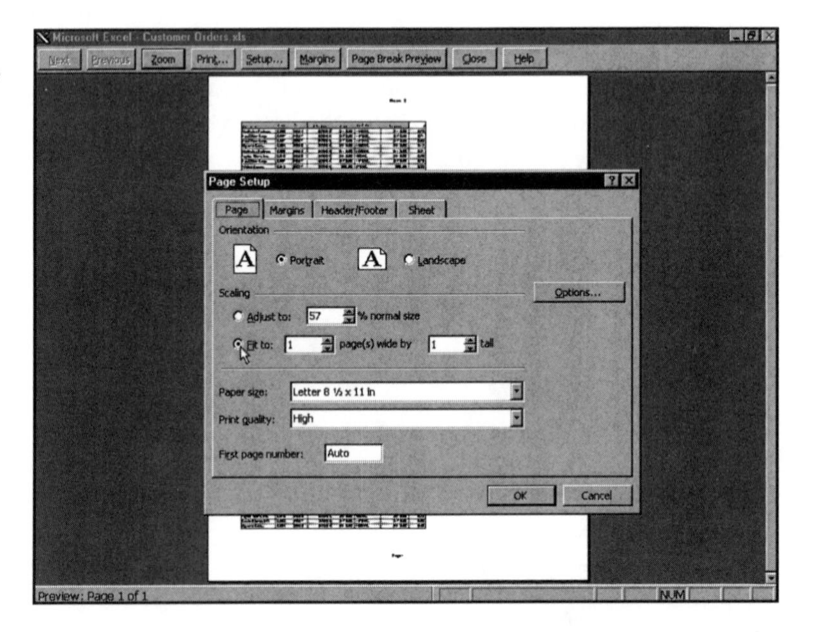

Fig. 5.9
Shrink your print job to fit on one page or several.

This is great for a worksheet that almost, but doesn't quite, fit on one page. If you have a single column stranded on page two, this option saves you a lot of fussing.

But for a longer report, shrinking to fit may make your printout completely unreadable. For situations like that, try adjusting the number of pages in the Fit to Page(s) text box. You can also adjust the scaling. With enough tinkering, you'll get it right sooner or later!

Which way do you want the paper to go?

This is a quick and easy adjustment that's more my style (because it's quick and easy). Take a piece of paper and hold it so that the longer edges are vertical. That's called **portrait** orientation. Now turn it sideways so that what was the left side is now the bottom edge. This is called **landscape** orientation. You can print either way by selecting Portrait or Landscape on the Page tab (refer to Figure 5.9).

For worksheets wider than they are long, landscape orientation is the best choice.

A few minor adjustments: column width and margins

If you love to tinker, you'll love being able to adjust margins and column widths manually. And it's not always mere tinkering. Sometimes, no matter how often you adjust the margin settings in the Margins tab, the page still doesn't look right. Click the Print Preview button on the toolbar. In the Print Preview window, click Margins. Now you can see exactly what you're doing (see Figure 5.10).

Put the pointer on any one of the broken lines. It turns into the double-headed black arrow, and you can drag the lines up and down or from side to side to fine-tune the margins. Aim the pointer at the markers at the top of the page to adjust the column width.

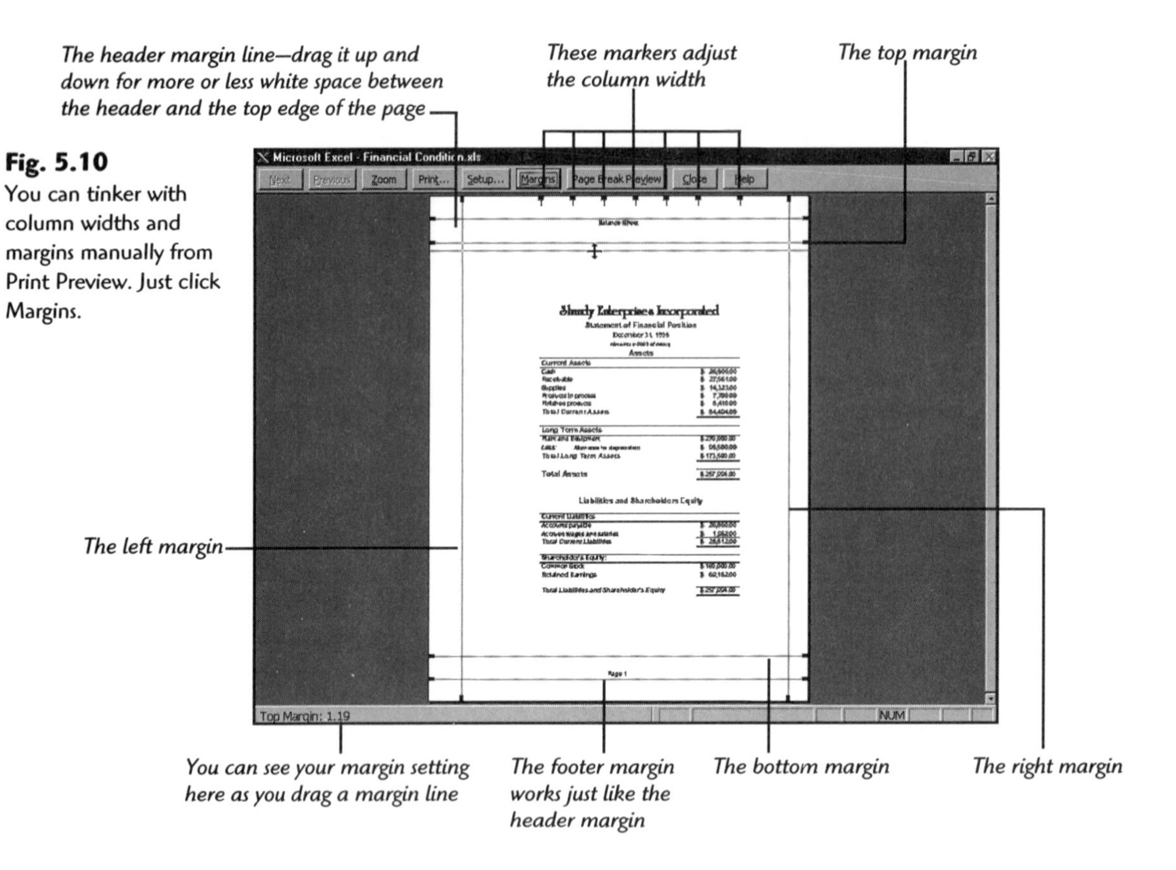

Fig. 5.10
You can tinker with column widths and margins manually from Print Preview. Just click Margins.

Head to toe: headers and footers

You may want something more exotic than the sheet name for the header and the page number for the footer. That's what Excel gives you by default, but you don't have to settle for it. The Header/Footer tab on the Page Setup dialog box gives you plenty of other options.

Click File, Page Setup and click the Header/Footer tab. The two drop-down lists have prepackaged headers and footers that come with the program.

If you don't see anything you like, click Custom Header or Custom Footer. Figure 5.11 shows the Header dialog box.

You can type whatever you want in the text boxes. Click the buttons to insert codes for the date, time, and so on. Then preview your work in the boxes on the Header/Footer tab.

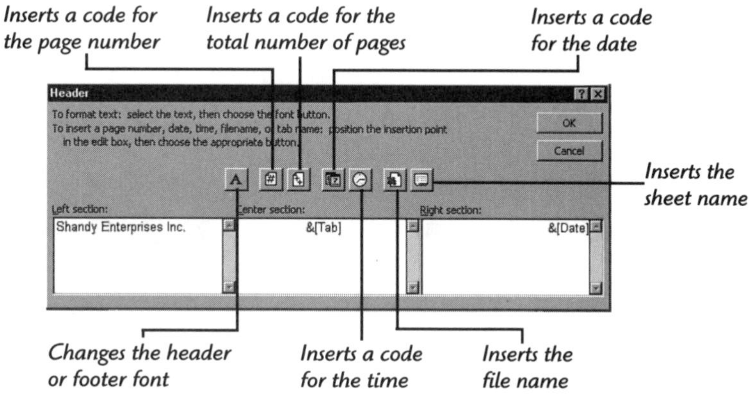

Inserts a code for the page number
Inserts a code for the total number of pages
Inserts a code for the date
Inserts the sheet name
Changes the header or footer font
Inserts a code for the time
Inserts the file name

Fig. 5.11
Create your own headers and footers with these buttons.

I could really use a page break!

When you print a worksheet that will run to several pages, Excel automatically starts a new page after the end of each full page of data. Broken lines, called **page breaks**, appear on the worksheet to show you where one page ends and the next begins.

But you may want your page to break somewhere else—before a new head, for example.

To see where Excel breaks the pages on your worksheet, click View, Page Break Preview. That shows you the pages where different parts of the worksheet are going to wind up, as shown in Figure 5.12.

While you're in Page Break Preview mode, you can drag a page break to a different section of the worksheet. Or, if you don't like what Excel has done, you can supply your own page breaks:

1. Select the row below the one where you want the page to break—just click the row heading.
2. Click Insert, Page Break.
3. Your manually inserted page break shows up as a solid line in Page Break Preview mode (see Figure 5.13).

To break a page at a column, select the column after the one where you want to break the page (click the column heading), then click Insert, Page Break. Want to get rid of your manual page breaks? Select the row below, or the column after, the manual page break. Click Insert, Remove Page Break to finish the job.

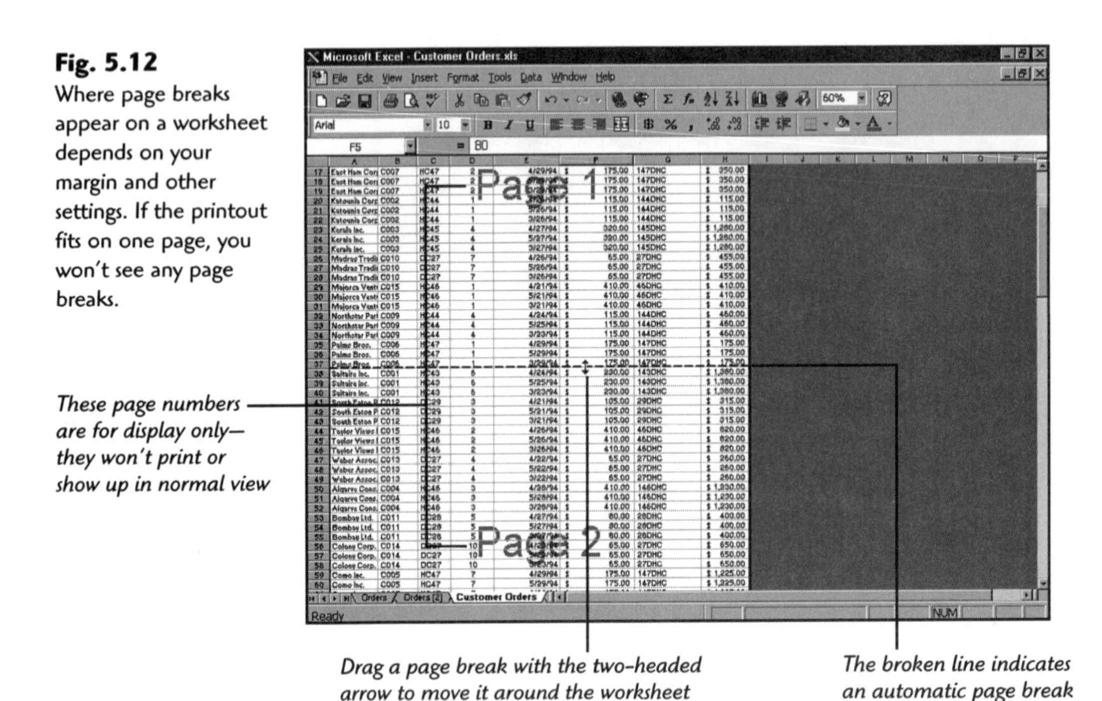

Fig. 5.12
Where page breaks appear on a worksheet depends on your margin and other settings. If the printout fits on one page, you won't see any page breaks.

Fig. 5.13
A manual page break is a solid line; an automatic page break is a broken line.

The Select All button

Manual page break

Automatic page break

I have manual page breaks in the wrong places all over this worksheet. How do I get rid of them all at once?

Here's the easy way to clear several manual page breaks at the same time. Click the Select All button—that unmarked but powerful little gadget at the juncture of the row and column headings (refer to Figure 5.13). Then click Insert, Reset All Breaks. That'll zap all the manual breaks.

Skip the office copier—there's a copier in Excel

Howmany times have you done this tedious chore? You have piles of copies to collate, so you laboriously turn page 1 face down, plop page two on top of it, and so on. Then you start on the next pile. Photocopiers that automatically collate copies were a great advance for those of us stuck with jobs like that.

Here's some good news: Excel collates copies for you. When you have a workbook or worksheet that spans multiple pages, and you need several copies, click File, Print to open the Print dialog box.

Use the arrows to select the Number of Copies, then click the Collate check box, as shown in Figure 5.14.

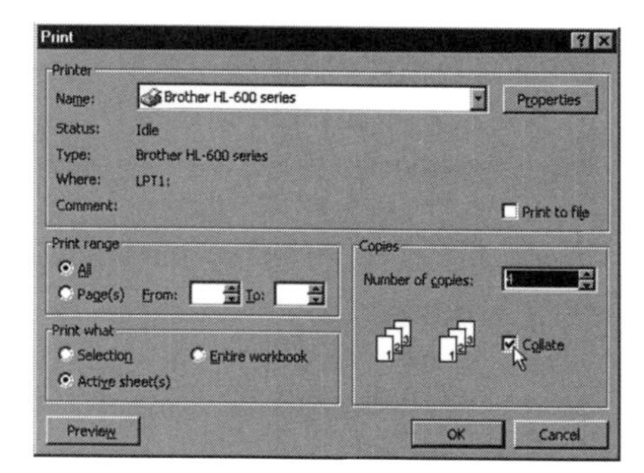

Fig. 5.14
One quick click saves you a lot of tedious hand collating when you have multiple copies to print.

Working with Worksheets and Workbooks

In this chapter:

- Why should I bother with multiple worksheets?
- I need to add more sheets
- I can't find my workbook!
- Can I put this in another workbook?
- This stuff has to go in another worksheet

Excel workbooks have worksheets for the same reason that printed books have pages—there's just no better way to store and present data . . . .

Sherlock Holmes kept pipe tobacco handy in the toe of a Persian slipper. He impaled his correspondence on the mantelpiece with a dagger. After reading the newspapers on train trips, he'd roll them into a ball and toss them in the overhead rack. He once carved Queen Victoria's initials on the wall of his room—with revolver shots.

He was less eccentric when it came to work. Holmes kept extensive scrapbooks, filled with newspaper clippings and notes from his cases. He knew the importance of orderly files. When the game was afoot, Holmes wanted his critical data within reach.

We want our critical data to be just as orderly. Important workbooks have to be at our fingertips, and the worksheets inside them need to be meticulously organized.

Too much effort? Not really. With Excel, it's elementary!

Do I really need all these sheets?

Chances are you don't stuff all your vital papers into a single file. Instead, you organize them in file folders, and then arrange the folders in hanging file holders.

You could stick all your different kinds of data in a single worksheet. With about 4.2 million cells per sheet, it's certainly big enough to hold it all. But it sure isn't the easiest way to keep track of everything! Consider:

- Clicking sheet tabs is much handier than scrolling across vast expanses of worksheet. With multiple sheets, you keep all your data in easy reach.
- Cells in one worksheet that refer to data in another sheet are easy to set up.
- You can use different worksheets for separate components of a workbook—income statement on one sheet, cash flow on another, and balance sheet on a third, for example.
- Or keep different elements of a workbook, like charts and macros, on separate sheets.

- No matter how many sheets it has, a workbook is still a single file—everything you need is in one place.

Shuffling sheets

It's easy to flip from sheet to sheet in a workbook. Just click the tab of the worksheet you want.

Keyboard artists can press Ctrl+Page Up or Ctrl+Page Down to go from sheet to sheet.

You can also adjust how many sheet tabs are displayed, as shown in Figure 6.1.

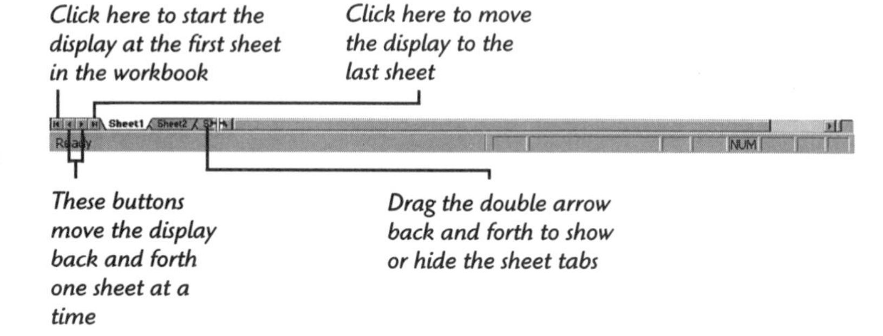

Fig. 6.1
Show or hide as many tabs as you want by clicking scroll buttons or dragging. Go from sheet to sheet by clicking sheet tabs.

Remember to double-click the sheet tab to name your sheet.

How do I add sheets I need and get rid of sheets I don't?

When you start a new Excel workbook, you get three worksheets. If you fill those up, you can add more if you like. If you have extras, you can delete them.

Inserting sheets

This is really easy:

1. New sheets are inserted to the left of the active sheet, so click the sheet tab to the right of where you want the new worksheet.
2. Click Insert, Worksheet to instantly pop a new blank worksheet into the workbook.

Deleting sheets

This is even easier:

1. Right-click the sheet tab of the sheet you want to delete; you get the shortcut menu shown in Figure 6.2.

Fig. 6.2
You have to right-click the sheet tab for this shortcut menu; miss the sheet tab, and right-clicking gives you a different menu.

2. Click Delete.
3. You'll get a dialog box with a stern warning that you're about to permanently delete the selected sheet. Click OK if you're sure.

When Excel says permanently, it means business. Undo doesn't work here. Before you delete a sheet, be sure you really want it deleted.

To get rid of more than one sheet at a time, click the sheet tabs while pressing Ctrl. Each tab is highlighted. Then click the right mouse button for the shortcut menu and click Delete.

Similarly, click Insert, Worksheet to add as many new sheets as you've selected existing sheets.

I know how many sheets I want in my workbooks, and it's not what Excel automatically gives me. Can't I avoid doing these gyrations every time I start a workbook?

Sure. Click Tools, Options. Click the General tab and pick a new number for Sheets in New Workbook. Every time you open a new workbook, you'll start with that number of sheets.

From many worksheets, one efficient workbook

You can do whatever you want with multiple worksheets. One handy use is to have one sheet show summary data, drawn from detailed breakdowns on other sheets.

That offers a few advantages. You can print or display only your summary, without having to wade through the detail. Some of the detail needs adjusting? Make the changes on the detail worksheet, without disturbing anything on the summary sheet (which you've spent hours formatting) except for the one number you're fixing.

And you don't lose anything, because the detail is all still there. It's just on another sheet.

Copying cells from one worksheet to another

Figure 6.3 shows the Shandy Enterprises balance sheet. Notice that the Cash amount is blank.

Our CFO hasn't gone to Rio or anything, so we know our cash is still on hand. It's just broken out for us on the worksheet labeled Cash. Now all we have to do is move our cash total to the right cell on our balance sheet. To make a linked copy of a cell from one worksheet to another:

1. Starting in the destination worksheet, select the cell you want to copy *to* and click the Edit Formula button on the formula bar.
2. Now click the sheet tab we're copying *from*. The sheet we began with has its tab highlighted, and the reference for the sheet we're copying from appears in the formula bar on the new sheet.

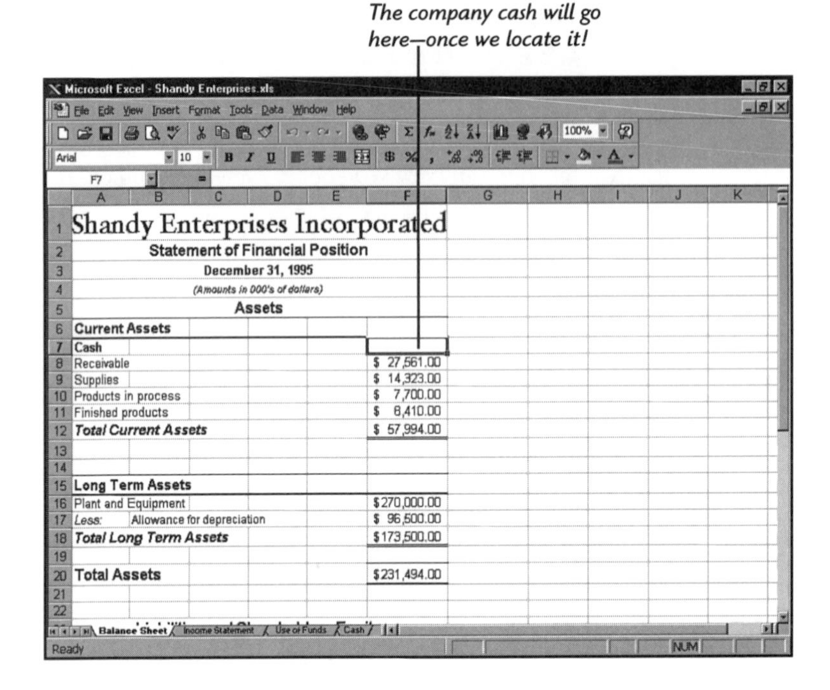

Fig. 6.3
Notice the sheet names on the tabs. Also, the gaping hole where our cash ought to be.

3 Click the cell we're copying. The marquee, that moving border, appears around it, as shown in Figure 6.4.

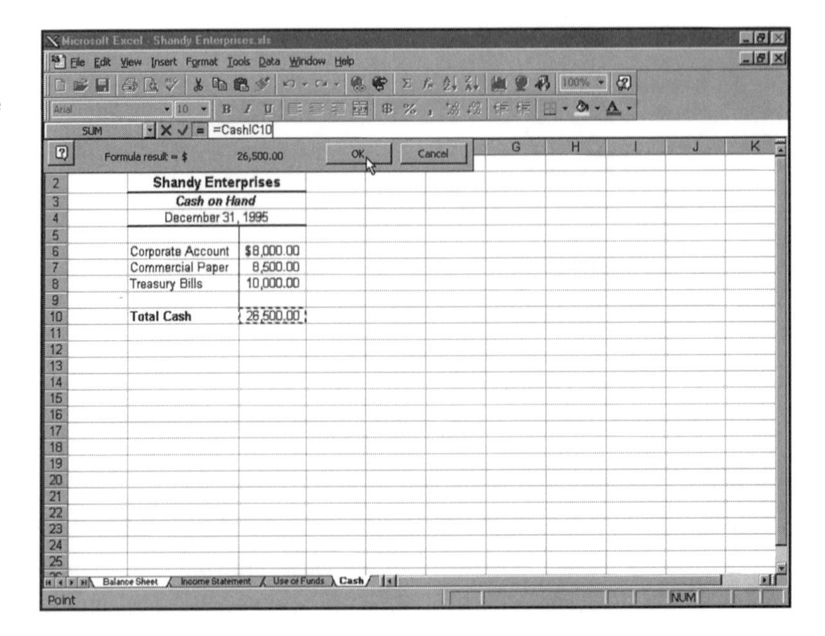

Fig. 6.4
The shareholders will be relieved to hear we aren't broke after all.

4. Click OK on the formula bar (or press Enter), and we're done. Our cash is just where it should be, and the CFO is off the hook. Figure 6.5 shows where the copied cell winds up.

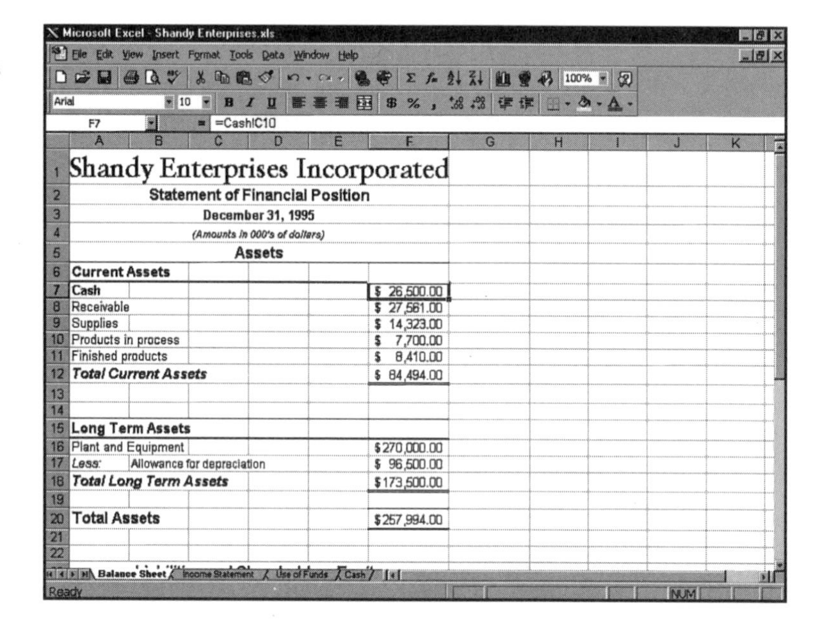

	A	B	C	D	E	F
1	Shandy Enterprises Incorporated					
2	Statement of Financial Position					
3	December 31, 1995					
4	(Amounts in 000's of dollars)					
5	Assets					
6	Current Assets					
7	Cash					$ 26,500.00
8	Receivable					$ 27,561.00
9	Supplies					$ 14,323.00
10	Products in process					$ 7,700.00
11	Finished products					$ 8,410.00
12	Total Current Assets					$ 84,494.00
13						
14						
15	Long Term Assets					
16	Plant and Equipment					$270,000.00
17	Less:	Allowance for depreciation				$ 96,500.00
18	Total Long Term Assets					$173,500.00
19						
20	Total Assets					$257,994.00

Fig. 6.5
The formula bar shows the sheet reference `Cash!` and the cell reference `C10` from the cash worksheet.

If we make any changes on the Cash worksheet, they'll be reflected automatically on the Balance Sheet worksheet. We didn't have to worry about absolute and relative cell references. Relative to the cell we copied to, the reference `Cash!C10` is exactly what we want because it includes the sheet reference `Cash!`.

Check out Chapter 8 for more information about cell references.

A straight copy from one sheet to another *will* change the cell reference. If we'd copied C10 on the cash worksheet by clicking the Copy button, then clicking the destination sheet tab and pasting, the `SUM` formula wouldn't have worked. Without the sheet address, the pasted formula would have referenced cells on the destination worksheet. Moral of the story: include the sheet address when copying formulas from one sheet to another.

Refer to multiple worksheets with 3-D references

The next time you do a little research on Croatian poetry, you might look up the 17th-century poet Giovanni Gondola. Hunt through the encyclopedia, find the reference—and instead of an article, you get something like this: "Gondola, Giovanni. See Gundulic, Ivan (p. 765)."

A cross-reference like that can lead you to other valuable information (it can also drive you up the wall). Sheet addresses in Excel are like cross-references. `Cash!C10` is just like telling Excel to "See the Sheet 'Cash,' cell C10" when it looks for data in a cell.

If you want to refer to the same range on several sheets in a workbook, you can use a **3-D reference**. For example, Universal Racquet Sports has regional sales on two separate worksheets. We want to consolidate those sales on a third sheet, as shown in Figures 6.6 and 6.7. To create the 3-D reference:

1 Click the cell where you want the 3-D reference and begin the formula. Because we're totaling values here, we'll use Excel's automatic adding machine, AutoSum. Click the AutoSum button on the toolbar.

TIP **When you click the AutoSum button, AutoSum suggests a range to** total, either above or to the left or right of the selected cell, depending on where your data is. Just ignore the suggestion. As soon as you select a different range, which we do by clicking the first sheet tab, AutoSum's suggested range disappears.

2 Click the tab for the first sheet in the range, `East` for us.

3 Press Shift while clicking the tab for the last sheet in the range, or `West`. If your 3-D reference includes more than three sheets, Shift+click any additional sheets. In this example, all three sheet tabs are highlighted, as shown in Figure 6.6.

4 Select the cell or range to include in the formula, B9 in the example.

5 Press Enter, and we're done. Figure 6.7 shows a windowed view of all three worksheets.

The formula in progress appears in the formula bar

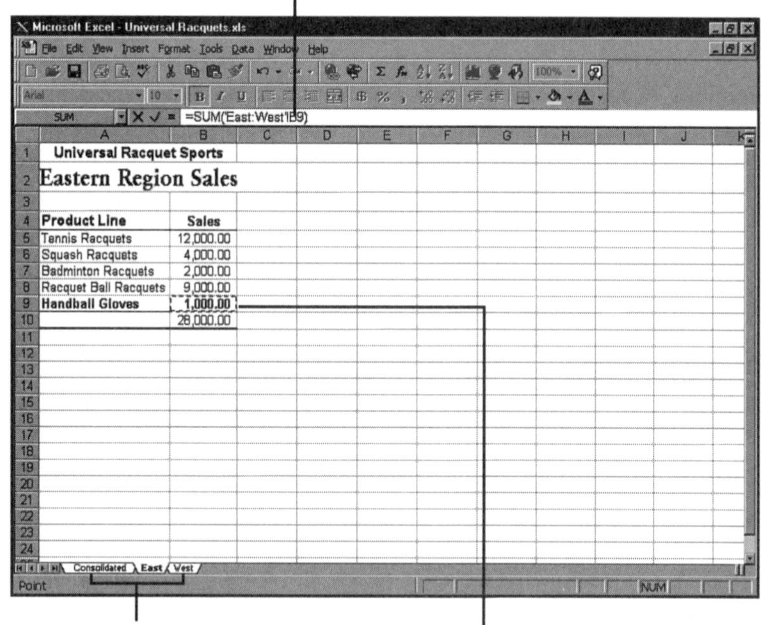

Fig. 6.6
Creating a 3-D reference by pointing and clicking. It's easier done than said.

Click the first sheet of the range, then Shift+click the last sheet of the range—all three sheets are highlighted

Selecting the cell or range from the active sheet puts the marquee around it

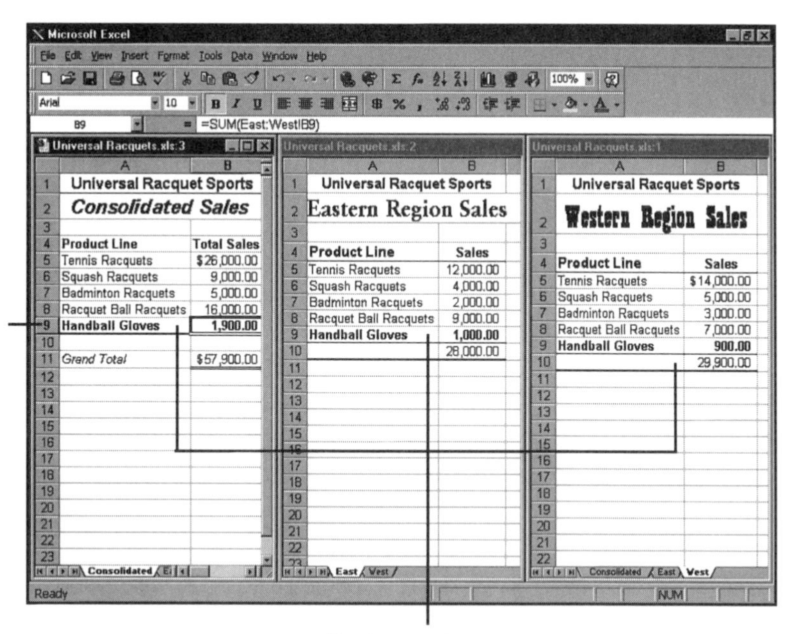

Fig. 6.7
=SUM(East:West!B9) gives us our consolidated Handball Gloves sales.

The values we're summing up are in cell B9 in each sheet

The layout of the three sheets is identical

3-D references like this only work when the same cell address is referenced in all the sheets. In the example, B9 is the cell address common to all three sheets; if the value we needed had been in a cell other than B9 on the middle sheet, that value would have been ignored. When you set up sheets with 3-D references, just make sure that the sheet layouts are identical.

No, wait! I don't want to do this after all

Change your mind after you've selected a range of sheets? Click another sheet tab outside the range and the selected sheets are deselected. Or right-click a sheet in the range and select Ungroup Sheets from the shortcut menu.

Copying and moving worksheets in the same workbook

Copying worksheets in Excel is a lot more efficient than making copies on the office photocopier. It's just not as social.

1 Click the tab of the sheet you want to copy.

2 Press Ctrl and drag the sheet along the tabs at the bottom of the worksheet. Two things happen: the little sheet icon follows the pointer across the tabs, and a black triangle appears between each sheet tab to show you where your copy's going to wind up (see Figure 6.8.)

3 Release the mouse button, and the copy slips into place. Excel uses whatever sheet name was on the tab and adds a (2) to identify the copy, as shown in Figure 6.9. You might want to rename this sheet to avoid confusion.

To shuffle the order of the worksheets by moving a sheet between two others, just drag the sheet tab. The black triangle shows you where the sheet will go.

Fig. 6.8
Ctrl+dragging a sheet tab makes a copy of the sheet.

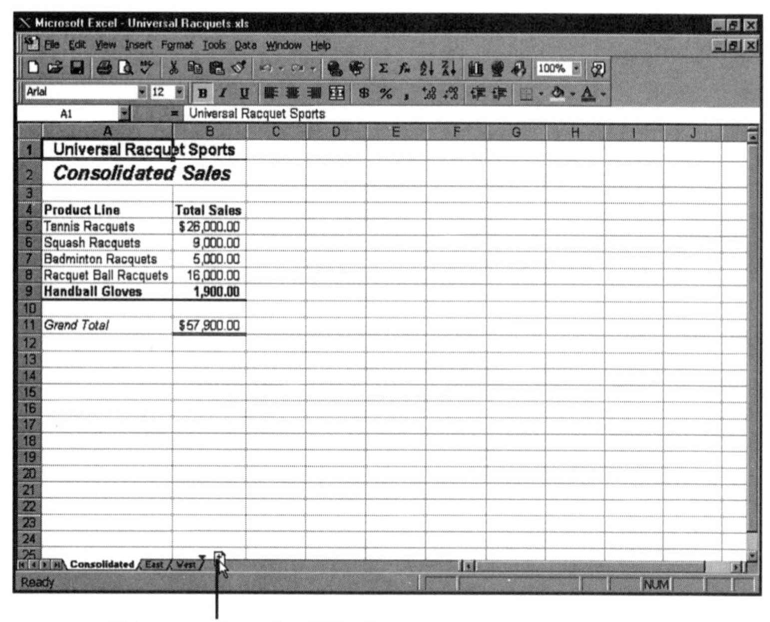

This copy will go after "West"

Fig. 6.9
A copy of the original sheet slips into place—no smudges or smears.

Copying and moving from workbook to workbook

Copying a sheet from one workbook to another is just as straightforward:

1. Open the two workbooks.
2. Click Window, Arrange, Vertical, OK. That puts both workbooks in view.
3. Click the tab of the sheet you want to copy, and Ctrl+drag it to the new workbook. The black marker shows you where it will wind up, as shown in Figure 6.10.

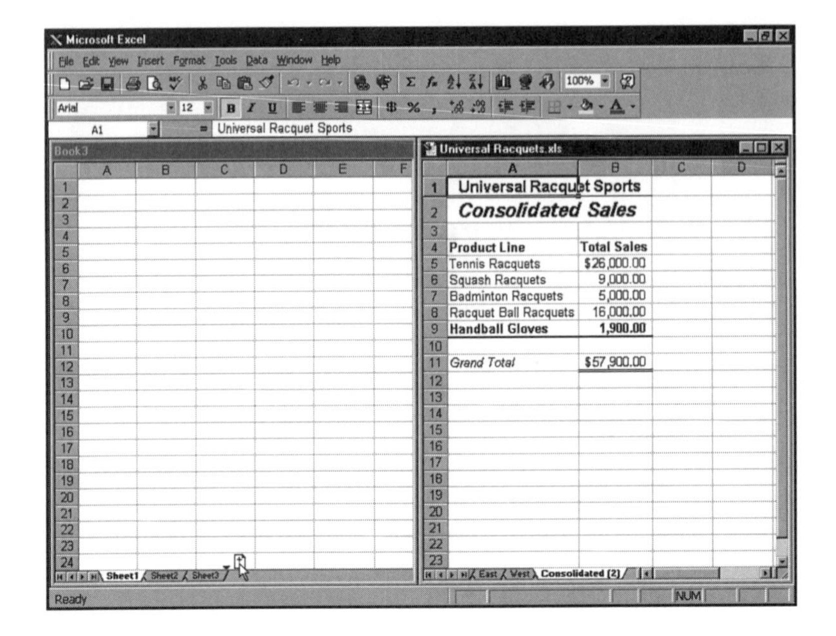

Fig. 6.10
Copying a sheet from workbook to workbook requires a little window work.

To move a sheet from one workbook to another, just drag the sheet instead of using Ctrl+drag.

CAUTION **Undo doesn't work for these maneuvers. If you don't like what** you've done, you'll have to drag moved sheets back by hand and delete unwanted copies with the shortcut menu.

How can I work on several sheets at once?

To edit or format several sheets at once, group them. Use the Shift key to select a range of sheets, just as though you were creating a 3-D reference. Whatever you do in one sheet will be done to the same cells in the other sheets.

If you want to group sheets that aren't contiguous, click the first sheet tab, then Ctrl+click your other selections.

TIP **If you change your mind, ungroup the sheets. Right-click any** sheet tab in the range and choose Ungroup Sheets from the shortcut menu.

How do I find my workbook?

Someday I'll put my home library in order. I can see it now—alphabetized rows of books, by subject and author, neatly arranged on shelves. It'll be grand. In the meantime, I prowl through the piles when I need something. The dustiest volumes tend to be the least useful, so I get to those last.

It's not exactly the Dewey decimal system. But then, I have a choice, unlike the public library. Their piles would be a little unwieldy. That's why they have a card catalog.

As your workbook collection grows, it's going to get a little unwieldy too. You'll need a catalog, and Excel provides a dandy.

Just where are my workbooks?

Windows 95 replaces directories and subdirectories with folders and subfolders. What's the difference? None. Only the names have been changed. The basic idea is the same: a hierarchy of parent folders containing subsidiary subfolders, just like the old directories and subdirectories.

When you save a workbook, Excel files it for you in the My Documents folder. The program also saves information about when you created the workbook and what's in it, just like a card in the card catalog at the library. Excel even saves a snapshot of the workbook for you to look at. My local library doesn't do that!

TIP **If you want Excel to save workbooks to a default folder other** than My Documents, click Tools, Options. Click the General tab in the Options dialog box, and type a new folder name in the Default File Location text box.

Plain English, please!

Excel stores all kinds of other information whenever you create a workbook, such as how much disk space the workbook occupies and even how long it took you to create it. Workbook information like that is called properties, and you can display it from the Open dialog box. Click the Properties button on the Open dialog box toolbar for a summary, or click the Commands and Settings button and choose Properties for more detail.

To get at Excel's card catalog, click the Open button on the toolbar to open the Open dialog box shown in Figure 6.11.

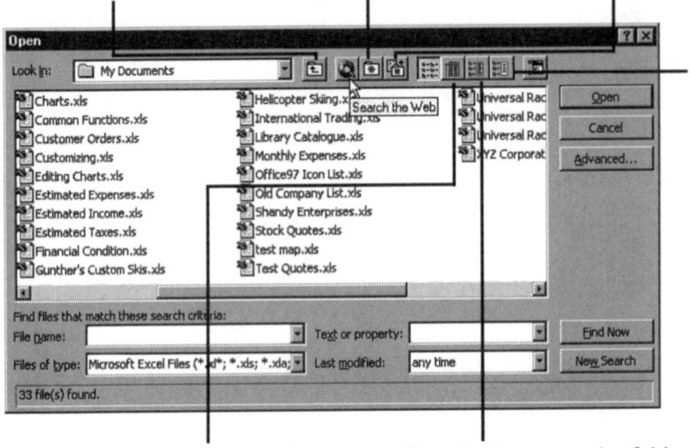

Up One Level displays the folder containing the current subfolder

Look In Favorites displays a special folder with frequently used files

Add To Favorites adds the selected file or file folder to the Favorites folder

Preview shows you a snapshot of the upper-left corner of the first worksheet in the workbook

List gives you the display shown here

Details shows you the folder where the workbook is stored, the size of the workbook, and the date it was last modified

Fig. 6.11
The Open dialog box lets you do your file managing chores in one place.

If you want to flip to another folder, click the Look In drop-down arrow, click the disk drive icon for the drive containing the folder you want, and scroll until you get to your folder.

Double-click the folder, and its contents are displayed in the Open dialog box. Unless you've already used the Open dialog box to explore other folders, the My Documents folder and its contents is displayed, the way it looks in Figure 6.11.

My workbook name doesn't tell me enough

The long file names allowed in Windows 95 let you identify your workbooks with much more descriptive names than the old eight-character monikers we used to be stuck with. Even so, you may find yourself asking "What's in that workbook, anyway?"

Click the Preview button on the Open dialog box toolbar to see a snapshot of the selected workbook. You'll only see the upper-left corner of the first worksheet in the workbook, but it'll at least give you a clue about what's there, as shown in Figure 6.12.

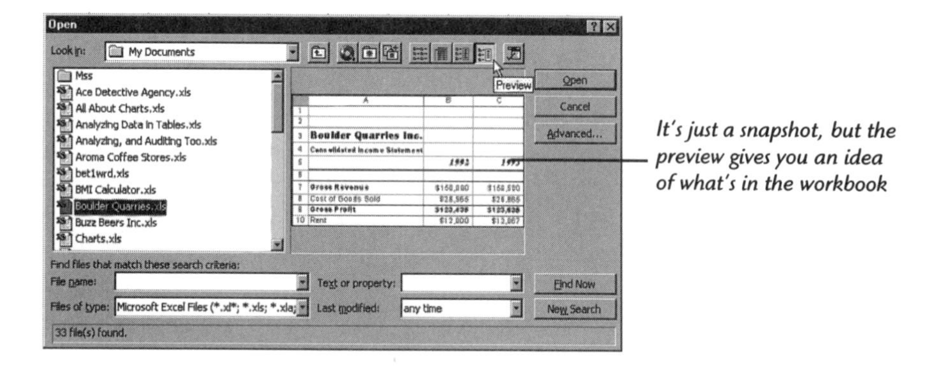

Fig. 6.12
Click from workbook to workbook to see the preview in the Open dialog box.

***How come all I see is* `No preview is available for this file?`**

There's a quick fix: double-click the file to open it, then choose File, Properties. Click the Summary tab, and select the Save Preview Picture check box. Click OK, then save and exit the file. The next time you want to view it in the Open dialog box preview window, you'll see a preview picture.

To get the most out of previewing, make sure the upper-left corner of the first worksheet in all your workbooks contains something that gives you a hint about what's in the rest of the workbook. Chart sheets make for especially uninformative previews, for example, unless you've got a chart title in the upper-left corner of the sheet.

Where's the rename command?

Whether you knew it as REN in DOS, or some variation of Rename File in Windows, the rename command has been sacrificed on the alter of progress. It will not be missed. To rename a file in Excel, click the file's name on the list in the Open dialog box to select it. Click the file name again, and the insertion point appears. Type the new name and press Enter.

That's all there is to renaming files. Just make sure you use two distinct clicks; one to select the file, and the second to conjure up the insertion point. A double-click, as opposed to two clicks, will open the file.

If you find yourself opening files instead of renaming them when you attempt two successive clicks, try a right-click instead. Right-click the file name, choose Rename on the shortcut menu, and type your new name.

How about Copy and Delete?

To get at other file management commands, such as Print or Copy, just right-click the file name. That pops up a shortcut menu with those items and more.

If you want to make a quick backup copy to floppy disk, right-click the file name for the shortcut menu, point at Send To, and click the floppy drive choice, as shown in Figure 6.13.

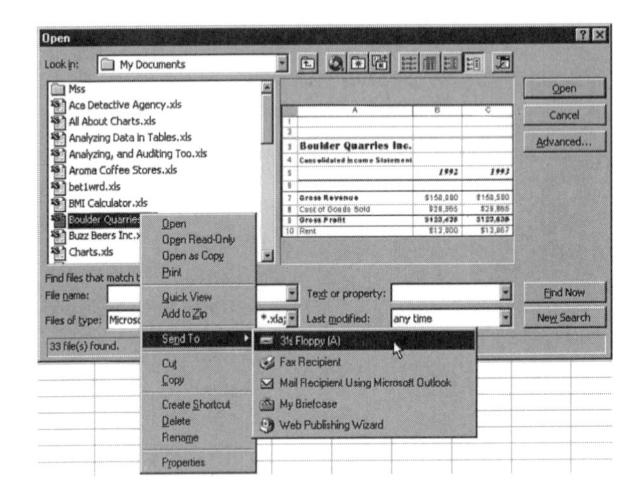

Fig. 6.13
Backing up vital files is fast work from the shortcut menu; just right-click the file name to pop it up.

To select two or more files for printing, copying, or sending to floppy, click the first file, then Ctrl+click each additional file. After you select the files you want, right-click for the shortcut menu and choose a command.

Although you can do a lot of file management chores without leaving Excel, you can't do everything. If you want to create a new folder, you have to use the Windows Explorer or My Computer.

Seek and ye shall Find

We all do it. We'll christen a workbook with a totally forgettable name, and then promptly forget it. What's more, to forget a file name is to guarantee that you'll need the file again.

Fortunately, you don't need to remember file names to locate a file in Excel. Anything about the file that you *can* remember is enough; it could be a client name, a worksheet title, or even a column label. Click the Open button on the toolbar, type whatever you remember about the file in the Text Or Property text box, and click the Find Now button.

Click New Search to clear the text box and try again if you need to.

Part III: Formulas and Functions

Not Just a Pretty Face: Formatting Makes Data Easier to Read

In this chapter:

- **If the numbers add up, who cares how they look?**
- **I just want to make this mess readable—quickly**
- **Fonts? Colors? How am I supposed to know what to use?**
- **I've created a work of art! How do I do it again?**
- **How can I stop someone (like me) from messing up my work?**

Once the numbers add up, the right formatting gets your work the attention it deserves . . . .

He can pop up anywhere. At conventions, in lecture halls, during meetings, there always seems to be one: the mumbler. He drones on and on, in a deadly monotone that puts audiences to sleep. He might have something interesting to say, but who's listening? By the time you've finished your umpteenth doodle, all you want is a well-marked exit.

The shouter is just as bad. We've all heard him. He rants, he pounds the table. His speech may or may not be thought-provoking. His manner is just plain provoking. Your only thought is "Put a sock in it, buddy."

Our worksheets have a point to get across too. The numbers say something. The message might be for corporate headquarters or just for ourselves. But if the worksheet screams—or whispers—the message gets lost (see Figure 7.1).

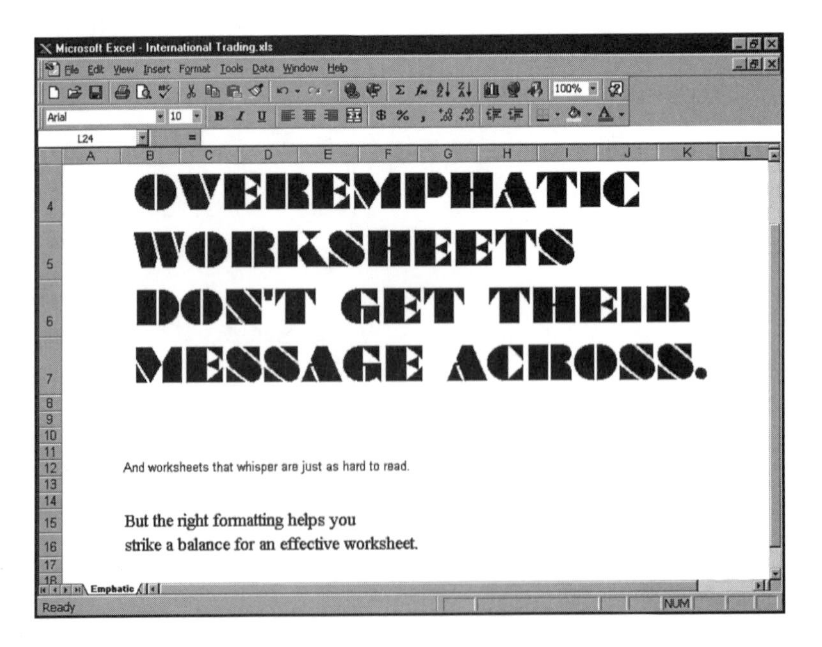

Fig. 7.1
The only thing worse than a mumbler is a shouter. And the only thing worse than a shouter is the guy who spits when he talks to you. At least that's one problem a worksheet can't have.

Instead, use a judicious mix of fonts, borders, and colors. Your message will get through loud and clear.

The Formatting toolbar

Ever look around at all the junk you own and wonder how much of it you really need? I do sometimes. If there were a dumpster handy at times like that, my house would be a lot less cluttered.

Some things really are useful, though. One such item is my Swiss Army knife. Blade, scissors, screwdriver, and bottle opener, all in one portable little tool.

Excel's Formatting toolbar is like your worksheet's Swiss Army knife. It's loaded with useful gadgets, and it's right where you want it. Let's take a closer look at the Formatting toolbar.

Formatting terms you might want to know

Font means typeface as far as Excel is concerned—those families of lettering and numbering types with names like Letter Gothic and Times New Roman.

Times New Roman is called a **serif** font; it has those little tails, or serifs, on each letter. Serif fonts are considered easier to read, because the tails direct the eye from one letter to the next. That's why they're often used in body text (like the text in this book).

> Here is an example of type set in a serif font.

Sans serif fonts, like Letter Gothic, have no tails. You often see them in headings and titles.

> Here is an example of type set in a sans serif font.

A **border** or **rule** is just underlining, with a few twists. You can put the line above or to either side of the cell contents, and you can choose double or single lines in different weights. A **palette** is just what you'd expect: a selection of colors (or borders) from which to choose.

Formatting toolbar puzzles solved

Most of the buttons on the Formatting toolbar are pretty self-explanatory. Select the cell, click the button, and get commas, dollar signs, and so on. One or two toolbar items need a little more explanation.

To bold, italicize, or underline only part of the cell, double-click the cell or click the formula bar. Highlight the bit of the cell contents you want by dragging with the mouse or using the Shift+arrow key, then click the Format button. This doesn't work for numbers or formulas. If you have to underline or bold part of a number, change it to text first by typing an apostrophe (') in front of it.

The Formatting toolbar, for push-button formatting

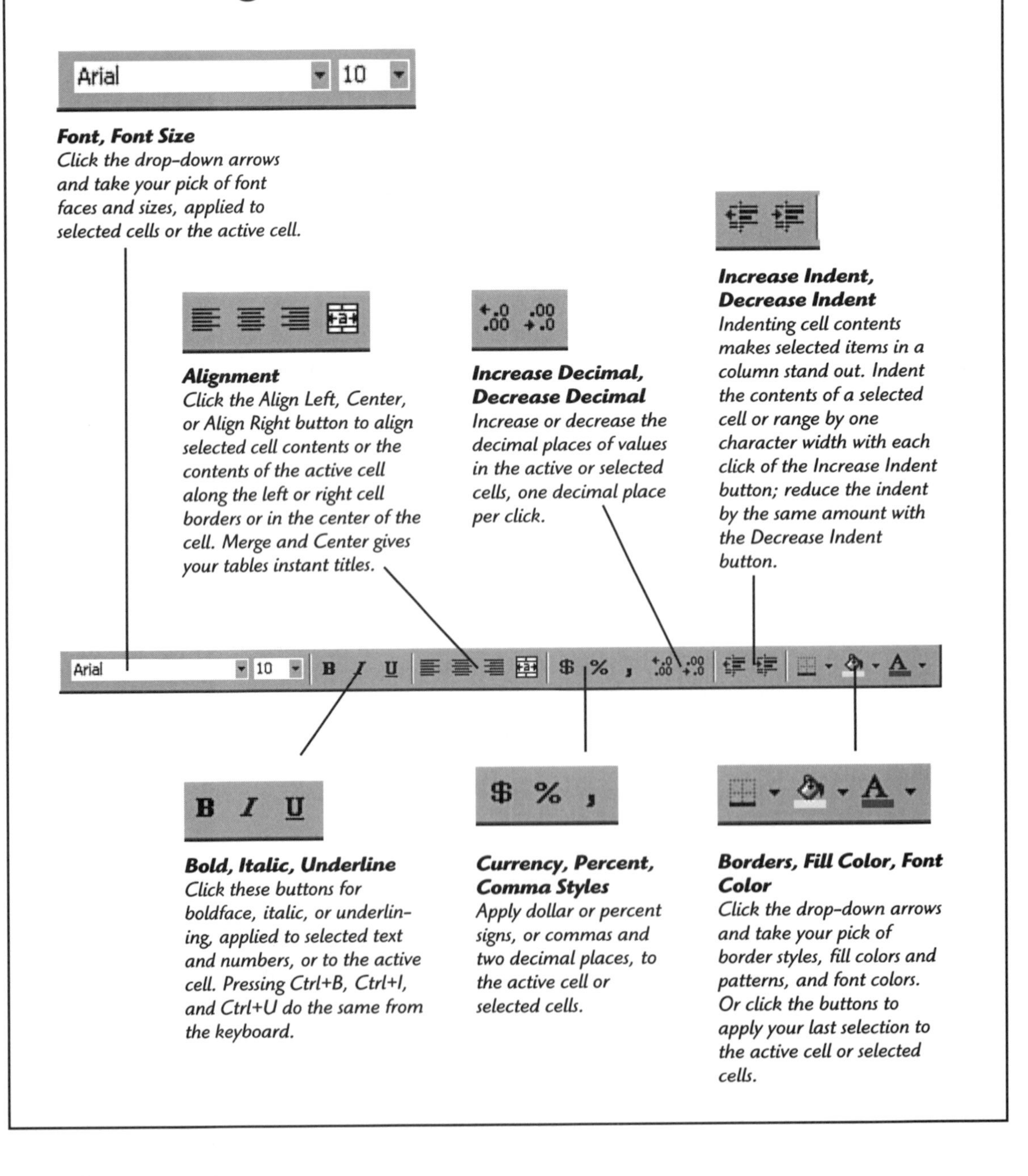

What is "Merge and Center"

It's really just what it says, but what *that* is may not be completely obvious. Here's how you create a centered title with the Merge and Center button:

1. Select the cell at the left border of where you want to center. In the selected cell, type your title or whatever it is you want centered.

2. Press Enter. Select the range of columns across which you want the text centered. The cell with your typing in it is the left border of the range.

3. Click the Merge and Center button.

Say you want to center a title over a table you've created. If the table runs from column B to column F, type the title in a cell in column B, select the range through column F, and click the button. The result looks like Figure 7.2.

Then click the Merge and Center button

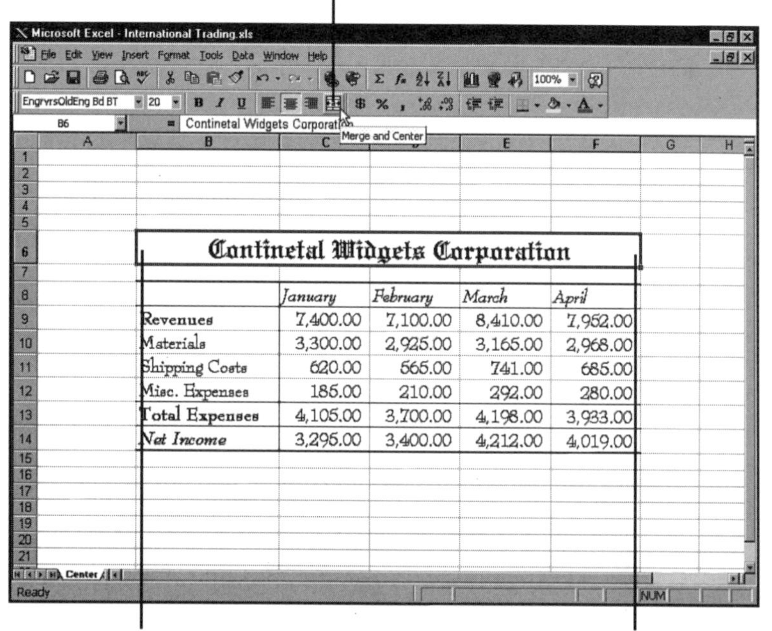

Type the title above the left border of the table

Select the cells through the table's right border

Fig. 7.2
Merge and Center gives titles a balanced look.

How do I add borders?

Borders—underlines, double underlines, even lines that go all the way around a cell—make text and numbers stand out. Grand totals are often given double underlines to really make them jump off the page.

Excel has plenty of borders you can use. To add a border:

1. Select the cell or range.

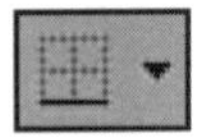

2. Click the drop-down arrow next to the Borders button. That gives you the Borders palette.
3. Click any border on the palette. The border is instantly added to your cell or range.

Figure 7.3 shows a few sample borders, with the grid lines turned off so you can see them better.

TIP **If you want the "inside" borders to be thinner than the thick** "outside" border, apply the inside ones first. Otherwise, you'll wipe out the outside border.

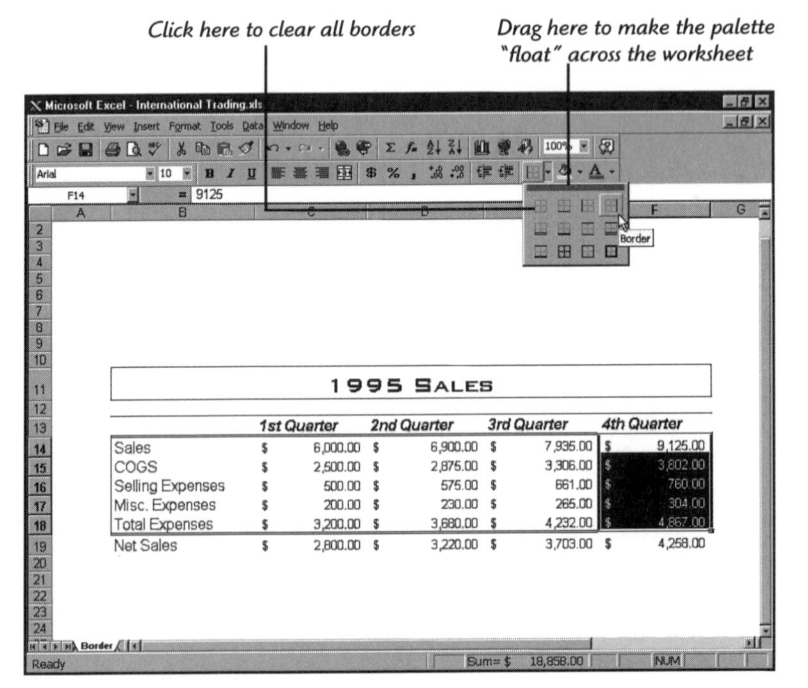

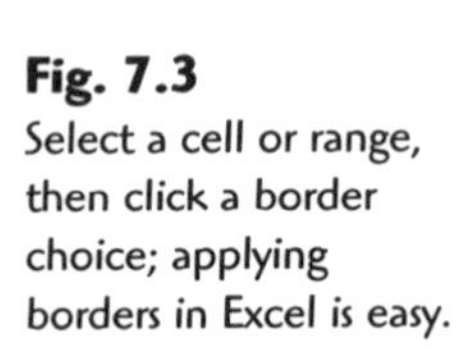

Fig. 7.3
Select a cell or range, then click a border choice; applying borders in Excel is easy.

To "tear off" the Borders palette so that it floats anywhere on the worksheet, just point at the gray strip across the top of the palette and drag. To get rid of the floating palette again, click the close button on the palette title bar. By the way, the border in the upper-left corner of the palette isn't a border. Click it to clear all borders from selected cells.

To get rid of formatting, such as borders, centering, dollar signs, and commas, delete doesn't delete. Use Edit, Clear, Formats instead.

I'm getting the toolbar blues

The Formatting toolbar is a great tool, but it only gives you access to the most common options. If you want more choices, select Format, Cells.

The Format Cells dialog box and tabs have all the features of the Formatting toolbar, and many more besides. Choose different formats for currency, date, time, and other numerical data on the Number tab. Wrap or justify text and pick different alignment options on the Alignment tab.

The Border tab of the Format Cells dialog box has all the choices of the Formatting toolbar Borders palette, along with a few other options. You'll find diagonal borders that cut across a cell, and a menu of line styles for border lines. Want a colored border? Click the Color drop-down arrow on the Borders tab of the Format Cells dialog box and make your selection from the palette of colors.

If you want to insert a hard return within a cell (to put your text onto two or more lines in the cell), press Alt+Enter at the end of a line.

The Font tab is particularly useful. It gives you a preview of all the available fonts, as shown in Figure 7.4.

Right-click any cell to pop up a shortcut menu. Select Format Cells to go right to the dialog box.

To change fonts, first select the cells where you want the different font to apply. The cells can be empty or occupied. Then click the Font drop-down arrow on the Formatting toolbar and choose from the list. Or right-click the selected cells, choose Format Cells from the short-cut menu, and click the Font tab of the Format Cells dialog box. Select a Font and Size, then click OK.

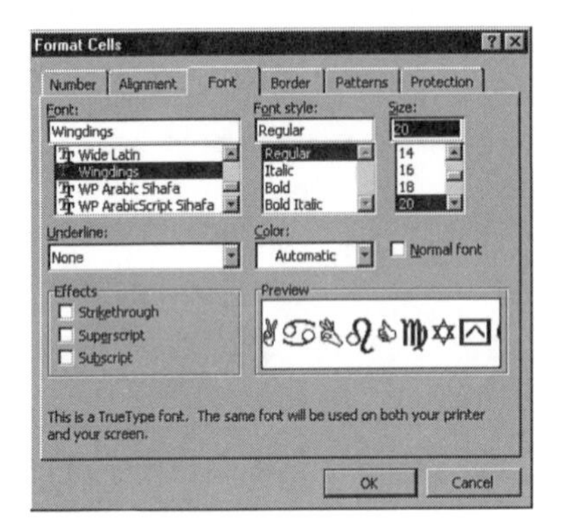

Fig. 7.4
Ever wondered what Wingdings are? Now you know.

Fonts in fancy dress: create special effects with WordArt

Kings and Queens, faced with the fact of looking like ordinary men and women, but burdened by the professional obligation to stand out in a crowd, hit on a simple expedient. They put on ermine robes and jeweled crowns. If your treasury can afford it, that's an effective way to say "look at me." Ordinary worksheets requiring extraordinary attention can pull off a similar stunt with Excel's WordArt feature. WordArt takes fonts and dresses them in flamboyant clothes, for worksheets that clamor "look at me."

To put WordArt to work on attention-getting worksheet titles:

1. Leave plenty of room at the top of your worksheet and select a cell near where you want your title to appear. WordArt is easily moved, so you don't need to be precise.
2. Click Insert, Picture, WordArt. That pops up the WordArt Gallery shown in Figure 7.5.
3. Choose any of the WordArt styles and click OK.
4. In the Edit WordArt Text dialog box that appears next, type the text of your title. Try to keep it short; the longer the text, the more distorted

the characters will be. Click OK, and the title, dressed up in WordArt, pops into the worksheet, as shown in Figure 7.6.

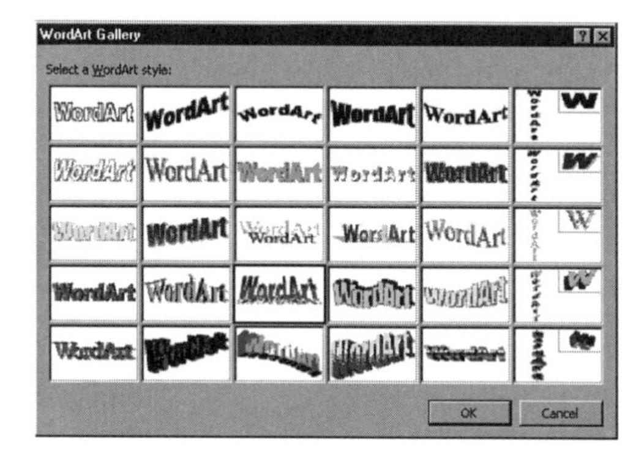

Fig. 7.5
The WordArt Gallery is stocked with colorful special effects for text.

Drag the diamond to change the angle of the WordArt characters

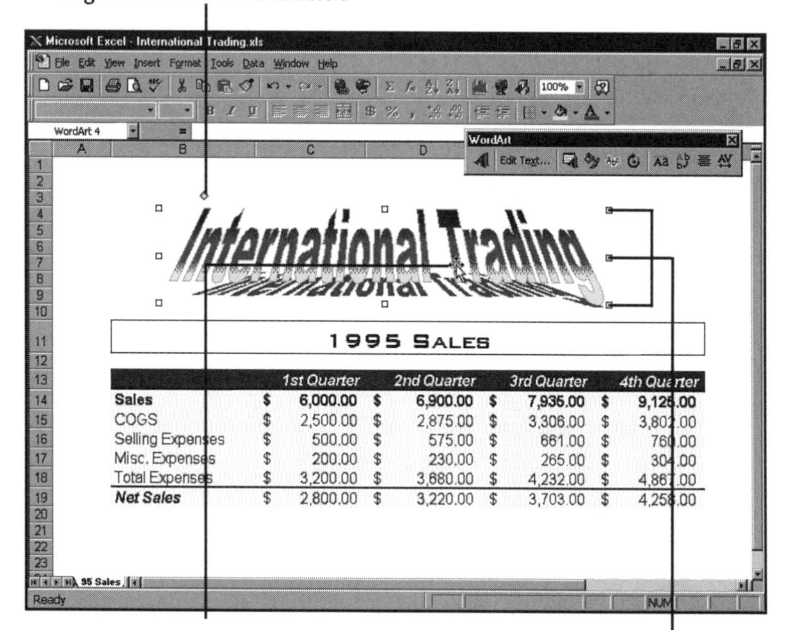

Fig. 7.6
The WordArt toolbar appears automatically when you insert WordArt in the worksheet.

Drag with the four-headed arrow to move the WordArt object around the sheet

Drag a handle to stretch or shrink the title in any direction

TIP **To turn off the worksheet gridlines display, click Tools, Options,** View. Deselect the Gridlines check box and click OK.

5. Drag the handles to stretch or shrink the WordArt object. To move the object, drag it with the four-headed arrow. If you click outside the WordArt object, the handles disappear; click the WordArt to get them back.

6. Use the WordArt toolbar to alter your creation. If any of the toolbar buttons are obscure, press Shift+F1, then click a button for a Help description of its function. If you accidentally close the toolbar and want it back, right-click the Standard toolbar and choose WordArt from the toolbars menu that pops up.

7. When you've finished moving, editing, and formatting your WordArt title, click anywhere outside the title to get rid of the handles and the WordArt toolbar. Don't forget to click the Save button on the Standard toolbar to save your work.

If you need to do any further tinkering with your WordArt creation, click it to bring up the handles and the WordArt toolbar. Want to get rid of the thing entirely? Click the WordArt object and press Delete.

Make it look good fast with AutoFormat

Some people deploy a battery of waxes and polishes and take hours to wash the family wheels. Some just go to the car wash.

You can spend hours fussing with every formatting detail in Excel worksheets too. But if you don't have the time, the fast alternative is Excel's "car wash": the AutoFormat feature. It gives you a polished format for tables, lists, and other data, instantly.

Select a cell in your table, click Format, AutoFormat, and drive right in. Figures 7.7 and 7.8 show you what it's all about.

Click OK when you're done, and AutoFormat sends you on your way with a gleaming worksheet (see Figure 7.9).

If you don't like what AutoFormat has done, just click the Undo button. Or select the range, and choose Edit, Clear, Formats.

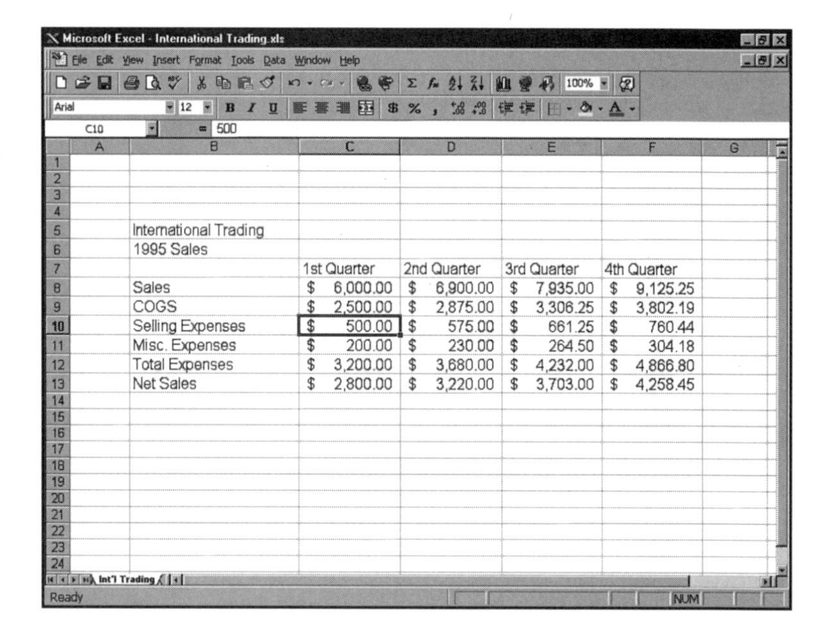

Fig. 7.7
The Before picture. This table doesn't exactly gleam, so drive it into AutoFormat for a quick once-over.

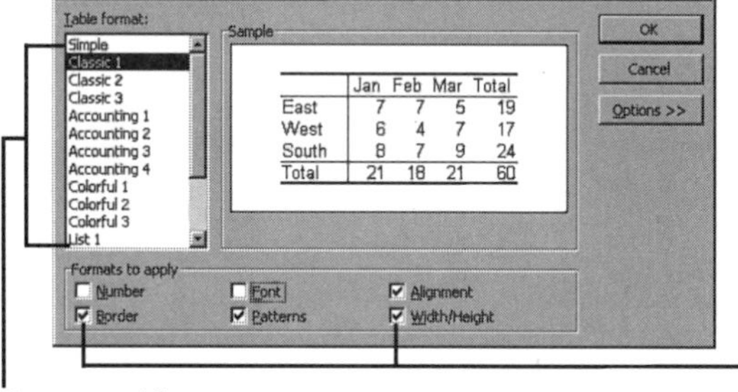

Fig. 7.8
Click the Options button in this dialog box to select from the Formats to Apply choices.

I just AutoFormatted my table, and the column width is all screwed up. What do I do?

If you AutoFormat a table with wide titles, you'll run into this little problem. There are three fixes:

- Deselect Width/Height in the Formats to Apply check boxes of the AutoFormat dialog box.
- Don't include the titles in the range you AutoFormat—do them by hand instead.
- Center the titles across the columns before you AutoFormat.

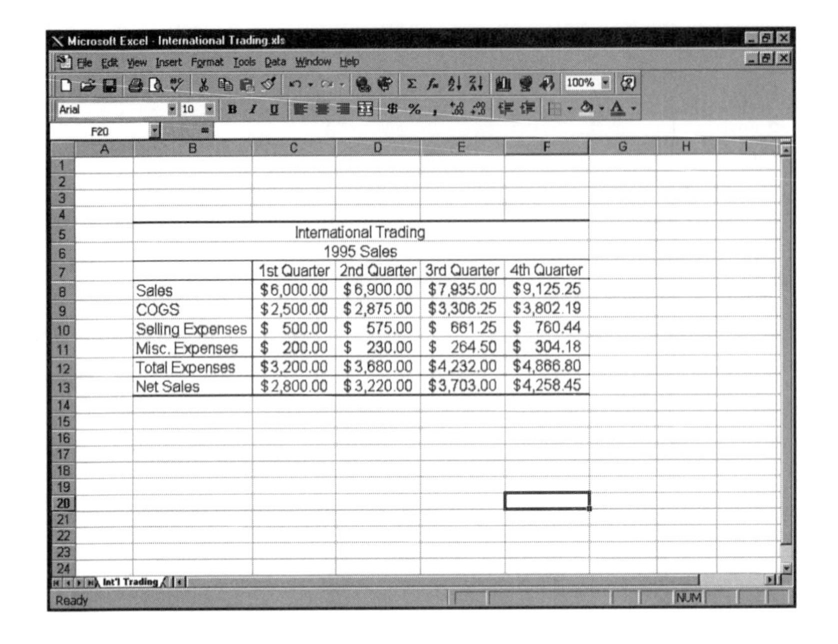

	1st Quarter	2nd Quarter	3rd Quarter	4th Quarter
Sales	$6,000.00	$6,900.00	$7,935.00	$9,125.25
COGS	$2,500.00	$2,875.00	$3,306.25	$3,802.19
Selling Expenses	$ 500.00	$ 575.00	$ 661.25	$ 760.44
Misc. Expenses	$ 200.00	$ 230.00	$ 264.50	$ 304.18
Total Expenses	$3,200.00	$3,680.00	$4,232.00	$4,866.80
Net Sales	$2,800.00	$3,220.00	$3,703.00	$4,258.45

Fig. 7.9
After the AutoFormat makeover. Interior cleaning is extra.

Feel free to tinker with the formatting once AutoFormat's done its work. I did for some of the following figures.

AutoFormat is quick and easy, but there's one drawback to using it: if the range you AutoFormat already contains formatting, that formatting gets wiped out. It's best to AutoFormat first, then add other formatting as needed. That's how I did it in the example.

Color me purple: adding color and patterns

Polite worksheets don't wave their arms around and jump up and down to get attention. On the other hand, we don't want our work to be a wallflower. Adding a little color or a pattern can make critical parts of the worksheet stand out. Well-dressed, but not showy, is the watchword.

Patterns, for a pattern worksheet

What's the first thing that comes to mind when you look at rows and columns of numbers or text? Borrrring. No matter what we do, our work isn't going to win the Nobel prize for literature. Still, breaking up the monotony of serried ranks of data can at least make the worksheet readable. And if it doesn't scintillate, blame the content. Figure 7.10 shows one way of giving International Trading Corporation's results a little eye appeal.

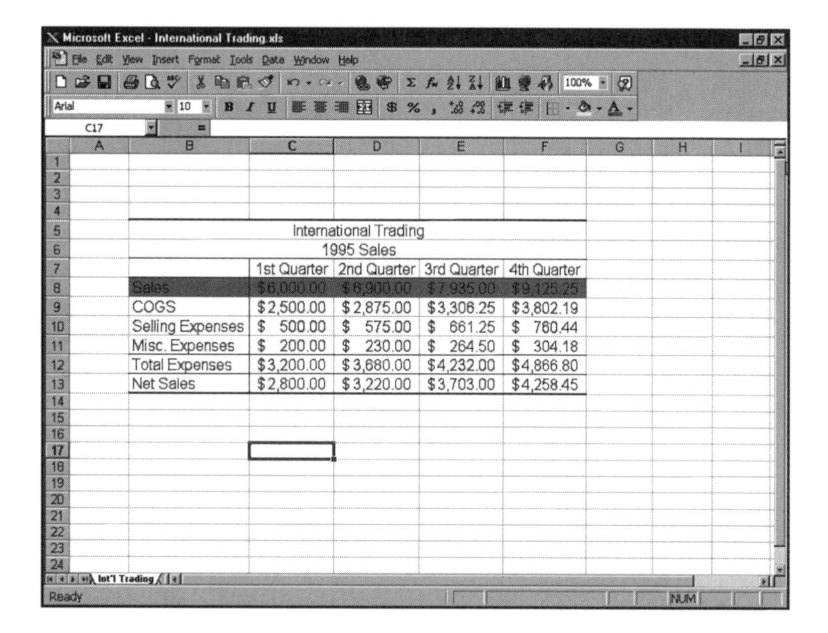

Fig. 7.10
Adding patterns or colors to important rows and columns makes them stand out without shouting.

1. Select the column or row you want patterned or colored.
2. Click Format, Cells, Patterns. (Or right-click a cell in the range and choose Format Cells, Patterns.)
3. Click your choice of color from the Color palette.
4. Click Pattern to add dots, lines, cross-hatching—whatever you like. Click a color to add colored patterns.

Figure 7.11 shows you the menu of Patterns in the Format Cells dialog box.

Losing a pattern

If you don't like your patterns and colors, lose them. Choose Format, Cells and click the Patterns tab of the Format Cells dialog box. Click No Color to get rid of colors. The white box in the upper-left corner of the Pattern palette eradicates your patterns. Our old standby Edit, Clear, Formats does the same thing, but be careful—that command also wipes out any other formatting in the cell or range.

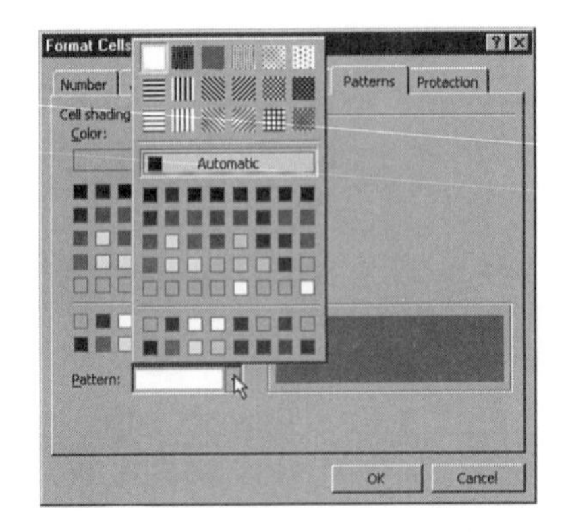

Fig. 7.11
Both patterns and colors are found under the Cell Shading category. Colored patterns can make for some startling effects, but you don't want to go overboard.

TIP **Colored fonts and backgrounds may all look fine on the screen,** but they don't necessarily translate well to print. Use Print Preview to see how your artistic effects will look in the harsh glare of the printer.

To copy a format from one place to another, call the painter

Ever watch a small child paint? My kids used to like to smear some paint on a piece of paper, dip a brush in it, then smear other bits of the paper with the same color. They called it art, and who was I to argue? Some people get paid pretty well for that kind of thing.

The Format Painter doesn't make a mess, but it works on the same principle. You dip the brush into a formatted cell, and "paint" the same format in another cell (just the formatting, not the rest of the cell contents).

It works on ranges of cells, too. Let's add another shaded line to the table shown in Figure 7.10 using the Format Painter.

Black and white in color?

In Excel, both colors and patterns are called **shading**. Excel considers grays to be colors and, strictly speaking, Excel is right. Black, white, and gray are sometimes called achromatic colors, as opposed to chromatic colors like red, blue, and green, or nonchromatic colors like brown and pink. Blame Sir Isaac Newton, who first demonstrated that color was a quality of light.

1 Select the range with the formatting we want, then click the Format Painter button (see Figure 7.12). The pointer acquires a little paintbrush.

The Format Painter button

Fig. 7.12
When you select a cell or range and click the Format Painter button, the pointer gets a little brush, and the selected cell or range acquires a marquee.

The pointer grows a paintbrush when you click the Format Painter Button

2 Now select the cell or range you want to paint with the new format. When you release the mouse button, the formatting is painted in. Figure 7.13 shows the results.

If you don't like the paint job, click the Undo button. And if you want to paint several ranges, double-click the Format Painter. It'll stay on until you click it again, and you can paint as many cells as you like.

Conditional Formatting makes worksheets come alive

Excel is designed to handle changing data with ease. When you want to highlight changes in your numbers with formatting that changes automatically, try Excel's new Conditional Formatting.

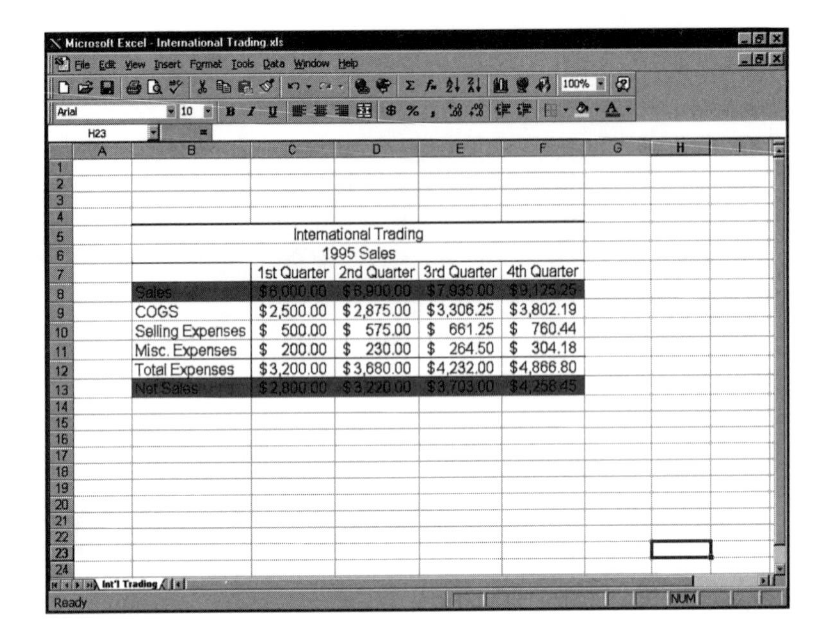

Fig. 7.13
Using the Format Painter to apply existing formatting to other cells saves a lot of steps.

Conditional Formatting lets you create formatting touches that apply to data only under the conditions you determine. If you're tracking a stock that you bought at $30, and you want to see at a glance those months in which the stock hit $50 or higher, set up Conditional Formatting that shows the closing price in boldface if it climbs to $50 or more:

1. Select the cell or range to which the Conditional Formatting will apply.
2. Click Format, Conditional Formatting. In the Conditional Formatting dialog box, set a Cell Value that's greater than or equal to 50, as shown in Figure 7.14.
3. Click the Format button in the Conditional Formatting dialog box. In the Format Cells dialog box that pops up, choose any font, patterns, or border formatting you care to apply and click OK.
4. Click OK in the Conditional Formatting dialog box. Whenever values of 50 or greater are entered in the selected row, they'll automatically display in the selected formatting.

You might find Conditional Formatting very handy in a large worksheet crowded with data. If you want key numbers to stand out under prescribed conditions, apply Conditional Formatting to them.

Fig. 7.14
Once you set the parameters, Conditional Formatting triggers format changes as the data changes.

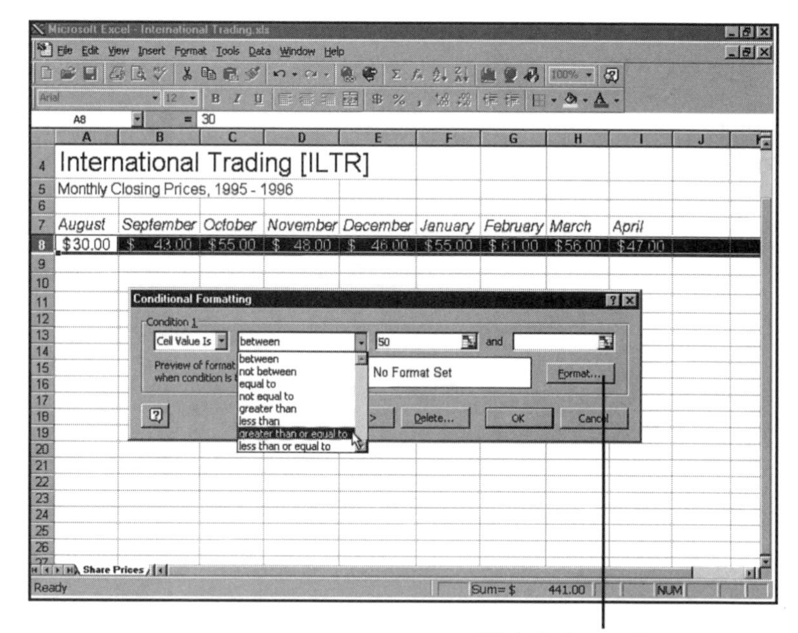

Click the Format button to set additional conditions

Do it with Style: saving and using styles

After tinkering with patterns, fonts, colors, and borders, you might be pleased with the result. You might also dread the prospect of doing it all again for the next worksheet.

So don't. Save your work as a **style**, and reuse it:

1. Select the cell containing the formatting you want to save.
2. Click Format, Style to open up the Style dialog box.
3. Give your style a name, and decide which formatting elements you want to keep or lose (see Figure 7.15).
4. Click Add and OK to save your style.

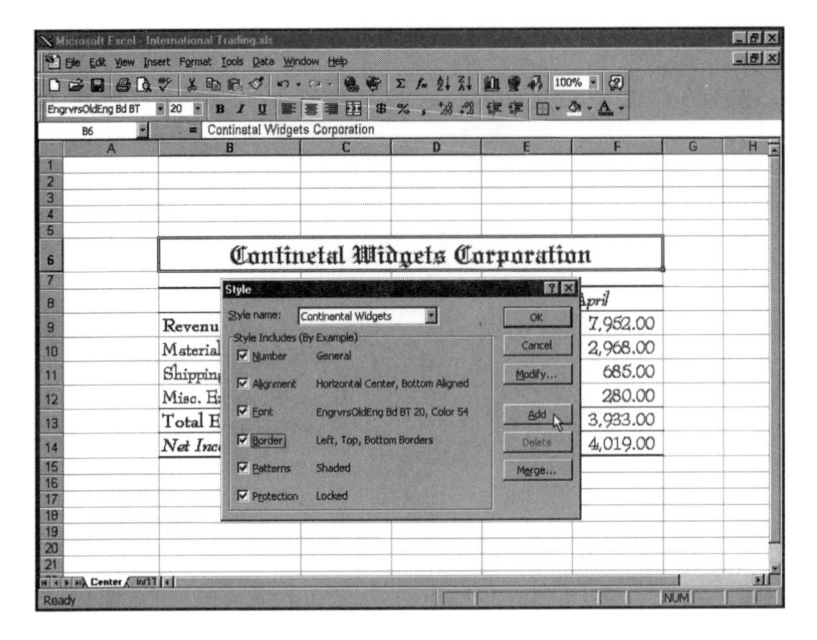

Fig. 7.15
If you've concocted a mix of formatting elements you want to use again, save it with Style.

> ### *Plain English, please!*
>
> A **style** is a saved combination of formatting that you name and reuse. Excel has a built-in style that you use whenever you start typing in a new worksheet. Those plain-looking characters you see are formatted in Excel's Normal style.

The next time you want a cell or range formatted in the style you saved, just select it. Then choose Format, Style, click the Style Name box, and click your style name.

I selected a range I formatted, saved it as a style, and all the formatting got wiped out! What did I do wrong?

First, click the Undo button to restore your formatting. Then learn the grim truth: saving a style only works for the formatting in a single cell, or a range of cells with identical formatting. If you try to save the style of a range containing different formatting, the style saves only the formatting common to all the cells. If they're all different, nothing gets saved.

Creating a style from scratch

You can also build a style from the ground up. Select Format, Style. In the Style dialog box, name the new style, then click Modify. That takes you right to the Format Cells dialog box, and you can add all the colors, fonts, patterns, shading, and borders you want.

To save the new style and apply it to a selected cell or range, click OK in the Style dialog box. If you want to save the style without applying it, click Add, then Close.

Defend your style: protecting cells, worksheets, and workbooks

We lock almost everything nowadays—homes, cars, even our bicycles. A nuisance, but we all know what can happen when we don't lock up.

Worksheets and workbooks sometimes need security too. That's why Excel lets you lock them. Why would you want to do that?

- After all the effort you've put in creating, formatting, and calculating your worksheets, you don't want somebody else's carelessness (or your own!) undoing your work.
- If you use Excel to create forms, you don't want casual users altering the form itself when they're just supposed to be using it for data entry.
- Parts of a workbook might contain valuable or confidential formulas that you want to keep hidden from other users.

Locking begins with unlocking: leaving cells and ranges unprotected

Protecting a worksheet locks every cell. Once protected, no changes can be made until the sheet is unprotected again.

Chances are, you'll need to leave some cells or ranges unlocked in a protected worksheet. One common reason is to permit data entry in a form, while the form itself stays locked.

Before you protect a sheet, you have to set up the unlocked cells. Here's how to do it:

1. Select the cell or range and choose Format, Cells, Protection.
2. Locked is selected by default. Click the box to unlock the cells you've selected.

The cells you've selected remain unlocked when the worksheet itself is protected.

Protecting worksheets and workbooks

From the Tools menu, click Protection, Protect Sheet. You have a few options:

- Password lets you enter a password of your choice. Pick a word you won't forget, then write it down and put it in a safe place. Once protected with a password, the sheet can't be unprotected without it. You don't have to password-protect your worksheet. But if you do, treat that password like an heirloom.
- Contents locks the cells on the sheet; no changes or deletions are allowed.
- Objects prevents changes to charts or graphical objects.
- Scenarios locks any scenarios you've created.

Select all, some, or none of these options, then click OK to protect the worksheet. If you opted for a password, the Confirm Password dialog box appears. Retype the same password, then click OK.

To protect the entire workbook, click Tools, Protection, Protect Workbook.

Hiding protected cells

You may want to prevent others from seeing certain parts of a protected worksheet. Valuable formulas, for example, can be cloaked from view with the Hidden command.

Select the cells you want to hide, then click Format, Cells, and click the Protection tab. Click the Hidden check box on the Protection tab.

When you protect the worksheet, formulas in the selected cells are hidden from view. Hiding cells only works in protected worksheets.

TIP **Hiding cells with the Format, Cells, Protection command hides** formulas, not values or the results of formulas. If a hidden cell contains the formula =(2+2), you'd see the value 4 in the worksheet. The formula bar, where the formula would normally be seen, is blanked out. To hide other cell contents, use Format, Row, Hide or Format, Column, Hide.

Hiding rows and columns

Just to add variety to life, Excel offers another way to hide. Say you really want to make your totals jump off the page, but you don't care about showing all the detail that went into the totals.

Select the rows or columns, then click Format, Row (or Column), Hide. Your detail is still there, but now it's out of sight. To make it visible again, choose Format, Row (or Column), Unhide.

See how it looks in Figure 7.16, which shows the same table with hidden and unhidden rows.

Before Hiding...

	1st Quarter	2nd Quarter	3rd Quarter	4th Quarter
Sales	$ 6,000	$ 6,900	$ 7,935	$ 9,125
COGS	2,500	2,875	3,306	3,802
Selling Expenses	500	575	661	760
Misc. Expenses	200	230	265	304
Total Expenses	$ 3,200	$ 3,680	$ 4,232	$ 4,867
Net Sales	$ 2,800	$ 3,220	$ 3,703	$ 4,258

And after.

	1st Quarter	2nd Quarter	3rd Quarter	4th Quarter
Sales	$ 6,000	$ 6,900	$ 7,935	$ 9,125
COGS	2,500	2,875	3,306	3,802
Net Sales	$ 2,800	$ 3,220	$ 3,703	$ 4,258

Fig. 7.16
Same table, different look. Rows 22:24 in the bottom table are still there; they're just hidden from view.

If you print a worksheet with hidden rows or columns, they'll be hidden on the printout, too. And you can't hide cells or ranges on protected sheets. Unprotect the sheet first, hide, then protect again.

Hiding the entire sheet or workbook

Say you're working in several workbooks at once. Your screen is a mess of windows and workbooks, and you're beginning to lose track of where things are.

Do what I do when my desk gets too messy—shove things out of sight. To hide a workbook, click Window, Hide. Click Unhide and select the workbook name to get it back again.

You can pull the same trick with worksheets, but with a different command. Select Format, Sheet, Hide instead. To restore a hidden sheet, choose Format, Sheet, Unhide.

Formulas: Excel's Recipe for Calculations

In this chapter:

- **If Excel really is a giant calculator, how do I make it calculate?**
- **My cell references keep referring to the wrong cells**
- **Why would I want to call my cells names?**
- **This formula has the right ingredients, but the wrong results**
- **How does one array formula do the work of many regular formulas?**

Formulas are directions to Excel on how to calculate your data. Writing your own formulas is no harder than giving directions to a passerby . . . .

A **formula** is like a recipe:

1. Take one tablespoon of vinegar.
2. Add two tablespoons of olive oil.
3. Add salt and pepper to taste.

The result is salad dressing.

1. Take the number 6.
2. Multiply it by the number 5.
3. Then add the number 2.

That gives you 32.

Same thing, really. Except that we use shorthand for formulas instead of writing them out. We'd say instead (6*5)+2 = 32. Just like recipes, formulas can be simple, medium, or complex. But whether it's a soufflé or a present value calculation, following a series of ordered steps is what gets you your result.

Writing formulas in Excel is just as easy as jotting down your favorite recipe for another cook. And Excel is one cook you can count on to follow your recipes to the letter.

Witches' brew: what goes into a formula?

When the three witches in *Macbeth* get together for a little "Double, double, toil and trouble," they raid the larder for Eye of Newt, Toe of Frog, Wool of Bat, Tongue of Dog, and other delicacies. The result they want? Big trouble for Macbeth.

Finance MBAs concocting formulas like to toss in things like cumulative normal probability density functions. The result they're after? The value of a stock option.

Both know that if you want the correct result, you have to use the right ingredients, and you have to give the right instructions on what to do with the ingredients. In an Excel formula, the ingredients are **values**, and the instructions are **operators**.

- Values are the "oil and vinegar" of the formula. The numbers, dates, times, and text you type in to your worksheets are all values. When you add 5+2, 5 and 2 are the values.
- Operators are the instructions about what to do with the values. Because you can't tell a formula to "mix well until smooth," you use a kind of shorthand. Multiplication, division, addition, and subtraction are operators, except that we get even more terse and use symbols.

Values are also called **operands**. They can also be **constants** or **constant values.** When they're enclosed in parentheses, values are called **arguments**. And much of the time, your formulas will use **cell references**, such as C1 or D4, that refer to values in those cells. By whatever name, values refer to the ingredients in the formula, as opposed to the instructions about what to do with the ingredients. ”

The = sign is the essential ingredient

No matter what other ingredients you put into an Excel formula, one item is always included. Formulas *always* begin with the equal sign (=).

For Excel to calculate 2+2, the formula has to read =2+2. You can get creative with your other ingredients, but not this one. You could finish Einstein's last project and write a formula that solves Unified Field Theory, but if it doesn't start with an = sign, Excel gives you a blank stare.

Before you start writing a formula in Excel, click the Edit Formula button on the formula bar. That activates the formula bar, and automatically inserts the crucial equal sign at the beginning of the formula.

Get me the operator

Excel has all kinds of operators. Arithmetic operators do just what you expect: add, subtract, multiply, and divide. Here's a list of the arithmetic operator keys and what they do.

Press this key or button...	In this kind of calculation...	To get this result
+	5+3 (Addition)	8
–	6–4 (Subtraction)	2
*	8*4 (Multiplication)	32
/	9/3 (Division)	3
^	4^2 (Exponentiation)	16
%	.6 (Percentage)	60%

Q&A ***I entered the same operators and numbers twice and got two different results. Can't Excel do plain old math?***

It can, but it attacks arithmetic operators in order. If you got two results with the same operators and numbers, it's because you entered them a little differently. Excel does multiplication and division first, then tackles addition and subtraction. For example, if you entered 8+2*5, you would get 18. Excel multiplies 2*5, and then adds 8. But if you entered (8+2)*5, you would get 50, because Excel calculates whatever's in parentheses first.

How can I spot a missing parenthesis in my formula?

If your formula starts to bristle with multiple pairs of parentheses, it's easy to leave out one of a pair. And doing that, as we've seen, changes the result. Excel has two great tricks to help you keep track of your parentheses. To identify which parentheses go together, nested pairs of parentheses are shown in different colors. The outermost ones are black, the next ones in are green, the ones after that are magenta, and so on.

To find a missing parenthesis, click the formula bar and use the arrow keys to move the cursor through the formula. Excel shows each pair of parentheses in bold as the cursor passes by, like this:

=**(**(C8+C4)/2**)**+((D5+E3)/B1)

If you're missing one of a pair, or if you've added an extra parenthesis by mistake, the lone parenthesis won't be bold.

Comparison operators

Comparison operators are: =, >, <, >= (greater than or equal to), <= (less than or equal to), and <> (not equal to).

When you stick a comparison operator in a formula, the result is TRUE or FALSE. Those are called **logical values**. What do you do with them?

Say you create a worksheet that checks whether clients have paid their bills. You decide that if a client's outstanding balance is $2.00 or less, you won't bother generating another bill.

You might put the client's name in one column, his prior account balance in the next column, and his latest payment and the new balance after that. In the last column, put a formula—that "greater than 2" comparison—to decide whether to generate another bill. A TRUE value could automatically send the client another bill. It would look like Figure 8.1.

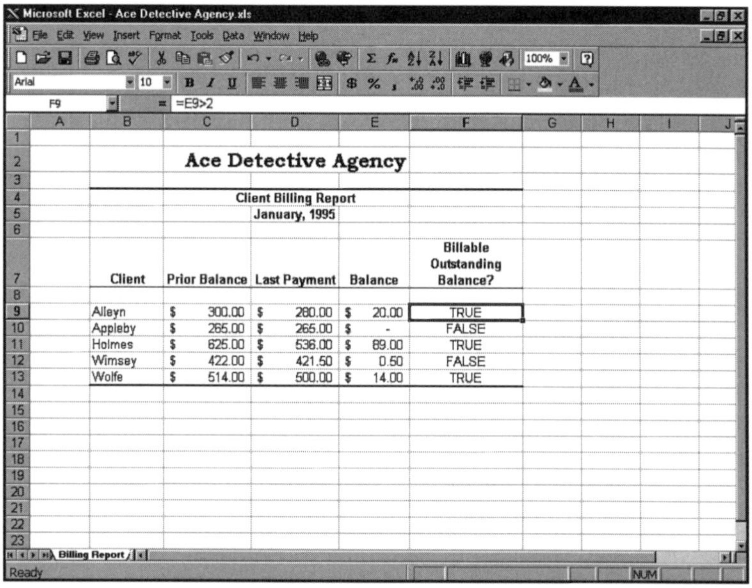

Microsoft Excel - Ace Detective Agency.xls

F9 = =E9>2

Ace Detective Agency

Client Billing Report
January, 1995

Client	Prior Balance	Last Payment	Balance	Billable Outstanding Balance?
Alleyn	$ 300.00	$ 280.00	$ 20.00	TRUE
Appleby	$ 265.00	$ 265.00	$ -	FALSE
Holmes	$ 625.00	$ 536.00	$ 89.00	TRUE
Wimsey	$ 422.00	$ 421.50	$ 0.50	FALSE
Wolfe	$ 514.00	$ 500.00	$ 14.00	TRUE

Fig. 8.1
Comparison operators at work. The formula bar shows the formula *=E9>2* that returns the TRUE or FALSE values.

Reference operators

The colon (:) that you use to define a range is called the **range operator**. A1 and D4 are cell references. A1:D4 is the range that includes all the cells from

A1 through D4. The range operator is one of several **reference operators**. You use reference operators in formulas to grab values in cells or ranges and plug them into the formula.

If you want to include all the cells in a row or column in your formula, you enter **E:E** for all of column E. Enter **3:8** for all the cells in rows 3 through 8.

The comma (,) is another reference operator. It's called the **union operator**, because it joins together two or more cell or range references. A1,D4 means cell A1 and cell D4. A1:D4,F1:H4 means the range A1:D4 and the range F1:H4.

TIP **When you use the mouse to select a range to include in a formula,** Excel supplies the range operator (:) for you. And when you select nonadjacent cells or ranges, Excel inserts the union operator (,) for you as well.

Cell references, for useful formulas

If I wrote "To what are you referring to?", you might put this book down and turn on the idiot box. Bad grammar really jars. We like our writing crisp and precise.

Excel requires the same precision from formulas. References have to be exact. In a formula like =2+2, the references are unequivocal. The result is equally unequivocal—and obvious—which makes the formula pretty useless. Something like this has a lot more going for it: =C2+C3.

Written with cell references, we can put whatever values we want in C2 and C3, and our formula dutifully adds them together. We just have to make sure we have the right cells.

References made easy

What's the foolproof way of getting the right cell or range in the right spot in your formula? Grab it with the mouse:

1 Select the cell where you want to put the formula.

2 Click the Edit Formula button on the formula bar.

3 Select the cell you want *in* the formula. For a range, select the beginning of the range and drag to the end of it. The marquee, that moving border, appears around the cell or range you're adding to the formula.

4. Now type the operator—comparison, arithmetic, or whatever—that you want in the formula.

5. Select another cell or range. If it's the last cell or range in the formula, press Enter, click the Formula Bar Enter button, or click OK in the formula bar. Any of the three methods saves your formula in the selected cell.

You'll see the cell or range addresses appear in both the cell and the formula bar as you click cells. Figure 8.2 shows a formula being built by selecting cells.

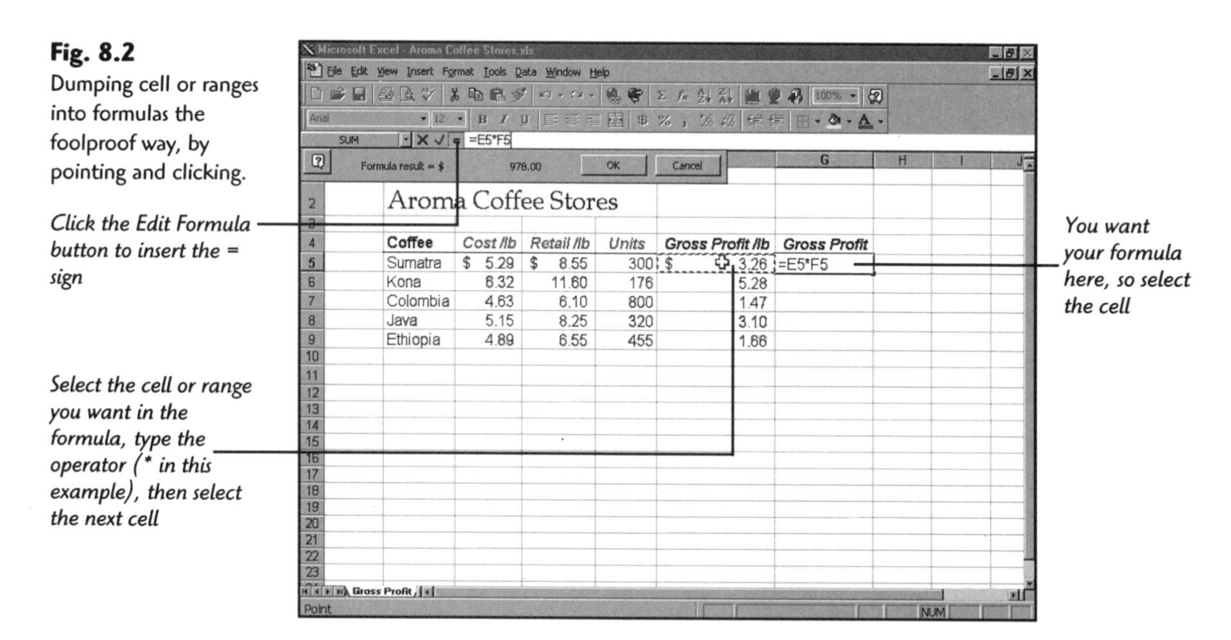

Fig. 8.2
Dumping cell or ranges into formulas the foolproof way, by pointing and clicking.

How do I change the cell references in a formula?

Cut or copy the formula and paste it somewhere else, and the references change automatically. If you want the formula to stay where it is, but you need its references changed, just edit it.

Press F2 or double-click the cell with the formula in it. Move the insertion point to where you want to make the change and use Delete or Backspace to zap the old cell reference. Then just select the new cell with the mouse.

What's the difference between a relative and an absolute reference?

Formulas with absolute cell references always refer to those cells, no matter where you move the formula.

When you enter cell references in a formula by pointing and clicking, they are relative references (until you change them). If you move the formula, the cell references change relative to where the formula is moved.

That's fine, as long as the formula doesn't have to refer to the same cell all the time. But if your formula requires a value in a particular cell, you want to refer to that cell with an absolute reference.

Some cell references have to be absolute

The example in Figure 8.3 shows a situation where you'd want an absolute reference.

We've got the T Bill rate in C3. We're using it as the risk-free rate of interest in some Net Present Value (NPV) calculations. We want to include it no matter where we copy the NPV formula so we can compare these two beers we're thinking of introducing.

Relative versus absolute references in real life

We use relative and absolute references all the time. You just may not think of them that way.

When your new colleague wanders into your office and asks the way to the fax machine, you could tell her to go down the hall and take a left at the exit sign. That's a **relative reference**. It works, as long as you are both in your office. But go upstairs to the water cooler and the reference changes relative to where you are. Give her the same directions up there, and she'd get lost.

Instead of that relative reference, you might say: "The fax machine is in the mailroom, third floor, room 315." That's an **absolute reference**. The location is fixed, no matter where you happen to move. Your directions will work at lunch, or at the water cooler, or wherever you go to avoid your desk.

We put our NPV formula in G5 and include the reference to C3. We're in G5. By C3, Excel thinks we mean "use the cell two rows above this one and four columns to the left." And that's where C3 *is*, in relation to G5. Figure 8.3 gives you an idea of what we're talking about.

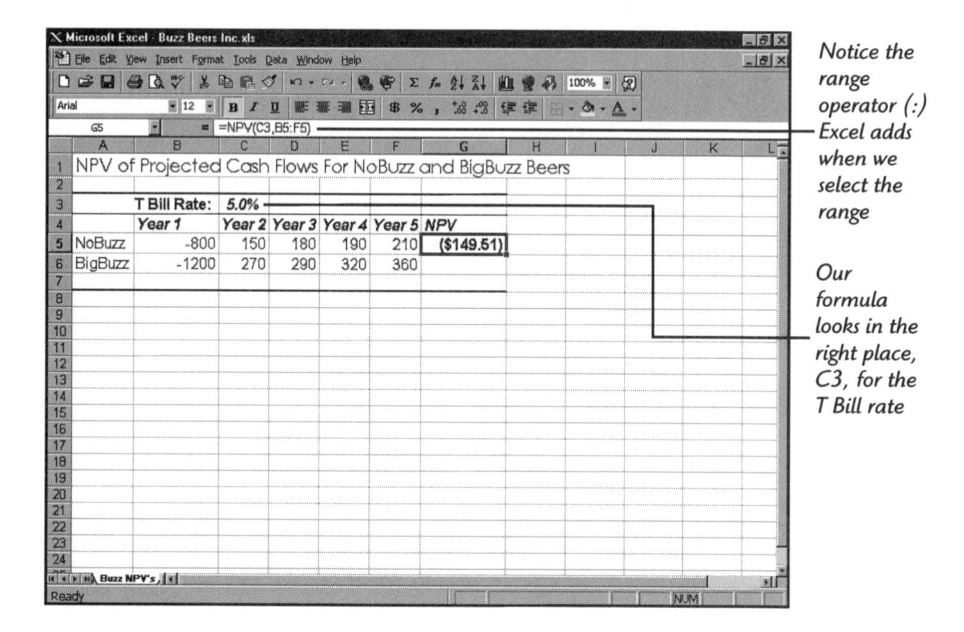

Fig. 8.3
As long as our formula is in the right spot in relation to the cells it references, all is well.

Now we copy the formula into G6 to get the NPV for the second beer. Excel is still looking for the T Bill rate two rows up and four columns over! Relative to G6, that's C4, and there's nothing there except an old column title.

Instead of a useful result, we get an Excel error message, `#VALUE!`, as shown in Figure 8.4.

How can I tell where my formula went wrong?

In a small worksheet like the one in Figure 8.4, it's pretty easy to see the fly in our formula's ointment. On a big worksheet crowded with data (or at two o'clock in the morning if you're working late), spotting a formula misstep might not be so simple. If your formula returns an error value, like `#VALUE!`, Excel has a terrific tool to help you figure out where you went wrong.

To track down formula errors, put Excel's worksheet auditor to work:

1 Click the cell containing the error value.

2 Choose Tools, Auditing, Trace Error. Arrows leading from the incorrect formula to the cells or ranges that went into the formula appear on the worksheet, as shown in Figure 8.5.

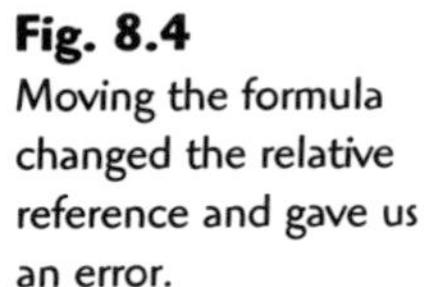

Fig. 8.4
Moving the formula changed the relative reference and gave us an error.

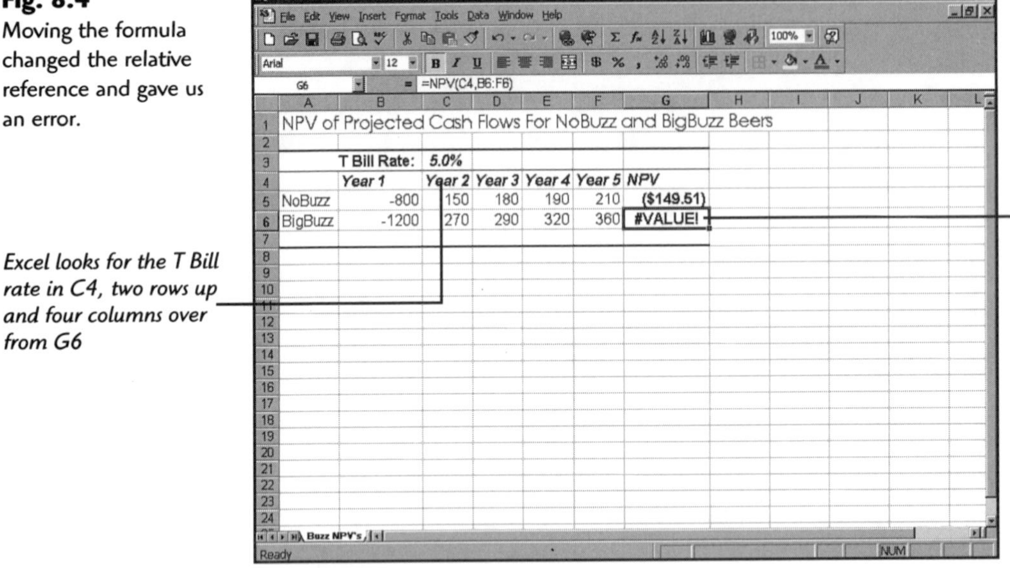

Excel looks for the T Bill rate in C4, two rows up and four columns over from G6

An error message is returned because the formula required a number and found text instead

Fig. 8.5
When you can't figure out where your error came from, use Excel's auditing tools to track down the errant cells.

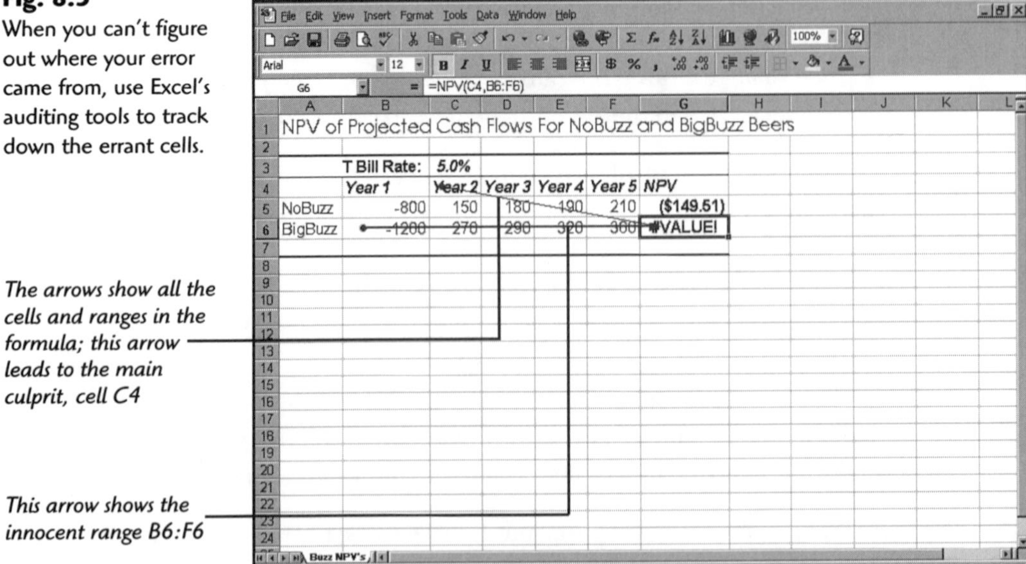

The arrows show all the cells and ranges in the formula; this arrow leads to the main culprit, cell C4

This arrow shows the innocent range B6:F6

3 After you locate the cell that produced the error with the help of the auditing arrows, choose Tools, Auditing, Remove All Arrows to clear the arrows from the screen.

See Chapter 14 for more information on Excel's handy worksheet detective, the auditing feature.

Relative references: written in chalk

In this example, C3 is a relative reference. It changes relative to where we move the formula. Because we don't want that, we'll just tell Excel to stop making automatic cell reference changes by converting C3 in the formula from a relative to an absolute reference.

Absolute references: carved in stone

You type a $ sign to make absolute references. C3 is the same thing as saying "third floor, room 315" in the previous sidebar example. Stick the absolute reference in our formula, and no matter where we copy it, the formula will refer to cell C3. Figure 8.6 shows the effect of making C3 an absolute instead of a relative reference.

To save yourself some typing, convert C3 to an absolute reference with the F4 key. Click the reference C3 in the formula bar, then press F4 to insert the $ symbols automatically.

Okay, I confess. We cheated. We used the NPV function in that last example instead of typing out the formula for NPV, which is shown in Figure 8.7.

As you can see in Figure 8.7, the NPV formula would be a bear to type. Because Excel has functions for complicated formulas like NPV, it's worlds easier to take advantage of them. To insert a function like NPV in a new formula, click the Edit Formula button on the formula bar. That activates the formula bar, and turns the Name box into the Functions box. Click the Functions box drop-down arrow and choose a function from the list. There are plenty of other Excel functions that we'll look at in Chapters 9 and 10.

And we didn't really cheat anyway. Functions *are* formulas, and formulas can contain functions, just like ours did.

With the absolute reference C3, the formula can be pasted anywhere on the worksheet and always refer to cell C3

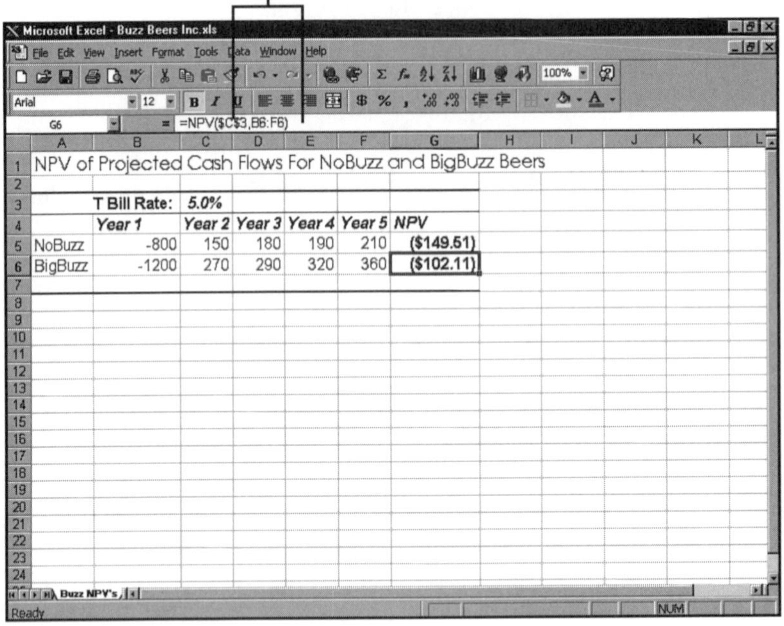

Microsoft Excel - Buzz Beers Inc.xls

G6 =NPV(C3,B6:F6)

	A	B	C	D	E	F	G
1	NPV of Projected Cash Flows For NoBuzz and BigBuzz Beers						
2							
3		T Bill Rate:	5.0%				
4		Year 1	Year 2	Year 3	Year 4	Year 5	NPV
5	NoBuzz	-800	150	180	190	210	($149.51)
6	BigBuzz	-1200	270	290	320	360	($102.11)

Fig. 8.6
Making cell C3 an absolute reference fixed our formula problem. (It still looks like a poor investment, though.)

$$= \sum_{i=1}^{n} \frac{values_i}{(1+rate)^i}$$

Fig. 8.7
The formula for NPV. Kind of looks like a porcupine, and it's just about as cuddly.

When absolute or relative won't do, use mixed references

Range references don't have to be absolutely absolute, or absolutely relative either. You might want to fix a column of values in place but change the rows as you move formulas. $C3 does just that. Or use C$3 to fix the row and change the column.

Use the reference key, F4, to enter mixed references. First, click the cell reference in the formula bar so the insertion point is positioned inside the reference.

If the cell reference in the formula is C5, for example, put the insertion point between C and 5. Then press F4. Pressing F4 repeatedly cycles through the four possible combinations of absolute row and relative column, absolute column and relative row, fully relative, and fully absolute references.

Named cells and ranges make references easier

If a San Franciscan told you he lived seven blocks south of the North Bay and ten blocks west of the East Bay, you'd probably work out where he lived—eventually. You'd also give him a funny look. But if he said, "I live on Lombard Street," you'd know where he lived instantly. Name a street, and locations are a lot easier to find.

C4-D4 also conveys a certain amount of information, but not much. Sales—Expenses tells you a lot more. That's why Excel's Name commands are so handy. They let you give a plain text name to any cell or range.

Named cells and ranges can be moved, copied, or entered in formulas, just like cells with ordinary addresses. Need convincing? Consider this:

- You probably knew what C5*D6+H11 was all about weeks ago when you wrote it. Now it might as well be alphabet soup. But if you'd written Commission*Sales+Draw, there'd be no need to scratch your head over it.
- It's easier to spot mistakes in your formulas. You might not catch C5*D5 when you didn't mean to enter it, but you'd certainly notice Sales*Expenses if what you meant was Sales–Expenses.
- Names make getting around a worksheet easier. Pick a named cell or range from the list in the Name box, and you're there.

OK, so how do I create a name?

You have two choices. First, the quick way:

1. Select the cell or range you want to name.
2. Click the Name box drop-down arrow (see Figure 8.8).

3 Type in any name you want. You have 255 characters to play with. Just don't use any spaces, don't use a number for the first character, don't use any punctuation (except for periods), and don't use a name that looks like a cell address.

4 Press Enter.

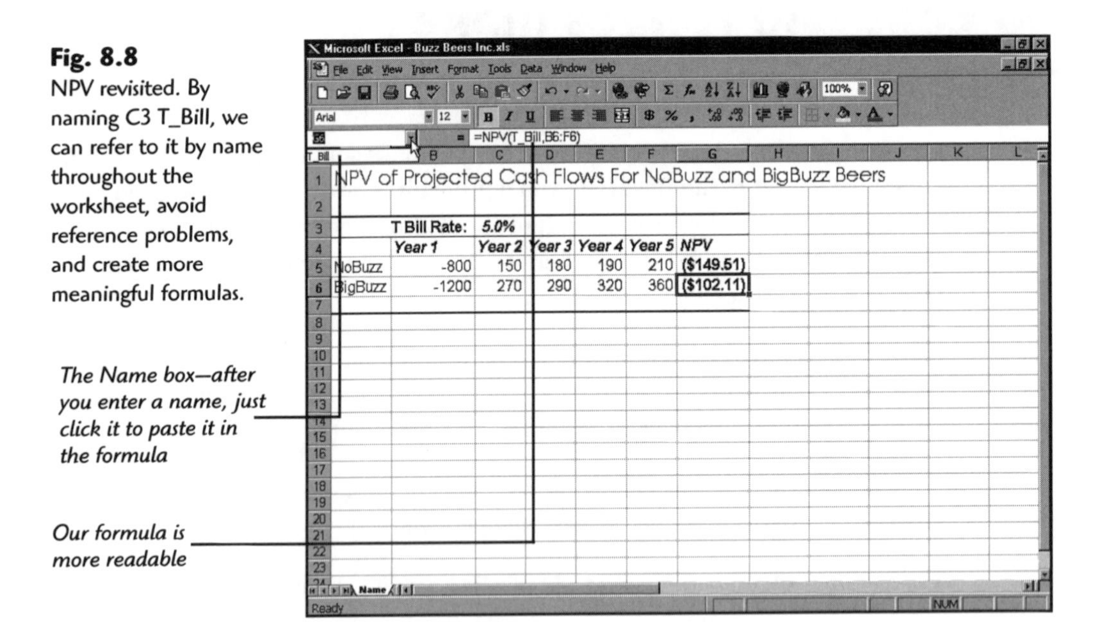

Fig. 8.8
NPV revisited. By naming C3 T_Bill, we can refer to it by name throughout the worksheet, avoid reference problems, and create more meaningful formulas.

Easy enough, but why bother?

Take our Net Present Value calculations as an example. We ran into a slight problem of absolute and relative references, which we'd have avoided by using a name.

Had we called the cell with the T Bill rate `T_Bill` instead of C3, our copied formula would have worked perfectly. Because names create an absolute reference, they're perfect for frequently used constants like the one in Figure 8.8.

TIP **Another way to name a cell or range: make your selection, then** press Ctrl+F3 to pop up the Define Name dialog box. Use the Define Name dialog box to delete names too.

More about names

The Insert menu's Name command is your other choice for naming cells and ranges, and it includes a few more options. After you select the cell or range, click Insert, Name, Define to name it. Excel suggests names from your row or column titles. From the Insert, Name menu:

- Select Define to enter names in the Define Name dialog box. Click the Refers To text box, then select the cell or range. Type a name in the Names In Workbook text box. Click the Add button if you're naming more than one cell or range.
- Select Create to grab your row or column titles, or both, to name ranges.
- Select Paste to paste names into formulas. Select the cell, moving the cursor to where you want the name, and click the name on the list. (Paste List just duplicates the Name box.)
- Naming a cell or range referenced in an existing formula doesn't replace the old references. Apply works like Search and Replace. Name the cell or range, select Insert, Name, Apply; then click the name on the list. Apply searches your formulas and replaces the old references with the new name.

You also use Insert, Name, Define to get rid of names. Just select the named cell in the Define Name dialog box and click the Delete button.

Deleting a name doesn't remove it from any formulas it might be in, it just zaps the name from the list. If you deleted a name and forgot that it was still in a formula, Excel reminds you by gently shouting `#NAME?` where your result used to be.

What are arrays, and what do I use them for?

The formulas we've looked at so far used two or more values and came up with one result. An **array formula** takes a range of values and produces as many results as there are values in the range.

Think of it this way. An array takes matching pairs of data, performs a calculation, and puts the results in a corresponding range. Arrays are like those elaborate ballroom scenes Hollywood used to love, where two lines of single dancers pair off one by one to make a third line of couples.

Arrays: an example

In Figure 8.9, we want to calculate the gross profit for each type of coffee: profit per unit * total units = gross profit. The idea is to multiply all the values in column E by all the values in column F, and dump the corresponding result of each calculation into column G.

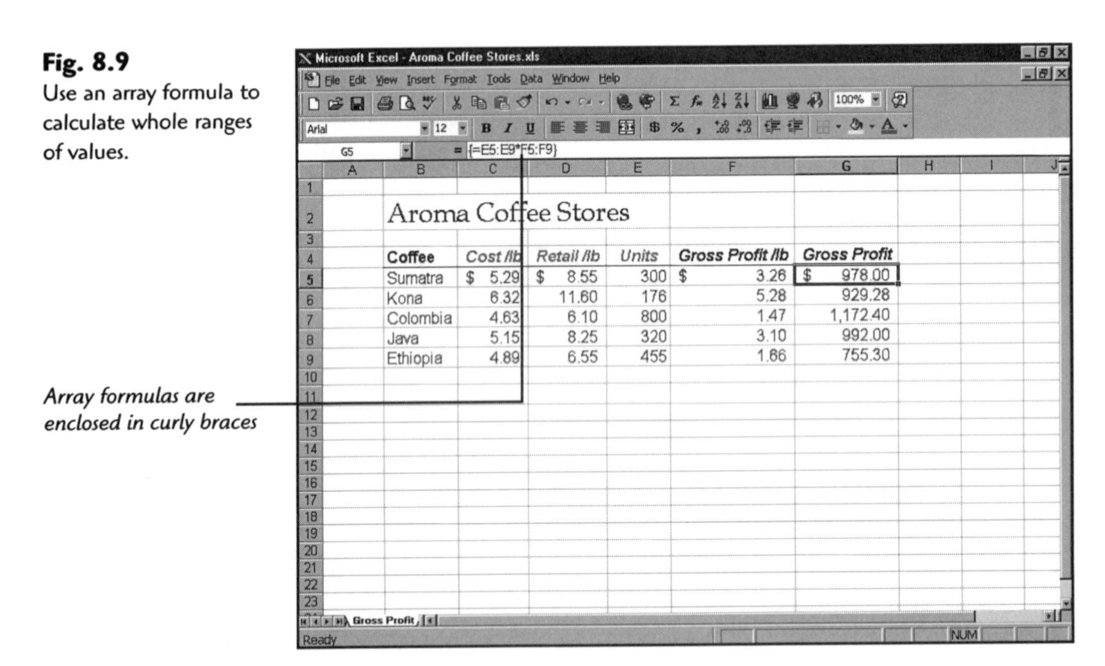

Coffee	Cost /lb	Retail /lb	Units	Gross Profit /lb	Gross Profit
Sumatra	$ 5.29	$ 8.55	300	$ 3.26	$ 978.00
Kona	6.32	11.60	176	5.28	929.28
Colombia	4.63	6.10	800	1.47	1,172.40
Java	5.15	8.25	320	3.10	992.00
Ethiopia	4.89	6.55	455	1.66	755.30

Fig. 8.9
Use an array formula to calculate whole ranges of values.

We could use our tried-and-true method: create the formula **=E5*F5** in cell G5, then use the fill handle to copy the formula all the way down the column.

Or we can use an array to get the same result more efficiently.

How do I create an array?

There are three things you need to know about arrays:

- The shape and size of the range the results are going into has to be the same shape and size as the ranges you're operating on.

- An array formula is enclosed in curly braces ({}) but you don't type them. Excel supplies the braces for you.
- Pressing Enter doesn't enter an array formula. Instead, press Shift+Ctrl+Enter.

Armed with these facts, let's backtrack and perform the array calculation shown in Figure 8.9.

1. Select the range the results are going into (in this case, G5:G9).
2. Click the Edit Formula button to start the formula.
3. Select the first range of the formula (E5:E9) followed by an operator (see Figure 8.10).

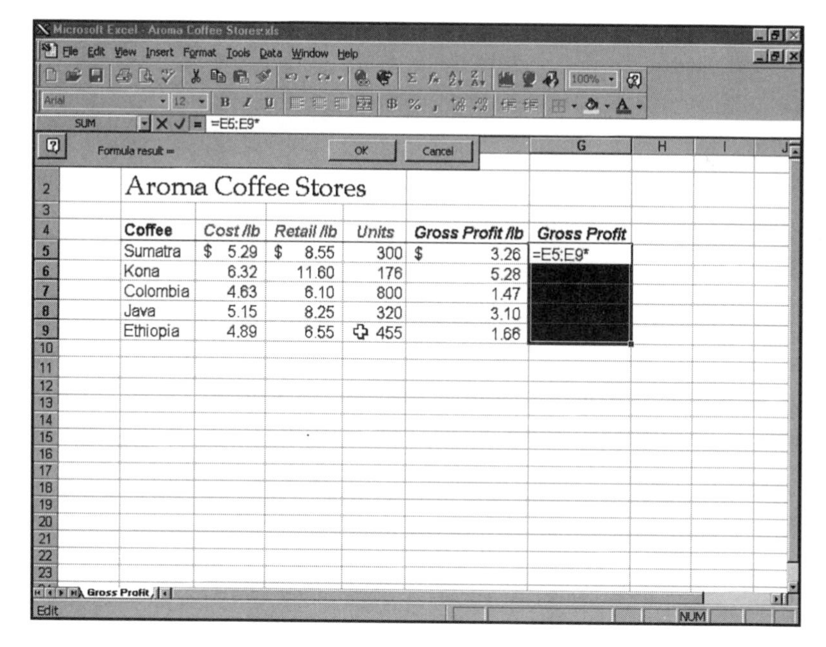

Fig. 8.10
Start an array calculation by selecting the range for the results to show up in. Notice that it's the same shape and size as the ranges for the input.

4. Select the second range, F5:F9 (see Figure 8.11).
5. Press Shift+Ctrl+Enter to tell Excel you're not entering just any old formula, but an array formula. In return, you get your results and a pair of curly braces, gratis, just as you saw in Figure 8.9.

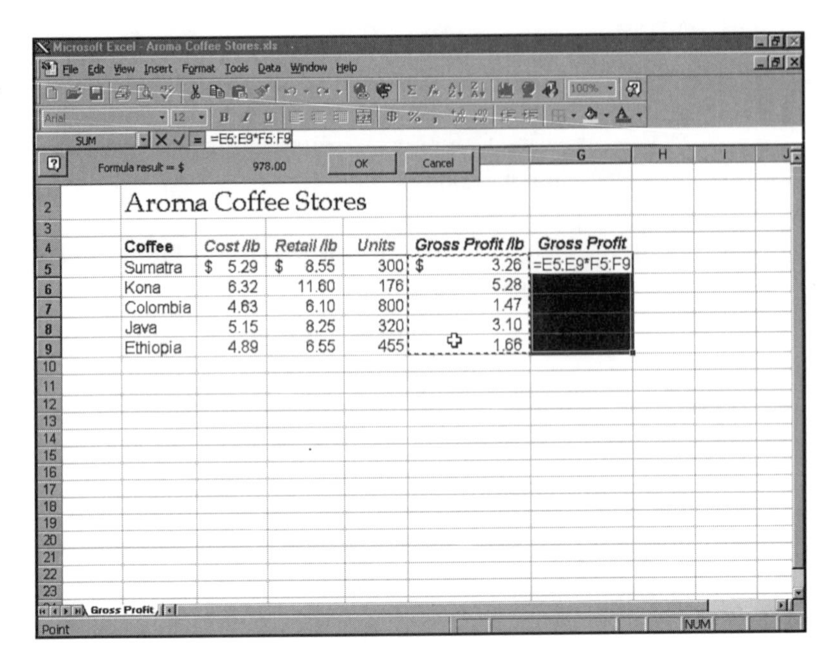

	Coffee	Cost /lb	Retail /lb	Units	Gross Profit /lb	Gross Profit
2	Aroma Coffee Stores					
4	Coffee	Cost /lb	Retail /lb	Units	Gross Profit /lb	Gross Profit
5	Sumatra	$ 5.29	$ 8.55	300	$ 3.26	=E5:E9*F5:F9
6	Kona	6.32	11.60	176	5.28	
7	Colombia	4.63	6.10	800	1.47	
8	Java	5.15	8.25	320	3.10	
9	Ethiopia	4.89	6.55	455	1.66	

Fig. 8.11
Select the input ranges, separated by an operator.

So what does {=E5:E9*F5:F9} mean exactly?

The array formula we wrote is a kind of hyper-shorthand. It tells Excel to multiply E5 times F5 and put the result in the first cell of a selected range, then multiply E6 times F6 and put the result in the second cell, and so on.

You can edit an array formula just like any other formula, but you can't edit individual cells in an array. You have to select the entire array range. You also can't delete or insert rows in an array without redoing the whole thing. Just remember that Excel treats an array as one unit.

Why should I use arrays?

Arrays are a way to do a lot of calculations with one compact formula. Looking at our little example, you might say, "Why bother?"

Well, there are more than 16,000 rows on an Excel worksheet. Copying a formula with the fill handle down even a tenth of those rows would get very old, very fast. And if the worksheet were stuffed with that many calculations, your computer would probably choke.

One array formula can do the work of 1,600. Arrays save time and memory in big calculations.

Same values, different results

Those curly braces around an array formula make a big difference in calculations. =E5:E9*F5:F9, without the braces, tells Excel to multiply the range E5:E9 times the range F5:F9 and return a single product. That's impossible, because when you use (*), Excel requires a single value on either side of the operator. All you'd get is the error message #VALUE!.

Putting the array braces around the same formula tells Excel to multiply each value in column E by each value in column F and put each resulting product in a third column. Amazing what a pair of braces can do.

What Are Functions?

In this chapter:

- **Why a function? (And why not a formula?)**
- **Instant Totals with AutoSum? That's functional!**
- **If functions are so easy to use, how come my function won't function?**
- **I need to work with dates and times (and why did time begin in 1900?)**

Functions are the fast and foolproof way to tap Excel's calculating power. And with more than 200 of them, Excel has a function for every occasion . . . .

People have been making bread for at least five thousand years. And, with a lot of variations, we've been making it the same way: mix the ingredients, make dough, knead the dough, let the dough rise, knead it again, bake it. Of course, it's easy to make a mistake somewhere along the line; there are a lot of steps, and it's easy to take a wrong one.

Writing formulas, as we did in Chapter 8, is like making bread by hand. It works, but it's laborious, and it's easy to make a mistake.

Functions, on the other hand, are like automatic bread makers. Throw in your data, click Finish, and bingo! Out pops the result. Magic? No. Convenient? You bet.

Ingredients of the function

As we saw in Chapter 8, formulas have two basic parts: values, and instructions about what to do to them. Functions have the same setup.

- There's the **function** itself, which tells Excel what to do. It's like those formula operators, +, –, /, and *, except that a single function can hold lots of operators. Better still, it always executes the operators in the right order. No worries about where to put what sign. The function is like the bread-making machine.
- And there are the **arguments**. That's yet another name for the values, references, or text that you're operating on. Arguments are the data you put into the function to get results. They're like the flour and water and salt and yeast that go into the bread-making machine. Different functions take different kinds and amounts of arguments. For some functions, arguments are numbers or text. Others take dates and times. Some functions take no arguments at all; others take as many as you care to dump in.

There's another thing that functions and formulas have in common: both begin with the = sign. Leave it out, and your function is nonfunctional. Functions inserted with the Paste Function button or the formula bar Functions list come with a ready-made equal sign; if you type a function yourself, click the Edit Formula button first to add that vital = sign.

A simple formula can duplicate the work of a lot of functions. But there's no reason to. Fact is, it's much easier—and faster—to use functions *instead* of formulas whenever you can.

Case in point: AutoSum, the fastest and easiest Excel function of all.

AutoSum: the "ka-ching!" function

Remember those big old clunky cash registers? There was something satisfying about that ka-ching! sound they made every time the clerk hit the Total key. The modern electronic versions may be more efficient, but they're a little cold-blooded.

AutoSum works like the Total key on a cash register. It sits right up on the toolbar, only one click away. Use it to quickly add columns or rows of numbers. (Sorry, no sound effects.)

1. Select the cell below a column or to the right of a row of numbers that you want totaled.

2. Click the AutoSum button.
3. AutoSum looks up or to the left for the numbers to total and suggests a range, putting a marquee around its suggestion.
4. If AutoSum guessed right, click the AutoSum button again, or press Enter, or click the Enter button on the formula bar. Any of the four methods completes AutoSum's operation and sticks the total in the selected cell. Why so many ways to do the same thing? Excel is nothing if not accommodating, and you can choose the option that's most comfortable for you. If you want a different range, select the range first, then click AutoSum. Total many rows or columns at once if you like.
5. AutoSum writes the SUM function for you, totaling the selected range. The column total is neatly added to the bottom of each column. Figure 9.1 shows AutoSum suggesting a range to total and writing a SUM function.

TIP **This also works for nonadjacent ranges. Select each range, click** AutoSum, and totals appear below columns or to the right of rows.

AutoSum writes the SUM function automatically, using the suggested range as the argument

Press Enter or click AutoSum again, and the sum displays in the selected cell

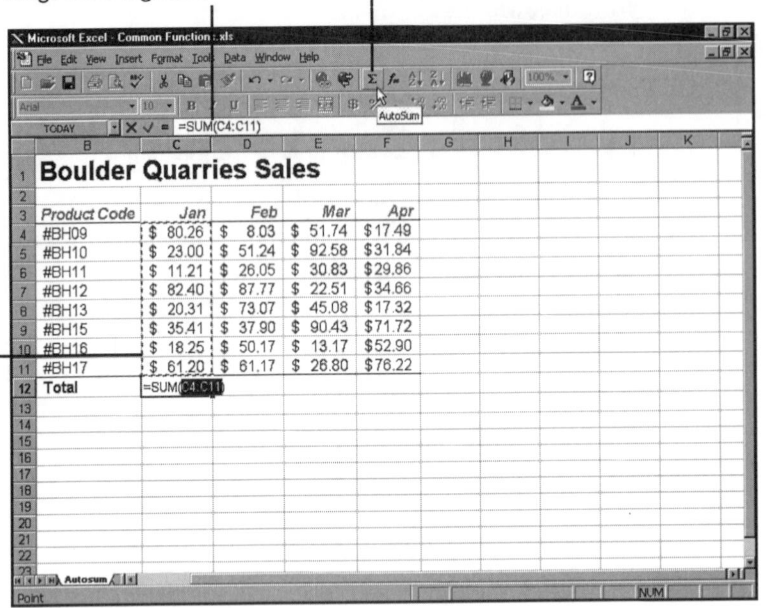

Fig. 9.1
AutoSum totals rows or columns speedily. Here, AutoSum writes a function to sum the column.

AutoSum throws a marquee around the column above the selected cell to indicate the range to total

TIP **Tired of mousing around? With the active cell anywhere within** your data, press Ctrl+Shift+* (the asterisk on the keyboard 8 key, not the number pad multiplication sign) to select an entire table, then click AutoSum to total each column. AutoSum ignores anything that isn't a number.

What's there to argue about?

The function AutoSum cooked up for us in Figure 9.1 reads like this: `=SUM(C4:C11)` (the equal sign, followed by the function name, followed by the argument in parentheses). That's the syntax for functions in general. If a function takes more than one argument, separate them with commas.

We could have written a formula to get the same result:`=(C4+C5+C6+C7+C8+C9+C10+C11)`. And it would have worked perfectly well. But it would have been a little like going to the corner store when you need a quart of milk—the corner store in the next town.

TIP **If you want to type a function (SUM, for example), type it in** lowercase letters. If the function is typed correctly, Excel automatically converts the lowercase letters to uppercase. If you wind up with a #NAME? error, it means the function wasn't typed correctly.

Let functions do the work

Some functions can be a little unruly. They require many arguments, and the arguments have to be of the right type, entered with the right syntax. The more complex the function, the harder it is to keep it all straight.

Excel makes writing functions easy. It guides us, step-by-step, through the most complex functions.

Click the Paste Function button, and the Paste Function dialog box appears. This dialog box performs a number of, well, functions. The Paste Function dialog box:

- Lists functions and describes their uses
- Prompts for the right type and number of arguments at each step
- Provides quick descriptions of each function and of each argument in a function
- Helps you edit functions already in the worksheet
- Writes the function with its arguments, then puts it in a selected cell

Figure 9.2 shows the Paste Function dialog box.

Fig. 9.2
Click the Paste Function button to pop up a list of all the available functions.

The Most Recently Used category in the Function Category list displays common functions when you first start using Excel. Once you put the Functions to work, it also displays—you guessed it—the functions you've used most recently.

You can always write functions on your own if you really want to. But it's a lot easier to use the Paste Function dialog box. Let's take a look at how much time and trouble a few common functions can save you.

Everyday functions

SUM is a function you'll use all the time, and the quickest way to get at it is with the AutoSum button. To use other common functions (or any function, for that matter), just click the Paste Function button.

Finding averages

Select a range of values, right-click the status bar, and select Average. The mean average of the values appears in the AutoCalculate box on the status bar (see Figure 9.3).

Fig. 9.3
Finding the mean average of a range of values is no mean feat with AutoCalculate.

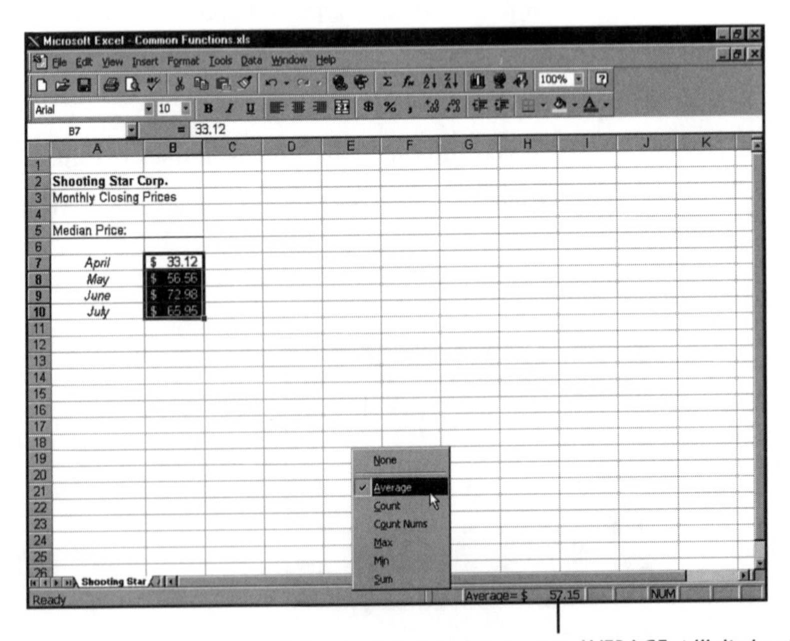

As long as AutoCalculate is set to AVERAGE, it'll display the mean average of any other ranges of values you select

But suppose you want to find the median average of a range of values—the middle value of a range. Just use the MEDIAN function and the Paste Function dialog box.

To quickly find the median average of a series of values:

1. Select the cell where you want the result.

2. Click the Paste Function button and select Statistical from the Function Category list. Scroll down the Function Name list, and double-click MEDIAN (see Figure 9.4).

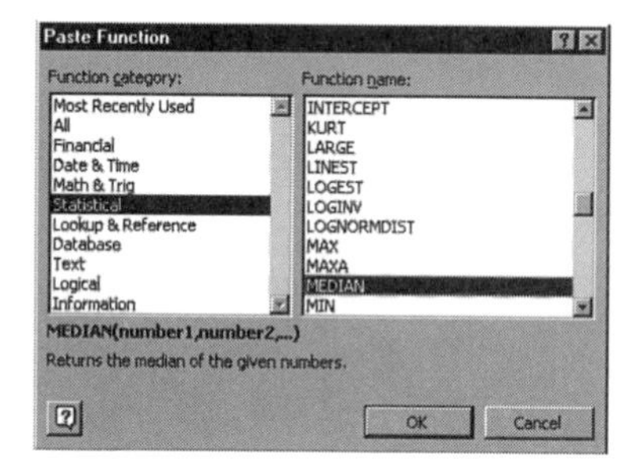

Fig. 9.4
Read the syntax and description of the selected function in the lower-left corner of the Paste Function dialog box.

3. The Median dialog box pops up under the formula bar. The cursor should be in the Number 1 text box (if it isn't, click the box). Use the mouse to select a range to average—B7:B10 in this example (see Figure 9.5). You can also enter each value individually in the Number 1 and Number 2 text boxes (Excel adds more as needed), but it's faster to select a range. If the dialog box gets in the way of the cells you want to select, either drag it to one side, or click the Collapse Dialog Box button to hide all of the dialog box except for the text box you're working in.

4. The result appears at the bottom of the Median dialog box. Click OK, and the median value is dumped in the selected cell, as shown in Figure 9.6.

If you look closely at the Median dialog box in Figure 9.5, you'll notice that **Number 1** is in boldface, but Number 2 is not. Functions have both required arguments and optional arguments. Required arguments are in boldface; you must enter a value for them to continue building the function. Values that are optional aren't bold.

Fig. 9.5
Although function dialog boxes don't have title bars, you can still drag them out of the way.

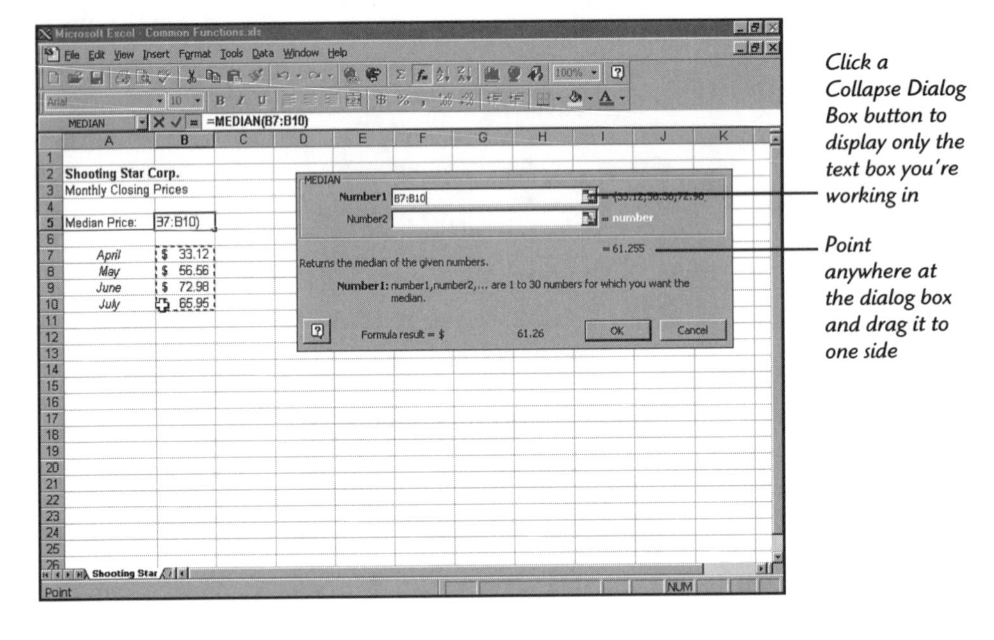

Fig. 9.6
When you click OK in a function dialog box, the result goes in whatever cell you first selected.

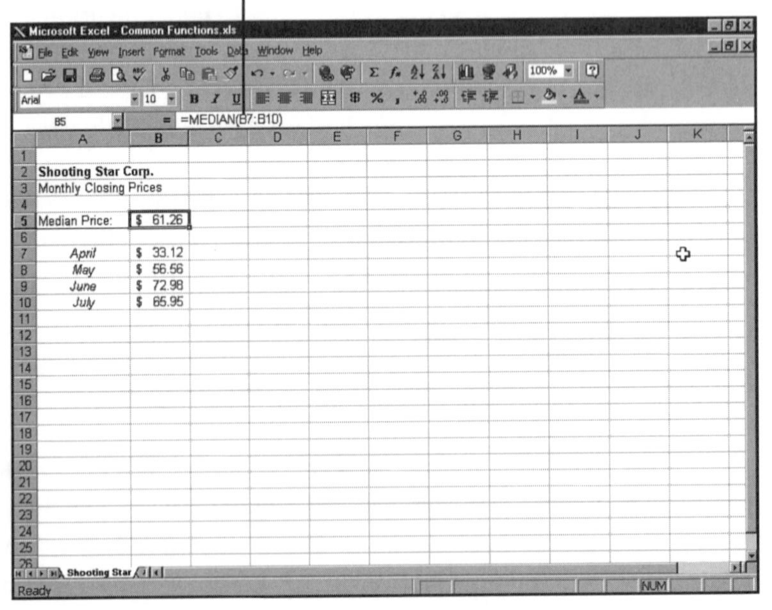

When the formula bar is activated, the Name box turns into the Functions button. Click the button to insert the displayed function, or click the drop-down arrow for a list of your most recently used functions.

TIP **The AVERAGE function returns the mean; MEDIAN returns the** middle value for an odd number of values. If you use MEDIAN for an even number of values, MEDIAN calculates the mean of the middle two values and returns that.

How do I know what function I'm supposed to use?

You know what it is you want to calculate, but you have no idea what Excel function to use for the calculation. The function names are—well, functional, but a bit on the cryptic side. So what to do? Call on the Office Assistant.

Click the Office Assistant Button in the Paste Function dialog box, and choose Help With This Feature in the Office Assistant balloon. Type a description of what you're trying to calculate, and click Search. The Office Assistant produces a list of Recommended functions in the Function Name box. Select any of the recommended functions, and read the description of what it does. If the description doesn't provide enough information, click Help on Selected Function in the Office Assistant balloon.

Q&A ***I know what function I need, but I don't know the category it falls into. How do I find it?***

Select All in the Function Category list box (refer to Figure 9.2). That gives you an alphabetical listing of all the functions. Click the Function Name list box, then type the first letter of the function you're looking for to scroll right to it.

IF (and if not)

The IF function is a handy Excel tool that tests the contents of a cell and returns a logical value based on the results of the test.

> ### Plain English, please!
>
> A **logical value** is a fancy way of saying True or False. So why not just say True or False? Because they really are values. Excel converts True to the value 1 and False to the value 0 if you use cells containing True or False in calculations. Let's say that C4 contains a 2, and D5 contains the logical value True. C4+D5 would equal 3, because Excel evaluates True as 1.

Use the IF function for any True/False statement. The kicker is that you can make the resulting values more meaningful than just True or False.

In Figure 9.7, Ace Detective Agency is trying to keep track of its clients' billing history. Ace is having trouble with its bookkeeper, and wants to include clear instructions on what to do about overdue balances.

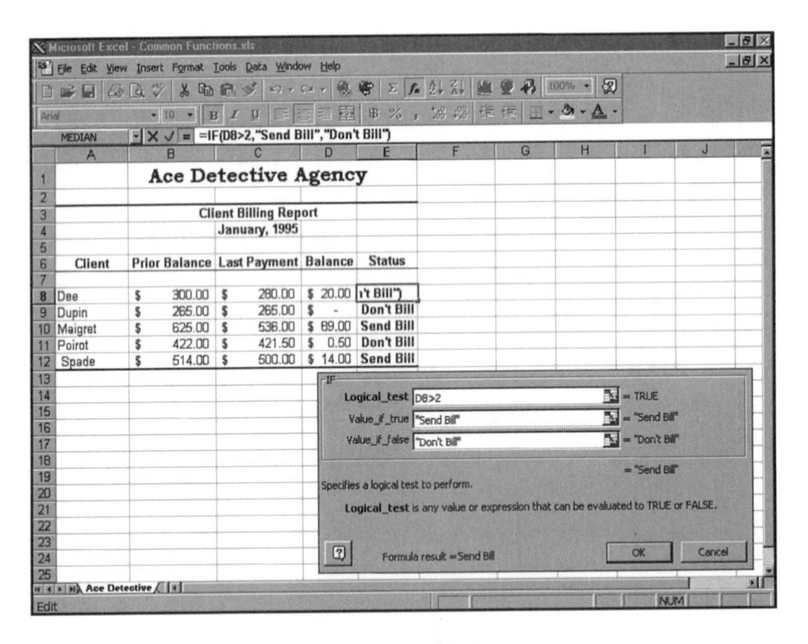

Fig. 9.7 Excel supplies the quotes in the Value_if_true and Value_if_false boxes, so you don't need to type them.

Ace wants to rebill clients with balances over $2.00. It constructs a simple test to check the outstanding balance: `D8>2`. To let the bookkeeper know exactly what to do, Ace uses the IF function to return a value of `"Send Bill"` if the balance meets the test, and `"Don't Bill"` if it doesn't.

Count Nums counts numbers

Students everywhere cheered when the word processor came along. Those thousand-word assignments got finished a lot faster, because you didn't have to hand-count your word total any more. Word processors total up word counts accurately and quickly.

The Count Nums function in Excel does the same trick with worksheet numbers. Select a range, right-click the status bar, choose Count Nums, and AutoCalculate displays a count of the numbers in the range. Count Nums also counts dates, times, and logical values—anything, in short, that can be converted to a number. Count Nums ignores text or blank cells that can't be converted to a number.

Sometimes numbers don't look like numbers, but Count Nums will count them anyway. In Figure 9.8, Count Nums includes D9 in its number count, even though it's a minus sign (–). D9 is actually a zero, but the Accounting Category of the Format, Cells command formats it this way.

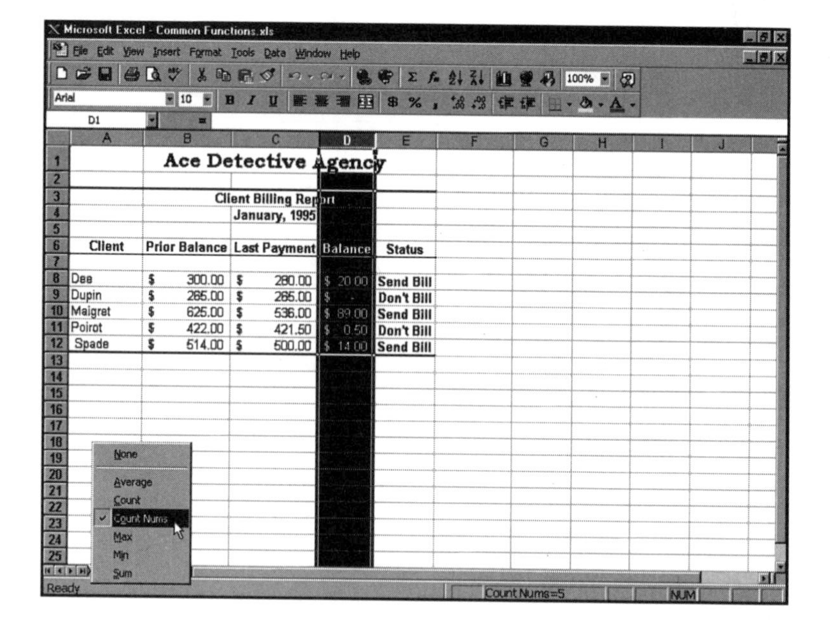

Fig. 9.8
Count Nums did ignore the blank cells and text in column D, returning a value of 5 because there are five numbers in the column.

To insert counts of numbers in a selected cell, use the COUNT function in the Paste Function dialog box. The Paste Function dialog box COUNT function is the equivalent of using the Count Nums option on the AutoCalculate menu.

How come when I used the COUNT function to insert a count of the numbers in my column, I got Excel's error message about circular references?

When you clicked the Paste Function button, the active cell was in the same column you were trying to count. COUNT can't count its own count. Just saying it is circular.

Count counts everything

What if you need to count something other than numbers—the total number of clients in a table, for example? To get a read on every occupied cell in a range, select the range, right-click the status bar, and choose Count from the AutoCalculate menu. That counts both numbers and text, but ignores blank cells. To insert a count of the occupied cells in a range, including text, use the COUNTA function from the Paste Function dialog box (see Figure 9.9).

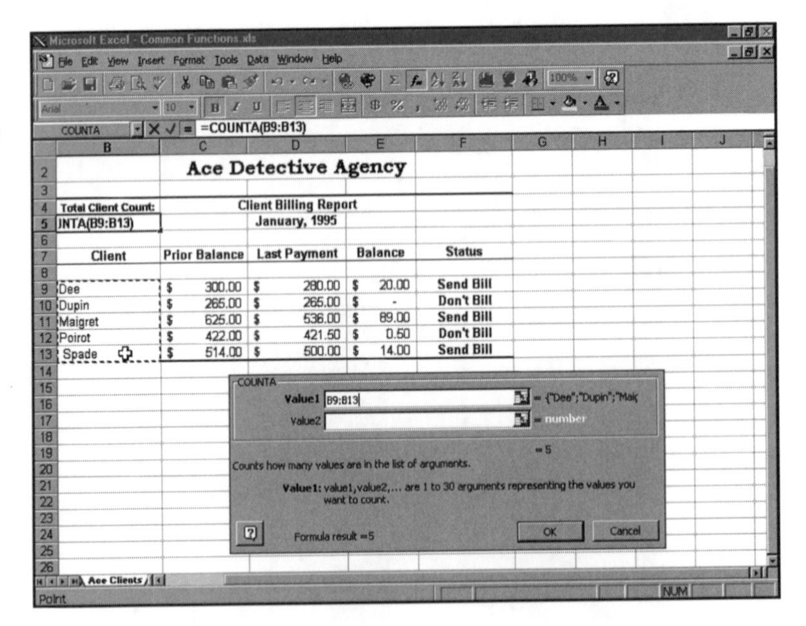

Fig. 9.9
Unlike the COUNT function, COUNTA counts all the occupied cells in a range, including text.

Then and now: date and time functions

When we travel abroad, we convert dollars to foreign currency. You hand over dollars and get the equivalent in francs, sterling, or whatever. You have the same amount of cash (less those pesky fees); it's just in a different form.

Excel does the same kind of thing with dates and times. When you enter a date or time, Excel converts it to a serial number. Same time, same date, just in a different form. It may look the same to you, but Excel knows otherwise.

Plain English, please!

A **serial number** is one in a series of numbers. 0,1,2,3,4,5 is a series; any digit in the series is a serial number.

The Excel calendar begins on January 1, 1900

When you type a date in Excel, it shows up as a normal calendar date on your worksheet. But as far as Excel is concerned, your date is actually a number in a series from 1 to 65,380. Why would it think that? Because from January 1, 1900 through December 31, 2078, there are 65,380 days.

Enter a date from 1/1/1900 to 12/31/2078 and Excel stores it as the corresponding number in the series. 5/31/57, for example, is stored as 20,971. That's because there are 20,971 days between 1/1/1900 and 5/31/57. Treating dates this way lets Excel make calculations involving dates, and lets you use dates as formulas as well as constants.

Can I flip between serial and calendar dates?

The DATE function prompts you to enter the year, month, and day. The function then returns the corresponding date. How the date is displayed on the worksheet depends on the formatting of the cell where the date appears. But no matter how the date is displayed, Excel stores it as a serial number. Figure 9.10 shows you the DATE function.

To display a serial date as a calendar date, right-click the cell to open the shortcut menu. Select Format, Cells, click the Number tab, and choose a Date Type.

To display a date as a serial number, choose Number on the Category list of the Format Cells dialog box Number tab.

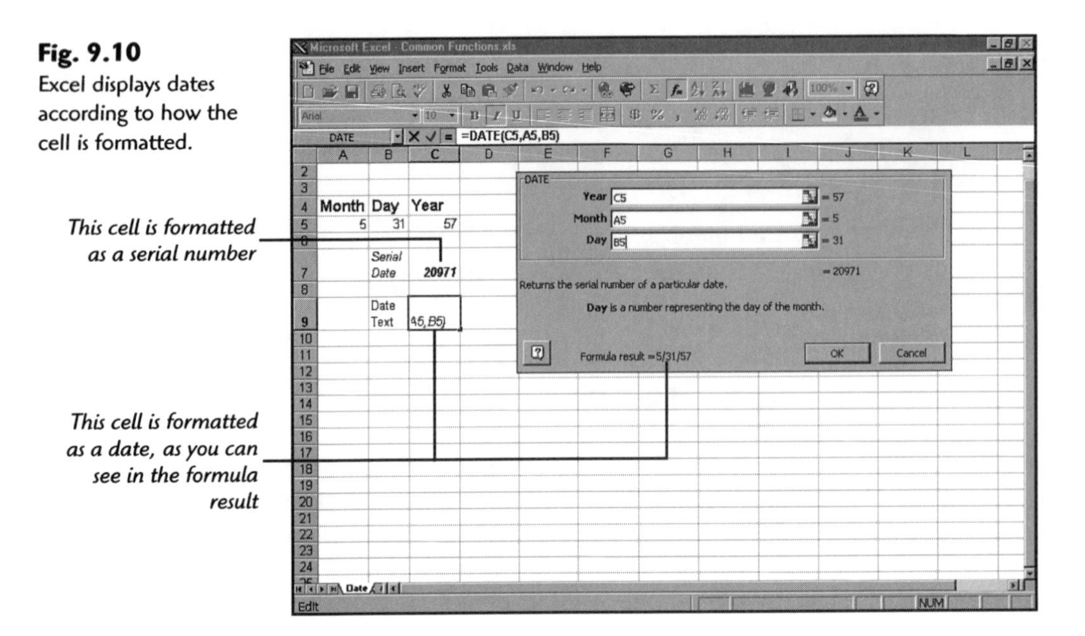

Fig. 9.10
Excel displays dates according to how the cell is formatted.

How many days are there between these two dates?

You're planning a critical project, and you need to allocate your scarce days judiciously. You know the start and end dates. Now you want to know how many days to allocate to each phase of the project. You *could* sit down with a calendar. Or you could save precious time and use the DAYS360 function instead. DAYS360 calculates the number of days between any two dates.

Use the completion date of one phase of the project as the start date of the next phase. The planned completion of the project is the end date. Set up this way, it's easy to build a timeline with DAYS360.

Figure 9.11 shows how such a timeline might look.

CAUTION

This timeline might be handy, but use it only as an estimate. DAYS360 uses a 360-day year and 12, 30-day months to make its calculations. No leap years, and no odd-numbered months. If only life were that simple.

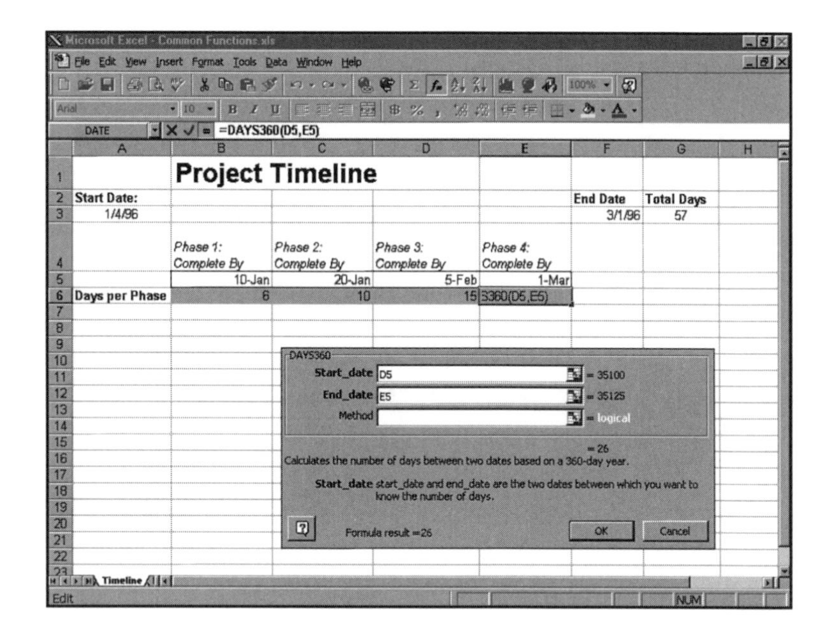

Fig. 9.11
Use the DAYS360 function to calculate the number of days between any two dates.

Only a fraction of the time

Excel takes a similar approach to time. Hours, minutes, and seconds are stored as serial numbers between 0 and .99999999. That series of decimal fractions represents all the times, down to the second, between 00:00:00 and 23:59:59 on the 24-hour clock.

Enter **13:52** (or 1:52 PM) and Excel stores it as .5777…8. Just as incomprehensible as our date of 20,971? The time is only displayed as a serial number if you format the cell as a number.

Use the TIME function to enter times without making mistakes. TIME prompts you for the hour (0 to 23), the minute (0 to 59), and the second (also 0 to 59). TIME stores the resulting time as a decimal fraction, and displays the time in whatever format you've chosen.

Don't look NOW

To plug the current time and date into your worksheet, use the NOW function. The time and date will be updated whenever you recalculate your worksheet.

TIP **To stop Excel from updating NOW, change the cell from a function** to a value. Right-click the cell and choose Copy from the shortcut menu. Right-click the cell again and choose Paste Special. In the Paste Special dialog box, click Values and choose OK. You're pasting the NOW function over with a value instead, which freezes the date and time. In the blink of an eye, NOW becomes then.

If all you need is the current date with no time display, use the TODAY function. The TODAY function updates automatically. To insert today's date that won't update tomorrow, press Ctrl+;.

10 Functions You'll Use Often

In this chapter:

- **Figure my loan payment? Analyze my investment? Now these are functions I can really use!**
- **Asset seen better days? Don't deprecate it—use a function to depreciate it.**
- **Statistical functions, for statistics and other lies**
- **Produce a number, any (random) number, with RAND**

Statistical and financial calculations yield fascinating results—but getting them requires lots of dull arithmetic. Excel functions do the arithmetic automatically, letting you skip right to the finish

If something around the house needs building or fixing, you reach for the toolbox. There's a tool in there, somewhere, that's right for the job. Excel's tools are its functions. Whatever the job, there's a function that'll get it done. And unlike my toolbox, Excel's tools are always in their rightful place—no rummaging needed. What's more, every Excel function comes with instructions on how to use it. That's more than I can say for my tools.

Financial functions

Making financial calculations like Net Present Value and Internal Rate of Return used to mean scanning endless tables or peering at tiny calculator screens. Excel's financial functions eliminate those hassles.

Payments and annuities

Getting ready to buy a new home or car? The PMT function is a terrific tool for analyzing loans and annuities. As long as you're consistent about the arguments you enter, using PMT is a snap.

Say you're refinancing your mortgage with a 7%, 15-year loan. The balance of the loan is $150,000. Call on the PMT function to calculate the monthly payment. Just be sure to convert all the other numbers to monthly amounts first.

- The rate is an annual figure, so divide it by 12 to get the rate per month.
- It's a 15-year mortgage, with 12 payments a year. 12*15=180 for the total number of monthly payments.

Set up the PMT function as shown in Figure 10.1, and you'll see the monthly payment appear in the PMT function dialog box.

IPMT figures interest

Say you want to dig a little deeper into this mortgage question. Use IPMT to calculate the amount of interest you're paying in any given period. Set up IPMT the same way we set up PMT. In the Per (period) text box, enter the number of the period you're wondering about.

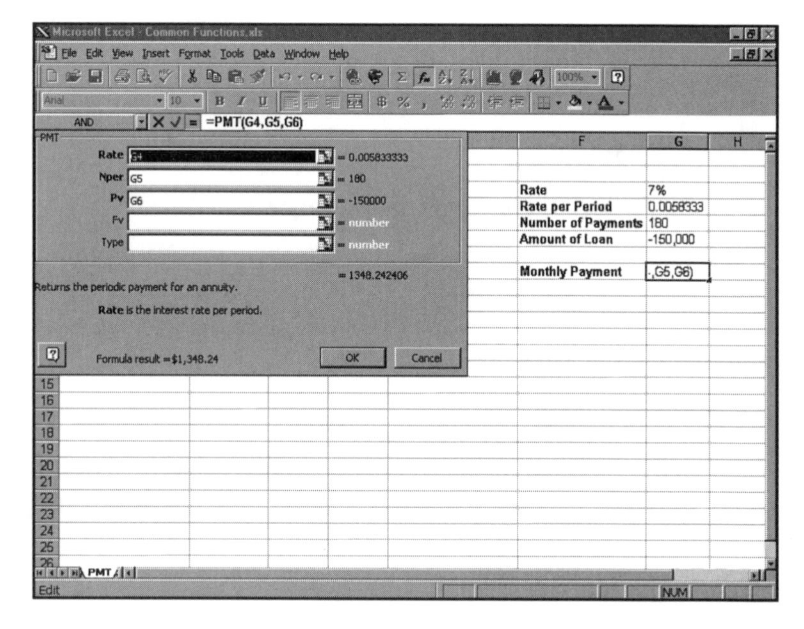

Fig. 10.1
PMT is handy, but be careful to make the arguments consistent. Here, we've converted everything to monthly amounts because we're after the monthly payment.

In the example, that would be a number between 1 and 180, representing all the payment periods for the life of the mortgage.

Figure 10.2 shows the IPMT function, with the amount of interest in period 90 shown in the Formula Result area.

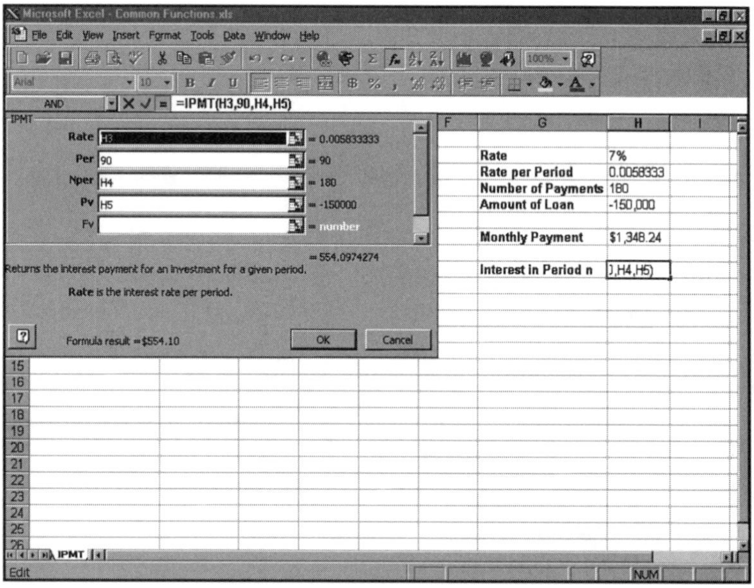

Fig. 10.2
To get the amount of the principle payment in any period, subtract the interest from the total payment.

PV and NPV

Present Value and Net Present Value are involved calculations based on a simple idea: a dollar today is worth more than a dollar a year from now.

Plain English, please!

Present Value (PV) is the value today of an amount received in the future, discounted by a selected interest rate. **Future Value** (FV) is what today's amount will be worth at a future date, inflated by whatever interest rate the amount will earn. **Net Present Value** (NPV) subtracts the initial investment from the sum of a discounted stream of future payments. NPV answers the question, "How much is this investment REALLY worth?"

NPV tells us when a million isn't a million

Congratulations! We've just won the lottery, and the payout is a million dollars!

That million-dollar jackpot will be paid out over 10 years. We'll get $50,000 a year for the first five years, and $150,000 a year for the last five years. So why aren't you jumping up and down? Is it because you're not really getting one million? Five times 50,000 plus five times 150,000 equals a million—or does it? Figure 10.3 shows otherwise.

$643,517 isn't exactly a million, is it? We want the Net Present Value of our lottery investment, so we have to figure in our initial outlay. After all, we spent $5 on that lottery ticket!

Neither a borrower nor a lender be?

If you give me a dollar right now (thank you!), I'm going to rush down to the bank and put it in my savings account. My account pays interest of, say, 3%. By a year from today, that dollar will have earned three cents (actually a little over three cents with compounding). It'll be worth $1.03. That's called **future value**.

And what is that future $1.03 worth today? $1.00. That's **present value**. So if I tell you I'll pay your dollar back in a year, you're being cheated. Why? Because that year-from-now dollar is really worth about $.97 today. You should insist on getting $1.03 if I keep your dollar for a year.

Fig. 10.3
A dollar today is worth more than a dollar tomorrow. A million bucks paid out over 10 years is not really a million bucks.

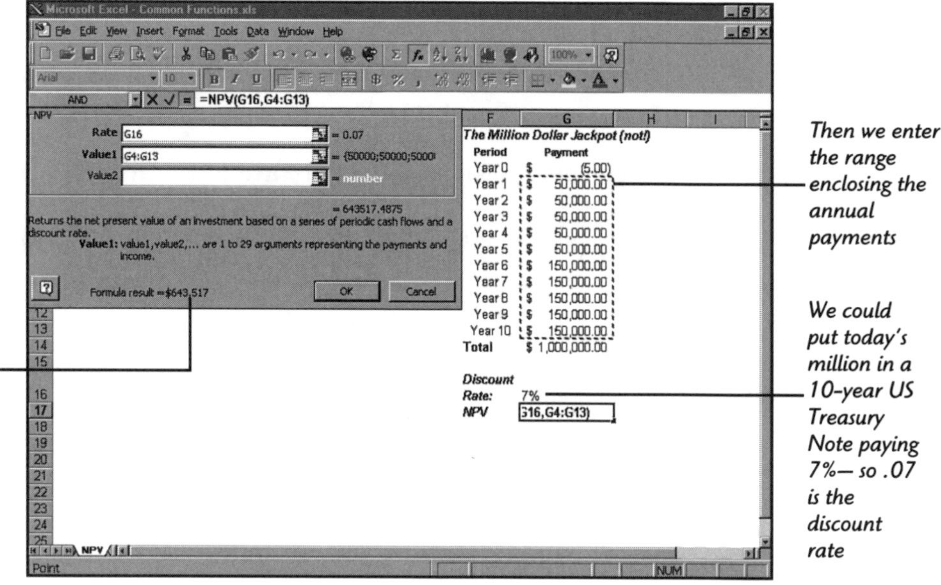

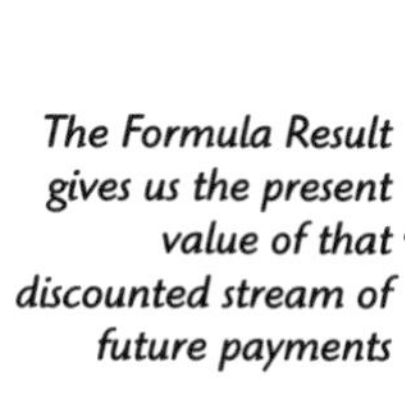

So:

```
NPV = (investment) + PV of Income Stream
($5.00) + $643,517 = $643,512
```

NPV calculations are usually set up like this. Our investment, the $5 we spent on the lottery ticket, was money we paid out, so it's a negative number. We don't include it in the range calculated by the NPV function because we've already paid it. NPV calculates future investments and income that occur at regular intervals.

TIP **Do include the initial investment in the NPV function calculation** if you plan to make the investment at the end of the first year.

NPV is one of the best tools around for evaluating an investment. Financial analysts often look at a project by saying, "If the NPV is a positive number, we should do it." What they mean is that the investment pays out more than it costs. And if we think of our lottery prize that way, we shouldn't feel too badly about not getting a full million.

But it's still not a million.

IRR or MIRR?

We could also take this approach to an investment: what rate of return would I have to get to make the NPV of an investment equal to zero?

That rate is called the **Internal Rate of Return** (IRR). IRR is often used to make financial decisions. It gives us a comparison between the return thrown off by the investment and the opportunity cost of capital. If the IRR exceeds the return offered by the market, the investment we're considering must be pretty good. If it doesn't, why bother?

Figure 10.4 shows one way to set up the IRR function.

Plain English, please!

The **opportunity cost of capital** is the rate of return we could get in the market, on a Treasury for example, that we pass up to make another investment.

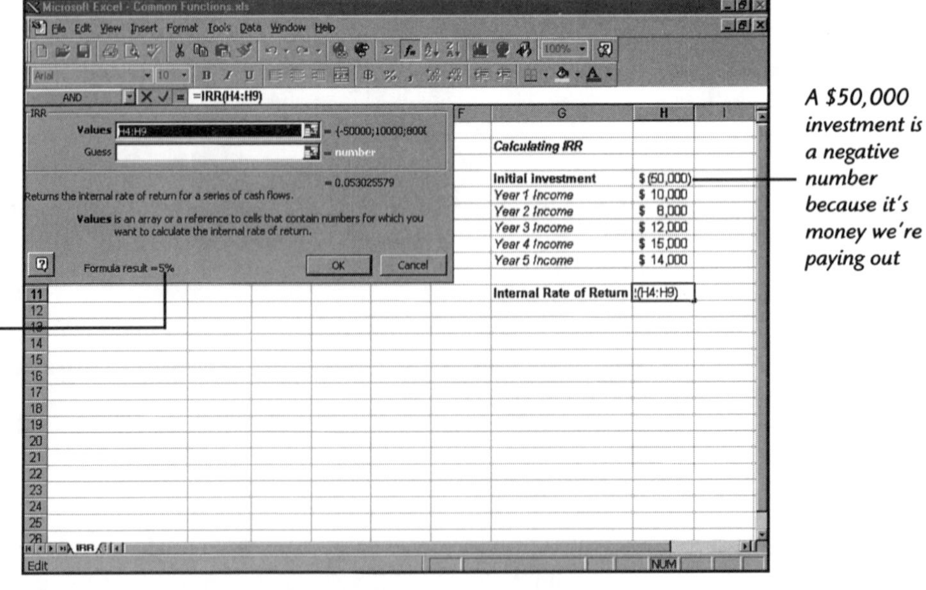

Fig. 10.4
IRR calculates the discount rate that makes the NPV of an investment equal to zero.

With an IRR of 5%, should we make this investment? Not if we can get more in a Treasury

A $50,000 investment is a negative number because it's money we're paying out

The only way to calculate IRR is by trial and error, or iteration. You have to keep plugging in discount rates until you find one that makes the NPV equal zero. We let Excel do that for us, and the program takes 20 shots at it. In our lottery investment, the rate would be impossibly huge. Excel would give up after 20 tries and just shout `#NUM?`.

In the IRR dialog box shown in Figure 10.4, the Guess text box is where you enter your estimate of what the return should be. You don't have to make an estimate though. If you don't, Excel uses 10% as a guess and starts its trial-and-error process from there.

MIRR

There are a few problems with IRR. One is the fact that two different discount rates can make NPV equal to zero for the same investment! Excel tries to find the IRR that makes the most sense in a case like that.

A second problem reflects the real world. If you take out a loan to build an office building, you pay the bank one rate. When your tenants start to make rental payments, you stick those rentals in a money market fund and get an entirely different rate.

How can you find one IRR that reflects both rates? You can't. Use **Modified Internal Rate of Return** (MIRR) instead. Excel's MIRR function performs an IRR calculation, but allows you to enter both the rate you pay for borrowed funds, and the rate you get by reinvesting your income stream.

Figuring depreciation

Ah, the company rust-mobile. The battered wagon is practically new, and it's already falling apart. Plenty of hard driving by too many different drivers has given it a few premature gray hairs. It's a hunk of junk, but you regard it with a kindly eye.

And not only because the dings and scratches make interesting patterns. The depreciation it generates each year probably saves you more in taxes than the heap is really worth.

Plain English, please!

Depreciation allocates the cost of an asset over the asset's useful life. Useful life is usually taken to mean the time that elapses before you have to replace the asset. The idea is that as you use the asset over time, you account for, in each period, the expense of gradually using it up. Depreciation is an accounting fiction that tries to reflect the true cost over time of an asset. Depreciation is also mighty useful at tax time. ”

SLN, the straight line depreciation function

The **straight line depreciation** method takes the difference between the rust-mobile's cost and its resale value (the term of art is **salvage value**), divided by the number of years of useful life of the machine. The SLN function saves you the arithmetic, as shown in Figure 10.5.

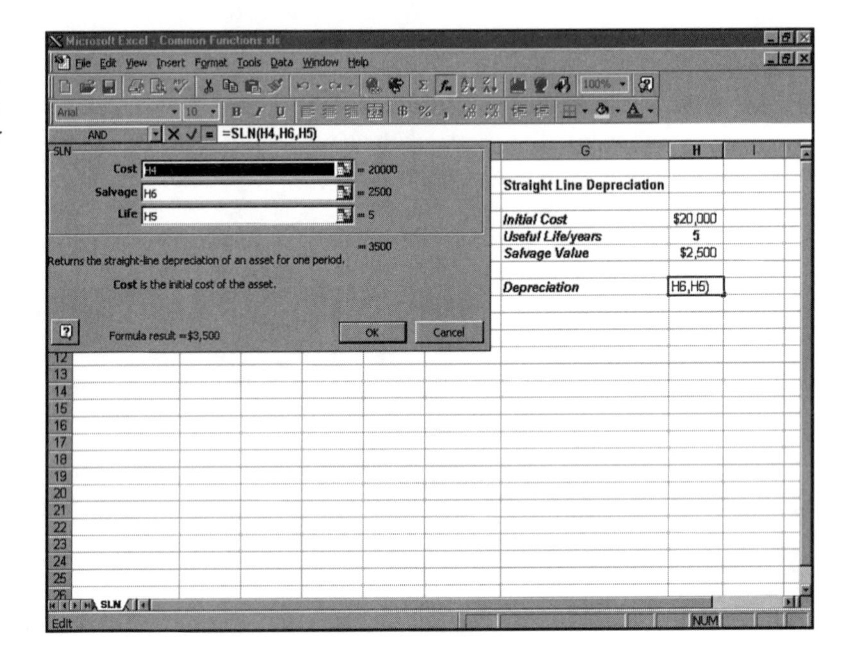

Fig. 10.5
Just plug the numbers into the SLN function to see how much your wreck is really worth.

SYD

Sum-of-the-years-digits (SYD) is a more interesting way to depreciate that heap. It's a widely used method that depreciates the asset faster at the beginning of its life. You get a bigger depreciation charge, earlier. Because a tax saving today is worth more than a tax saving tomorrow, SYD and other accelerated depreciation schemes are popular with the accounting set.

SYD calculates the depreciation for each period separately. Take a look at the difference between the depreciation in year one on the worksheet and the depreciation in year five, shown in the SYD function's Formula Result in Figure 10.6. As you can see, we get a much bigger depreciation charge out of year one than we do out of year five.

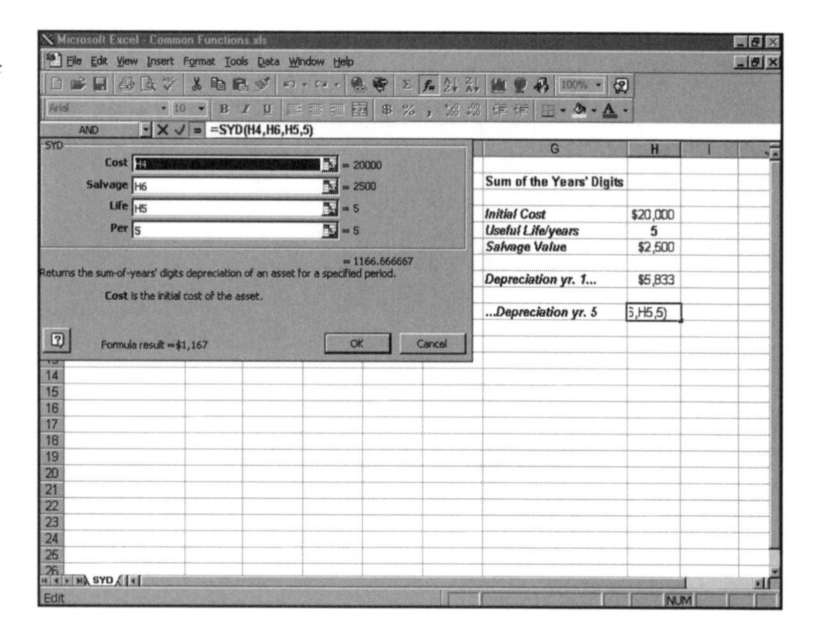

Fig. 10.6
With SYD, each year of useful life is a distinct period.

Statistics and other lies

Mark Twain wrote in his autobiography: "There are three kinds of lies—lies, damned lies, and statistics." And don't worry about offending statisticians with this crack, by the way. They quote it themselves, with relish. With the help of Excel functions, you can concoct any type of lie—er, statistic—in a few easy steps.

Getting a line on data: linear and growth trends

Suppose you own a new office furniture store. Business has been good for the past few months, but you wonder about the future. What's the next quarter going to be like?

One common statistical tool can give you a clue. If you plotted your past six months' sales figures on a piece of graph paper, then tried to draw a line that passed as close as possible to each point, extending the line *into the future* would give you your answer. That's sometimes called the **best-fit line**—the line that best fits the data. It's also called a **trend line**.

How do I create a trend?

Trying to draw a best-fit line just by looking at your data points could make you go cross-eyed. Excel saves your vision by finding the line for you. Excel uses the **least squares method** to do it.

Plain English, please!

Mathematician Carl Friedrich Gauss came up with the **least squares method** two hundred years ago, and promptly used it to discover the first observed asteroid, Ceres.

The least squares method measures how far bits of data are from a line drawn through the bits, producing an equation that describes the line. That's the best-fit line, also called a **regression line** or **trend line**. The whole procedure is called **regression analysis**.

Excel saves you the trouble of messing around with graph paper and equations. When you need to create a linear (as in straight-line) trend, use the fill handle. Here's how to do it:

1 Select the range enclosing your data, B4 through B10 in Figure 10.7.

2 At the bottom of the selected range, grab the fill handle with the *right* mouse button and drag to the end of the range enclosing the blank cells you want filled in, B11 through B13 in Figure 10.7. Release the mouse button and the shortcut menu pops up.

3 Clicking Linear Trend produces the results shown in Figure 10.8.

The selected blank cells at the end of the range are then filled in from points further along the line.

Hey, I tried this but the Linear Trend option on the shortcut menu is grayed out. What gives?

You selected the last cell in the range and tried to drag from there, instead of first selecting the range enclosing your data and then dragging. A fine point, but critical. How do I know what you did? Because I do it all the time myself.

You can do the same thing by highlighting the entire range, including blank cells, and then choosing Edit, Fill, Series from the menu. Selecting AutoFill in the Series dialog box duplicates what we just did.

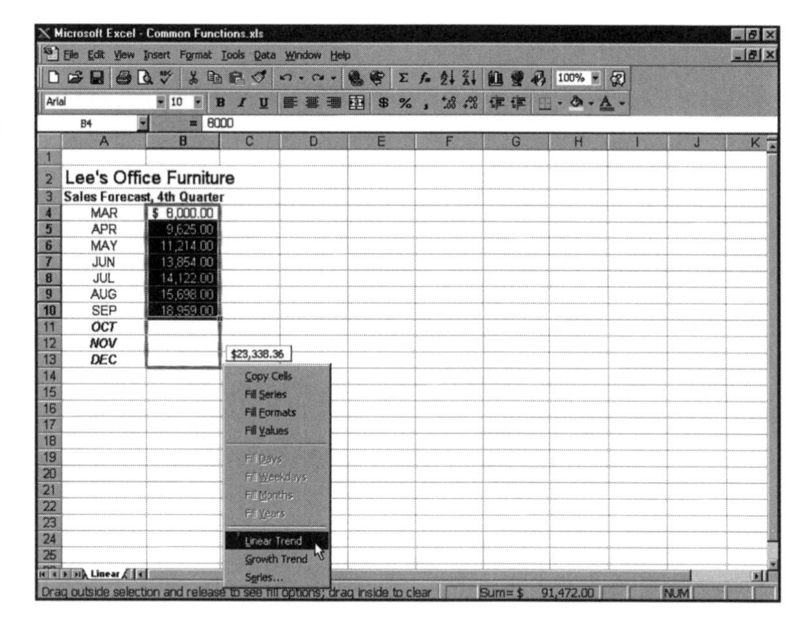

Fig. 10.7
Grab the fill handle with the right mouse button and drag to the end of the period you want to analyze.

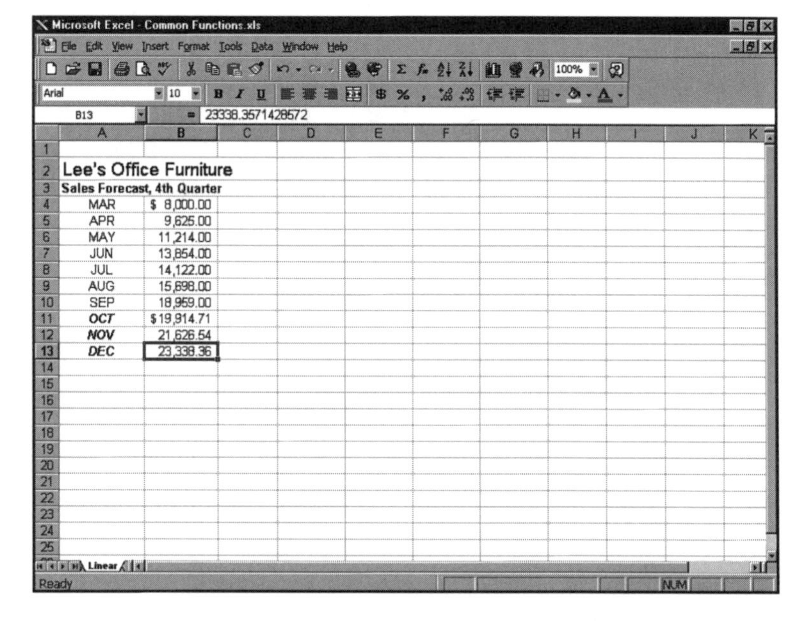

Fig. 10.8
Selecting Linear Trend from the shortcut menu told Excel to find the best-fit, trend, or regression line (take your pick of names).

Selecting Linear, or selecting the Trend check box in the Series dialog box (click Edit, Fill, Series to get there) replaces the original data with data created from the trend line produced from the original set. You might gain a trend, but you lose your original data.

Going beyond the line: growth trends

Maybe you're an optimist. You expect more than linear growth for that new office furniture store. If you anticipate sales really taking off, create a growth trend, as shown in Figure 10.9.

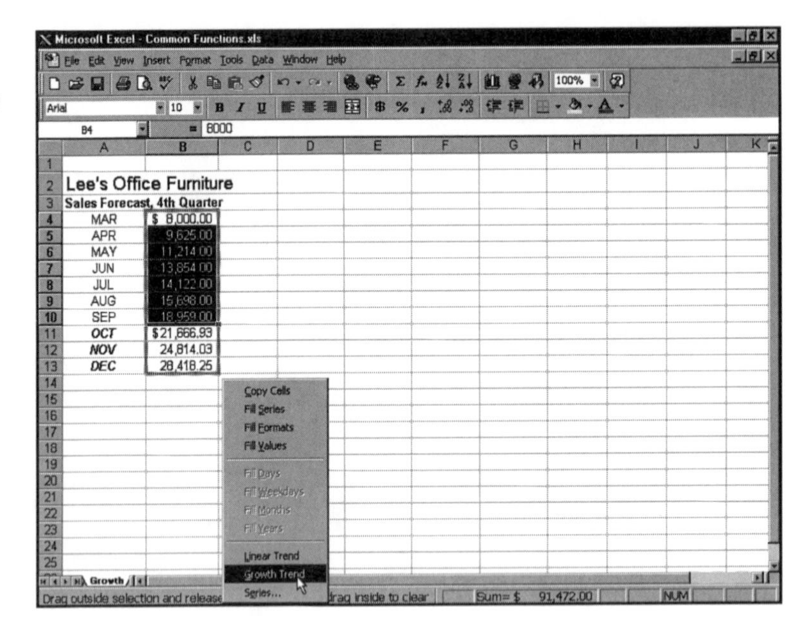

Fig. 10.9
The difference between a linear trend and a growth trend is, well, exponential!

The linear trend in Figure 10.8 predicted sales rising in future periods based on fixed increases. A growth trend bases predictions on constantly growing, or exponential, increases from period to period.

For more complex forecasts and progressions, including finding the best-fit lines for arrays, use statistical functions like TREND and GROWTH.

Deviating from the mean: STDEV and STDEVP

What's the idea behind **standard deviation**? Take some data, average it, then calculate how far from the average is each individual bit of data. The standard deviation is a measure of the data's scatter.

STDEV function

There are two ways of getting at standard deviation. One is to take all the data, or the **whole population**, as statisticians say. That works for some things, but not for very large populations. Too much work.

So we take a random sample from the whole population and calculate the standard deviation of the sample. That can be pretty accurate, and it saves a lot of work. Either method involves lots of tedious computation, which we completely avoid with Excel's STDEV function.

What's standard deviation for?

Say you're a potter, making 100 clay pots a day. You don't care if every pot is exactly the same size, but you want them all to be fairly alike. You're no statistician, but you do know that standard deviation is a gauge of how far from an average size your pots are. The smaller the standard deviation, the closer the pots are to the average size.

So you take a sample of 10 pots, measure them around the middle, and find the standard deviation of those measurements (see Figure 10.10).

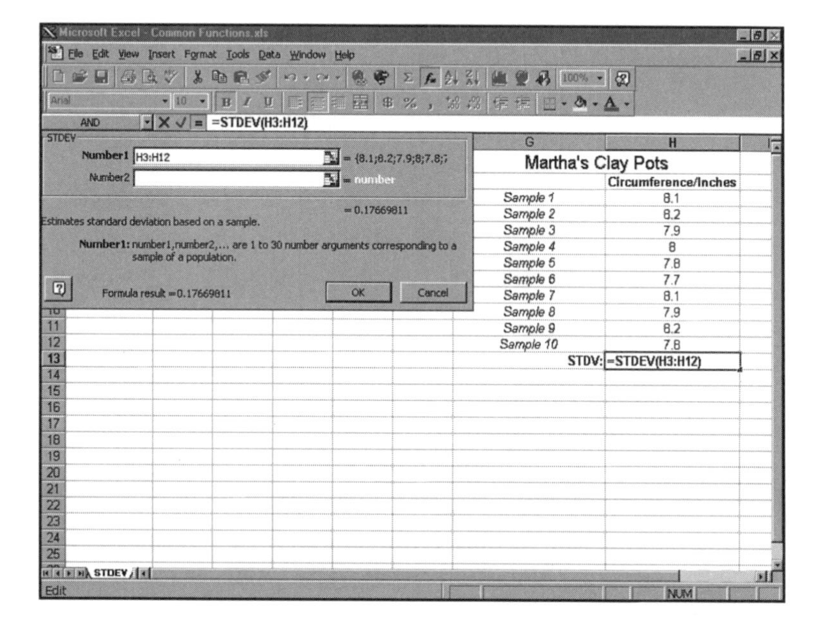

Fig. 10.10
With a standard deviation of less than two-tenths of an inch, these pots are more like precision tools.

The STDEV function only works for samples of a population. For entire populations, the calculation is different, and so is the function. Had the whole day's production of a hundred pots been measured, we would have used the STDEVP function.

Standard deviation is not the most intuitive concept around, but statisticians have come up with a general rule of thumb to help us get a grip on it. The rule of thumb says that for any set of values, more than 90% of them are within three standard deviations of the mean average of the values.

Add more functions? It's only logical

The IF function lets us apply logical tests to cells and return values of our choosing. For example:

```
=IF(C12>10,"Great","Lousy")
```

would give us `Great` whenever C12 was greater than 10, and `Lousy` whenever it wasn't.

Excel lets you put one function inside another to create more complicated decisions. IF is often joined with AND and OR for **nested** functions, in which one function is an argument in another function.

Let's say you've been following the stock of Shooting Star Corporation. If the stock price trades within a range of $20 to $25, you want to buy it. A price higher than $25 makes it too expensive. If the price falls below $20, you expect Shooting Star to keep falling and you don't want to risk buying it at all.

The AND function nested in the IF function helps make your decision clear. Plug in the current price, and the function tells you to buy or don't buy.

1 Start building the first function, IF. Select the cell where you want the `value_if_true` and `value_if_false` to appear and click the Paste Function button. Under Function Category, select Logical, and double-click IF in the Function Name box. The IF function dialog box pops up, as shown in Figure 10.11.

2 Click the formula bar Functions drop-down arrow (see Figure 10.12). If the function you want appears on the list, select it. Otherwise, select More Functions to open the Paste Function dialog box. In the Paste Function dialog box, select Logical from the Function Category list, then double-click AND under Function Name.

3 In the AND function dialog box, enter the conditions that have to be met by our nested function (see Figure 10.13).

4 Click in the formula bar and press End to move the insertion point to the end of the formula in progress. The IF function dialog box reappears.

5 Type **Buy** in the `Value_if_true` text box, and **Don't Buy** in the `Value_if_false` text box, as shown in Figure 10.14. There's no need to type the quotation marks shown in Figure 10.14—Excel supplies those automatically.

Fig. 10.11
Nesting functions begins with building the first function.

Click the formula bar Functions drop-down arrow to insert nested functions (functions used as arguments in another function)

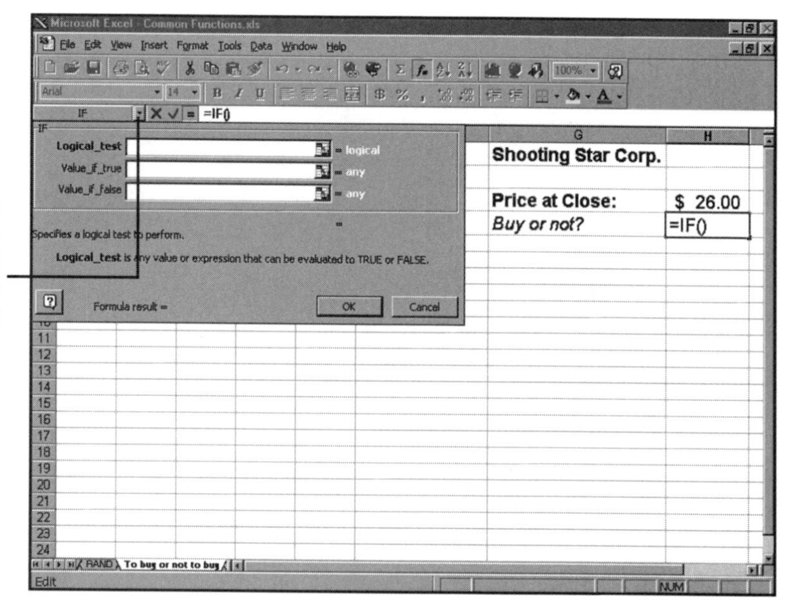

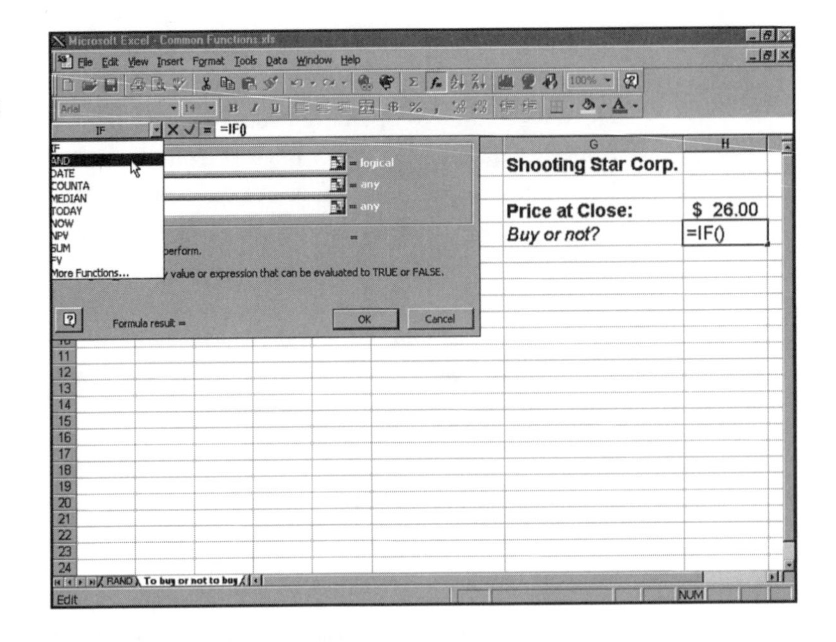

Fig. 10.12
If you've used the function you're going to nest recently, it appears on the list. Otherwise, choose More Functions.

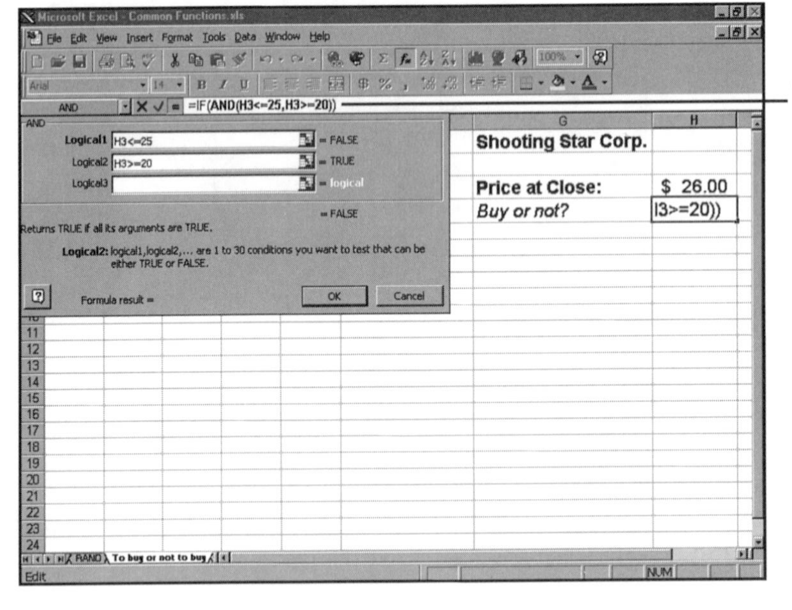

Click here and press End to return to the IF function dialog box

Fig. 10.13
The closing price in H3 has to be *<=25 and >=20* to meet our conditions.

6 The formula bar in Figure 10.14 shows the nearly completed nested function. Click OK in the IF function dialog box, and we're done.

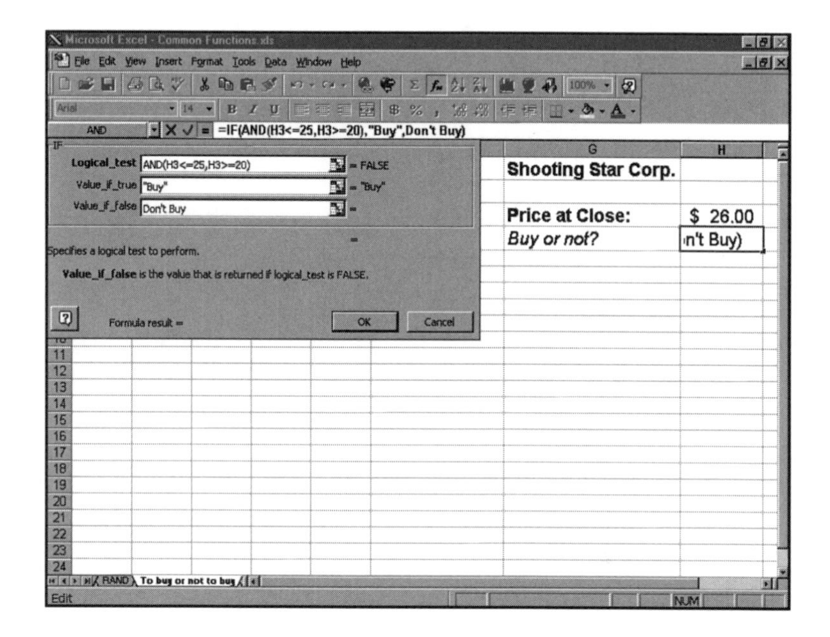

Fig. 10.14
The logical_test is the AND function and its arguments.

Shooting Star closing prices of $20 to $25 entered in C3 will return a value of `Buy`. Any other price, and our function returns `Don't Buy`.

RAND—because the world can be a random kind of place

Excel offers many more functions than we've covered here, but we're running out of room. We'll mention just one more. Among the mathematical functions is a handy tool for producing random numbers.

The RAND function takes no arguments, and it produces a new random number between 0 and 1 every time you recalculate the worksheet or press F9, as shown in Figure 10.15.

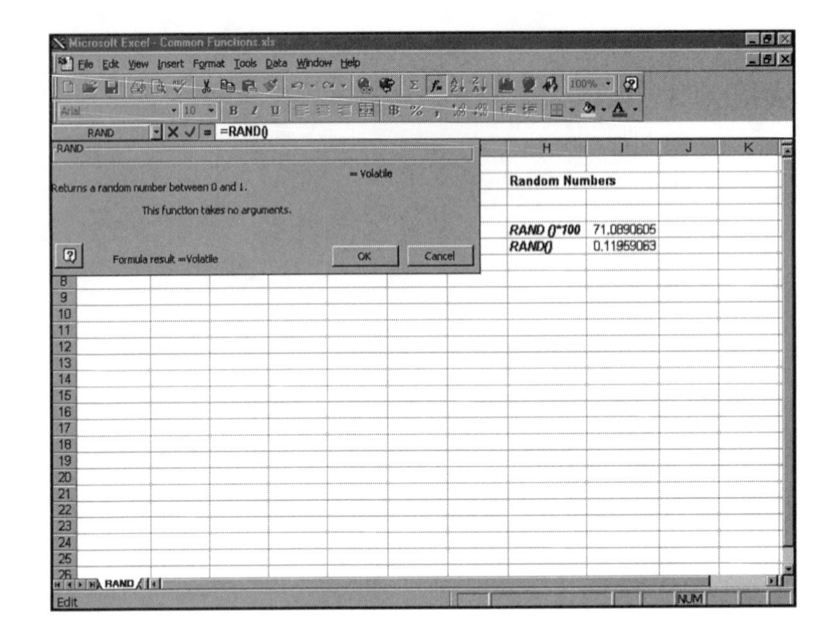

Fig. 10.15
To produce numbers greater than one, multiply the RAND function by 100.

To insert a random number in the selected cell, just click OK in the RAND dialog box.

TIP **To stop numbers produced by RAND from changing randomly** every time you recalculate, copy the numbers, then choose Edit, Paste Special. Choose Values to paste the values over the volatile number.

Part IV: Working with Charts

11 Charts Explained (in English)

In this chapter:

- **What do I need to know to create a chart?**
- **How do I know what type of chart to use?**
- **I want my chart right on the worksheet with my data**
- **Can I put my chart on another sheet?**
- **The Chart Wizard makes charting easy?**

Charts tell the story of your data in a single colorful picture. Creating an effective chart with Excel is a matter of point and click . . . .

Step out of an office building onto a city street and you're in a riot of traffic, crowds, and noise. It's hard to take it all in. Then ride the elevator to the fiftieth floor. With the city at your feet, you can take it all in at a glance.

Charts let you view your data from the fiftieth floor. Like the panorama from a high floor, charts provide insights you might never get at ground level. Up on 50, you can see the relationship between uptown and downtown, east side and west. Charts are good at illustrating those kinds of relationships in your data.

What do I need to know about charts?

Most charts arrange data between a vertical arm, the **y axis**, and a horizontal arm, the **x axis**. They're just like the rows and columns in Excel. And just as you locate data on a worksheet by its row and column position, each bit of data on a chart is positioned along the horizontal and vertical axes.

Those bits of data are called **data points**. Several data points make a data series. Remind you of anything? Right. Cells and ranges.

What should I know about axes?

The two chart axes represent **categories** and **values**. A category is the item you're charting, and a value is the amount of each item. By displaying categories and values along the x and y axes, charts show the relationships between them at a glance.

The y axis

The y axis is also the values axis. Why is that? The y axis on the following page shows sales in thousands of dollars. Each of those little lines along the scale, called **tick marks**, represents a value.

In our example, those values are a function of the month in which the sales took place. In January, we had $2,000,000 in sales. That figure varies month by month. In February, we had $2,150,000 in sales. You might say that each of those values depends on the month in which it occurred.

Anatomy of an Excel chart

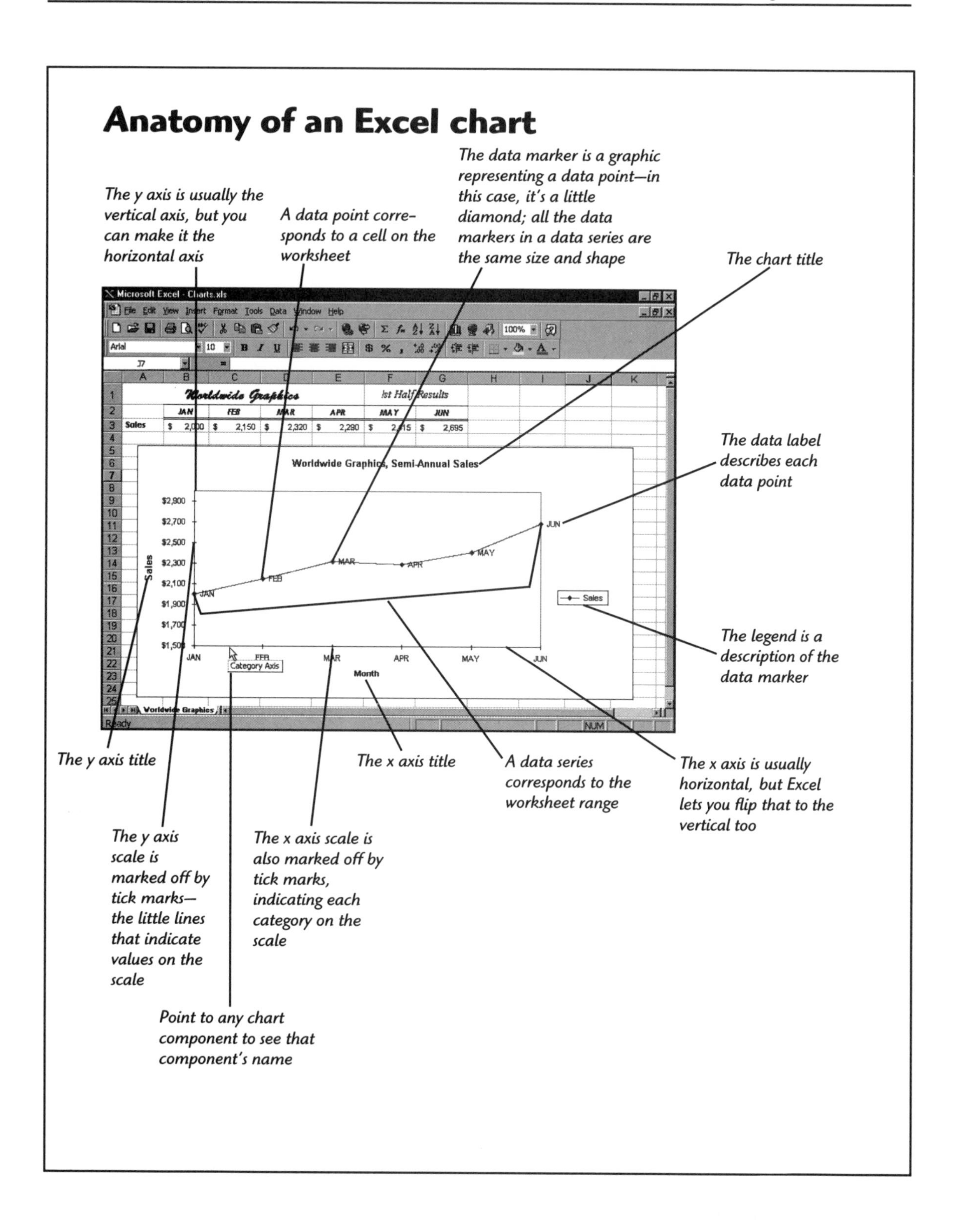

So each sales value varies, depending on the month. It's a dependent variable. And that's why the y, or values, axis is also said to represent the dependent variable.

The x axis

The x axis is the categories axis. It's also called the independent variable axis. You control it. Not that you can control the months of the year, but you do decide which months to include in your chart. You might make the same decision about which salespeople to include in a chart showing sales per salesperson. In that case, sales would be the **dependent variable**, salesperson the **independent variable**.

Where do I put my chart?

You have two choices. The chart on the previous page is an **embedded** chart. We stuck it right into the data worksheet. Embedded charts work well in reports, when you might want the data and the chart to sit side by side.

The other choice is to use what's called a **chart sheet**, in which you take a separate worksheet and stick the chart on it. It'll refer to data that's sitting on a different sheet. If you don't care about having the chart and the data side by side, or if you're going to turn your chart into an overhead projection or a slide, that's the way to go.

We'll take a stab at creating both types of charts.

What, now chart jargon?

If you find this whole notion of independent and dependent variables as counter-intuitive as I do, read on. After all, a month doesn't seem really *independent*. It varies according to the time of year. And a year really depends on the year that preceded it. And so on.

Here's one way to think about it: when you change an independent variable, the dependent variable's value also changes. It's not that the independent variable is really independent, just that the value of the dependent variable depends on *it*. I asked an engineer pal of mine about this, and he said that the terminology comes from lab experiments. As he put it, "The paradigm is not that useful in the world outside the laboratory." Took the words right out of my mouth.

Where do I start? See the Chart Wizard

Someday we'll all carry around computers the size of a wallet. Any time we have a decision to make or need information, expert advice and libraries of facts will be at our fingertips.

In the meantime, we have Excel's Chart Wizard. It guides us through the steps in creating a chart. All we have to do is select the data and make a few decisions along the way.

How do I choose the data for my chart?

The first question to ask when you create a chart is a basic one: what exactly am I charting? Excel makes the answer pretty basic, too: just select your data, as shown in Figure 11.1.

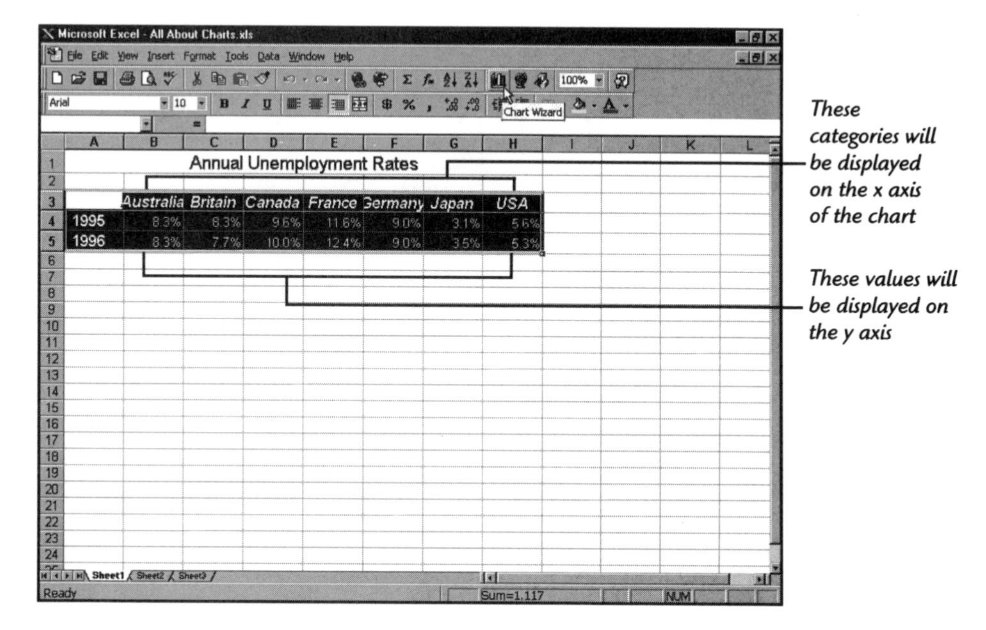

Fig. 11.1
The first step in building a chart: select the range enclosing your data.

What if I want to chart data that's not parked side by side?

Remember the nonadjacent ranges we looked at in Chapter 1? Select the first range, then select additional nonadjacent ranges by Ctrl+dragging. The Chart Wizard doesn't mind using nonadjacent ranges one bit.

If you want to include row and column titles in your chart (you probably do), include them in the selected range, but nothing you do here is final. Any data selections you make can be changed with ease in Step 2 of the Chart Wizard.

Different charts for different data

After you select your data, click the Chart Wizard button on the Standard toolbar. A dizzying selection of charts pops up, as shown in Figure 11.2.

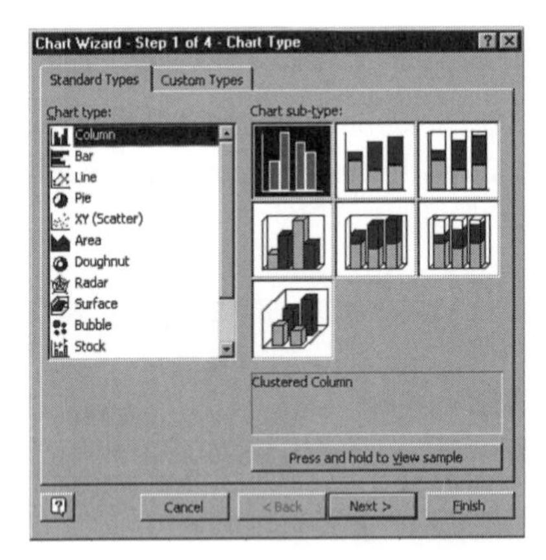

Fig. 11.2
Decisions, decisions. Picking the right chart for the right data isn't hard if you follow a few guidelines.

What kind of chart should you choose? There are 14 different standard chart types, and each basic type has a further selection of up to 10 subtypes. You'll also find a slew of additional charts with fancy formatting on the Custom Types tab of the Chart Wizard dialog box. So what do you do?

There's a short answer and a long answer. The short answer: pick the right chart for the type of data you're charting. But because that really doesn't get us much farther, keep reading.

Charts by default: column charts

The default is a choice of column charts (refer to Figure 11.2). Click a column Chart Sub-type, then click the Press and Hold to View Sample button to see how your data looks in that type of chart (see Figure 11.3).

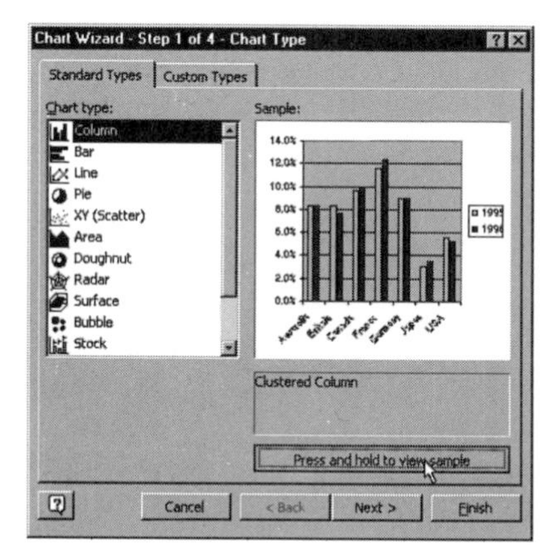

Fig. 11.3
The Chart Wizard's Sample window shows you if your choice of chart makes sense for the selected data.

Q&A ***Why is the Chart Wizard's Sample window blank?***

You see a sample chart only if you select your data first. If your Sample window is empty, click Next in the Chart Wizard dialog box. In the Chart Wizard's Step 2, click the Data Range tab, then select the range holding your data. The Chart Wizard dialog box remains in view as you select the range on the worksheet. Click Back to return to Step 1, and you'll see a sample chart when you click the Press and Hold to View Sample button.

Column charts are good for showing comparisons between distinct items in one time period, or changes in distinct items over several periods. You might use them for comparing annual sales for each of the last five years. You can throw in expenses, too, and compare sales and expenses side by side for each of those five years.

Bar charts

Bar charts are like column charts, except that the axes are flipped around. The x or category axis becomes vertical, and the y or value axis is laid out horizontally (see Figure 11.4).

Bar charts are used like column charts. Because those horizontal bars look a little like they're in a race against each other, bar charts are good for illustrating values of different items in one time period. Which salesperson has the most sales in a single month? A bar chart is good for showing that kind of thing.

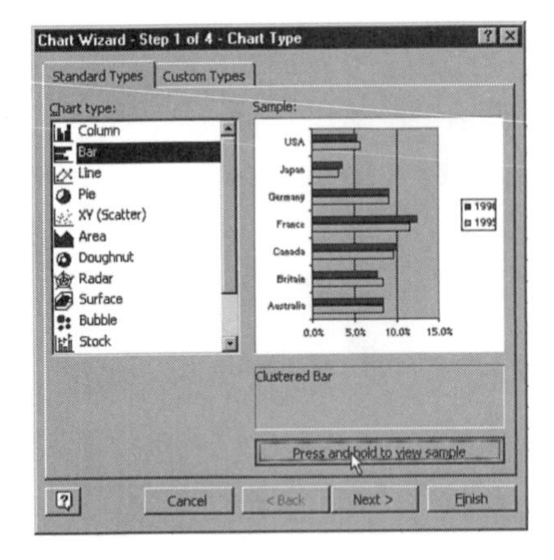

Fig. 11.4
Bar charts are close cousins of column charts, except that their axes are reversed.

Cylinders, pyramids, and cone charts

Bar and column charts are simple and effective, but they have a "been there, done that" quality; they're so widely used that you might find them a shade dull. Excel has some nifty variations on the bar and column theme. Like bar and column charts, **cylinder, pyramid,** and **cone** charts show comparisons between distinct items in one time period, or changes in distinct items over several periods. The unusual shapes of the cone, cylinder, and pyramid data series add a little drama to your data. Figure 11.5 shows the three chart types.

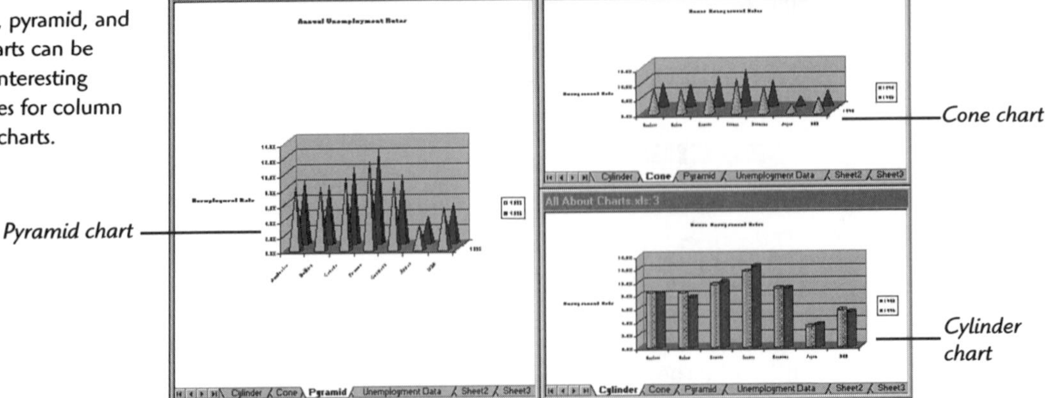

Fig. 11.5
Cylinder, pyramid, and cone charts can be used as interesting substitutes for column and bar charts.

Line and Stock charts

Line charts are good at illustrating changes over time, in one item or several. The chart shown in the Anatomy of an Excel Chart on page 219 is an example of a line chart.

How's your stock doing over time? How's it doing compared to the S&P 500? That's the idea behind **stock charts**. Closely related to line charts, stock charts show changes over time (see Figure 11.6).

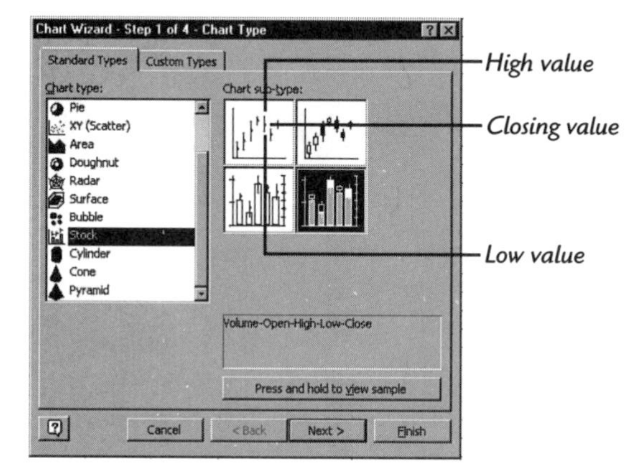

Fig. 11.6
Stock charts display the good (or bad) news about a stock at a glance.

Plain English, please!

The sample chart in Figure 11.6 displays a **high-low bar**. Those small vertical lines each represent a specific time period. The top of the line shows a high value for the period, the bottom the low value, and the little horizontal mark the closing value.

You'll see this kind of chart in *The Wall Street Journal* all the time, illustrating the performance of the Dow Jones Averages. It's handy, because it simultaneously shows the performance of the Dow on one day, and over the course of many days.

Food for thought: pie charts

Want to see just how much of your budget is getting eaten up by overhead? Create a **pie chart**. They're a great way of dramatizing that sort of problem. Pie charts show the relationship between the whole and the parts. Total budget and individual budget items, a whole investment portfolio and specific investments—pie charts answer "How much of the whole is this part?" questions.

If you want to highlight one or more parts of the whole, you can break up a pie chart like some of the pie chart sub-types in shown Figure 11.7.

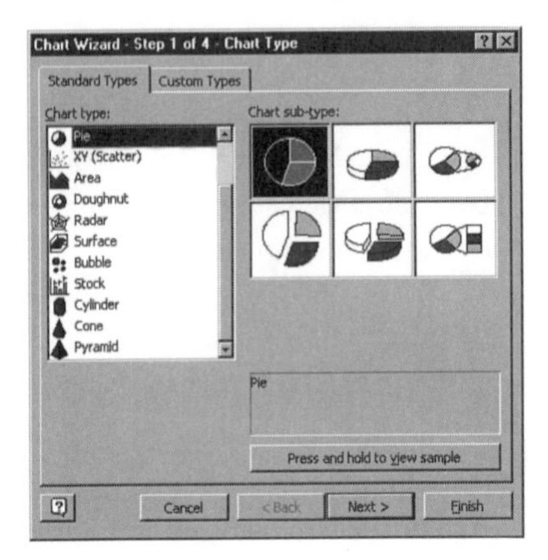

Fig. 11.7
Use pie charts for comparing the parts with the whole.

Q&A *Why doesn't my pie chart have slices?*

Pie charts can only show one data series. Think of data in a table: pie charts can show one row of multiple columns of values, or multiple rows of one column of values. They can't show multiple rows *and* multiple columns of values. For example, you could illustrate your different budget components in one year, but not over several years. Or you could show your entire budget totals over several years, but not the individual budget components in each of those years. If you try to illustrate more than one data series in a pie chart, you can wind up with a sliceless pie.

No glazed looks: doughnut charts

Apart from the fact that they constitute another major food group, **doughnut charts** are similar to pie charts in other ways. They also show how various parts are proportional to the whole.

There's one big difference. Doughnuts can show different data series by adding concentric rings. In Figure 11.8, the makeup of a portfolio is shown in two different years, one year in each ring.

Area charts

Area charts are like line charts, and are used to show similar things—change over time. Area charts also share a trait of pie charts, in that they show proportional comparisons. Say you're tracking how many units of soap powder and liquid soap you've shipped over time. The top line represents total units shipped. The two areas illustrate soap powder and liquid soap units (see Figure 11.9).

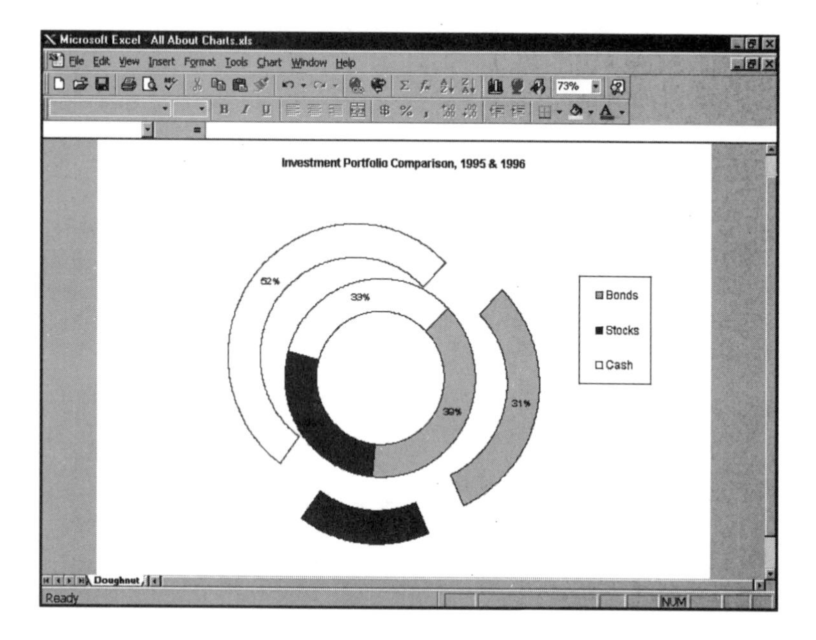

Fig. 11.8
Doughnuts can show multiple data series, but I find them hard to read.

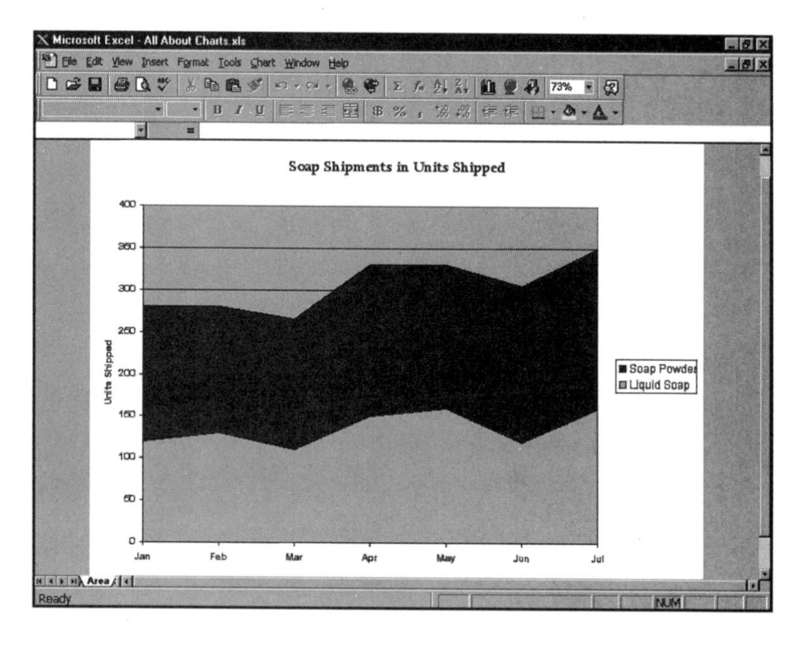

Fig. 11.9
Area charts illustrate change over time and proportional relationships between parts and wholes.

Radar and scatter charts

Radar charts look a little like rooftop TV antennas after they've been hit by lightning. Except for some specialized applications, you might find them just about as useful. They show relationships between different data series, and between each series and all the series, all at the same time. With that much going on at once, they can be difficult to interpret. Radar charts are sometimes used for complex project management applications.

Scatter charts are widely used in statistics. They can illustrate the strength of the relationship between data points, and the strength of the relationship between the data points and a mean value.

Figure 11.10 shows a side-by-side view of a radar chart and a scatter chart, also called a scattergram.

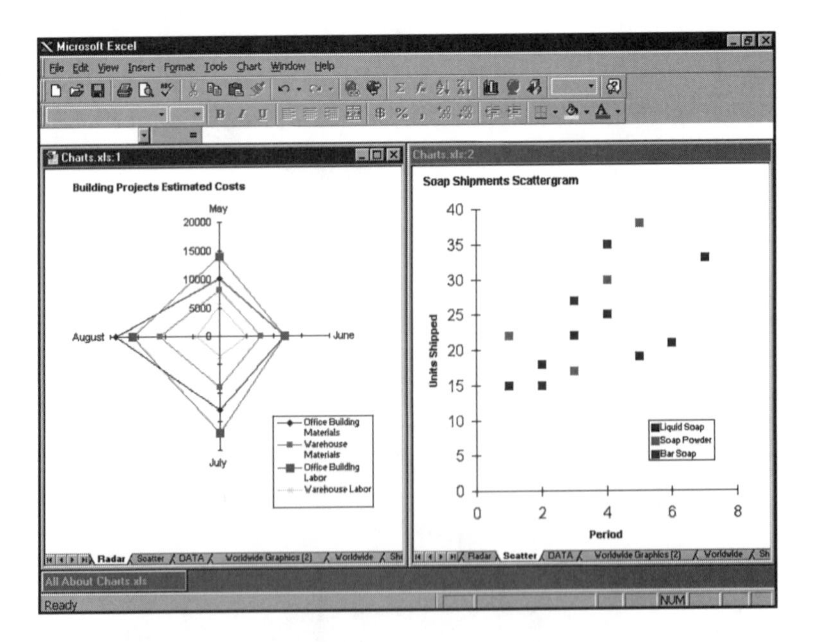

Fig. 11.10
Scatter charts are good for showing trends; radar charts aren't the easiest to interpret.

Both of the charts in Figure 11.10 were created with the As New Sheet option in Step 4 of the Chart Wizard. That option puts a chart on its own chart sheet. To size chart sheets to fill a window, as I did in Figure 11.9, choose Tools, Options and click the Chart tab. Select Chart Sizes with Window Frame. Now, whatever the size of your window, the chart will fill it.

If you do select the Chart Sizes with Window Frame option, resizing your windows might distort the chart. If that happens, you can move titles and legends around and adjust the size of the chart plot area to eliminate the distorted look. To adjust the size of a chart on its own chart sheet, choose File, Page Setup. Click the Chart tab, then click Custom under Printed Chart Size. Click OK, and drag the frame that pops up around the chart to resize it.

Scatter charts also show change over time, which makes them kin to line charts. When do you use line charts and when should you use a scatter chart instead?

- Use line charts to track changes over time that are measured in regular intervals, like evenly-spaced days, weeks, or months.
- Use scatter charts if the time intervals are not evenly spaced. If you're tracking shipments every day, but certain items aren't shipped at all on particular days, use a scatter chart. It shows irregular intervals, whereas a line chart would give a misleading impression of continuity.

Bubble trouble? Not with bubble charts

Like scatter charts, Excel's new bubble charts show the relationship between different data series. Bubble charts simultaneously display data values; the bigger the bubble, the higher the value (see Figure 11.13 for an example of a bubble chart).

3-D charts

The difference between most 2-D and 3-D charts is cosmetic. 3-D charts look cooler, but their uses are similar to their 2-D cousins.

The exception is the family of 3-D charts called **surface charts**. They're used to illustrate relationships between more than one variable, or among large amounts of data that would be tough to interpret otherwise. Like a topographical map, they show highs and lows in a big set of data.

Figure 11.11 shows a surface chart.

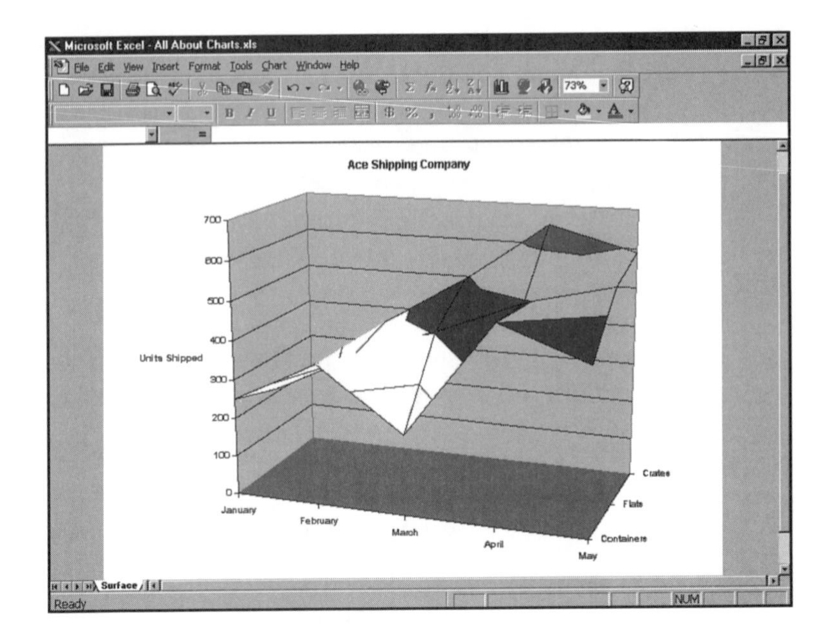

Fig. 11.11
Surface charts can illustrate big data sets with clarity, and they look cool, too.

Custom charts for fancy formatting fast

Click the Custom Types tab of the Chart Wizard Step 1 dialog box for a selection of charts that come ready-made with fancy formatting. All the Custom Types are variations on the standard charts, with the addition of colored backgrounds and unusually shaped data series. Figure 11.12 shows one custom option.

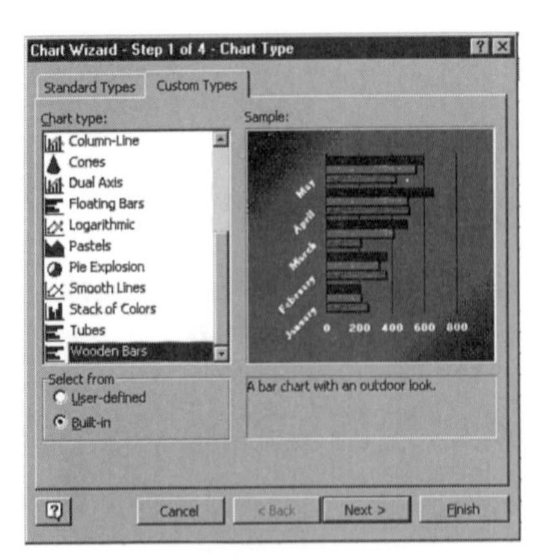

Fig. 11.12
Wooden bars make an ideal charting choice for lumber companies.

Help! I still don't know what chart type to use

Variety is a good thing, but Excel's Chart Wizard offers so many choices of chart types that you might find yourself undecided after exploring a few options. Fortunately, charts are one area where the Office Assistant really shines. If you want to dig a little deeper into this question of what chart to use for your data, call on the Office Assistant for further assistance:

1 Select a chart from the Chart Type list in the Standard Types tab in Step 1 of the Chart Wizard.

2 Click the Office Assistant button in the Chart Wizard dialog box and choose Help with this feature in the Office Assistant balloon that pops up.

3 Choose Example of the Selected Type in the next Office Assistant balloon. The Examples of Chart Types window appears (see Figure 11.13).

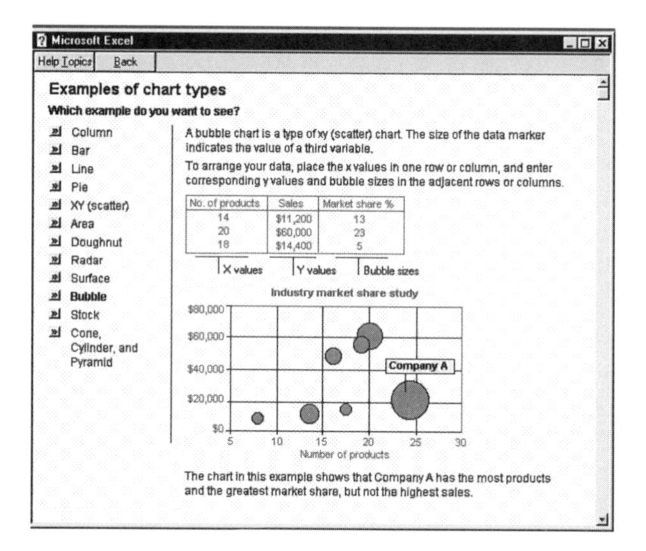

Fig. 11.13
Click any of the chart types in the window to see more examples.

The Examples of Chart Types window shows how each chart type looks with sample data, and the different kinds of data that each type is used for. If you're in doubt about the right chart for your data, study the samples and examples that the Office Assistant keeps up its sleeve.

I want my chart and my data side by side

Charts make terrific illustrations in a report because they dramatize and clarify the raw numbers. Figure 11.1 showed unemployment rates in various industrial countries for 1995 and 1996. Fascinating, no? OK, now let's put them in a chart and see if we can't liven things up a little.

1 If you still have the Chart Wizard open, click Cancel or press Esc to close it and start over. Select the range you want to chart, then click the Chart Wizard button.

2 Step 1 of the Chart Wizard pops up. Just to see what happens, choose Pie from the Chart Type list. Click the Press and Hold to View Sample button. As you can see in Figure 11.14, this is not exactly what we want.

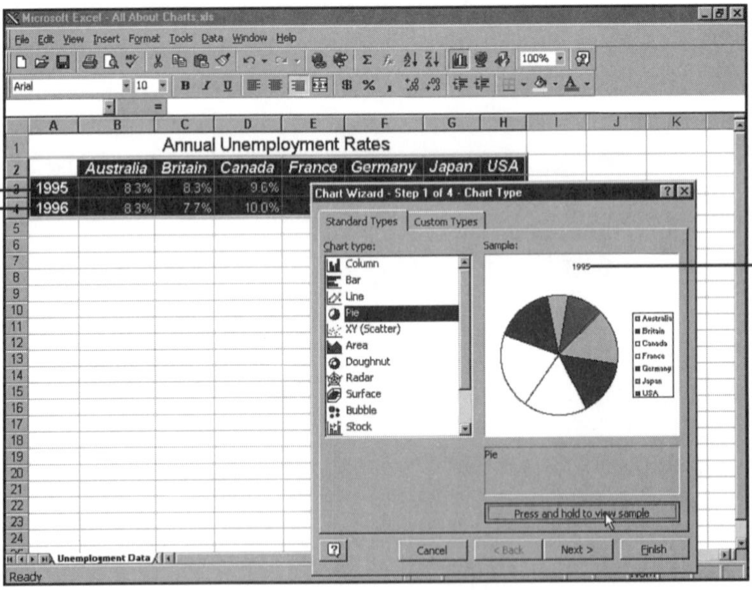

Fig. 11.14
Because pie charts take only one data series, this chart can't show our year-to-year comparison.

Our data includes both 1995 and 1996 series

Because a pie chart can only handle one data series at a time, only 1995 is charted

3 We'll choose another type of chart. We're comparing two data series, unemployment rates in 1995 and 1996, and we have seven distinct countries to look at. We don't care about comparing parts to the whole, and we're only dealing with two time periods. A column, bar, cone, cylinder, or pyramid chart would work here. Select any of those options from the Chart Type list, then double-click one of the Chart Sub-types. I've selected a 3-D Clustered Bar chart in the following figures.

4 That gets us Step 2 of the Chart Wizard. The range we've selected is displayed in the Data Range text box. Here's the place to select a new range if you need to.

5 Our range is the entire table, which is what we want. Click the Series tab of the Chart Wizard dialog box to view the different data series in the selected range. To remove data series from the chart in progress, make your selection on the Series list and click Remove (see Figure 11.15.).

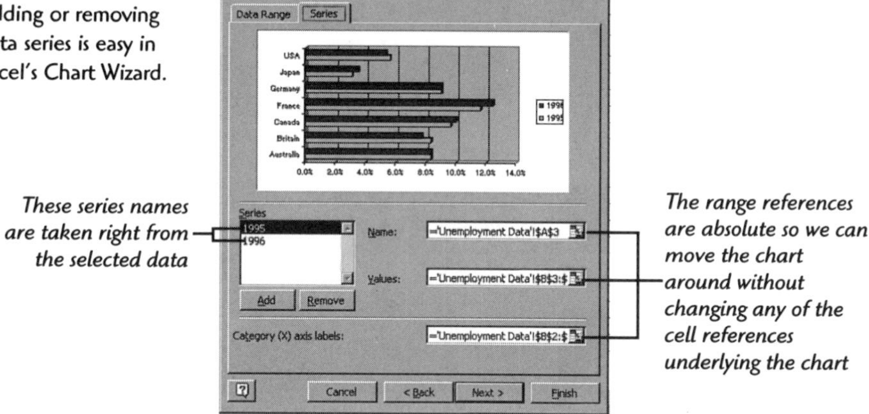

Fig. 11.15
Adding or removing data series is easy in Excel's Chart Wizard.

6 Click Next for Step 3 of the Chart Wizard (see Figure 11.16). Here's where you add a legend if the Wizard hasn't already. You'll also want to label your axes and title the chart. A good chart is self-explanatory. If it makes you scratch your head and wonder what it means, labeling it will probably solve the problem.

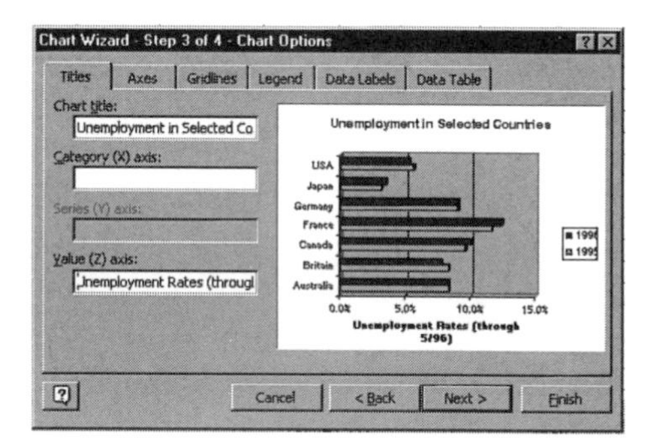

Fig. 11.16
Charts without titles and labels don't say much; add them here.

7 Click Next again for Step 4 of the Chart Wizard. Do you want your chart on its own worksheet, or embedded on the worksheet with your data? We want the latter, so choose As Object In the selected chart sheet, as shown in Figure 11.17.

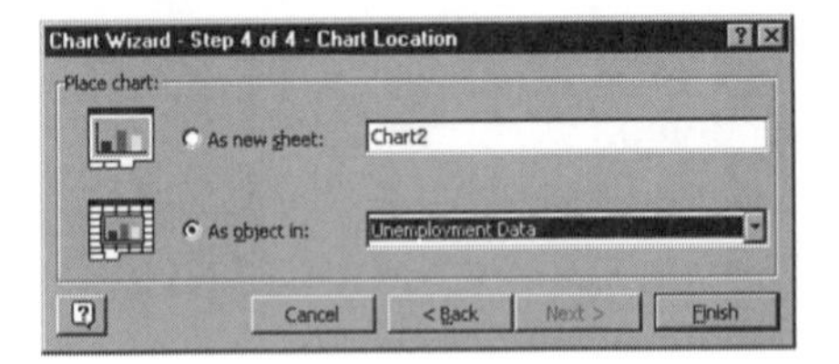

Fig. 11.17
Charts placed on the worksheet with the data let you see the number detail and the big picture illustration at the same time.

8 Now click Finish. Figure 11.18 shows the final result, complete with chart title and x axis title added in Step 3 of the Chart Wizard.

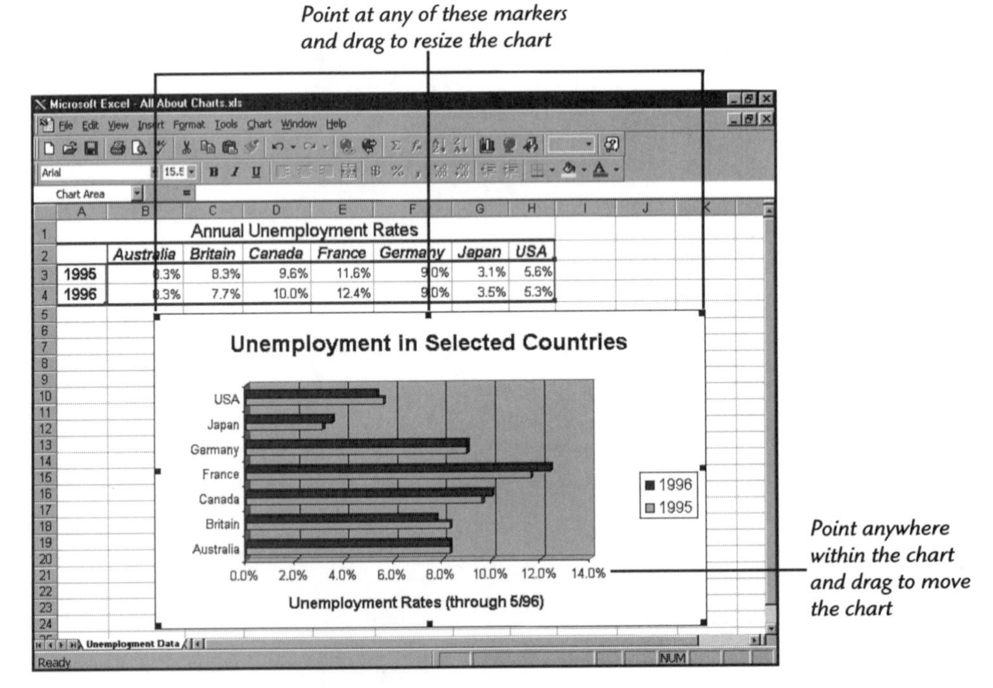

Fig. 11.18
The chart makes the numbers a little more interesting. It also shows that the Japanese could teach the French a lot about keeping unemployment rates down.

Click anywhere outside the chart to deselect it and get rid of the handles—those black markers around the chart which you drag to resize and move charts.

Why did the Chart Wizard give me numbers for my x axis labels?

The Chart Wizard was looking for your axis labels in the wrong row. Just tell it to look again. Click the border around the finished chart to select it, then click the Chart Wizard button. Click Next to go to of the Chart Wizard. Click the Series tab of the Chart Wizard dialog box, then click the Collapse Dialog Box button in the Category (x) Axis Labels text box (that's the little button at the right end of the text box). Select the range that covers your categories. Click the Collapse Dialog Box button again to return to the Chart Wizard, click Next twice, and then click Finish to save your changes.

Putting the chart on another worksheet

If you don't need your chart on the same worksheet with your data, put the chart on its own sheet. A chart sheet fills up the Excel window. There's more room to edit the chart and, because the chart is bigger, you'll see it more clearly.

For a chart on a separate chart sheet:

1. Select the range to chart.

2. Click the Chart Wizard button and work your way through the Chart Wizard steps.
3. When you get to Step 4 of the Chart Wizard, choose As New Sheet for your chart location and click Finish. Excel inserts the new chart in a sheet labeled Chart 1.

How do I change this chart?

After you have the chart on the worksheet, you might not like what you see. Right-click anywhere inside the Chart Area to pop up the shortcut menu shown in Figure 11.19.

From there, you can change anything from the chart type, to the axis labels, to the colors Excel has chosen. For in-depth coverage of chart formatting and modifying, see Chapter 12.

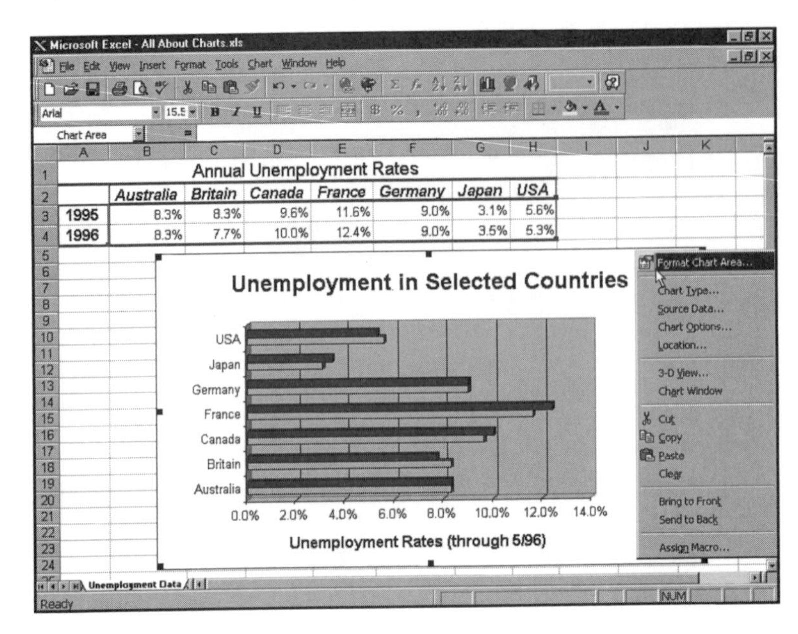

Fig. 11.19
To get this shortcut menu, you have to right-click the Chart Area; right-clicking different parts of the chart pops up different shortcut menus.

12 Editing Charts

In this chapter:

- **I need a different type of chart!**
- **The Chart toolbar makes life even easier**
- **How do I change the insides of this chart?**
- **I want different colors and patterns in my chart**
- **Can I add data to the chart?**

Useful charts say what we mean them to say, and that usually requires a little tweaking. With Excel's chart-editing tools, it's easy to get your chart exactly right . . . .

Edward Gibbon finished *The Decline and Fall of the Roman Empire* more than 200 years ago. It's considered a model of flawless writing and scholarship to this day. Gibbon was a perfectionist, but he didn't do much editing. In fact, he took pride in sending his rough first drafts straight to the printer.

Still, from the time he got the idea to the day he wrote his last sentence, it took Gibbon more than 20 years to finish his masterpiece. Although we want our charts to be perfect, we don't have quite as much time on our hands.

Because Excel makes editing charts as easy as creating them, we can make changes to cook up a perfect chart in no time at all.

I picked the wrong type of chart!

Ordered a doughnut when a pie is what you really wanted? Those 2-D columns look a little flat? Change 'em. The biggest alteration you can make to a chart is changing the chart type. That's also about the easiest change to make.

Do you walk to work, drive, or take the bus? Same destination, different ways of getting there. Excel gives you a similar choice when it comes to modifying charts. Just pick the one that suits you.

Excel has a box full of charts

To see all the available chart types, right-click your chart and choose Chart Type on the shortcut menu. That pops up the Chart Type dialog box, with menus of chart types and sub-types. If the Chart Type dialog box looks familiar, that's because it's the Chart Wizard Step 1 under a new name. Figure 12.1 shows the Chart Type dialog box.

Select a new Chart Type, then double-click any of the Chart Sub-types to instantly transform your chart.

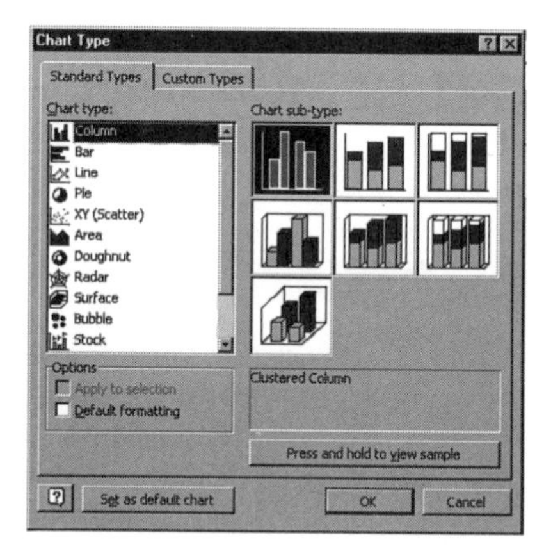

Fig. 12.1
The Chart Type dialog box offers a choice of all of Excel's charts.

Click the Chart toolbar for express service

Sometimes you just order the special instead of staring at a menu, especially if your lunch hour is short. For speedy chart transformations, call up the Chart toolbar: right-click any displayed toolbar and choose Chart on the toolbar menu. To change your chart, click the Chart Type drop-down arrow on the Chart toolbar, as shown in Figure 12.2.

Click any of those tiny images of charts, and your chart is instantly transformed into a different type. No questions asked, no dialog boxes to puzzle about. Not all the subtypes are displayed, but this is the fastest way to change your chart.

We got the 3-D Pyramid chart in Figure 12.3 with just one click.

If you're not sure which chart type is the best choice for your data, the toolbar lets you find the right one by speedy trial and error. And if no one is breathing down your neck for results, it's fun to play around with, too.

The Chart button next to the arrow on the toolbar changes to show your last selection.

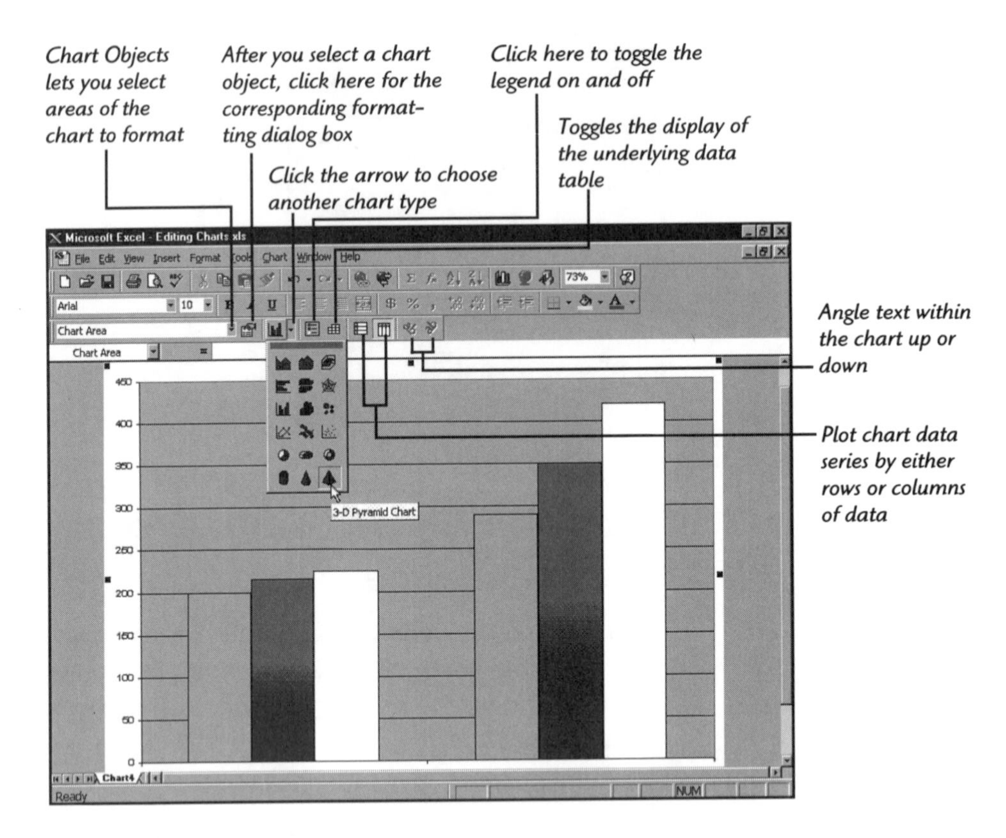

Fig. 12.2
The Chart toolbar has all the tools you'll need to format your chart.

Object lesson: making changes inside the chart

Step into a museum, and you find rooms filled with clearly labeled objects. Each object—statue, painting, or vase—has its place. And a label describing it.

A chart is a bit like that. It's made up of objects with labels. The difference is that most things on the chart can be changed. The axes, data markers, tick marks, titles, and legends are all objects. You can alter their size, color, scale, and font any way you like. Try doing that in a museum.

Changing the chart and plot areas, and anything else in your chart

The two biggest objects on a chart are the background, or **chart area**, and the **plot area**, the space between the two axes.

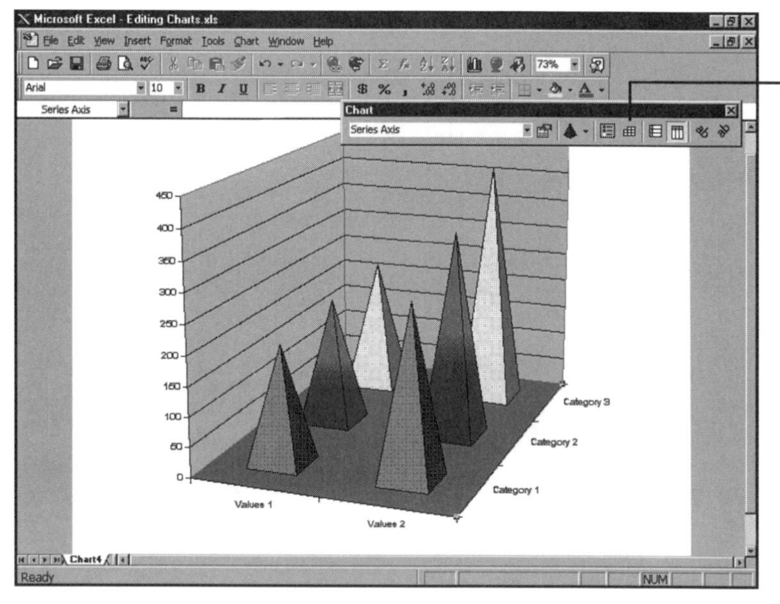

Fig. 12.3
Same data, different look. Changing the chart with the Chart toolbar is a fast way to get the best result through experimentation.

There are three ways to make changes to the chart and plot areas, and to any object in a chart:

- You can change the colors, patterns, shapes, and the formatting of any other chart object by double-clicking the object. For example, move the pointer between the axes and double-click to format the plot area; point anywhere outside the axes but within the background to make changes there. Double-clicking an object pops up the Format dialog box for that object.

- Point at any object in the chart, and a little Help Prompt appears with the object's name. Now right-click for the shortcut menu, and choose Format (see Figure 12.6). That gets you the Format dialog box for the object.

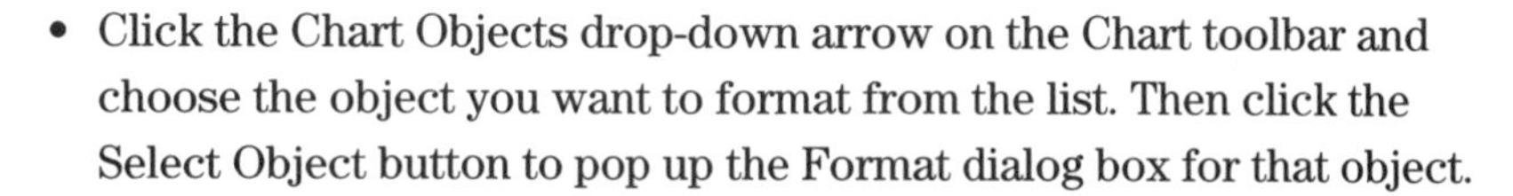

- Click the Chart Objects drop-down arrow on the Chart toolbar and choose the object you want to format from the list. Then click the Select Object button to pop up the Format dialog box for that object.

All three routes take you to the same place: the chart object's formatting dialog box. Choose the method that's most comfortable. Double-clicking an object to format it is the more direct method, but it's not always easy to double-click exactly what you want. That's especially true in a small or crowded chart. In situations like that, use the Chart toolbar to select and format precisely the object you're after. Or use my favorite method: right-click the object and choose Format from the shortcut menu.

Figure 12.4 shows you what we're talking about.

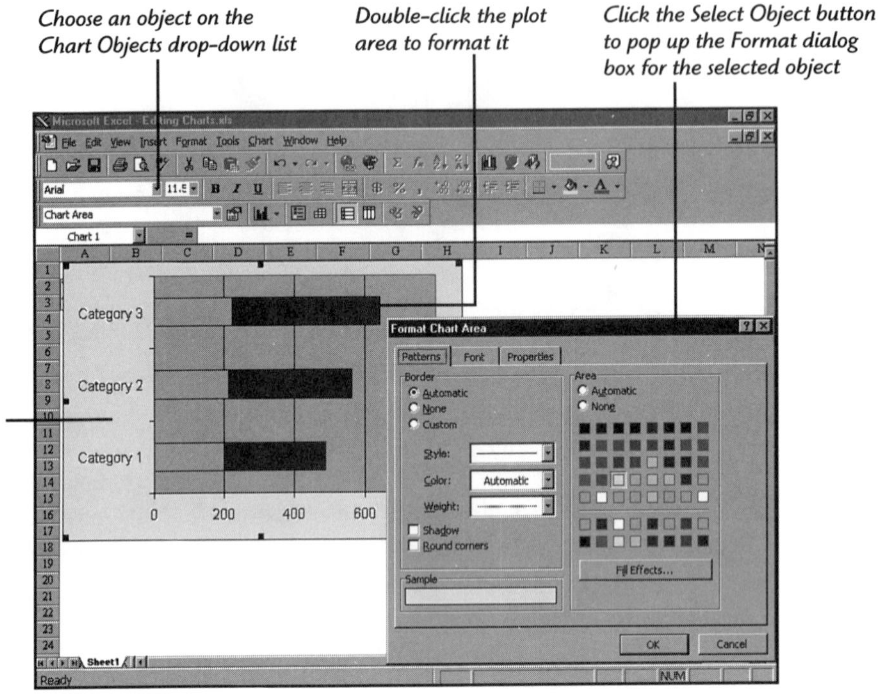

Fig. 12.4
Double-clicking any chart object pops up Format dialog boxes, where you can change colors, borders, or patterns.

3-D plot and chart areas

In 3-D charts, you get a few extra objects to format. There are plot and chart areas, and walls and floors inside the plot area. All can be enhanced with patterns and colors. Just double-click any one of them to bring up the Format dialog box, or right-click for the shortcut menu shown in Figure 12.5.

Selecting objects to format

Those columns or bars or lines you've created out of your data are pictures of data series, and they're made up of data points. They correspond to the cells and ranges holding the data they represent.

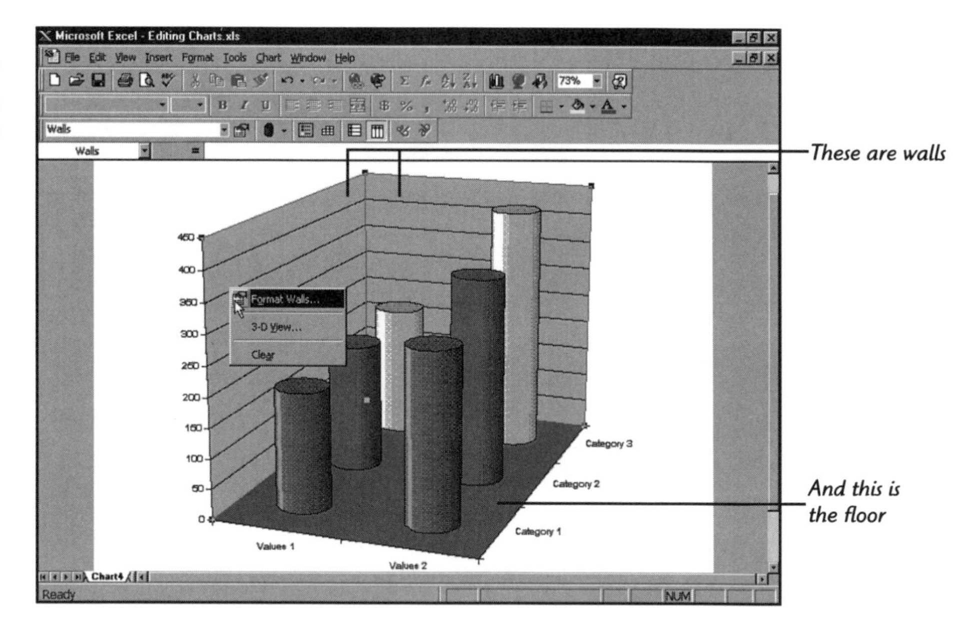

Fig. 12.5
You can splash a lot of color onto a 3-D chart by formatting the walls and floor. Just remember that your more startling effects may not look so great in black-and-white print.

They're also objects, and they can be colored, labeled, and even moved.

The **data markers**—those columns, lines, or bars in your charts—can be formatted one data marker at a time by selecting and formatting a data point. Or format all the markers for a data series at the same time by selecting and formatting a data series. The idea is the same in both cases. It's just a question of where you point:

- To format a data series, double-click anywhere along the line, or inside the bar, column, cone, or other object. Data series handles appear as little squares, and the Format dialog box for the selected object pops up. Or right-click an object for the shortcut menu and select Format Data Series from the menu.

- To format a data point, click once along the object to get the data series handles. Then click a data marker once to select the individual data point. Now right-click for the shortcut menu and choose Format Data Point, or double-click the selected data point.

Figure 12.6 might make it all more comprehensible.

Fig. 12.6
Formatting data points and data series requires some accurate clicking, but it can be done with a little care.

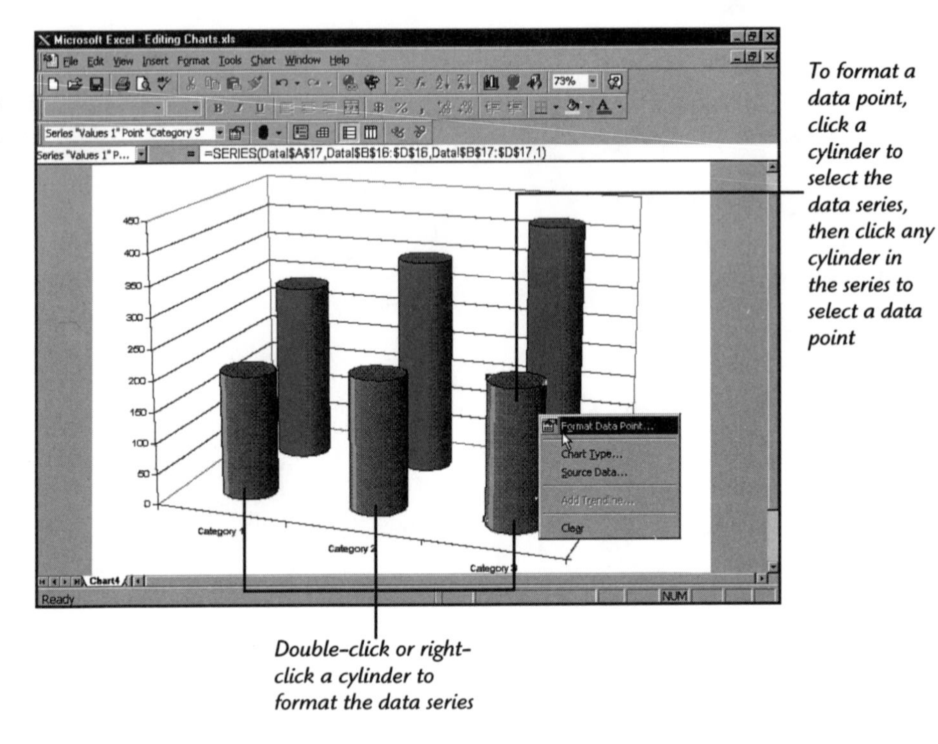

If your clicking is off, you'll wind up selecting grid lines, or chart areas, or walls. No disaster, but you'll have to try again.

TIP **To deselect any chart object after you've clicked it, just press Esc.**

Selecting titles and legends

The same idea applies to selecting all the labels inside the chart. Just point at a title or the legend and double-click to get the Format dialog box. Or right-click for the shortcut menu.

Formatting objects

After you select an object, there are plenty of things you can do with it. Some alterations will be for cosmetics, some for clarity. Both varieties can make your chart more useful.

Changing the axes

Maybe one of your products didn't make it out of the starting gate in time and recorded zero sales for the month. A salesperson misses a couple of weeks with the flu and has no sales. As a result, your chart shows a blank (see Figure 12.7).

Microsoft Excel - Editing Charts.xls
Data Series with Zero Value
Category 1 Category 2
Values 3
Values 2
Values 1
0 50 100 150 200 250 300 350 400
Value Axis
Zero Value
Ready
NUM

Double-click here to format the y (values) axis

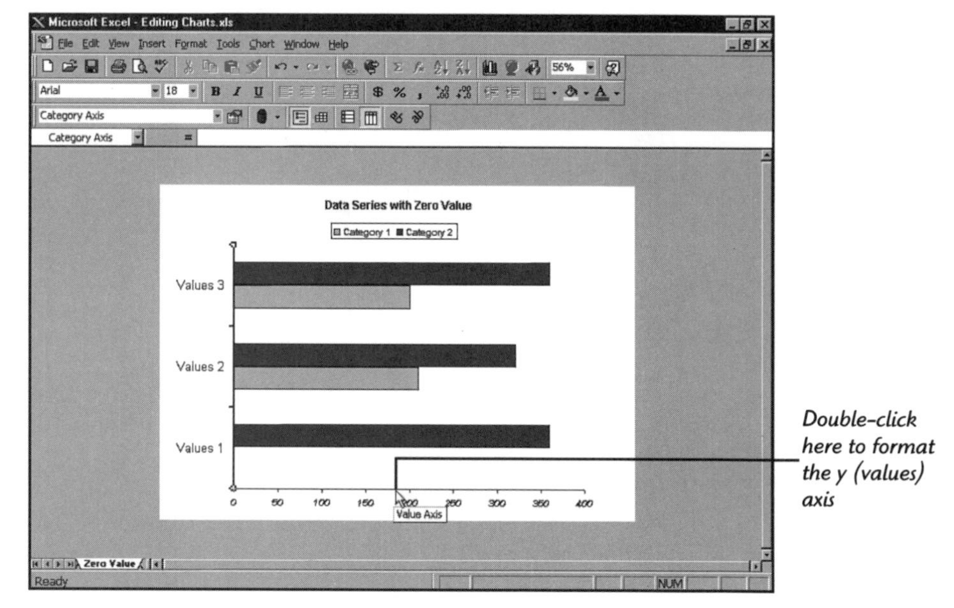

Fig. 12.7
Charting data series with zero values gives this kind of result: a bar chart with a missing bar.

It's easy to fix. Just change the scale of the axes. Double-click the y (values) axis to pop up the Format Axis dialog box, as shown in Figure 12.8.

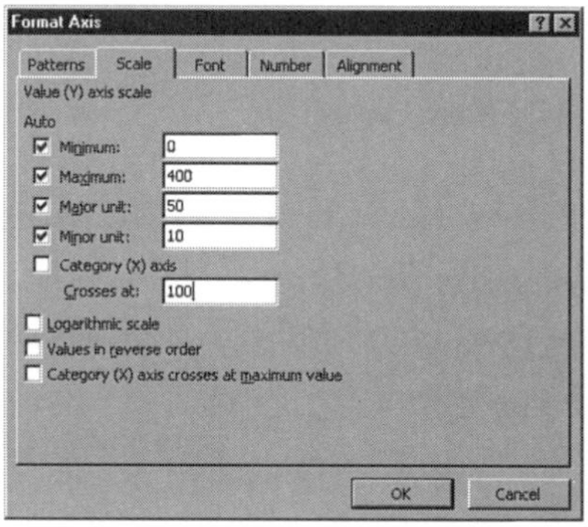

Format Axis
Patterns Scale Font Number Alignment
Value (Y) axis scale
Auto
Minimum: 0
Maximum: 400
Major unit: 50
Minor unit: 10
Category (X) axis
Crosses at: 100
Logarithmic scale
Values in reverse order
Category (X) axis crosses at maximum value
OK Cancel

Fig. 12.8
The Format Axis dialog box. Click the Scale tab to change the axis scaling.

By default, Excel crosses the axes at zero. Click in the Category (X) Axis Crosses At text box, and type in a new value. The x axis gets moved to cross the y axis at whatever value you set, making zero values stand out, as shown in Figure 12.9.

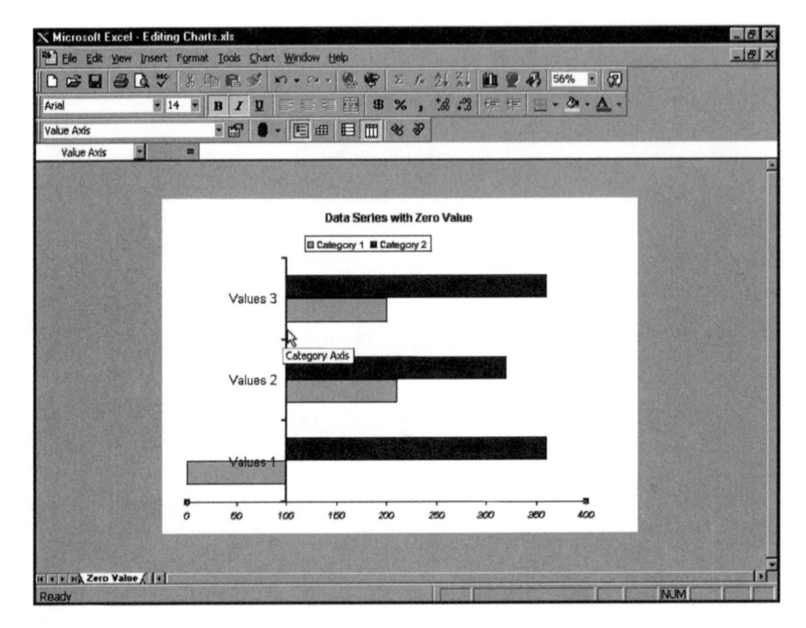

Fig. 12.9
Setting the x axis to cross the y axis at 100 makes zero values stand out. Just make sure your readers know you've moved the axis.

To let chart readers know you've moved it, double-click the X (categories) axis and click the Patterns tab in the Format Axis dialog box. Change the Weight, Color, or Style of the line to make it stand out.

Other axes changes

While you're visiting the Format Axis dialog box, select the other tabs to change the font or the number formatting.

Why are all my columns the same height?

You're charting small changes in values. To fix it, adjust the y axis scale. Double-click the y axis and click the Scale tab. Then enter a smaller range in the Minimum and Maximum text boxes.

Misleading charts do just that: change the y axis scale to exaggerate small changes. If you change the y axis scale, do it in modest increments. And if you see a chart for an investment that looks too good to be true, take a careful look at the y axis scale.

Changing the orientation of a 3-D chart

Take a look at the chart in Figure 12.10. The cylinders in the foreground are hiding the ones in the background. It's a common occurrence when you choose a 3-D chart of this type for multiple data series.

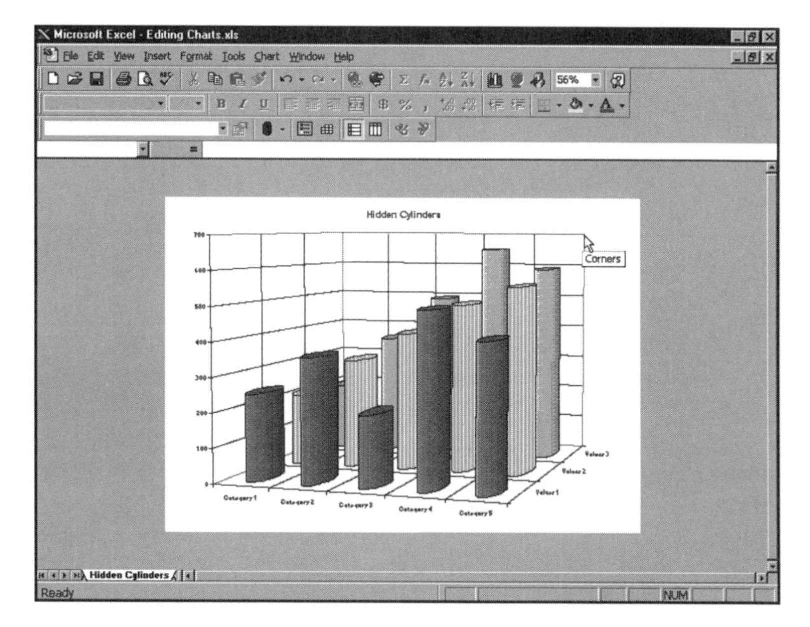

Fig. 12.10
When the foreground objects obscure background objects, you can't see the trees for the forest.

You could chose another type of chart (with this data, that might not be such a bad idea). But if you're wedded to a 3-D chart of this type, you can fix the "visibility" problem.

Point at any outer corner of the walls or floor of the plot area; the little Help Prompt appears and reads `Corners`. Now click. You'll get square black handles at each of the corners. Point at any of the handles, and the pointer becomes a crosshair. Drag with the crosshair, and the chart becomes a wire frame image that you can rotate in any direction, as shown in Figure 12.11.

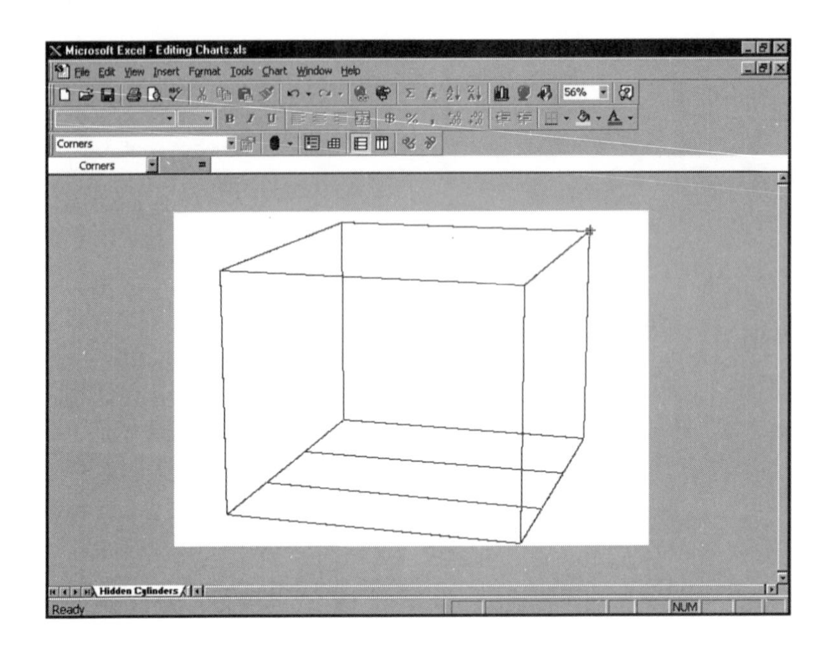

Fig. 12.11
Rotate the wire frame image of the chart in any direction. If you drag one of the handles out of sight, grab another one.

Release the mouse button, and the chart snaps back into view. From a different angle, we can see all the cylinders, as shown in Figure 12.12.

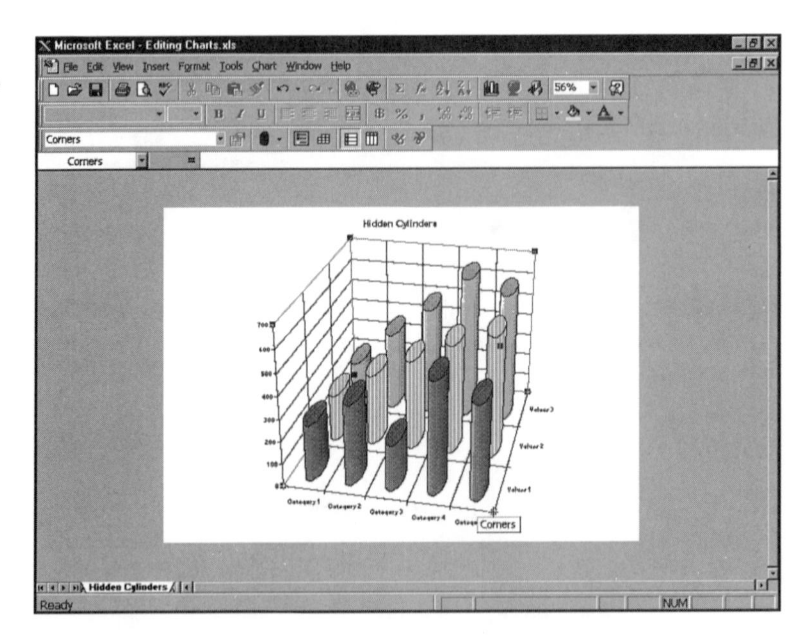

Fig. 12.12
Rotating the chart puts the hidden objects in view. But it still looks like a candidate for another chart type.

If any of your formatting or moving maneuvers goes awry, don't forget about the Undo button on the Standard toolbar. Click the Undo drop-down arrow and select all the changes you want to reverse.

Taking a slice of the pie

Pie charts show relationships between the parts and the whole very effectively. But if one of the values is small, its slice of the pie might be unnoticeable.

To fix that, pull out the slice:

1 Click anywhere on the pie to make the data series handles appear.

2 Click the handle on the slice you want to slip out, as shown in Figure 12.13.

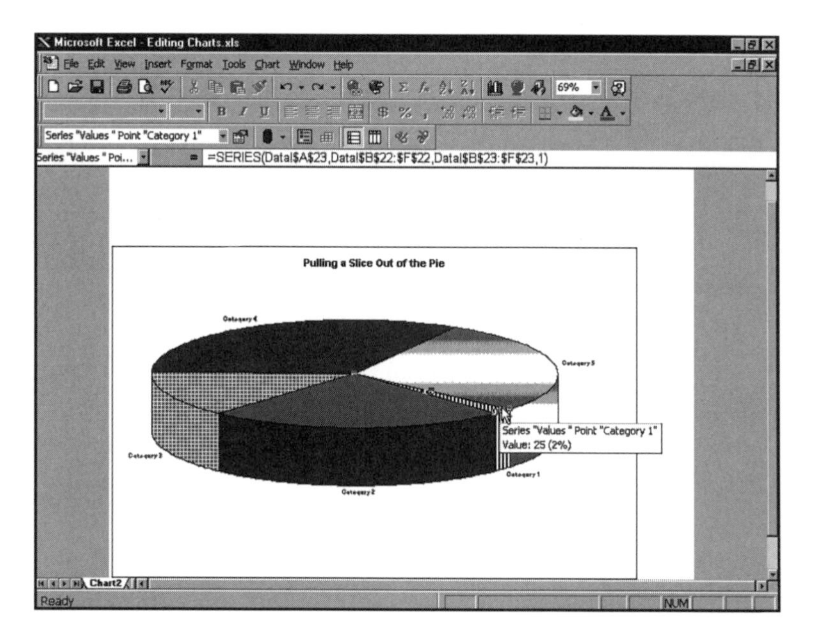

Fig. 12.13
Pulling a slice out of the pie is easy once you grab the right handle.

3 Drag the slice as far as you want it to go (see Figure 12.14).

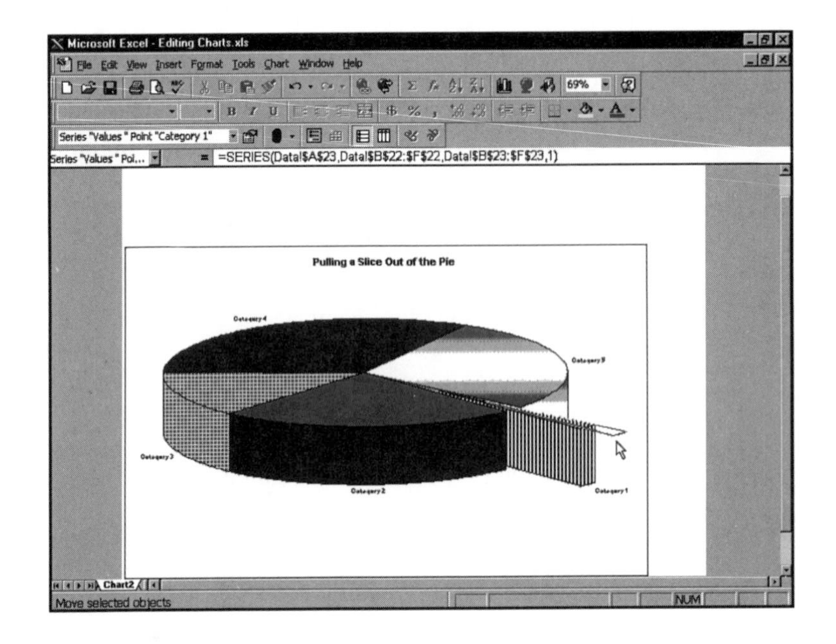

Fig. 12.14
If you want to reassemble your pie, just shove the slice back in and press Esc to get rid of the handles.

TIP **You can also break up the pie entirely. Click once to get the data** series handles, then drag any of them to crack the pie open.

Chart not saying much? Add data labels

Some charts scream, "Label me!" Figure 12.15 is one such chart.

To add some labels, double-click a pyramid to pop up the Format Data Series dialog box. Click the Data Labels tab and select Show Label, then click OK. As you can see in Figure 12.16, this is still not quite right.

Double-click any of those tiny labels to get the Format Data Labels dialog box, then click the Alignment tab, as shown in Figure 12.17.

Click the Font tab. Make them bigger, make them bolder, change their color, take your choice. Click the Alignment tab to change the labels' orientation, then click OK.

Now they're legible, but maybe the positioning is off. Click a label, and a gray border appears around it. Grab the edge of the border and drag the label into position. Figure 12.18 shows two formatted labels in place, and the third being dragged into position.

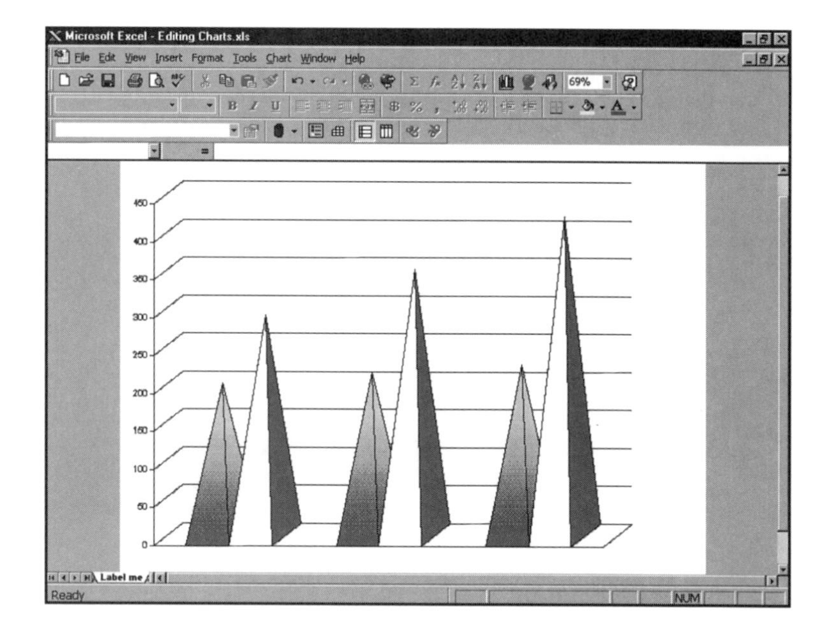

Fig. 12.15
This is one chart that could use a little explanation.

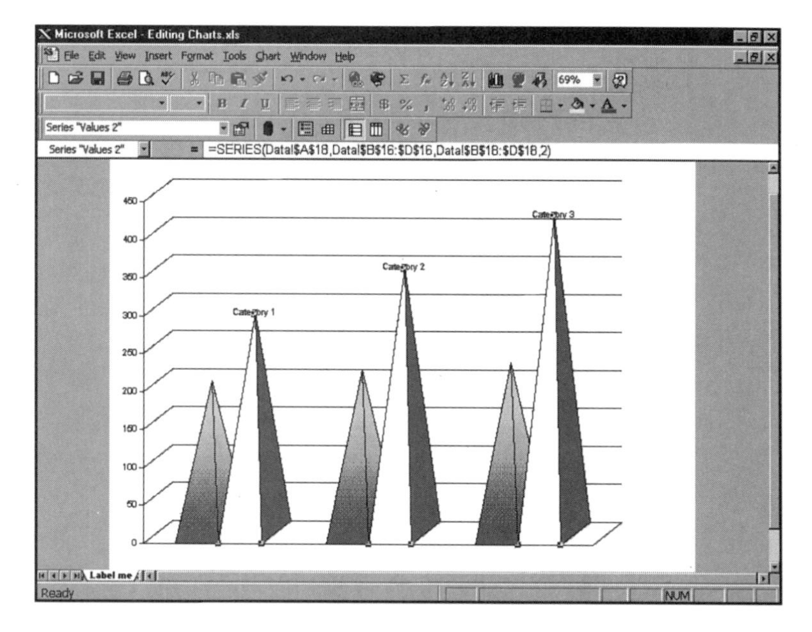

Fig. 12.16
This isn't much of an improvement, but we can fix it.

Moving and sizing labels can be a little tricky. If you go wrong, right-click a label for the shortcut menu. Select Clear to get rid of the labels; or choose Format Data Labels from the shortcut menu to try again.

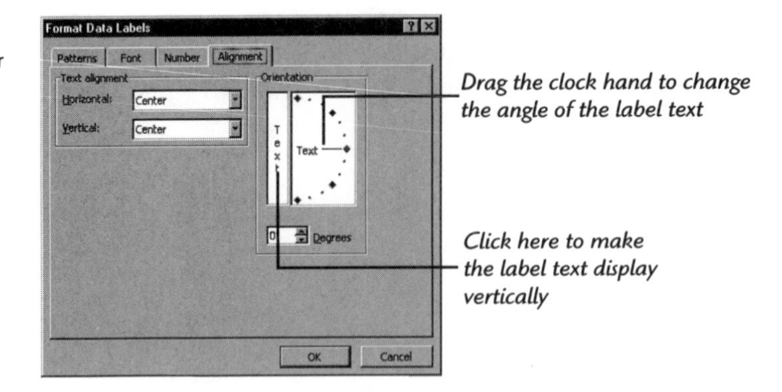

Fig. 12.17
This is where we fix our labels by affixing them to the columns. We need to do a little work on them first.

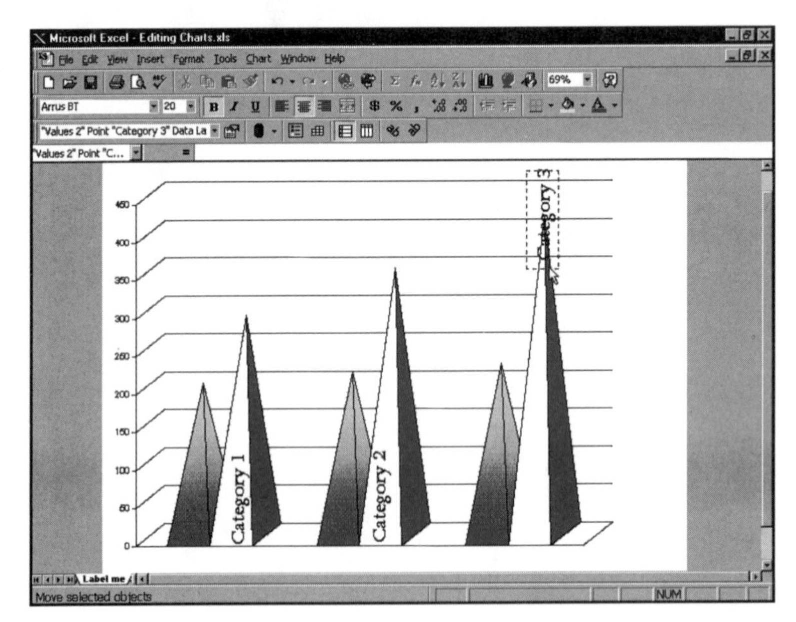

Fig. 12.18
The basic technique for moving objects like labels and titles around on a chart is click it, format it, and drag it into position.

Erected a plain pyramid? Format it with patterns and fill

The pyramids we labeled in Figure 12.18 are on the plain side. Labels help, but to make charts come alive, try applying fill and pattern effects to your chart objects. Double-click a chart data series to open the Format Data Series dialog box. Select the Patterns tab, and click the Fill Effects button. That pops up the Fill Effects dialog box. For some vivid (not to say livid) effects, choose the Gradient tab of the Fill Effects dialog box and click the Preset option.

Now click the Preset Colors drop-down arrow to see the choices shown in Figure 12.19.

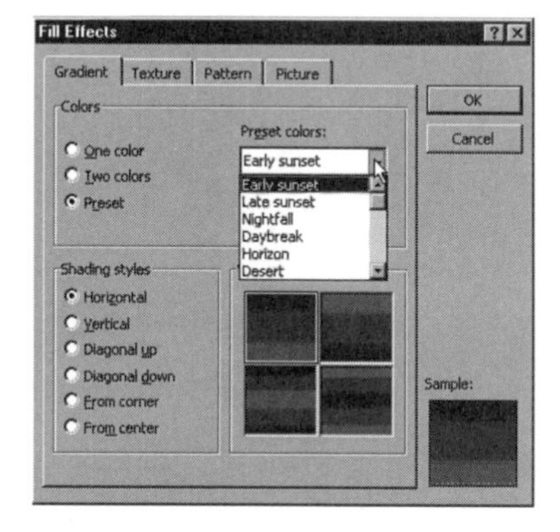

Fig. 12.19
Excel chart formatting allows for some colorful artistic effects.

If options like Late Sunset and Daybreak are too rich for your chart, click the Texture tab and select one of the Texture choices. Click OK, then click OK again in the Format Data Series dialog box. You'll return to find pyramids (or columns, or cones, or whatever you've chosen for your chart) that are plain no more (see Figure 12.20).

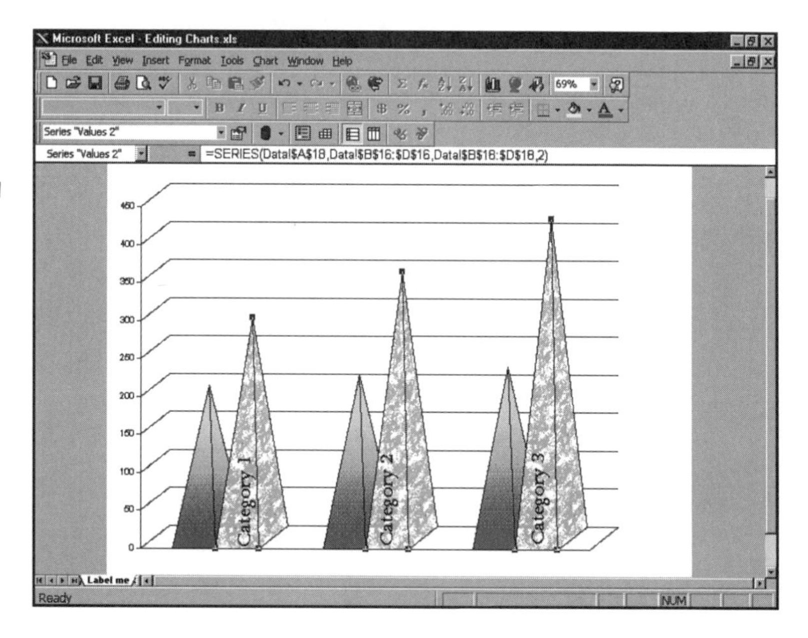

Fig. 12.20
There are dozens of chart formatting options in Excel, but for more dramatic charts quickly, apply fill and patterns to data series.

How do I add data to my chart?

You've just created and formatted a chart, you're all set to print it and go home, when—darn! Those latest shipping figures were hiding under your coffee mug.

Fortunately, you're using Excel. Adding data to a chart is just a drag and drop. Figure 12.21 shows the situation.

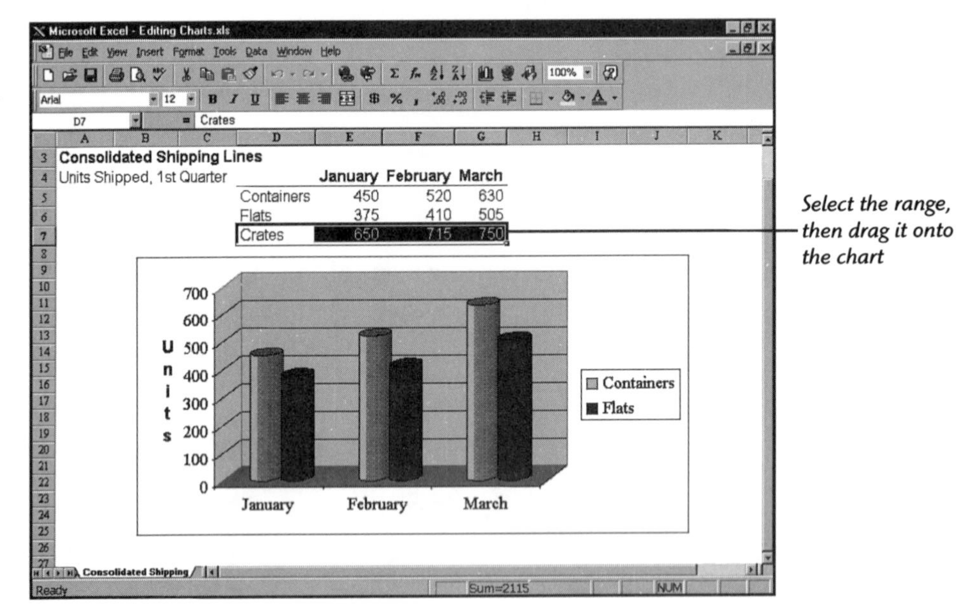

Select the range, then drag it onto the chart

Fig. 12.21
We charted containers and flats, but we forgot about the crates.

To add crates to the chart, select the range in the data table, point at the bottom edge, and drag it onto the chart.

When you release the mouse button, the data will simply be added to the chart. If Excel isn't sure about the layout of the data, the Paste Special dialog box appears. Check to see that Excel guessed right, then click OK.

Figure 12.22 shows the final result. The chart's finally done, and there's still time to make the train.

If you're working with a chart on a separate sheet and you want to add more data, click the chart sheet tab. Then choose Chart, Add Data; select the data, and click OK in the Add Data dialog box.

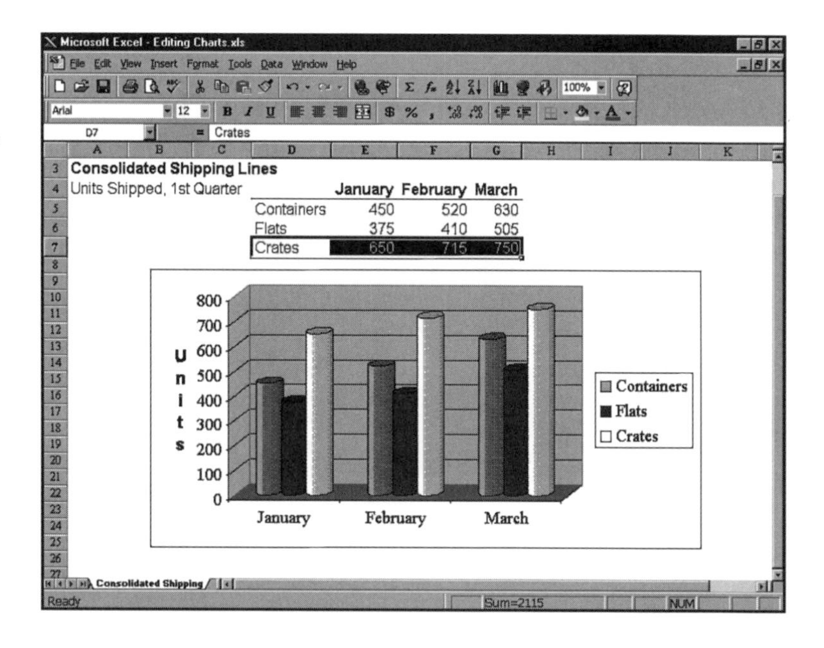

Fig. 12.22
A successful drag-and-drop operation added the data to the chart in no time flat.

I want to print my chart now

When it's time to put your work on paper, you'll find printing charts much like printing worksheets. The same rule also applies: preview before you print.

If your chart is embedded, it'll print along with your worksheet. Otherwise, select one or the other and use the print preview Setup and Margins commands to lay out the page.

Printing a chart sheet

You might want to have a chart sheet fill the printed page. To do that:

1 Click the Print Preview button on the Standard toolbar.

2 Select Setup and click the Chart tab.

3 Select Use Full Page and click OK.

4 If it looks right, click Print and choose OK in the Print dialog box. Otherwise, adjust the margins as you would for a worksheet.

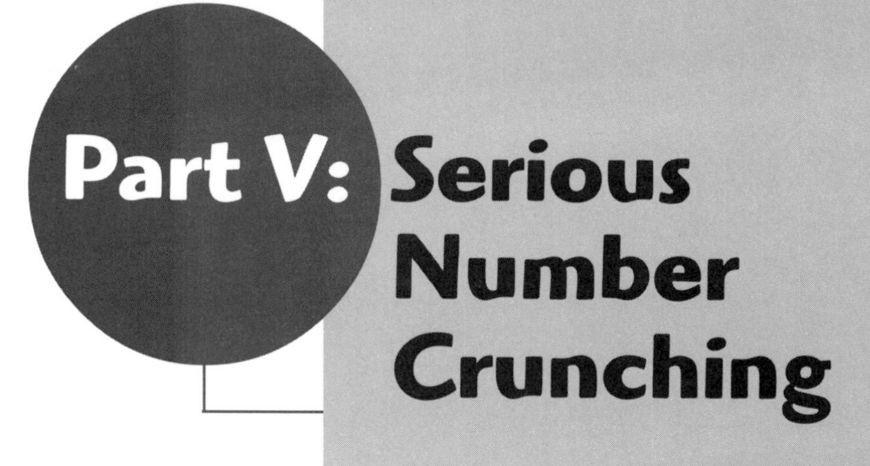

Part V: Serious Number Crunching

Analyzing Data in Tables

In this chapter:

- **What's a data table?**
- **These variable interest rates are driving me bonkers**
- **What is sensitivity analysis (and do I really need it)?**
- **I need to evaluate an investment**

You base business decisions on your analysis of the data. Excel has the tools to help make your analysis easy, speedy, and accurate. . . . .

Before the information age, gathering timely business data was anything but routine. Take one example: the London Rothschild bank had its own private mail service. One Rothschild "mailman" was stationed at the battle of Waterloo. As soon as Napoleon was defeated, the Rothschild man raced the news back to the bank in London. Long before anyone else had an inkling of the battle's outcome, Rothschild bought every British government bond in sight.

When news of the British victory hit the streets, the London bond market soared. Rothschild made a killing.

Business still prospers on timely information. But nowadays, data comes in electronic torrents, not in scraps of paper on horseback. Getting it is easy; making sense of it is another story. Excel's analytical tools can help. Sorting and evaluating information is a basic business chore. Excel won't corner the London bond market for us, but it can be a big help in extracting meaning from everyday business numbers.

How can I figure my loan payments when interest rates keep bouncing around?

Back in the Eisenhower era, inflation was low, growth was steady, and interest rates hardly budged. Shopping for a loan meant taking the going rate. Since then, we've had oil shocks, double-digit inflation, and money market accounts paying anywhere from 3% to more than 15% (remember those?).

Nowadays, bank rates fluctuate constantly. Delay getting your loan for a week or even a day, and you'll be offered a different rate. And with a different payment, all your numbers change. How can you track it?

Building a data table

One answer is a **data table**, an Excel tool that works just like a bottling plant. That soda you might have had at lunch began life on a conveyor belt. The belt passed the bottles through a machine that filled them. Then, as each bottle went down the line, it was capped, and then stacked in crates.

Excel's Data Table command takes rows or columns of values, passes them through a formula (conveyor-belt style), and then stacks the answers in a column or lays them out along a row.

Say we're shopping for a loan to buy a new warehouse. We have the perfect site, but the seller won't commit himself. The banks have a different loan rate for every day of his indecision. Meanwhile, we have to know what our payments are going to be so we can put a budget together.

Take a look at Figure 13.1.

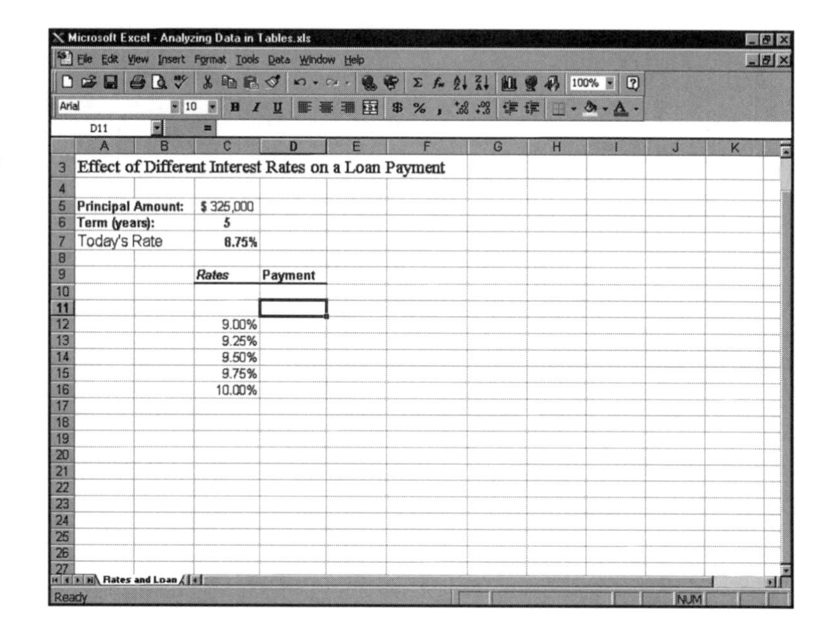

Fig. 13.1
With banks offering different loan rates every day, keeping track of payments is a job for Excel.

Begin building a table by entering the inputs. Here, the inputs are the interest rates in column C. We also need a formula to calculate today's payment, and for that we'll use the PMT Function.

1. Select the cell where we want the formula. In a data table, the formula has to be in the row above the column of input values, and one cell to the right of the first value. Here, it's D11.

2. Click the Paste Function button to pop up the Paste Function dialog box. In the Function Category list, select Financial. Then double-click PMT under Function Name to pop up the PMT dialog box.

3 Enter the rate, the number of periods, or term (nper), and the present value, or principal amount (pv). Remember to divide that annual rate by 12 and multiply the annual term by 12 to convert everything to monthly periods. It'll look like Figure 13.2.

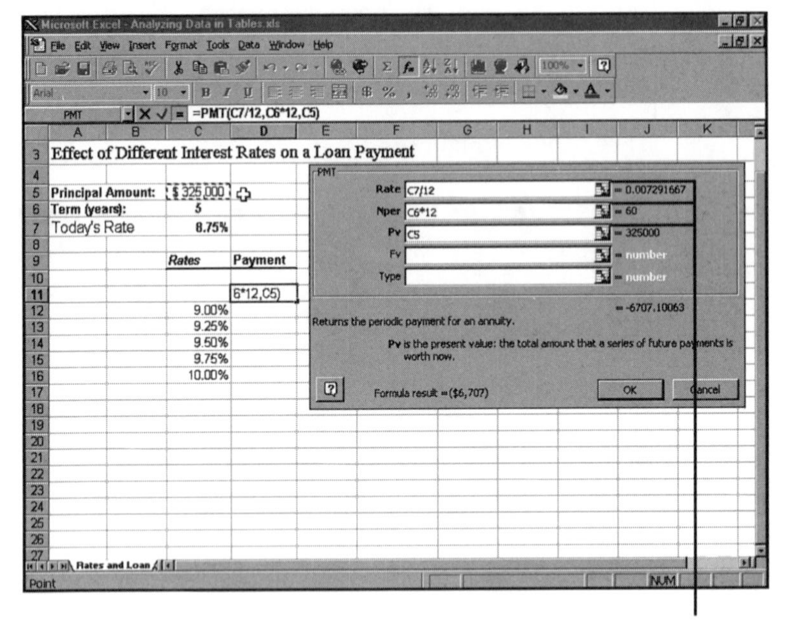

Fig. 13.2
Use the PMT Function to build your formula. Just remember to put the formula in the row above and one cell to the right of the first value.

If the PMT dialog box gets in the way of your cell selection, either drag it to one side or click the Collapse Dialog Box buttons in each text box

TIP **Insert the numbers into the PMT Function by clicking the box in** the PMT dialog box, then selecting the cell containing the value.

4 Click OK in the PMT dialog box to complete the formula. Now select the range holding the input values and the formula, C11:D16 in the example. The blank cells in the range will fill with payment values calculated by the Data Table command.

5 Select Data, Table, and the Table dialog box appears. Our inputs, the changing rates, are in a column. Click the Column Input Cell box.

6 Click the cell referenced in the formula whose changing value we're analyzing. Here, it's C7. That's where we put today's rate, and the cell referenced by the PMT Function we built (see Figure 13.3).

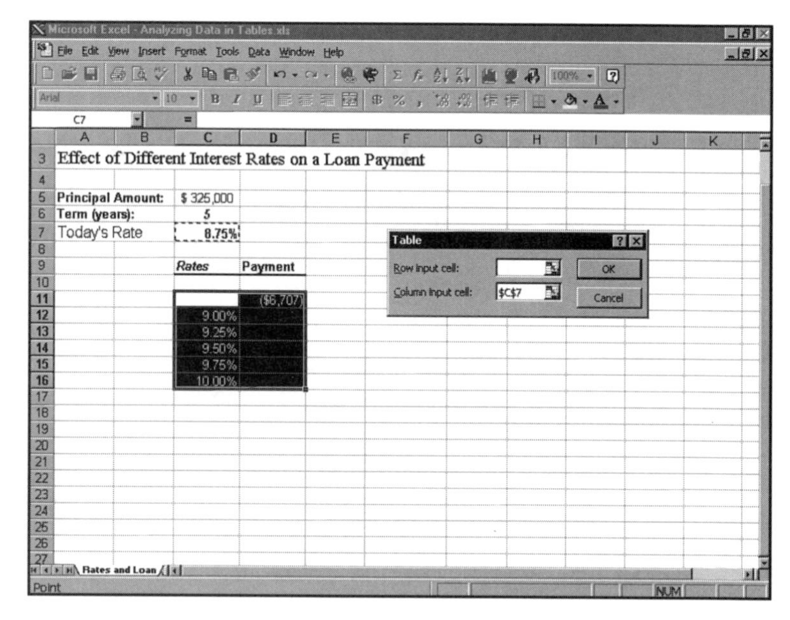

Fig. 13.3
The Column Input Cell is the cell referenced in a data table formula whose changing values we're analyzing.

7 Click OK, and our table is filled in, as shown in Figure 13.4. They're payments, so the numbers are negative.

Fig. 13.4
After you set them up, data tables supply a lot of information, speedily and automatically.

Microsoft Excel - Analyzing Data in Tables.xls

D16 = {=TABLE(,C7)}

Effect of Different Interest Rates on a Loan Payment

Row	A	B	C	D
5	Principal Amount:		$ 325,000	
6	Term (years):		5	
7	Today's Rate		8.75%	
9			Rates	Payment
11				($6,707)
12			9.00%	($6,746)
13			9.25%	($6,786)
14			9.50%	($6,826)
15			9.75%	($6,865)
16			10.00%	($6,905)

Rates and Loan — Ready — NUM

The data table fills in the calculated payments for each of the different interest rates

Now we can adjust our budget using these different payment amounts. The seller may dither for weeks, but at least we're armed with the right numbers.

I want to add more formulas to the data table

Maybe you want to know the amount of interest in that first payment for tax planning purposes. We can put the IPMT function in our table to get the interest component for each different rate.

Add additional formulas to the right of the original formula, on the same row. Then select the entire table, including the earlier values. That's C11:E16 in Figure 13.5. Click Data, Table, enter the interest rate as the Column Input Cell (C7 in Figure 13.5), and click OK. Figure 13.5 shows how it looks.

Fig. 13.5
Add formulas to the right of the first formula, select the range, choose Data, Table, and the new values fill in the column to the right.

Microsoft Excel - Analyzing Data in Tables.xls

E11 =IPMT(C7/12,1,60,C5)

Effect of Different Interest Rates on a Loan Payment

	A	B	C	D	E
5	Principal Amount:		$ 325,000		
6	Term (years):		5		
7	Today's Rate		8.75%		
9			*Rates*	Payment	Interest in Period 1
11				($6,707)	($2,370)
12			9.00%	($6,746)	($2,438)
13			9.25%	($6,786)	($2,505)
14			9.50%	($6,826)	($2,573)
15			9.75%	($6,865)	($2,641)
16			10.00%	($6,905)	($2,708)

Interest Amounts

Ready NUM

To figure the interest payment in periods 2…60, just add as many additional IPMT formulas as you like to the right of the first one.

TIP **PMT returns a negative number because it's an amount you pay** out. To display positive numbers, use the ABS function, which returns the absolute value of a number. The formula would look like this:

```
=ABS(PMT(C7/12,C6*12,C5))
```

Type it, or use the Paste Function button.

Building a data table with two inputs

Different rates affect the monthly payment on a loan. So do different terms. As we shop around for a loan, we're considering stretching out the loan to reduce the payment amount.

Just build a data table with two inputs: one to track different rates, and the other to evaluate different loan terms. Note that a two-input data table can handle two variables, but only one formula.

1 Set up a table like the one in Figure 13.6. Keep in mind that one input has to be in a column, the other in a row. The column inputs have to be below the formula, and the row inputs to the right of the formula. Here, the formula is in C10.

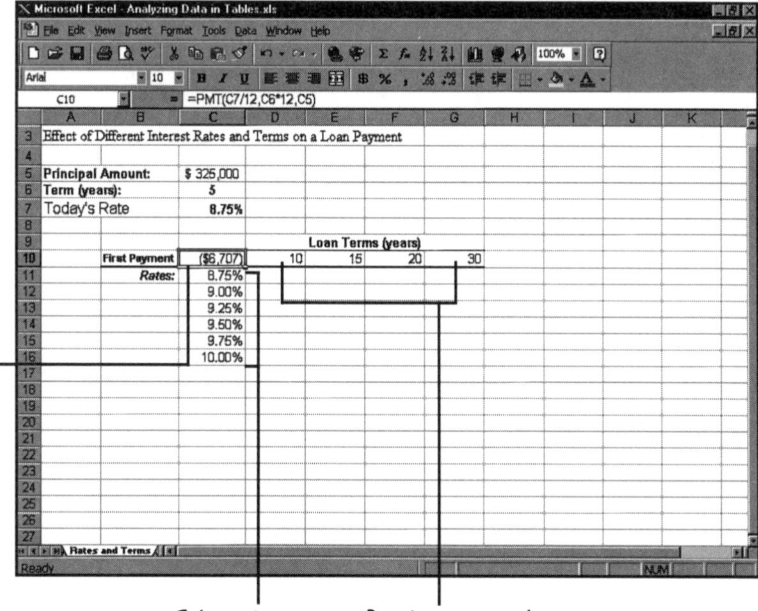

Fig. 13.6
One input in columns, the other in rows, is the ticket for two-input data tables. Column inputs go below the formula; row inputs to the right.

2 Select the range C10:G16.

3 Select Data, Table. The loan terms we want to look at are in a row to the right of the formula. So for Row Input Cell, click C6. That's the cell containing the loan term referred to in the formula.

4 For Column Input Cell, click cell C7. That contains the rate, and it's the cell referred to in the formula. The formula has to reference both input cells for this to work.

5 Click OK. Eureka! The values fill in, as shown in Figure 13.7. Notice how the table contains all the inputs and the formula in a rectangle. You'll probably think of more elegant arrangements for this kind of thing, but that's the required layout.

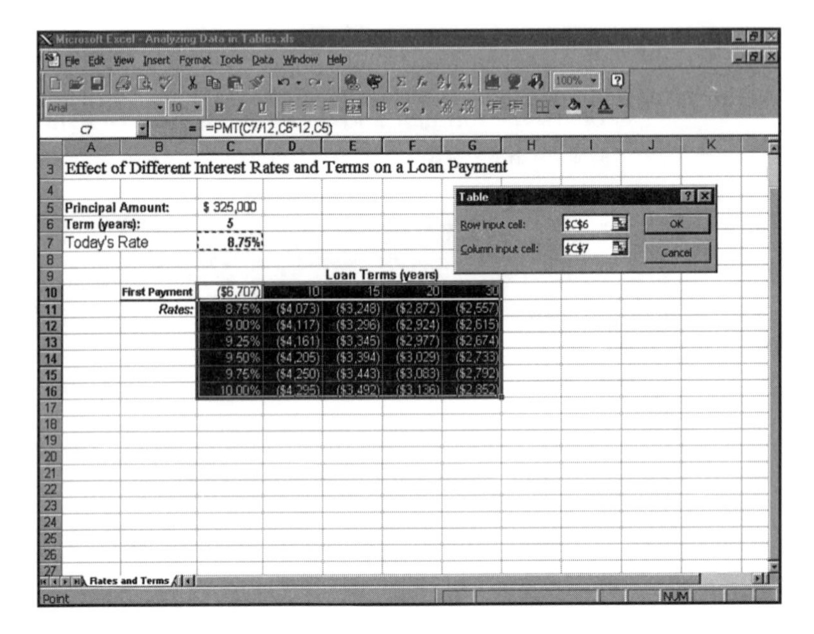

Fig. 13.7
The Data Table command fills in the different payments for the different rates and terms.

Q&A ***How come when I did this, I just get* `!Input Cell Reference Is Not Valid`*?***

The formula has to refer to both of the input cells you give to the Data Table command. Make sure the input cells you enter are the ones in your formula.

How can I tell if this investment is worth making?

Getting a loan to buy that warehouse is complicated enough. But do we need a new warehouse at all? Having extra storage space for more inventory is going to make us more money every year. Will we make enough to justify the cost of the warehouse? That's the kind of question Net Present Value (NPV) calculations are good at answering.

NPV helps evaluate investments

NPV figures the present value of those annual additions to income, or of any future cash flows, by discounting them. Think of packing a sandwich in a plastic bag. You squeeze the air out of the bag before sealing it up, leaving you with just sandwich to lug around. NPV deflates cash flows in the same way, sucking out the effects of interest over time, leaving the true value of the investment.

If we add up all the discounted future cash flows, that sum is what we're actually making from the investment. And if the sum of the discounted cash flows is more than our initial investment, we're making more than we spent. The investment is worth doing.

Discount rates: the fly in NPV's ointment

There's one big problem with NPV. We know our cash flows, we know our initial investment, but what do we use for a discount rate? There are dozens of different rates out there. Which one should we choose?

Using NPV and a data table, we can test them all.

Plain English, please!

Testing the effects of small changes like this is called **sensitivity analysis**. A fancy term for a simple idea, but what else would you call it? The resulting table is sometimes called a **table of answers**. ”

Combining data tables with NPV

Let's evaluate the effects of different discount rates on the Net Present Value of an investment. We just have to make sure we set it up properly. Figure 13.8 shows how we start.

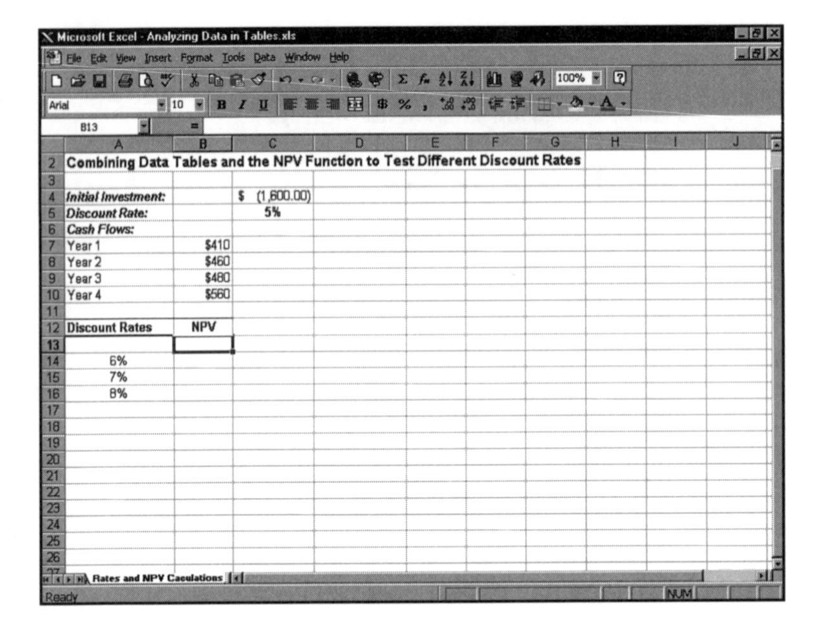

Fig. 13.8
The setup here is similar to the setup for our loan evaluation problem. Type in all known values, arrange the values to test in a column, and we're in business.

We plan to invest $1,600, and we estimate that we'll earn annual amounts as shown in years 1 through 4. Do those income flows justify our investment? And what's the effect of different rates on our calculation? Let's find out.

1. Because we're setting up a data table, our NPV formula goes in the cell above and one column to the right of the values we're testing (B13 in the example). We select B13, then click the Paste Function button.

2. The Paste Function dialog box appears. Under Function Category, select Financial. Then double-click NPV under Function Name.

3. Click in the Rate box, then select C5, where we've put our discount rate.

4. For Value 1, we'll use our initial investment, C4. Because we're not making the investment today, we need to discount it too.

5. Now select the range with our annual cash flows (B7:B10 in the example) for Value 2, and click to stick the formula in the cell. It looks like Figure 13.9.

6. Does this look familiar? Select the range containing the formula, discount rates, and adjacent blank cells. Then click Data, Table.

7. This time, our Column Input Cell is C5. That's also the cell referenced in our NPV formula, as shown in Figure 13.10.

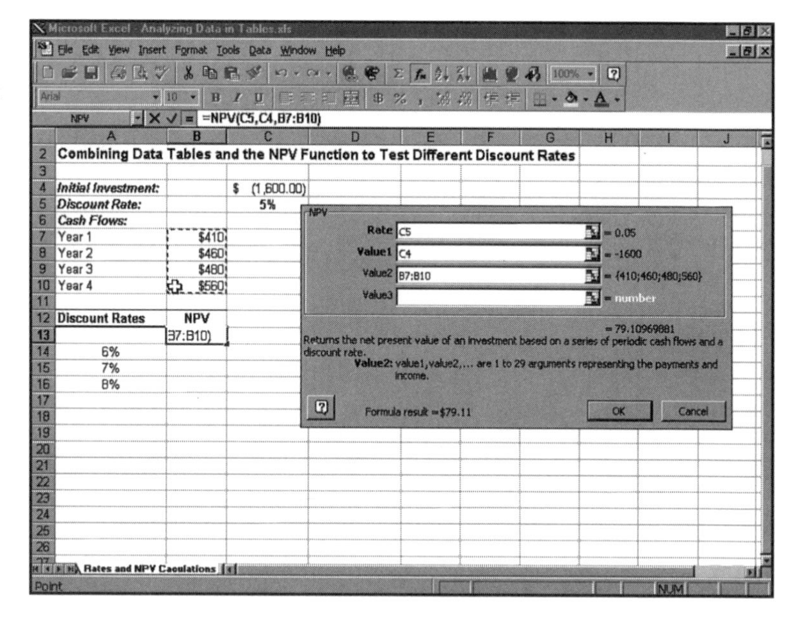

Fig. 13.9
If you've already made the investment, leave it out for now, then subtract it from the figure NPV comes up with.

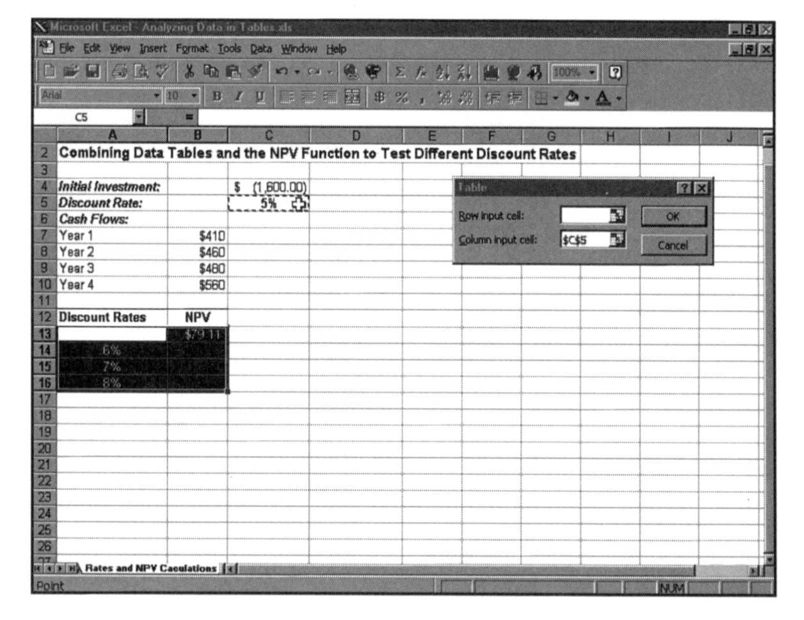

Fig. 13.10
The Column Input Cell is the variable we're testing, and the cell referenced in the NPV formula.

8 Click OK, and the different NPVs are filled in, as shown in Figure 13.11.

The investment looks fine until we get to a discount rate of 8% or more. At that point, it's not worth doing. We'd spend more than we made.

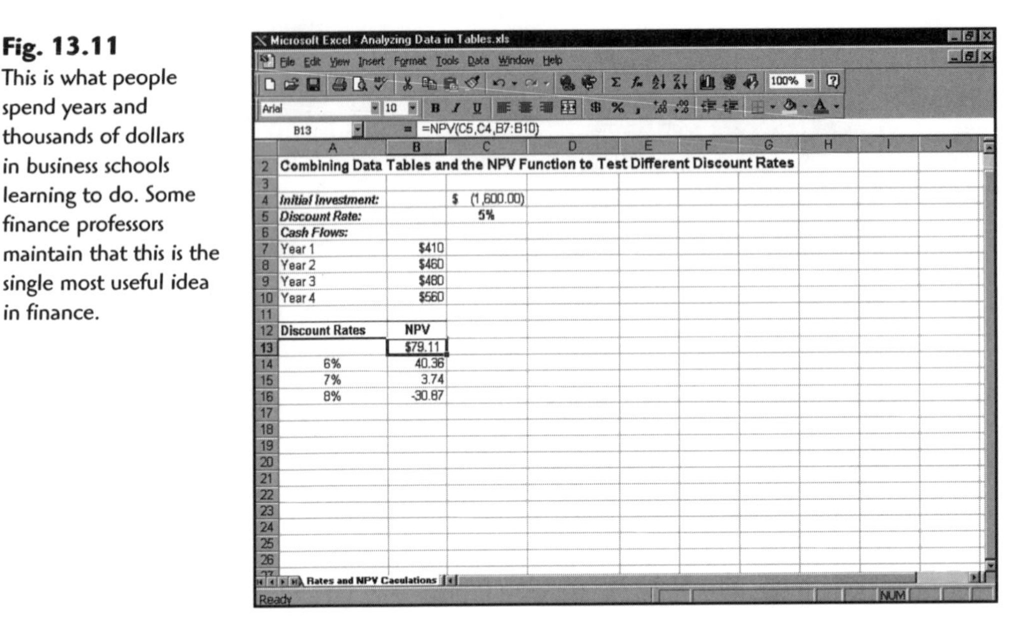

Fig. 13.11
This is what people spend years and thousands of dollars in business schools learning to do. Some finance professors maintain that this is the single most useful idea in finance.

Excel can't choose a discount rate for us. We still have to make that tough call ourselves. But at least we know what effect our choice is going to have.

If you need to test more variables, you can edit any of the data in a data table. Try different loan amounts or cash flows, for example. You can also edit the formula in the top row, which is the NPV or PMT formulas in our examples. The Data Table command has also added its own array formula to each of our tested values (remember those from Chapter 8?). They look like this:

```
{=TABLE(,C5)}
```

I need to add more data to my table

Maybe interest rates are even more volatile than usual. The Federal Reserve is jumpy, and the Board keeps fiddling with short-term rates. You can add data to a data table after you've set it up to handle additional values.

1. Add the new values at the bottom of the left column, below the original ones (begin adding in the cell to the right of the original values if your inputs are in a row). It should look like Figure 13.12.
2. Then select the whole table—formulas, new values, old values, and the original results.

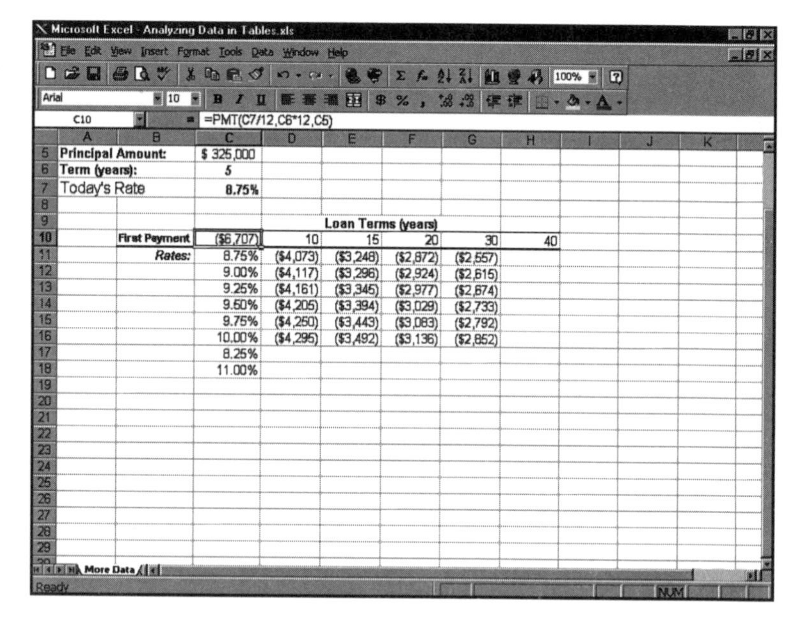

Microsoft Excel - Analyzing Data in Tables.xls

File Edit View Insert Format Tools Data Window Help

C10 =PMT(C7/12,C6*12,C5)

	A	B	C	D	E	F	G	H
5	Principal Amount:		$ 325,000					
6	Term (years):		5					
7	Today's Rate		8.75%					
8								
9						Loan Terms (years)		
10		First Payment	($6,707)	10	15	20	30	40
11		Rates:	8.75%	($4,073)	($3,248)	($2,872)	($2,557)	
12			9.00%	($4,117)	($3,296)	($2,924)	($2,615)	
13			9.25%	($4,161)	($3,345)	($2,977)	($2,674)	
14			9.50%	($4,205)	($3,394)	($3,029)	($2,733)	
15			9.75%	($4,250)	($3,443)	($3,083)	($2,792)	
16			10.00%	($4,295)	($3,492)	($3,136)	($2,852)	
17			8.25%					
18			11.00%					

More Data

Ready NUM

Fig. 13.12
Adding data to tables is easy. Put the new data below or to the right of the old data, or both.

3 Select Data, Table, and enter the original input cell or cells. It'll look like Figure 13.13.

Microsoft Excel - Analyzing Data in Tables.xls

File Edit View Insert Format Tools Data Window Help

C7 =PMT(C7/12,C6*12,C5)

	A	B	C	D	E	F	G	H
5	Principal Amount:		$ 325,000					
6	Term (years):		5					
7	Today's Rate		8.75%					
8								
9						Loan Terms (years)		
10		First Payment	($6,707)	10	15	20	30	40
11		Rates:	8.75%	($4,073)	($3,248)	($2,872)	($2,557)	
12			9.00%	($4,117)	($3,296)	($2,924)	($2,615)	
13			9.25%	($4,161)	($3,345)	($2,977)	($2,674)	
14			9.50%	($4,205)	($3,394)	($3,029)	($2,733)	
15			9.75%	($4,250)	($3,443)	($3,083)	($2,792)	
16			10.00%	($4,295)	($3,492)	($3,136)	($2,852)	
17			8.25%					
18			11.00%					

Table

Row input cell: C6 OK

Column input cell: C7 Cancel

More Data

Point NUM

Fig. 13.13
We're using the same formula, and testing the same variables, so we use the same cell inputs we used in Figure 13.7.

4 Click OK, and the table is recalculated with the new values. Figure 13.14 shows the results.

Fig. 13.14
The old values stay where they were, and the new ones are added to the table.

Microsoft Excel - Analyzing Data in Tables.xls

H18 = {=TABLE(C6,C7)}

	A	B	C	D	E	F	G	H
5	Principal Amount:		$ 325,000					
6	Term (years):		5					
7	Today's Rate		8.75%					
8								
9					Loan Terms (years)			
10		First Payment	($6,707)	10	15	20	30	40
11		Rates:	8.75%	($4,073)	($3,248)	($2,872)	($2,557)	($2,445)
12			9.00%	($4,117)	($3,296)	($2,924)	($2,615)	($2,507)
13			9.25%	($4,161)	($3,345)	($2,977)	($2,674)	($2,570)
14			9.50%	($4,205)	($3,394)	($3,029)	($2,733)	($2,633)
15			9.75%	($4,250)	($3,443)	($3,083)	($2,792)	($2,696)
16			10.00%	($4,295)	($3,492)	($3,136)	($2,852)	($2,760)
17			8.25%	($3,986)	($3,153)	($2,769)	($2,442)	($2,321)
18			11.00%	($4,477)	($3,694)	($3,355)	($3,095)	($3,017)

More Data

Q&A **_Why is my worksheet taking forever to recalculate?_**

When you add a data table to a worksheet, Excel recalculates the whole table each time you make changes on the sheet. If you have a big table, recalculating every cell might slow you down. To avoid this bottleneck, select Tools, Options, and click the Calculation tab. Select Automatic Except Tables. Everything on the worksheet but the table will be recalculated automatically. To recalculate the table after you do this, press F9, the Recalc key.

How do I get rid of table values?

Because a data table is an array, Excel treats it like a single unit. You can't get rid of an individual cell.

You can clear the results, though. Select all the values that the Data Table command has calculated. Then click Edit, Clear, Contents.

CAUTION **Don't include the formulas or inputs. If you do, you'll wipe out** the whole table. Unless, of course, that's what you want to do.

14 More Analyzing, and Auditing Too

In this chapter:

- **What is Goal Seek, and what's it good for?**
- **Can Excel solve break-even problems?**
- **I want to chart our break-even point**
- **With a tight budget, how can I find the right loan?**
- **I need to figure out where this worksheet went wrong**

Like a private consultant, Excel helps you come up with solutions to a range of business problems. Excel even solves the problem of worksheet errors . . . .

Mystery writers cheat. They toss out clues and strain your deductive powers (and sometimes your patience), before finally handing you the solution.

Of course, the writer knew who did it all along. In fact, the writer probably started with the solution and worked backwards, clue by clue, to create the mystery.

Some mysteries—in fiction or in business—are best approached solution-first anyway. Excel lets you do just that. It takes the result you have, or want, and gives you the values you need to get that result. Along the way, it can also find and eliminate worksheet red herrings.

And Excel doesn't mind if you skip to the end to see who-dunnit.

When are we going to make a profit? Ask Goal Seek

It's a classic problem. We've spent a lot of money bringing a product to market. We know what it costs to produce. We think we can sell it for a certain price. So how many units do we have to sell before we see a profit? When the number of units we sell produces exactly enough revenue to cover our costs, we've reached our **break-even** point.

Excel's Goal Seek command uses brute force to find the answer to break-even problems. It's like a tireless dart-thrower heaving darts at a target until the bull's eye is hit. Goal Seek looks at your formula, asks for the value you want, and then keeps plugging numbers into the formula. It doesn't quit until it finds the number that produces the value you asked for.

Breaking down break-evens

Let's put Goal Seek to work on a break-even problem. There are two parts to break-even formulas: a **cost function** and a **revenue function**.

- The cost function looks like this:

  Total Cost = Total Fixed Cost + (Total Variable Cost × Number of Units)

- The revenue function is simple:

  Total Revenue = Price per Unit × Number of Units.

We reach the break-even point when Total Cost = Total Revenue. A different way of saying the same thing: Total Revenue–Total Cost = 0. Sell fewer units than the number needed to reach the break-even point, and we show a loss. When the units sold exceed that number, we start to make a profit.

> **Plain English, please!**
>
> **Fixed costs** are those that don't change with changes in volume. **Variable costs** do vary with changes in volume. Take the cost of driving to work (please!). It has both fixed and variable components. The insurance, license fees, and purchase price remain the same whether you take the trip, or leave the car in the driveway and call in sick. They're fixed. The gas you use on the trip to work is a variable cost—the more you drive, the more you spend on gas.

Now we have our break-even formula. We'll use Goal Seek to figure out how many units we need to sell to reach the point where Total Revenues–Total Costs = 0.

Take a look at Figure 14.1. Total Fixed Costs are in C11, Total Variable Costs are in D12. Total Units will be in C14. Total Revenues are in C5. So our formula is `=C5-(C11+(D12*C14))`.

The long and short of it

Economists are always going on about the **long run** and the **short run**, as in "in the long run the economy will be harmed by drastically lowering interest rates, although in the short run the economy will benefit."

We know what they mean, more or less. Actually, those are technical terms that have pretty specific meanings, despite their vague sound. The long run means the period of time during which all inputs are variable. The short run refers to the period of time in which some inputs are fixed and some are variable.

Think of a car factory. In the short run, the cost of the factory itself is **fixed**. It stays the same, regardless of how many cars are produced. The labor and materials that go into each car are **variable costs**—make more cars, buy more steel, pay for more labor. But in the long run, the factory might be torn down and replaced. At that point, it too becomes a variable cost.

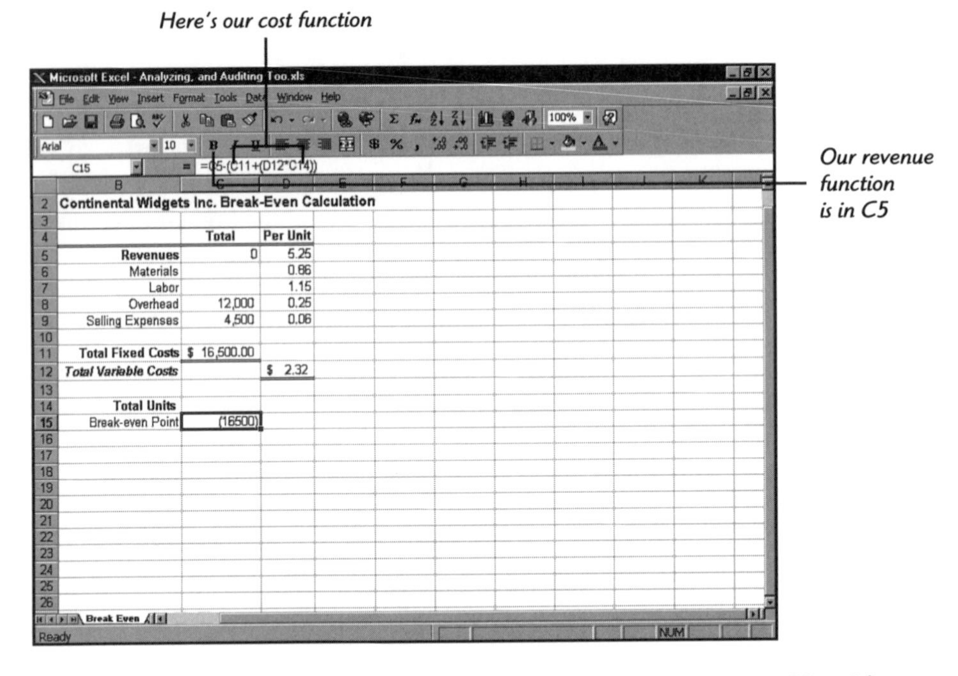

Fig. 14.1
The break-even point shows (16500) because the formula is subtracting Total Revenues from Total Costs. We have no Units at this point, hence no revenues.

Total Revenues are revenues per unit times total units, or `=D5*C14`. Now it's a big 0. It'll be filled in when Goal Seek finds our total units.

1 Click Tools, Goal Seek, and look at Figure 14.2.

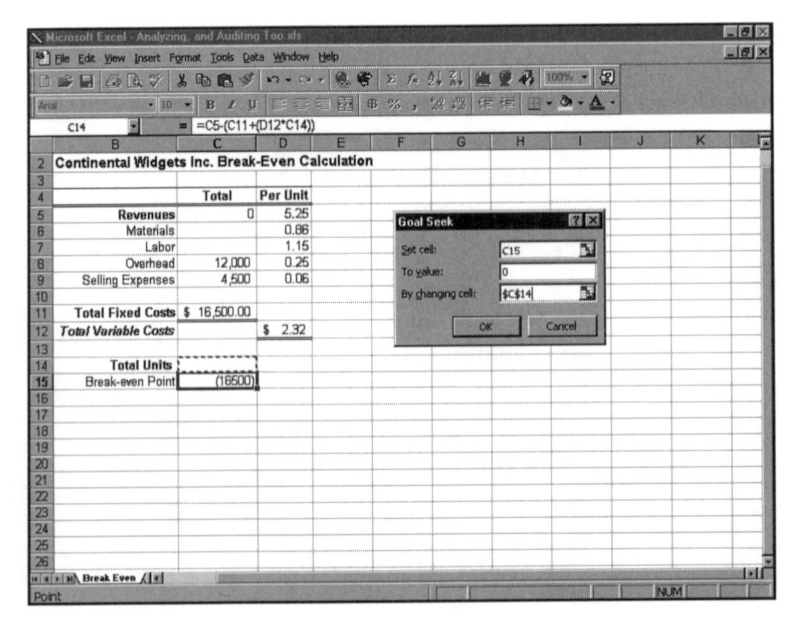

Fig. 14.2
Use the mouse to select cells for the Goal Seek text boxes. If the dialog box is in the way, drag it by the title bar, or click the Collapse Dialog Box buttons.

2 Set Cell is the formula we want Goal Seek to use. That's C15 here. We're commanding Goal Seek to set the formula to a specified value. If you put something other than a formula in here, you get an error message.

3 To Value is the result we want the formula to produce. That's 0 in the example, because break-even point equals Total Revenues – Total Costs = 0.

4 By Changing Cell is C14. We want to change that blank to the total number of units we need to produce to break even. It must be a cell that's referenced by the formula, or a cell that refers to another cell that's referenced in the formula. Goal Seek will keep plugging in numbers until it finds the one that makes our formula equal 0.

5 Click OK, and Goal Seek goes to work. When Goal Seek comes up with an answer, the Goal Seek Status dialog box pops up and displays the results, as shown in Figure 14.3.

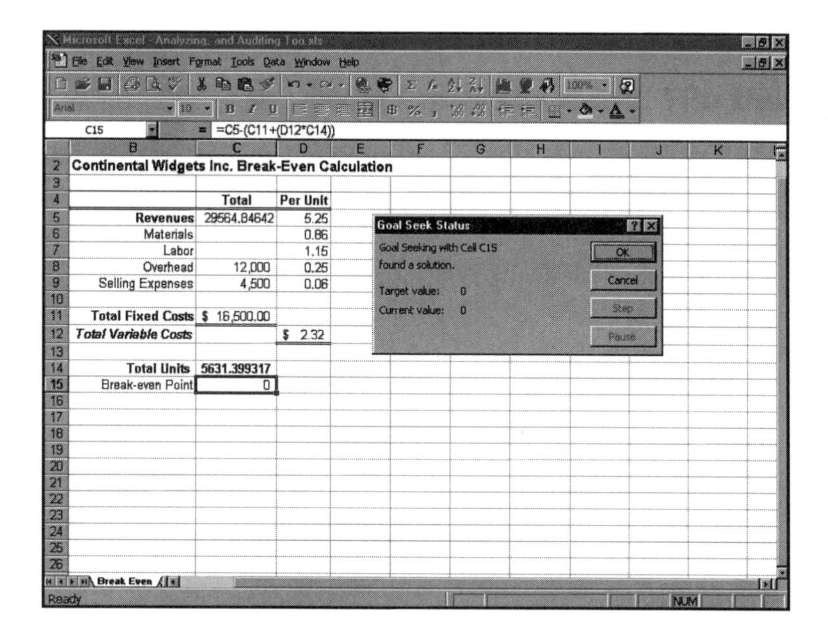

Fig. 14.3
Goal Seek has solved our break-even problem. Click OK in the Goal Seek Status dialog box to add the result to the worksheet.

Sell 5,631 units or fewer, and Continental Widgets shows a loss. We break even at 5,631.399 units, and when that 5,632nd widget goes out the door, we break out the champagne.

For anyone so inclined, a break-even problem like this one can also be solved algebraically. Because

```
Total Revenues-(Fixed Costs + (Variable Costs * Total Units)) = 0
```

is the break-even point, solve for Total Units:

```
Units = (Revenues-Fixed Costs)/Variable Costs
```

I tried this and got –7.28E–12 (or some other inscrutable number). What happened?

Goal Seek is accurate to more decimal places than you probably care about. That number is –.00000000...728, which is pretty darn close to zero. Because it looks confusing, right-click the cell and choose Format Cells on the shortcut menu. Click the Number tab in the Format Cells dialog box. Under Category, select Number and click OK. That formats the number into something more reasonable.

Goal Seek may come up with a number that makes no sense at all, no matter how you format it. It depends on the formula and the value you specify. In that case, use the Data Table command. You can produce a range of results that way, and some of them will make more sense (see the following section).

Charting break-even problems

Need another way to attack break-even problems? Chart them. By combining the Data Table command we looked at in Chapter 13 with cost and revenue functions, we can produce a range of total cost and total revenue figures. If we put those figures on a line chart, the point where the two lines intersect is the break-even point. Figure 14.4 shows how to set it up.

The revenue function is revenues per unit × number of units, or `E2*A7` here. The cost function is fixed cost + (variable cost × number of units), or `D7+(E8*A7)` in the example.

Now use the Data Table command to fill in the values for revenues and costs at the different levels of units.

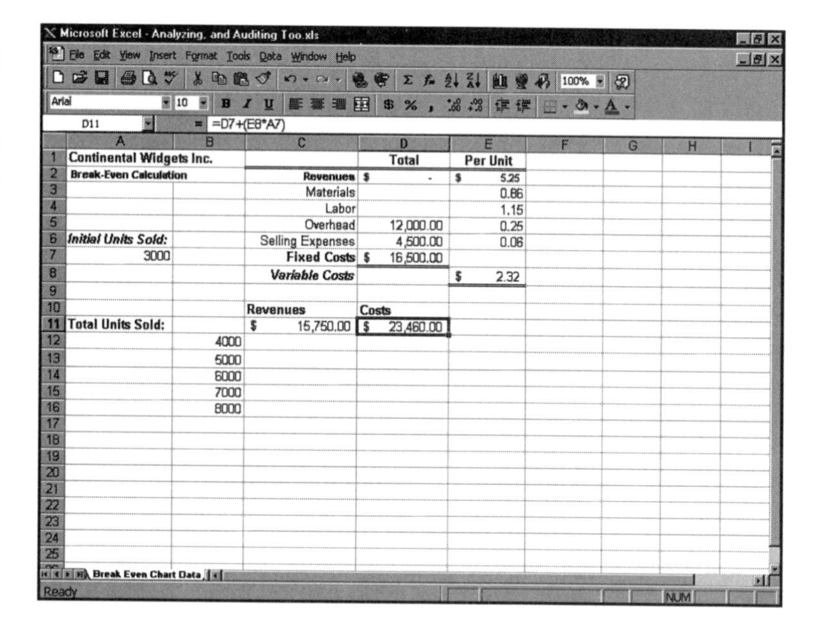

Fig. 14.4
The range of units sold is in column B. One row above and one column to the right of these values, enter the revenue and cost functions side by side.

1. Select the range enclosing all the input values and the two formulas (B11:D16 here).
2. Click Data, Table. Our data's in a column, so select the Column Input Cell box, as shown in Figure 14.5.
3. Select A7. I put a fairly arbitrary number there just to get the Data Table command started. The cell you select for column or row input has to be in the formulas the Data Table command uses, and it has to be outside the range of values and formulas selected for the data table. As long as you meet those conditions, it'll work.
4. Click OK and the values fill in, as shown in Figure 14.6.

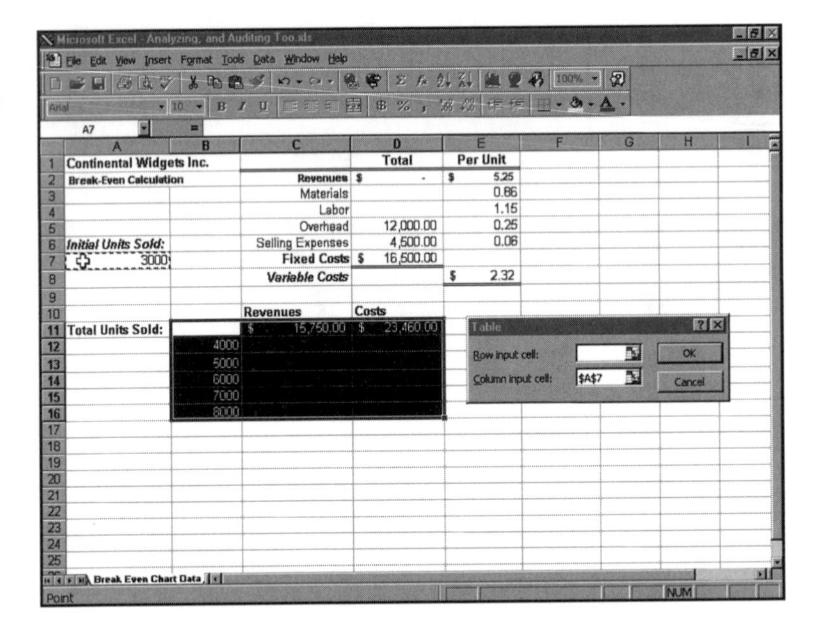

Fig. 14.5
A phony Initial Units Sold value, outside the data table range but referenced by the formulas in the range, gets around the data table's fussy layout requirements.

Fig. 14.6
Our break-even point, where revenues equal costs, is somewhere between 5,000 and 6,000 units sold.

Microsoft Excel - Analyzing, and Auditing Too.xls

C14 = {=TABLE(,A7)}

	A	B	C	D	E
1	Continental Widgets Inc.			Total	Per Unit
2	Break-Even Calculation		Revenues	$ 110,250.00	$ 5.25
3			Materials		0.86
4			Labor		1.15
5			Overhead	12,000.00	0.25
6	*Initial Units Sold:*		Selling Expenses	4,500.00	0.06
7	3000		Fixed Costs	$ 16,500.00	
8			*Variable Costs*		$ 2.32
9					
10			Revenues	Costs	
11	Total Units Sold:		$ 15,750.00	$ 23,460.00	
12		4000	21,000.00	25,780.00	
13		5000	26,250.00	28,100.00	
14		6000	31,500.00	30,420.00	
15		7000	36,750.00	32,740.00	
16		8000	42,000.00	35,060.00	

Break Even Chart Data

Ready NUM

Create the chart

Now we can use the Chart Wizard to chart the data. Select the range containing our values, C12 to D16. That leaves out the Initial Units Sold value, but it was phony anyway.

Click the Chart Wizard button and work your way through the Chart Wizard steps. You'll end up with something like Figure 14.7 (see Chapters 11 and 12 for details on creating and editing charts).

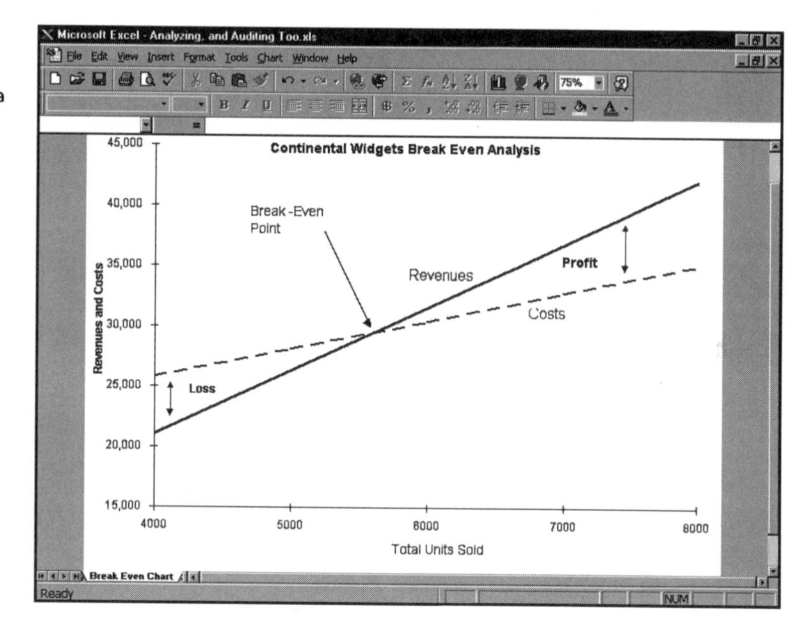

Fig. 14.7
I adjusted the y axis scale, and inserted data labels and axis titles. The arrows came from the Drawing toolbar. Click the Drawing button on the Standard toolbar to pop it up.

The intersection of the Revenues and Costs lines is the break-even point. The area between the lines above the break-even point represents profits; below break-even, losses.

What else can I do with Goal Seek?

Goal Seek will work for any formula for which you want a specific result, but don't know how to get it. Combining Goal Seek with Excel's many functions gives you a powerful problem-solving tool.

I know my payment...what rate do I need to get it?

We need to borrow $125,000 to build a new annex. The budget allows for a $1,000 monthly payment. One bank has offered a 15-year, 7% fixed-rate loan. Another bank has a range of lower-rate variable loans on offer.

We'll use the PMT function and Goal Seek to figure out which way to go. Let's calculate the payment on the fixed-rate loan first. Take a look at Figure 14.8.

To skip some typing, click the Paste Function button and select the PMT function

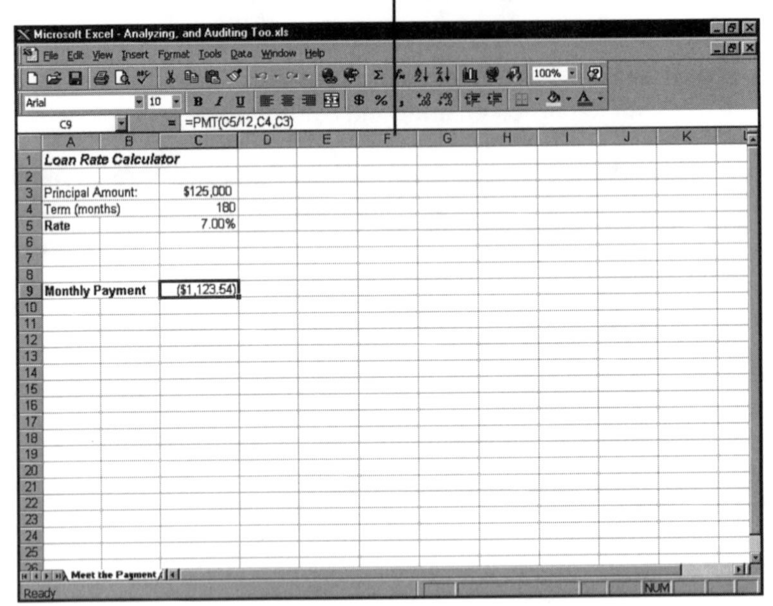

Fig. 14.8
The formula is in C9, `=PMT(C5/12,C4,C3)`. Type it in, or click the Paste Function button.

PMT comes up with a monthly payment of $1,123.54. Too much for the budget. This is a job for Goal Seek!

1. Select Tools, Goal Seek.
2. Set Cell is C9, which contains our PMT function.
3. For the To Value, enter **–1,000** (it's a payment, hence a negative number).
4. By Changing Cell is C5, where we put the rate. No need to worry about changing it to a monthly basis—we did that when we entered the function. It looks like Figure 14.9.

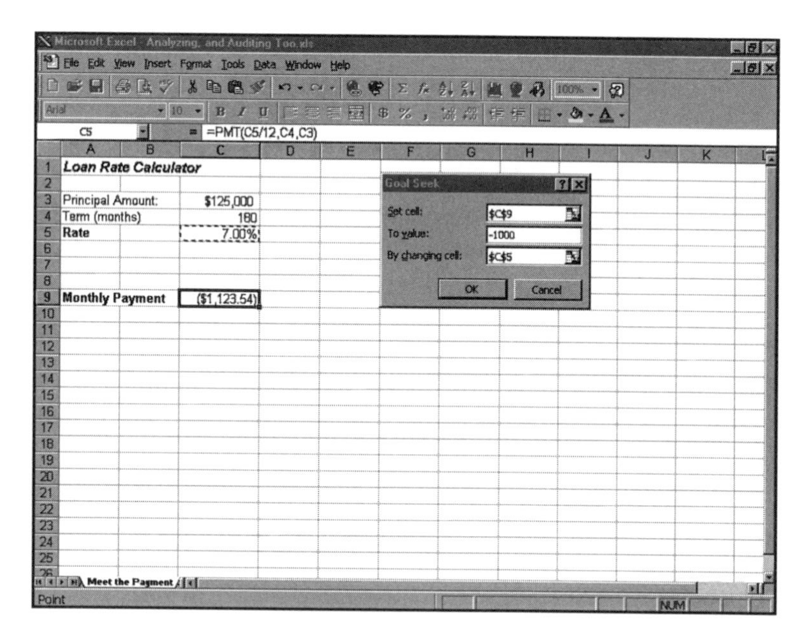

Fig. 14.9
We're setting the monthly payment to −1,000, the amount we want to pay.

CAUTION **Don't do what I did on my first attempt at this—enter a positive** number for the To Value box. We're looking for a payment, so we need to tell Goal Seek to find a payment. Goal Seek gets very confused if you instruct it otherwise in a problem like this.

5 Click OK, and Goal Seek finds our answer, as shown in Figure 14.10.

Fig. 14.10
We need a rate of 5.18% to get that monthly payment in under budget.

We'll need a lower, variable loan rate to make budget. Let's just hope the Fed doesn't raise rates again any time soon.

Solving with Solver

Goal Seek is a great gadget, but it has its limitations. It only works with one variable, for one thing. For another, you have to take what it gives you. If Goal Seek can't find a solution, there's no way to impose constraints on its search for another try.

Excel has a more powerful tool for solving problems with multivariable inputs. It's called Solver, and you get to it by clicking Tools, Solver.

I don't see Solver on the Tools menu!

Solver is an add-in. Its installation was an option when you ran Excel's Setup program. If Solver isn't on the Tools menu, select Tools, Add-Ins and click the Solver Add-In box. If it's not there either, you'll have to get out your Excel program disks or CD and run Setup. You won't have to reinstall the whole program—just the Solver add-in.

What's the cheapest, fastest, most efficient way to allocate scarce resources? Solver answers all kinds of complex optimization problems, such as:

- Finding the mix of stocks, bonds, and cash to minimize risk and maximize returns in a portfolio
- Figuring the optimal mix of products to build from a limited inventory of parts
- Analyzing different shipping routes to find the optimal amounts to ship by the least costly routes
- Building a schedule that makes the best use of available staff at the lowest cost
- Discovering the mix of short-term investments that maximizes both liquidity and returns

Solver is a potent but complex tool. There are Solver examples and sample worksheets built right into Excel. Click the Open button on the Standard toolbar and select the Solver subfolder in the Examples subfolder, which is found in the Excel folder. (Whew. We may start missing those old directories and subdirectories yet.) Then open Solverex and Solvsamp to study practical applications of Solver.

What's wrong with my worksheet? Auditing to trace errors

As you build complex worksheets, with formulas that refer to cells holding other formulas and functions nested inside of other functions, the chances of making a mistake increase with every step.

One error in a single formula can throw off the whole workbook. How do you track it down? Combing through dozens of formulas stuffed with cell references to other formulas could take days.

Fortunately, you don't have to. Excel has a detective standing by to find errors. Like a private eye, Auditing follows the trail from cell to cell, then unmasks the guilty party. It reveals a cell's ancestry by tracing all the other cells that contributed to it, exposing any closeted skeletons. Auditing also shows you at a glance all the cells related to a particular formula.

Its method? Elementary, my dear Watson. Auditing works by drawing arrows on your worksheet to show how cells relate to each other.

The Auditing toolbar

Whoever heard of a private eye who's on call 24 hours a day, doesn't charge a fee, and never nips from a bottle in the desk? Meet the Auditing toolbar.

Using the Auditing toolbar is the easiest way to put Excel's gumshoe to work. Click Tools, Auditing, Show Auditing Toolbar to summon it up.

The Auditing toolbar is its name, worksheet errors its game

Remove Precedent Arrows
When you click this button, all the arrows you drew with Trace Precedents disappear one level at a time with each click

New Comment
This button allows you to write yourself a memo about a particular cell

Remove Dependent Arrows
Click this button to get rid of all the arrows you drew with Trace Dependents

Remove All Arrows
This button is handy if you can't remember what you were tracing. It wipes out precedent and dependent arrows

Clear Validation Circles
Removes the circles displayed by the Circle Invalid Data command

Auditing

Circle Invalid Data
The Data Validation command lets you set conditions for the values in a given cell. If cell values don't meet those conditions, the cells are circled when you click the button

Trace Dependents
Select a cell, click this button, and arrows point to all the formulas that refer to the cell. Keep clicking for arrows to all the formulas that refer to the first one, level by level, one click at a time

Trace Error
If you get an error message, select the cell where it appeared and click this button. Arrows are drawn to all the cells that might have contributed to the error. If there are several cells containing errors, the arrows branch. You can pick the branch you want to follow first

Trace Precedents
Click here to see arrows pointing to all the cells referenced directly by that formula. Click again to see arrows pointing to all the cells referenced by the cells pointed to on the first click. Keep clicking to trace every cell that relates directly or indirectly to the selected formula

Where did this number come from?!

You might write a formula that references cells on the worksheet containing other formulas. If the result your formula produces makes you scratch your head, pop up the Auditing toolbar. To display the Auditing toolbar, click Tools, Auditing, Show Auditing Toolbar. Select the cells referenced in the formula and click the Trace Precedents button on the Auditing toolbar. Then select the formula itself and click the Trace Precedents button again.

The Trace Precedents arrows show you at a glance which values and formulas went into the formula that's giving you trouble. That makes it much easier to spot possible errors. Figure 14.11 shows a formula with all its precedents.

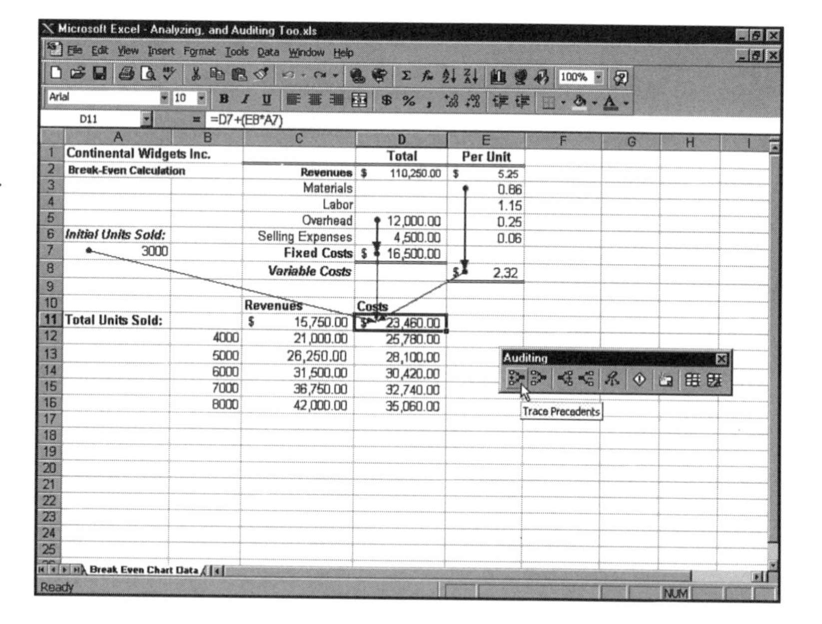

Fig. 14.11
Tracing precedents is a handy way to determine how you calculated a value arrived at by a formula.

The formula in D11 drew on A7, D7, and E8, shown by the first set of arrows. E8 and D7, in turn, are sums of the outlined ranges, shown by the second set of arrows.

We can see at a glance where the value produced by the formula came from. Figure 14.12 shows the answer to the question, "Where did I *use* this value?"

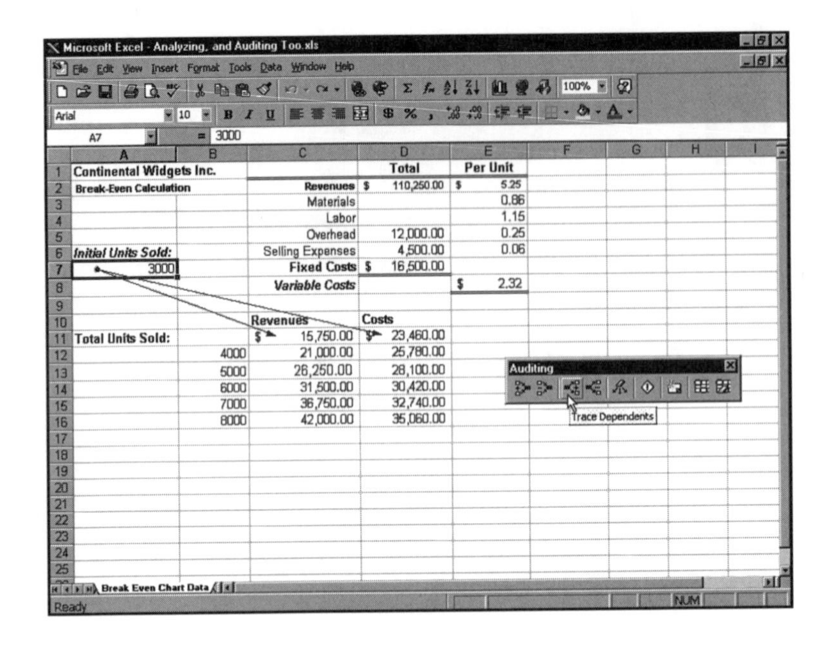

Fig. 14.12
Tracing dependents shows the formulas where that mysterious stray value wound up.

Auditing won't trace certain relationships between cells. Named constants are ignored, as are array results. It also doesn't come with a trench coat. Even so, you'll find Auditing a dependable worksheet private eye.

Part VI: Using Excel as a Database

15 Databases in a Nutshell

In this chapter:

- **What's a list?**
- **How should I set up my list?**
- **I want to enter data painlessly**
- **Sorting makes sense of big lists**
- **How can I get the information I need from my list?**

On a grocery list or office Rolodex, recording important information is part of daily life. Put your records in Excel worksheets and you can sort, analyze, and manage them any way you want. . . . .

Let's face it—there's nothing romantic about lists. Just listing something can make it seem mundane. A trip to Hawaii might be the thrill of a lifetime; write down a list of the sights you saw, and even *you* will find it dull reading.

But while lists may not inspire, we can't do without them. How useful would a library be without a card catalog? Or a telephone without a phone book? By wandering through the stacks or dialing numbers randomly, we could find what we wanted...eventually. But armed with the right list, organized in the right way, we get to the information we need right now.

Decide what sort of information you want organized, and Excel does the rest of the work. From arranging a list alphabetically to extracting buried details from obscure records in giant databases, Excel makes information useful by making it available.

You have it on the list

A **list** is just a worksheet, with columns and rows, text and numbers. But if you follow a few easy guidelines when you set up the worksheet, Excel treats it like a database.

What do you put in a list? Any sort of data you want. Employee records, salespeople's sales, parts inventories, client phone numbers and addresses, even your butterfly collection. Any information that can be stored, sorted, summarized, and retrieved is a perfect candidate for a list.

A database by any other name is a list

If you think a list sounds a lot like a database, you're right. In fact, past versions of Excel did call this kind of thing a database. So why is it a list now? Cynics might think it could have something to do with the fact that Excel's makers sell a separate database program. Noncynics might just view it as an Excel idiosyncrasy. If Excel calls spreadsheets "worksheets" and graphs "charts," why not call databases "lists?" We drive on one side of the road, the British and Japanese use the other. We all have our quirks, spreadsheet/worksheet programs with databases/lists included.

How should I set up my list?

A list is made up of three building blocks:

- **Records** are like Rolodex cards. Each record should be a complete entry for a particular item. If you're making a list of wines, you'd include the vintage, the winemaker, the vineyard, the variety of grape, the region, and the name of the wine. Maybe the distributor too—the record can be as detailed as you want. Here's an example of another sort of record: Moore, Jane, 555 Spruce Street, Smithtown, CA, 94100, 415-555-2678.

- **Fields** are each separate bits of data in a record. The vintage in a wine record is a field. Ms. Moore's phone number also is a field. Each field in a record can be searched or sorted. Want to find all your wines from 1989? Search the vintage field. Have your list produce a report on all of Ms. Moore's neighbors by sorting the street address and city fields. Break down your records into as many fields as you want. The more fields you create for the list, the more flexible it will be.

- The **header row** consists of the column titles at the beginning of the list. The titles label each field, and Excel uses them to sort, retrieve, and report on your list. The header row might have titles like First Name, Last Name, Vineyard, and so on. It's a good idea to format the header row in a way that distinguishes it from records and fields.

Break up your records into fields that'll hold the smallest bit of data you're likely to use. Instead of one field for Name, for example, have separate fields for Last Name and First Name. Addresses can be broken up into Street fields, ZIP Code fields, and so on. Doing so makes your list searchable, and sortable, by all those criteria.

In an Excel list, each column is a field, and each row is a record. The header row goes at the beginning of the list. It might look like Figure 15.1.

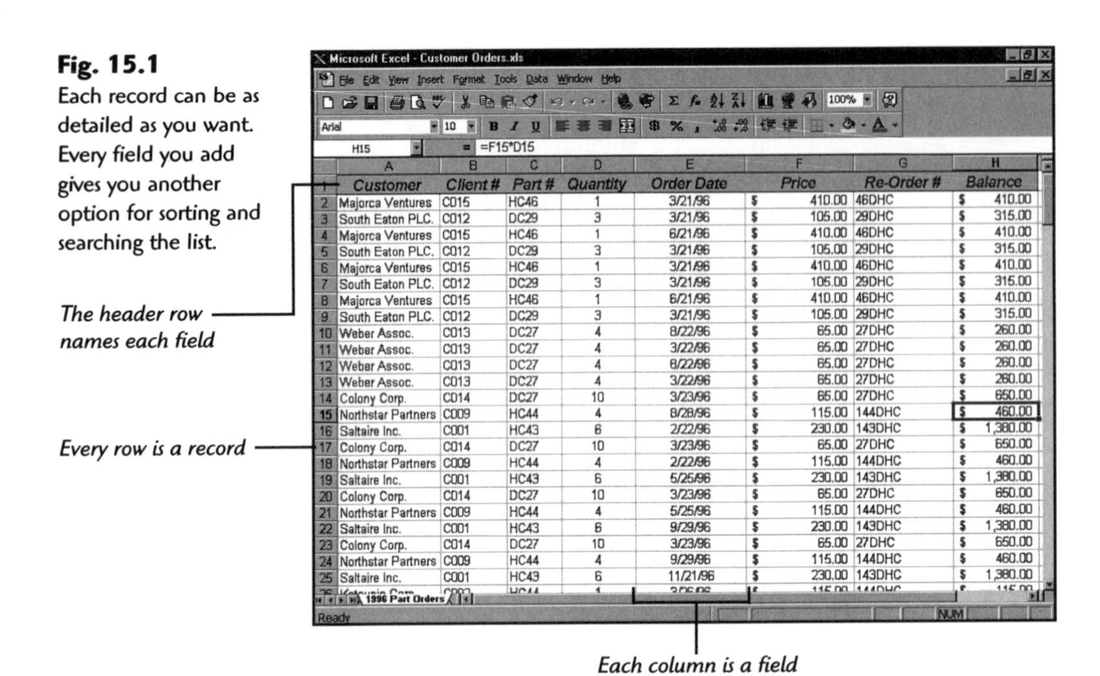

	Customer	Client #	Part #	Quantity	Order Date	Price	Re-Order #	Balance
2	Majorca Ventures	C015	HC46	1	3/21/96	$ 410.00	46DHC	$ 410.00
3	South Eaton PLC.	C012	DC29	3	3/21/96	$ 105.00	29DHC	$ 315.00
4	Majorca Ventures	C015	HC46	1	6/21/96	$ 410.00	46DHC	$ 410.00
5	South Eaton PLC.	C012	DC29	3	3/21/96	$ 105.00	29DHC	$ 315.00
6	Majorca Ventures	C015	HC46	1	3/21/96	$ 410.00	46DHC	$ 410.00
7	South Eaton PLC.	C012	DC29	3	3/21/96	$ 105.00	29DHC	$ 315.00
8	Majorca Ventures	C015	HC46	1	6/21/96	$ 410.00	46DHC	$ 410.00
9	South Eaton PLC.	C012	DC29	3	3/21/96	$ 105.00	29DHC	$ 315.00
10	Weber Assoc.	C013	DC27	4	8/22/96	$ 65.00	27DHC	$ 260.00
11	Weber Assoc.	C013	DC27	4	3/22/96	$ 65.00	27DHC	$ 260.00
12	Weber Assoc.	C013	DC27	4	8/22/96	$ 65.00	27DHC	$ 260.00
13	Weber Assoc.	C013	DC27	4	3/22/96	$ 65.00	27DHC	$ 260.00
14	Colony Corp.	C014	DC27	10	3/23/96	$ 65.00	27DHC	$ 650.00
15	Northstar Partners	C009	HC44	4	8/28/96	$ 115.00	144DHC	$ 460.00
16	Saltaire Inc.	C001	HC43	6	2/22/96	$ 230.00	143DHC	$ 1,380.00
17	Colony Corp.	C014	DC27	10	3/23/96	$ 65.00	27DHC	$ 650.00
18	Northstar Partners	C009	HC44	4	2/22/96	$ 115.00	144DHC	$ 460.00
19	Saltaire Inc.	C001	HC43	6	5/25/96	$ 230.00	143DHC	$ 1,380.00
20	Colony Corp.	C014	DC27	10	3/23/96	$ 65.00	27DHC	$ 650.00
21	Northstar Partners	C009	HC44	4	5/25/96	$ 115.00	144DHC	$ 460.00
22	Saltaire Inc.	C001	HC43	6	9/29/96	$ 230.00	143DHC	$ 1,380.00
23	Colony Corp.	C014	DC27	10	3/23/96	$ 65.00	27DHC	$ 650.00
24	Northstar Partners	C009	HC44	4	9/29/96	$ 115.00	144DHC	$ 460.00
25	Saltaire Inc.	C001	HC43	6	11/21/96	$ 230.00	143DHC	$ 1,380.00

Fig. 15.1
Each record can be as detailed as you want. Every field you add gives you another option for sorting and searching the list.

What should I know about setting up a list?

Although lists are just like regular worksheets, here are a few things you can do to make your lists more useful:

- Use a different font for the header row. Give it a border, a pattern, bold it or italicize it, whatever pleases you. You want to make sure it stands out from the records in some way.
- Create records that put similar data in matching fields. Last names should all go in the Last Name field. The column title in the header row should read "Last Name."
- Make your list more readable by formatting the columns, or fields, differently. You might format alternating records with a gray background, for example. Just remember that if you italicize or bold a field, it'll print that way in a report.
- Use capital letters or not, whatever's appropriate. Excel can search and sort either, ignoring case or not—your choice.
- Formulas also work fine in lists.

Set up the worksheet along these lines, and Excel turns into a powerful database program that can analyze and manage your data automatically and conveniently.

Pitfalls to avoid when setting up lists

There are also a few "don'ts" to watch out for when setting up your lists:

- Don't use blank rows or broken lines to separate the header row from the records. Excel doesn't like either one. Also, don't separate column titles in the header row with blank columns.
- Spaces within each field are fine, but don't start a field with spaces. That makes for problems in sorting and retrieving.
- Avoid putting other data on the same sheet with the list. If you must, surround the list with a blank row and column to let Excel know where the list ends and the other stuff begins. It's also a good idea to keep to one list per sheet.

How do I build my list the easy way?

Dinner parties in the Middle Ages were messy affairs. Guests ate with their fingers. In the absence of napkins, they wiped their hands on the stray dogs that milled around the banquet hall. When the proceedings dragged, banquetters would toss a bone amongst the dogs, then sit back and enjoy the fight. Great fun, especially with a team of servants standing by to clean things up afterward.

Most of us don't have servants to clean up after us nowadays. Maybe that's why our dinners are a little neater. We like our lists to be tidy too. If they get messy, we're the ones likely to be stuck with the job of cleaning them up.

There are three steps to making tidy lists:

1. Type the header row. In each column, label the fields for each record.
2. Click any cell in the header row, then choose Data, Form. A handy form pops up, with data entry boxes for each field created by your new column headings.

3 Enter the data for each field. Use the Tab key to move from box to box in the form. Then click New. The data form puts each entry in the appropriate column and you're ready to enter the next record. Click New when you're through, and the next record is placed at the bottom of the list (see Figure 15.2).

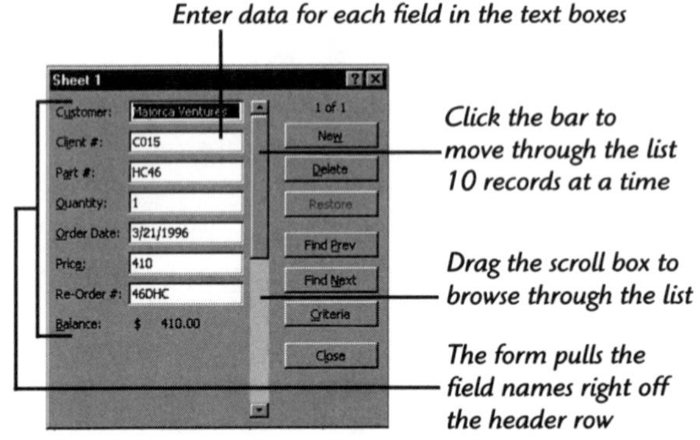

Fig. 15.2
The data form takes the sheet name for atitle. If you forget to select a header row cell before calling it up, Excel asks if you want to use the top row as a header row.

Using the data form

You *can* build a list by entering data in each field, cell by cell. And if your list includes many repeated entries, Excel's AutoComplete feature makes list-building directly in cells fast and convenient (see Chapter 2 for a detailed discussion of AutoComplete).

Otherwise, use the data form. Even for repetitive lists, data forms can improve the accuracy of those doing the data entry. On a crowded worksheet, it doesn't take much to enter data in the wrong column. You're much less likely to do that on the form.

Like a multiple-choice question, the data form forces you to stick to the straight and narrow. You don't have room for wild flights of fancy, but you can't do much damage either.

TIP

If you need wider text boxes on the form, widen one of the row header columns by dragging the right border of the column heading. The form uses the width of the widest header column for the width of the text boxes.

What do the buttons do?

The command buttons at the side of the data form give you a lot of control over your list. Take a look at Figure 15.3.

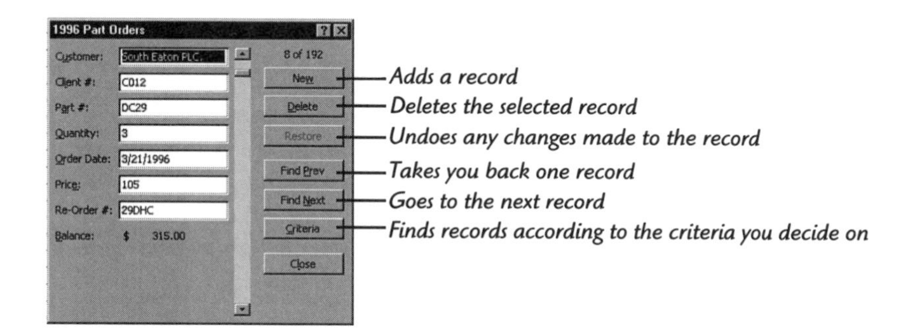

Fig. 15.3
Use the command buttons to manage your records.

CAUTION **Be careful when you use the Delete button. It works like the Edit,** Delete command. You get rid of the record and the row it occupied. All the other rows in the list slide up to fill the gap. If you use numbered records, that will renumber the records below the one you deleted.

Find records with the data form

When you click the Criteria button, the form changes into a search tool. Use the text boxes to search for records by any field, or combination of fields, you choose (see Figure 15.4).

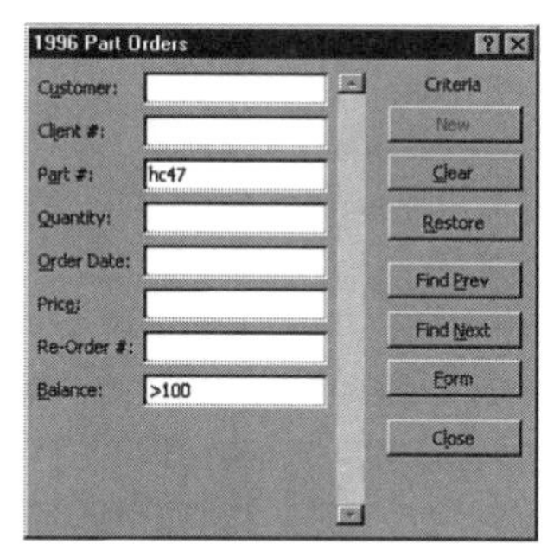

Fig. 15.4
Looking for a customer who ordered a certain part and has a balance more than $100? Click the Criteria button and enter those criteria in the form to find the record.

To enter new criteria, click Clear and start again. To search for a group of records, you can enter comparison criteria. Use comparison operators like =, <, and > to find subsets of the list that meet criteria, such as customers with balances >100 as shown in Figure 15.4.

How do I edit records?

Call up the record with the form, and you can edit the fields in the text boxes. Not formulas, though. The value calculated by the formula appears in the form, but there's no text box for that field. Same thing with protected cells.

I need to add a record to the middle of the list

The data form sticks new records at the end of the list. If you want to add a record anywhere else, select Insert, Rows. A blank row will be squeezed in above the row you were in when you started the operation.

All the records below the new one get shoved down one row.

This list is out of sorts!

If your phone books are like mine, they start life beautifully ordered. All the names are arranged alphabetically, and numbers and addresses are easy to find. Then you add a listing here, scratch out a listing there, and after a few weeks that pristine phone book begins to look a little chaotic. Wouldn't it be great to reorder all the listings and restore that clear alphabetical sequence? Short of cutting and pasting—the old-fashioned kind with scissors and glue—it can't be done.

That's one advantage Excel has over my disorderly phone books. No matter how many changes you make to an Excel list, you can order and reorder it anyway you like, as often as you like.

What does sorting do (and what can I do with it)?

Sorting an Excel list is like shuffling a deck of cards. Start with the ace of spades on top, shuffle, and it winds up on the bottom the deck. You can do the same thing with your records. This is a trick deck, though—one shuffle can order the cards from highest to lowest, lowest to highest, or put all cards of the same suite together. You can even stand the cards on end.

Select any cell in a list and click Data, Sort. The Sort dialog box pops up.

1 Click the Sort By drop-down arrow for a list of your fields (see Figure 15.5.) Select a field from the list, and all the records in the list will be reordered using that field as a starting point.

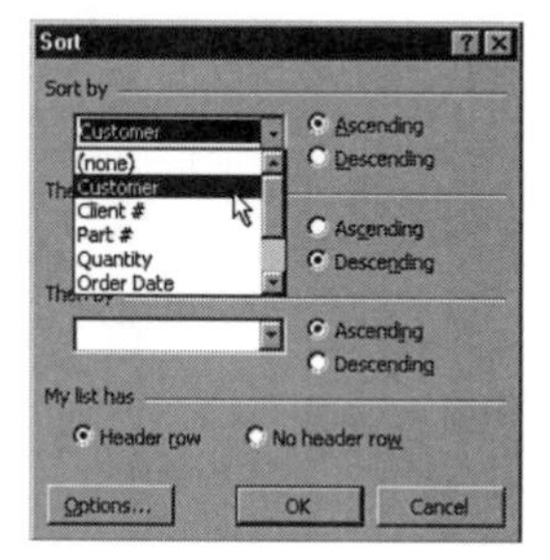

Fig. 15.5
Sorting lets you reorder your list in as many ways as you have fields to sort.

2 Select Ascending or Descending to decide the order of the sort. Ascending orders number from 1 to 10, letters from A to Z, and dates and times from earliest to latest. Descending takes the opposite track.

3 Then By lets you pick another field from the drop-down list and refine your sort further. It's like arranging the deck in order from ace to 2, *then by* spades, then clubs, and so on. Figures 15.6 and 15.7 show you how it works.

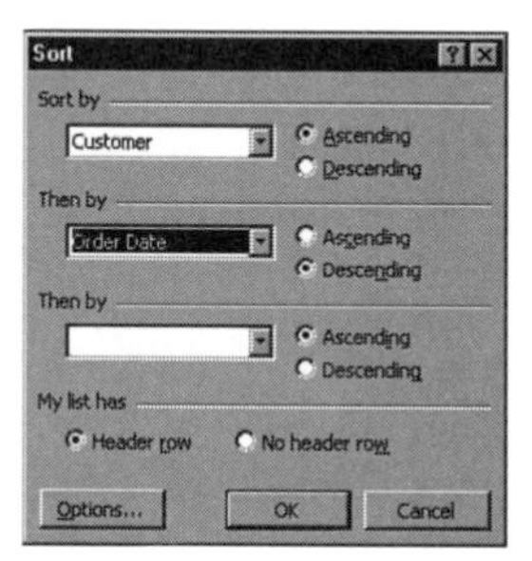

Fig. 15.6
Ascending by Customer puts the list in alphabetical order from A to Z. Then By Order Date Descending further sorts the list by order date, from a customer's latest order to the earliest.

Want to see the clients who've bought the most expensive parts most recently? Sort the list by Price, Descending, then by Order Date, Descending, as shown in Figure 15.8.

Fig. 15.7
Now we have an alphabetized list showing the latest customer orders first.

	Customer	Client #	Part #	Quantity	Order Date	Price	Re-Order #	Balance
2	Algarve Cons.	C004	HC46	3	6/28/96	$ 410.00	146DHC	$ 1,230.00
3	Algarve Cons.	C004	HC46	3	6/28/96	$ 410.00	146DHC	$ 1,230.00
4	Algarve Cons.	C004	HC46	3	6/28/96	$ 410.00	146DHC	$ 1,230.00
5	Algarve Cons.	C004	HC46	3	6/28/96	$ 410.00	146DHC	$ 1,230.00
6	Algarve Cons.	C004	HC46	3	5/28/96	$ 410.00	146DHC	$ 1,230.00
7	Algarve Cons.	C004	HC46	3	5/28/96	$ 410.00	146DHC	$ 1,230.00
8	Algarve Cons.	C004	HC46	3	5/28/96	$ 410.00	146DHC	$ 1,230.00
9	Algarve Cons.	C004	HC46	3	5/28/96	$ 410.00	146DHC	$ 1,230.00
10	Algarve Cons.	C004	HC46	3	3/28/96	$ 410.00	146DHC	$ 1,230.00
11	Algarve Cons.	C004	HC46	3	3/28/96	$ 410.00	146DHC	$ 1,230.00
12	Algarve Cons.	C004	HC46	3	3/28/96	$ 410.00	146DHC	$ 1,230.00
13	Algarve Cons.	C004	HC46	3	3/28/96	$ 410.00	146DHC	$ 1,230.00
14	Bombay Ltd.	C011	DC28	5	6/27/96	$ 80.00	28DHC	$ 400.00
15	Bombay Ltd.	C011	DC28	5	6/27/96	$ 80.00	28DHC	$ 400.00
16	Bombay Ltd.	C011	DC28	5	6/27/96	$ 80.00	28DHC	$ 400.00
17	Bombay Ltd.	C011	DC28	5	6/27/96	$ 80.00	28DHC	$ 400.00
18	Bombay Ltd.	C011	DC28	5	5/27/96	$ 80.00	28DHC	$ 400.00
19	Bombay Ltd.	C011	DC28	5	5/27/96	$ 80.00	28DHC	$ 400.00
20	Bombay Ltd.	C011	DC28	5	5/27/96	$ 80.00	28DHC	$ 400.00
21	Bombay Ltd.	C011	DC28	5	5/27/96	$ 80.00	28DHC	$ 400.00
22	Bombay Ltd.	C011	DC28	5	3/27/96	$ 80.00	28DHC	$ 400.00
23	Bombay Ltd.	C011	DC28	5	3/27/96	$ 80.00	28DHC	$ 400.00
24	Bombay Ltd.	C011	DC28	5	3/27/96	$ 80.00	28DHC	$ 400.00
25	Bombay Ltd.	C011	DC28	5	3/27/96	$ 80.00	28DHC	$ 400.00

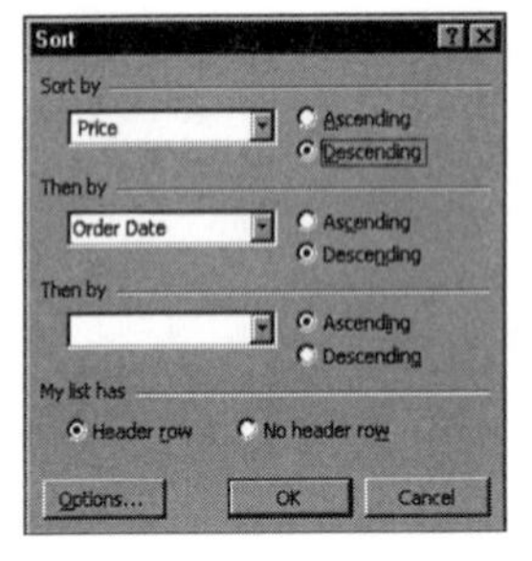

Fig. 15.8
Sorting gives you critical information from your list instantly. Sorted by these criteria, you could see who's placed the most recent order for the most expensive parts.

When you pop up the Sort dialog box in a sorted list, the last sort criteria you used are shown (refer to Figure 15.8).

Sorting it out further

Click the Options button to refine your sort method. Case Sensitive forces the sort to pay attention to the case of letters. Orientation lets you sort across the list instead of up and down. First Key Sort Order allows a custom sort by month or day, or by any other list you've created in Tools, Options, Custom Lists.

I sorted my list left to right and wound up with a whole column of `#REF!` error messages. What gives?

If one field in a list refers to another field, sorting across the list gets you this charming Excel error message. Click Undo right away to restore the list to its former state. Change the orientation back to Top to Bottom before sorting again. If you want to sort left to right across the list, you'll have to make all the cell references absolute.

I want my unsorted list back!

Sorting gives you plenty of ways to look at a list, but at the end of the day you might want your list restored to its original order.

The easy way to do that? Begin your list with a field called Record Number or something similar, then use the fill handle to fill the rows with a numbered series like R1, R2, and so on. When each record has a number, you can restore the original order by sorting on that field in ascending order. Figure 15.9 gives you the idea.

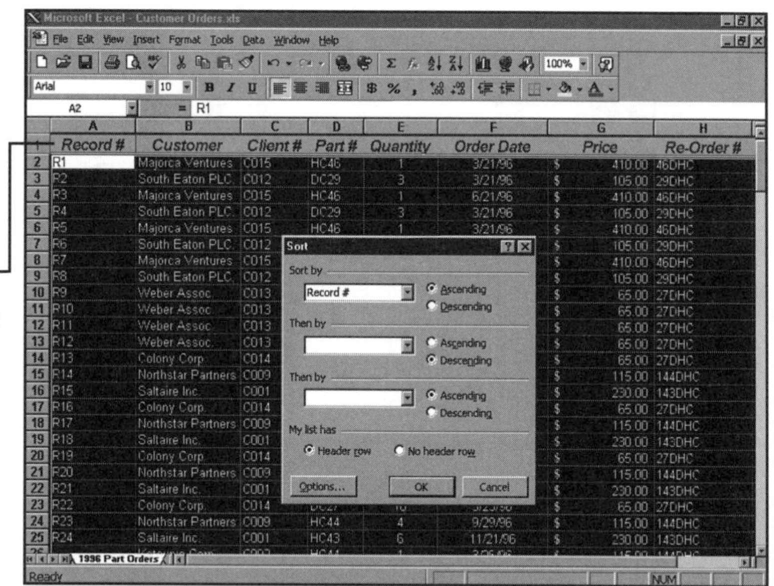

Fig. 15.9
When you set up a field to number all your records, you can snap the list back to its original state by sorting on that column.

Creating a field that numbers each record lets you sort on that field and return the list to its former state

TIP

For a quick sort, click a column heading to select it, then click the Sort Ascending or Sort Descending buttons on the toolbar. That sorts the whole list on the column (field) you selected in ascending or descending order.

Extract what you need with AutoFilter

What coffee addict doesn't know about filters? We want that burning black liquid, not the bitter grounds. So we filter them out. Paper filters, gold filters, everyone has a favorite type. The idea is always the same, though—keep what you want, eliminate what you don't.

Excel has a kind of coffee filter for lists called AutoFilter. And it does just what you'd expect—filters out the stuff you don't want, leaving only what you do want.

Using AutoFilter

Select Data, Filter, AutoFilter. Drop-down arrows appear in each column in the header row. Click an arrow, and a list appears of all the items in that field, as shown in Figure 15.10.

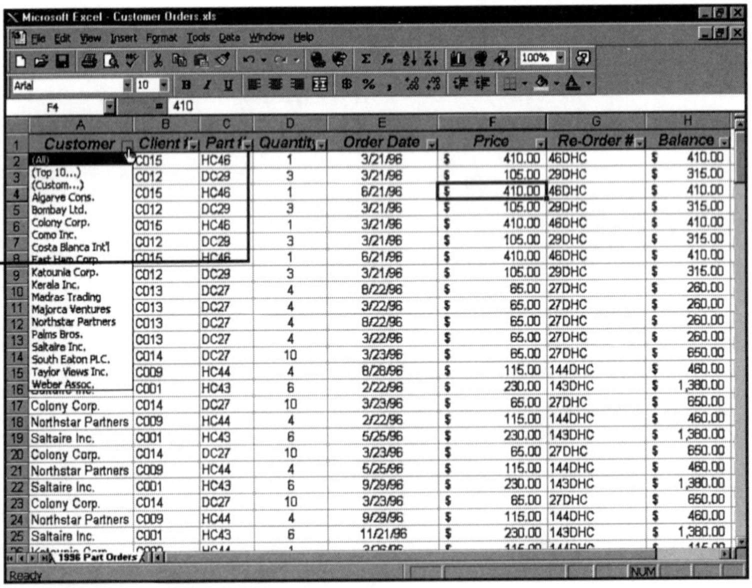

Fig. 15.10
AutoFilter gives you a menu of all the items in each field (column).

Click the drop-down arrows for a list of all the items in the field

This is just the beginning. Suppose we want to examine only the customers who ordered part number HC47. Scroll down the AutoFilter drop-down list to HC47 and click it. Figure 15.11 shows the result.

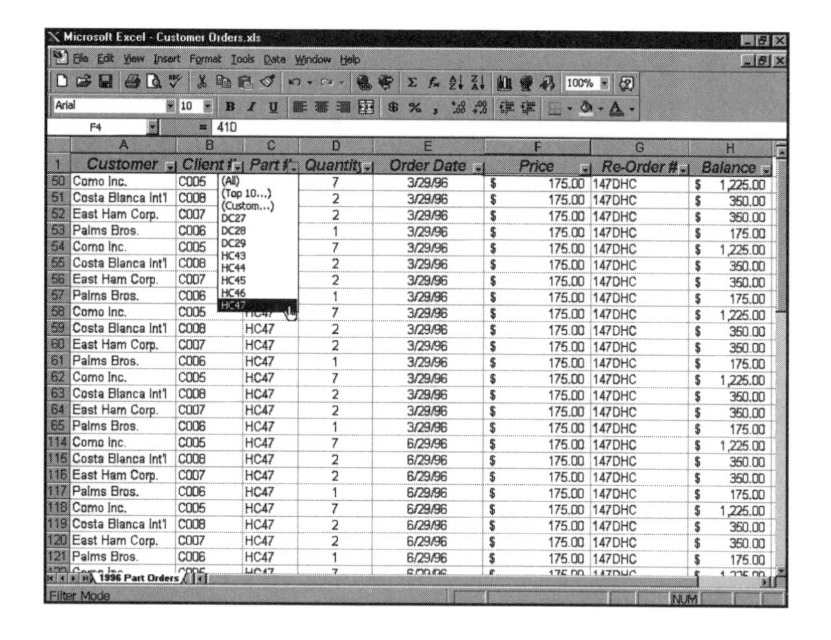

Fig. 15.11
Click an item to hide everything in the list except the records containing that item.

Everything in the list is hidden except those records containing HC47. We have an instant sublist of customers who ordered that part. Collapse the list still further by clicking the other arrows and choosing other items. See who ordered that part on a particular day, for example.

What happened to the rest of the list? It's there, just hidden. To restore the list, select Data, Filter, Show All; or choose All from the drop-down list.

AutoFilter with Top 10, for sorts without sorting

Sorting orders your list according to criteria you define, as you saw earlier in the chapter. But suppose you just want to see the highest or lowest values in the list? Maybe you want a quick read on your customers with the highest balances, for example. With the AutoFilter Top 10 option, you can do that without sorting the list.

Click the AutoFilter drop-down arrow in a column with numeric values, like balances. Select Top 10 from the AutoFilter drop-down list, and you get the Top 10 AutoFilter dialog box shown in Figure 15.12.

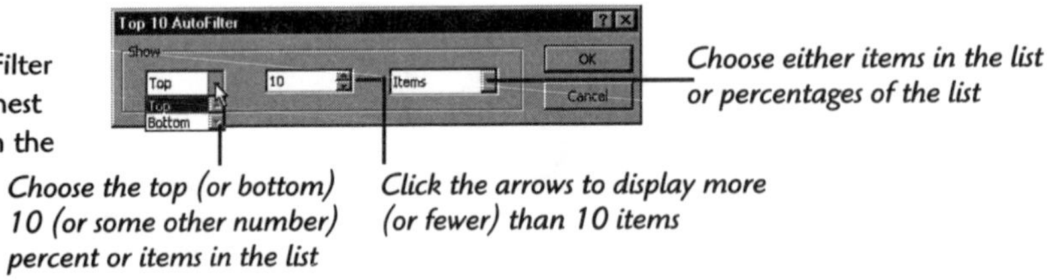

Fig. 15.12
Use Top 10 AutoFilter to display the highest or lowest values in the list.

Choose either items in the list or percentages of the list

Choose the top (or bottom) 10 (or some other number) percent or items in the list

Click the arrows to display more (or fewer) than 10 items

Although it's called Top 10, you can display any number of items at the top or bottom of the list, selected by their numeric values.

Customizing AutoFilter

We can narrow the AutoFilter drop-down list with the Custom option. Let's check the customers who placed orders between March 22 and March 29.

1. Click the AutoFilter drop-down arrow in the Order Date column and select **(Custom...)** (refer to Figure 15.10).
2. The Custom AutoFilter dialog box pops up. Click the upper-left drop-down arrow for a list of comparison conditions: Is Greater Than, Equals, Does Not Equal, Begins With, and so on. Select Is Greater Than, and it appears in the text box under the arrow.
3. Click the upper-right arrow for a list of all the items in the column. Now click 3/22/96 to dump that in the text box next to Is Greater Than.
4. Stay with it—the second time is easier. Click And, then click the lower-left arrow for more comparison conditions. Select Is Less Than.
5. Now click the lower-right arrow for the item list again. Click 3/29/96 to set the And criterion, as shown in Figure 15.13.

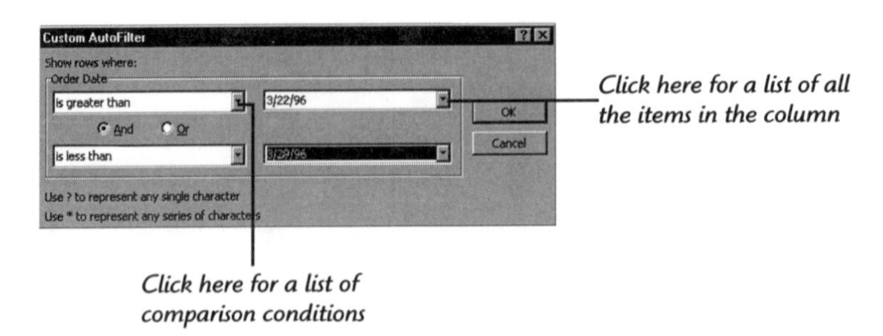

Fig. 15.13
Using the Custom AutoFilter dialog box is one of those things that's easier done than said. Worth trying though, because it's extremely handy.

6 Click OK in the Custom AutoFilter dialog box when you're done, and the range of records you've specified will be extracted and displayed.

To turn off AutoFilter, choose Data, Filter, AutoFilter. That gets rid of the AutoFilter drop-down arrows and restores the list display to the way it was before you selected AutoFilter.

For a quick report on items extracted with AutoFilter, click the Print button when your choices are displayed. Only the records you've extracted will print.

My list looks terrible

Is your list a confusing soup of text and numbers? Tidy it up with AutoFormat. Select Format, AutoFormat and scroll down to List 1, List 2, and List 3 for the three list formats. You can preview the formats in the Sample window.

Your whole list is selected automatically. To format just part of it, select the section first.

Figure 15.14 shows you one option for making the list more readable.

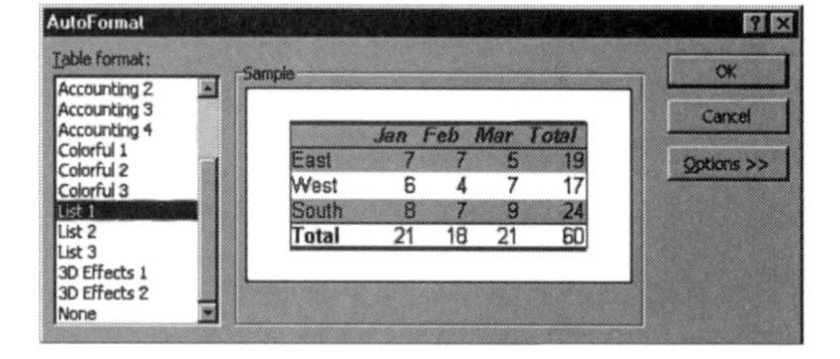

Fig. 15.14
AutoFormat can do wonders for an unsightly list. If you don't like the results, just click the Undo button.

16 Taming Monster Lists: Subtotals, Outlines, and Pivot Tables

In this chapter:

- **Outlines really cut this list down to size!**
- **How can I summarize this huge list?**
- **I want to print a subtotal report**
- **What is a pivot table?**
- **How can I get useful information from all this data?**

Before you know it, your little acorn of a list can grow to giant oak tree size. Excel has easy-to-use tools to cut the list back down to size. . . . .

Remember those "Can so! Cannot. Can so!..." playground squabbles? When poets Percy Shelley and Lord Byron drew Mary Shelley into a friendly exchange along those lines, the upshot wasn't the usual waste of time. "Bet you can't write a scary story," said Byron and Percy to Mary. "Can so!" she replied (or words to that effect). Then she sat down and wrote one of the greatest horror stories of all time: *Frankenstein.*

Entering records in a list is as easy and repetitive as saying "Can so!" It's automatic, and a little mindless. Before we know it, the worksheet is filled with data. Without much effort, the list grows to monstrous proportions.

But unlike Mary Shelley's monster, Excel lists never get out of hand. Excel's database commands extract useful information from vast expanses of worksheet data. They tame monster lists with ease.

Dr. F. should have had it so good.

Outlines let you see the trees in a forest of a list

When papers start to pile up in heaps on your desk, it's hard to find that one paper you need. Filing everything away is one answer, but who has the time (or the inclination) to poke around in filing cabinets? What we want to do is wave a wand and have everything we don't need disappear from view—only to have it all reappear with another wave when we do need it.

That can't be done with desktop heaps, but Excel has a gadget that works similar magic on heaps of data. **Outlines** let you group related data together, then stash it out of sight. When you need to see the data again, a click or two restores it to view.

When your forest of data starts to obscure a tree or two, create an outline:

1. Click a column heading in your list to select a field. If you want to group several fields, click the first heading, then Shift+click the last column heading. That selects the first and last columns, and all the columns in between.

You can't group nonadjacent data, so Ctrl+clicking nonadjacent columns won't work. If you try to group nonadjacent data, Excel gives you an error message.

2 Select Data, Group and Outline, Group. In the Group dialog box that pops up, choose either Rows or Columns, depending on what you're grouping together, and click OK. The Outline symbols appear in the worksheet, as shown in Figure 16.1.

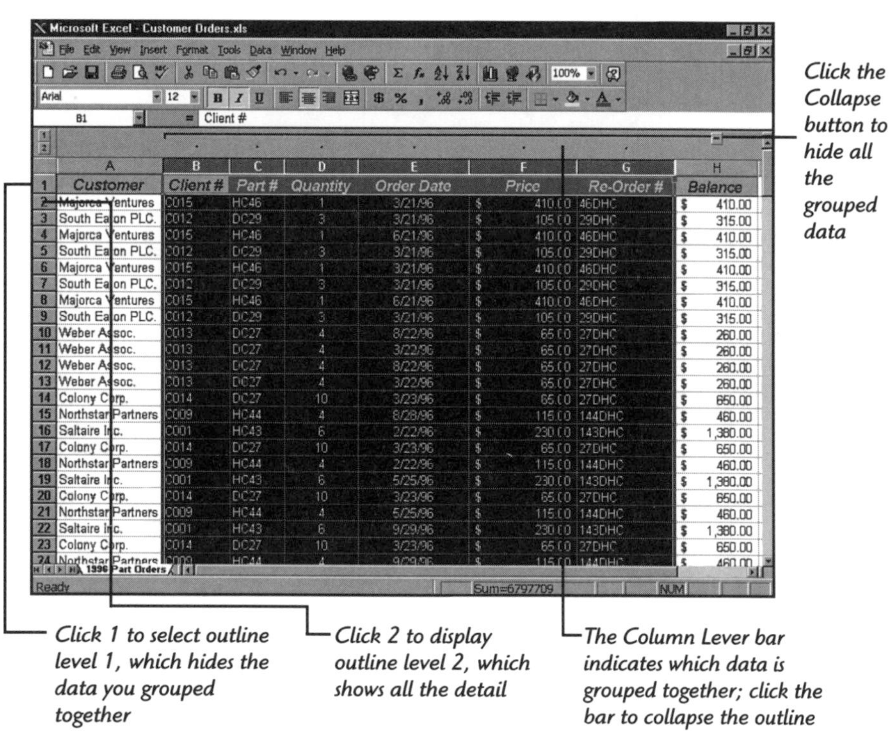

Fig. 16.1
When lists grow to monstrous proportions, use the outline tools to hide and display detail.

3 To hide the data you grouped, click the Column Lever bar or the Collapse button. That puts all the grouped data out of sight (see Figure 16.2).

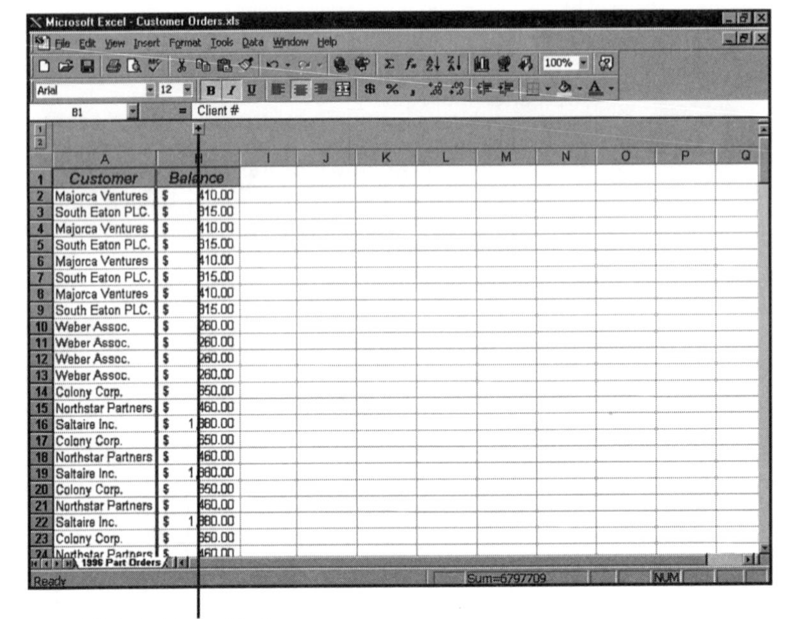

Fig. 16.2
Outlines let you exercise a lot of control over what portions of a list get displayed and printed.

Click the Expand button to display the detail in the list

For outlines with more than two levels, select grouped columns (or a single column), and choose Data, Group and Outline, Group again. After you group already-grouped data, you can refine the level of detail displayed by clicking the new outline level symbols that appear. You'll see a 3, a 4, and so on, depending on how many levels you create.

Outlines work the same way for rows. Click row headings to select the rows, then choose Data, Group and Outline, Group to group them together.

Q&A Why don't I see the outline symbols after I group data?

If the outline symbols don't display, click Tools, Options, View and click the Outline symbols check box.

When you print an outlined worksheet, only the displayed detail level is printed, making an outline a handy way to control print jobs.

To eliminate an outline level, click a row or column heading and choose Data, Group and Outline, Ungroup. In the Ungroup dialog box that appears, choose either Rows or Columns and click OK. Select Data, Group and Outline, Clear Outline to get rid of the outline altogether.

Get summary information with a subtotal

How do you cut a long story short? Read a summary. Same thing with lists. The longer your list grows, the more you'll need to view and analyze only parts of it at a time. Even sorted or filtered parts of the list can grow unmanageable. What you'll need is a summary, and the fastest way to summarize a list is with a **subtotal**. The Data Subtotals command gives you exactly that.

What is a subtotal, and what can I do with it?

Subtotals take a section of your list, apply a function like SUM to a selected field, then display the results. Like an outline, subtotals also let you control the level of worksheet detail that you print and display.

For subtotals to work, the list has to be sorted first. We arrange the list so that records with a common theme are grouped together. All the records pertaining to one customer might be one choice; records from a particular time period might be another (Chapter 15 tells you all you want to know about sorting lists). Once sorted, we can subtotal the groups of records to get our summary information. Here's how it works:

1. Decide what field or fields you want to subtotal, then sort the list so that those fields are grouped together. We want a subtotal for each customer, so we'll sort the list by Customer.
2. Select Data, Sort and choose Customer in the Sort By text box of the Sort dialog box (see Figure 16.3). Then click OK.

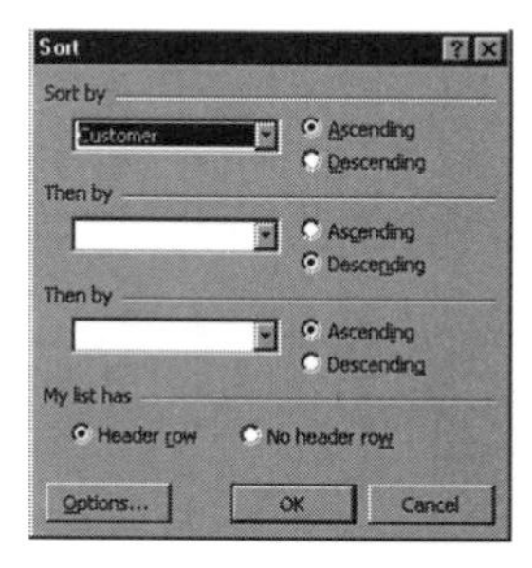

Fig. 16.3
Subtotaling starts with a sort, to group together the records whose field or fields you want to subtotal.

3. Click Data, Subtotals to open the Subtotal dialog box. Click the At Each Change In drop-down arrow for a list of all the fields in the database.

Here's where we tell Excel what groups of records to subtotal. We're after subtotals for each customer, so click Customer on the list.

4 Use Function gives you a choice of functions to apply to your subtotal. Sum is probably what you'll use most often. Among the other choices is Count, which counts how many records there are in each subtotal group. For now, we'll use Sum.

5 Add Subtotal To is where we choose what to subtotal. The drop-down list includes all the fields in the database. We're subtotaling Balance, so we'll click the Balance check box. It looks like Figure 16.4.

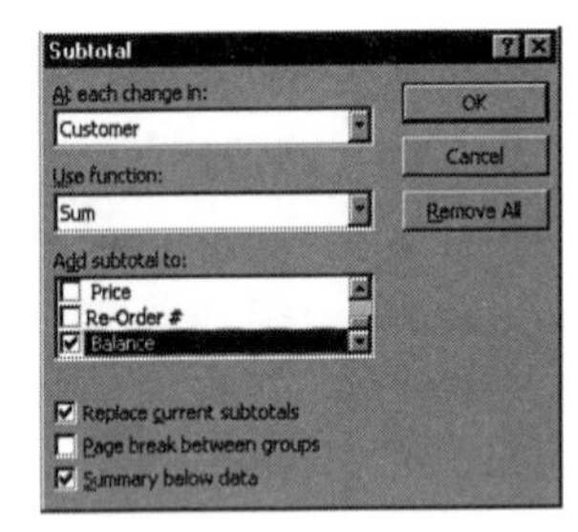

Fig. 16.4
The Subtotal dialog box lets you decide what and how to subtotal.

6 Click OK, and subtotals appear for each group of records (see Figure 16.5).

Fig. 16.5
The list with subtotals. A grand total appears at the bottom of the list.

These outline tools control the level of detail you see, print, or chart

Each subtotal is titled automatically

Microsoft Excel - Customer Orders.xls

H6 =SUBTOTAL(9,H2:H5)

	A	B	C	D	E	F	G	H
1	Customer	Client #	Part #	Quantity	Order Date	Price	Re-Order #	Balance
2	Algarve Cons.	C004	HC46	3	3/28/96	$ 410.00	146DHC	$ 1,230.00
3	Algarve Cons.	C004	HC46	3	3/28/96	$ 410.00	146DHC	$ 1,230.00
4	Algarve Cons.	C004	HC46	3	3/28/96	$ 410.00	146DHC	$ 1,230.00
5	Algarve Cons.	C004	HC46	3	3/28/96	$ 410.00	146DHC	$ 1,230.00
6	**Algarve Cons. Total**							$ 4,920.00
7	Bombay Ltd.	C011	DC28	5	3/27/96	$ 80.00	28DHC	$ 400.00
8	Bombay Ltd.	C011	DC28	5	3/27/96	$ 80.00	28DHC	$ 400.00
9	Bombay Ltd.	C011	DC28	5	3/27/96	$ 80.00	28DHC	$ 400.00
10	Bombay Ltd.	C011	DC28	5	3/27/96	$ 80.00	28DHC	$ 400.00
11	**Bombay Ltd. Total**							$ 1,600.00
12	Colony Corp.	C014	DC27	10	3/23/96	$ 65.00	27DHC	$ 650.00
13	Colony Corp.	C014	DC27	10	3/23/96	$ 65.00	27DHC	$ 650.00
14	Colony Corp.	C014	DC27	10	3/23/96	$ 65.00	27DHC	$ 650.00
15	Colony Corp.	C014	DC27	10	3/23/96	$ 65.00	27DHC	$ 650.00
16	**Colony Corp. Total**							$ 2,600.00
17	Como Inc.	C005	HC47	7	3/29/96	$ 175.00	147DHC	$ 1,225.00
18	Como Inc.	C005	HC47	7	3/29/96	$ 175.00	147DHC	$ 1,225.00
19	Como Inc.	C005	HC47	7	3/29/96	$ 175.00	147DHC	$ 1,225.00
20	Como Inc.	C005	HC47	7	3/29/96	$ 175.00	147DHC	$ 1,225.00
21	**Como Inc. Total**							$ 4,900.00
22	Costa Blanca Int'l	C008	HC47	2	3/29/96	$ 175.00	147DHC	$ 350.00
23	Costa Blanca Int'l	C008	HC47	2	3/29/96	$ 175.00	147DHC	$ 350.00
24	Costa Blanca Int'l	C008	HC47	2	3/29/96	$ 175.00	147DHC	$ 350.00
25	Costa Blanca Int'l	C008	HC47	2	3/29/96	$ 175.00	147DHC	$ 350.00
26	**Costa Blanca Int'l Total**							$ 1,400.00
27	East Ham Corp.	C007	HC47	2	3/29/96	$ 175.00	147DHC	$ 350.00

1996 Part Orders

Ready NUM

What else can I do with subtotals?

The numbered buttons and + and – symbols you saw in Figure 16.5 (they're the same outline tools we looked at earlier) turn your list into an accordion. It won't play "Lady of Spain," but you can collapse and expand the subtotaled list, just like an accordion expands and contracts. Click 3 to see all the detail, 2 for just the subtotals, or 1 for the Grand Total only.

Figure 16.6 shows the list with only the subtotals displayed.

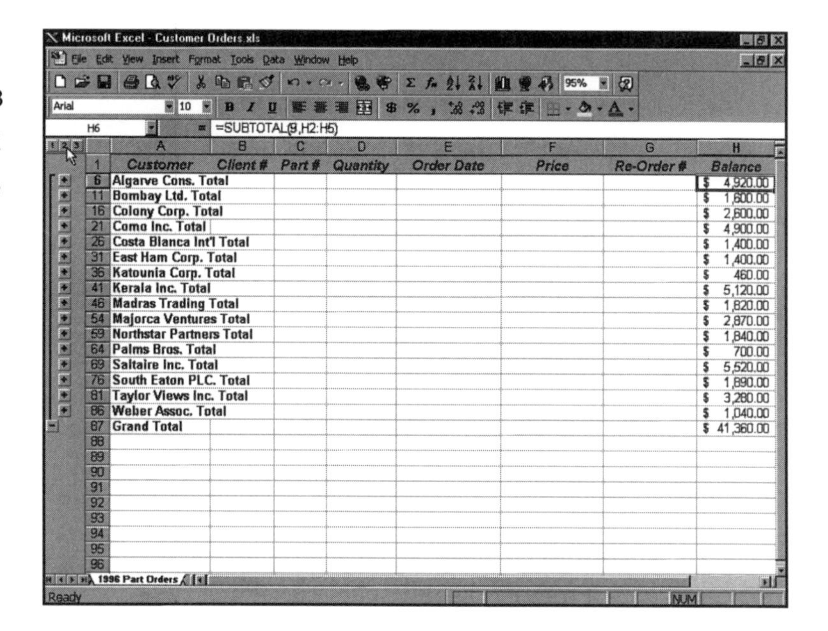

Fig. 16.6
Here, only the subtotals show. Click 3 to get back the detail. Expand each group of records by clicking the + buttons.

When you have the level of detail you want, preparing reports on your list is a breeze. Create a chart showing the balances for each customer, or print a subtotals report. The level of detail you choose to display controls the level of detail that you print or chart. That lets you decide exactly what you want to include or leave out.

Printing a subtotaled report

To make summary information in lists stand out, you can format the rows showing the subtotals with different fonts, borders, and patterns or color. Or do it the quick way and use AutoFormat. Figure 16.7 shows AutoFormat's List 3 option applied to the body of a list, excluding the header row.

Fig. 16.7
Apply AutoFormat to the entire list, or just a range, to make summary information stand out.

	Customer	Client #	Part #	Quantity	Order Date	Price	Re-Order #	Balance
2	Algarve Cons.	C004	HC46	3	3/28/96	$ 410.00	146DHC	$ 1,230.00
3	Algarve Cons.	C004	HC46	3	3/28/96	$ 410.00	146DHC	$ 1,230.00
4	Algarve Cons.	C004	HC46	3	3/28/96	$ 410.00	146DHC	$ 1,230.00
5	Algarve Cons.	C004	HC46	3	3/28/96	$ 410.00	146DHC	$ 1,230.00
6	*Algarve Cons. Total*							$ 4,920.00
7	Bombay Ltd.	C011	DC28	5	3/27/96	$ 80.00	28DHC	$ 400.00
8	Bombay Ltd.	C011	DC28	5	3/27/96	$ 80.00	28DHC	$ 400.00
9	Bombay Ltd.	C011	DC28	5	3/27/96	$ 80.00	28DHC	$ 400.00
10	Bombay Ltd.	C011	DC28	5	3/27/96	$ 80.00	28DHC	$ 400.00
11	*Bombay Ltd. Total*							$ 1,600.00
12	Colony Corp.	C014	DC27	10	3/23/96	$ 65.00	27DHC	$ 650.00
13	Colony Corp.	C014	DC27	10	3/23/96	$ 65.00	27DHC	$ 650.00
14	Colony Corp.	C014	DC27	10	3/23/96	$ 65.00	27DHC	$ 650.00
15	Colony Corp.	C014	DC27	10	3/23/96	$ 65.00	27DHC	$ 650.00
16	*Colony Corp. Total*							$ 2,600.00
17	Como Inc.	C005	HC47	7	3/29/96	$ 175.00	147DHC	$ 1,225.00
18	Como Inc.	C005	HC47	7	3/29/96	$ 175.00	147DHC	$ 1,225.00
19	Como Inc.	C005	HC47	7	3/29/96	$ 175.00	147DHC	$ 1,225.00
20	Como Inc.	C005	HC47	7	3/29/96	$ 175.00	147DHC	$ 1,225.00
21	*Como Inc. Total*							$ 4,900.00
22	Costa Blanca Int'l	C008	HC47	2	3/29/96	$ 175.00	147DHC	$ 350.00
23	Costa Blanca Int'l	C008	HC47	2	3/29/96	$ 175.00	147DHC	$ 350.00
24	Costa Blanca Int'l	C008	HC47	2	3/29/96	$ 175.00	147DHC	$ 350.00
25	Costa Blanca Int'l	C008	HC47	2	3/29/96	$ 175.00	147DHC	$ 350.00
26	*Costa Blanca Int'l Total*							$ 1,400.00

When the list looks right, select File, Print to print the report.

Q&A *I don't want subtotals after all. How do I get rid of them?*

If you subtotal, don't like what you see, and want to restore the list to its former state, click the Undo button, or select Data, Subtotals, and then click Remove All.

I need more information from my list

The Subtotals command lets you pull an amazing amount of useful information from your lists. You can subtotal more than one field from a group of records, as shown in Figure 16.8.

Use the Subtotal dialog box to add fields and to apply other functions. Here, we've subtotaled Price for each customer, and used Average to get the average price paid for each order.

Just deselect the Replace Current Subtotals check box in the Subtotal dialog box to keep the old subtotals and display them with the new ones. Excel adds a new subtotal line for each selection you make.

Fig. 16.8
Now the list shows totaled balances for each customer, and the average price paid by each customer.

Microsoft Excel - Customer Orders.xls

	A	B	C	D	E	F	G	H
1	*Customer*	*Client #*	*Part #*	*Quantity*	*Order Date*	*Price*	*Re-Order #*	*Balance*
2	Algarve Cons.	C004	HC46	3	3/28/96	$ 410.00	146DHC	$ 1,230.0
3	Algarve Cons.	C004	HC46	3	3/28/96	$ 410.00	146DHC	$ 1,230.0
4	Algarve Cons.	C004	HC46	3	3/28/96	$ 410.00	146DHC	$ 1,230.0
5	Algarve Cons.	C004	HC46	3	3/28/96	$ 410.00	146DHC	$ 1,230.0
6	**Algarve Cons. Average**					$ 410.00		
7	*Algarve Cons. Total*							$ 4,920.0
8	Bombay Ltd.	C011	DC28	5	3/27/96	$ 80.00	28DHC	$ 400.0
9	Bombay Ltd.	C011	DC28	5	3/27/96	$ 80.00	28DHC	$ 400.0
10	Bombay Ltd.	C011	DC28	5	3/27/96	$ 80.00	28DHC	$ 400.0
11	Bombay Ltd.	C011	DC28	5	3/27/96	$ 80.00	28DHC	$ 400.0
12	**Bombay Ltd. Average**					$ 80.00		
13	*Bombay Ltd. Total*							$ 1,600.0
14	Colony Corp.	C014	DC27	10	3/23/96	$ 65.00	27DHC	$ 650.0
15	Colony Corp.	C014	DC27	10	3/23/96	$ 65.00	27DHC	$ 650.0
16	Colony Corp.	C014	DC27	10	3/23/96	$ 65.00	27DHC	$ 650.0
17	Colony Corp.	C014	DC27	10	3/23/96	$ 65.00	27DHC	$ 650.0
18	**Colony Corp. Average**					$ 65.00		
19	*Colony Corp. Total*							$ 2,600.0
20	Como Inc.	C005	HC47	7	3/29/96	$ 175.00	147DHC	$ 1,225.0
21	Como Inc.	C005	HC47	7	3/29/96	$ 175.00	147DHC	$ 1,225.0
22	Como Inc.	C005	HC47	7	3/29/96	$ 175.00	147DHC	$ 1,225.0
23	Como Inc.	C005	HC47	7	3/29/96	$ 175.00	147DHC	$ 1,225.0
24	**Como Inc. Average**					$ 175.00		
25	*Como Inc. Total*							$ 4,900.0
26	Costa Blanca Int'l	C008	HC47	2	3/29/96	$ 175.00	147DHC	$ 350.0
27	Costa Blanca Int'l	C008	HC47	2	3/29/96	$ 175.00	147DHC	$ 350.0

1996 Part Orders

Ready NUM

Refining your subtotals by filtering

Subtotals also work for filtered lists. Click Data, Filter, AutoFilter. Select the filtering criteria from the drop-down lists for each column, then apply subtotals to the filtered data.

Pivot tables—for one-stop filtering, subtotaling, and sorting

Excel has lots of choices for pulling information out of lists of data. **Sorting** rearranges the data to let us view it from different angles. **Filtering** lets us pull particular chunks of data out of the list to see it more clearly. **Subtotaling** summarizes the data to give us the big picture.

Pivot tables do all three things at once. Confusing? Think of a room full of furniture and a really energetic decorator. First she moves all the furniture around. That's sorting. Then she gets rid of that ugly old cabinet and those hideous armchairs to open up some space. That's filtering. Tireless, she makes an inventory and breaks it down by the number of chairs, tables, pictures, and so on. That's subtotaling.

Then she grows a few more arms and legs and does it all at the same time (don't try this at home). That's a pivot table.

What do I need with a pivot table?

A pivot table is another tool for making sense of long lists of data. Because it summarizes, sorts, and filters all at once, pivot tables give you quick answers to questions about big databases. How many widgets did we sell in January? At what price? Who bought them? How many did each customer order?

Pivot tables let you answer all those questions in one breath. Or get your answers one at a time. They're a great tool for preparing reports or charts. They let you zero in on one element in your database, or sum up the whole thing with an overview.

Creating a pivot table

Let's build a pivot table and see how it works. We start with an existing list, and use the PivotTable Wizard to create the pivot table from the list.

Before creating a pivot table from your list, get rid of all the subtotals and filters. Pivot tables filter data any way you choose, and they can't be created at all from a subtotaled list.

1. Pivot tables start with a question about your list. What do you want to know? How about this: what customer bought how many of which part, and what did they pay and how much do they owe us? Whew. That should be enough to start with.
2. Select a cell in the list, and click Data, Pivot Table Report. The PivotTable Wizard pops up and asks where our data is coming from (see Figure 16.9). Choose the Microsoft Excel List or Database option.
3. Click Next for Step 2. Here we select the range the Wizard will operate on. If you already selected a cell in the database, the range displayed here should cover the whole list. Otherwise, use the mouse or the Shift+arrow key combination to select the entire list. The range will appear in the Range text box.

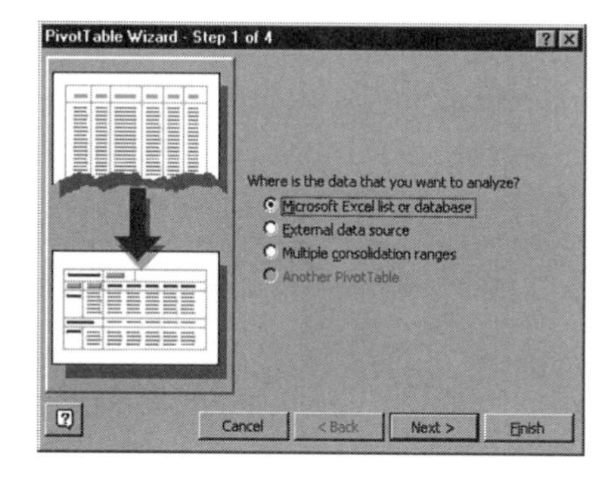

Fig. 16.9
Step 1 of the PivotTable Wizard gives you the chance to select the source of your data.

4 Click Next again, and it's decision time. Step 3 has two parts: on the left is a blank layout form, and on the right are buttons representing each field in the list. The idea here is simple. We use the mouse to drag the buttons over to the layout form, and dump them in the right spot. Take a look at Figure 16.10.

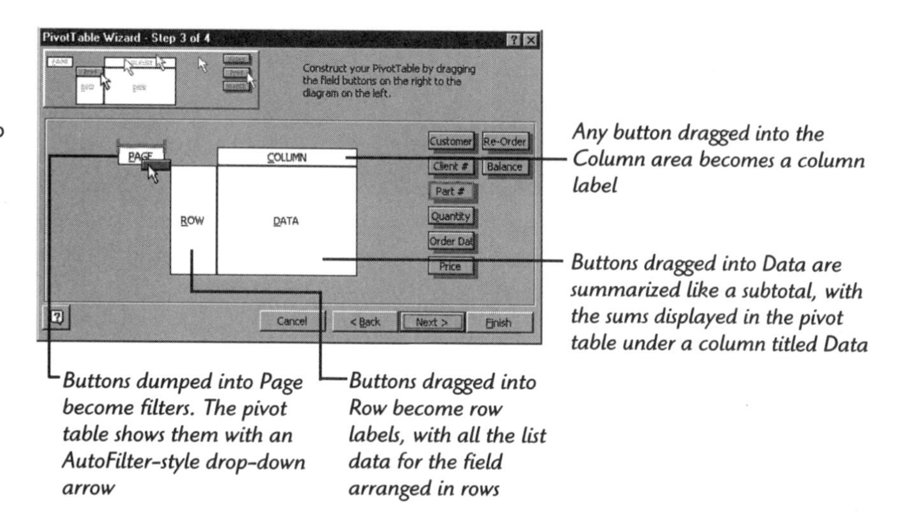

Fig. 16.10
The mechanics are easy—just drag-and-drop. Deciding what to put where is a little more involved. If you go wrong, it's easy to change things later.

5 We'll put our customers in rows and the price of each part in a column. Dumping the balances and quantities ordered into Data will sum them both up. Sticking Part # in Page will let us filter the data one part at a time, or display all the parts at once. It looks like Figure 16.11.

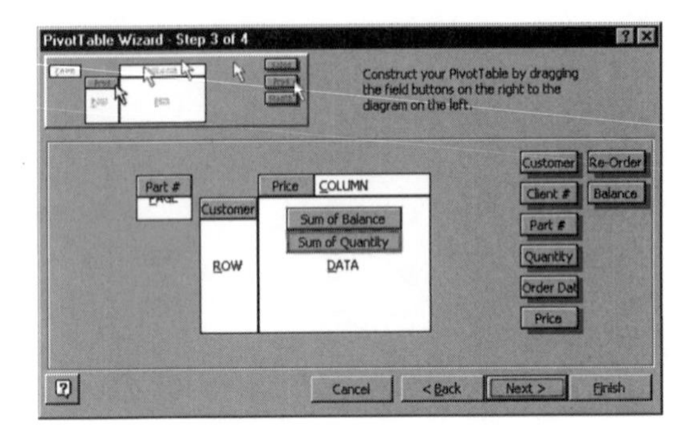

Fig. 16.11
If you don't like the way things turn out when you get to the pivot table proper, it's easy to go back and make changes.

6 Click Next for Step 4 and the finishing touches. Where do you want the pivot table? Click the New Worksheet option, which is the best place for it (see Figure 16.12).

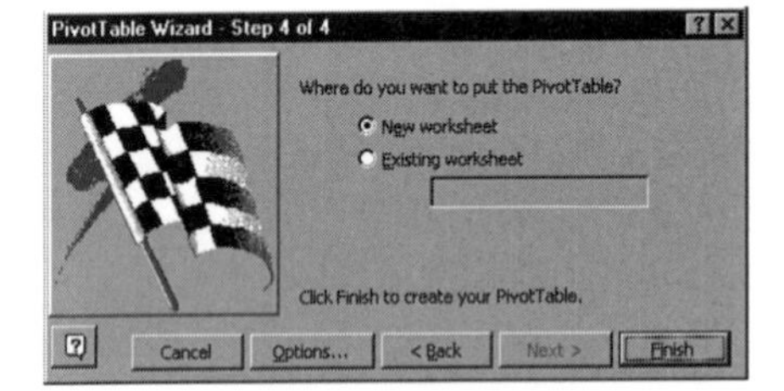

Fig. 16.12
Putting a pivot table report on a new worksheet is your best bet because it avoids the danger of overwriting your data!

7 Click Finish in the PivotTable Wizard Step 4 of 4 dialog box.

Figure 16.13 shows the completed table.

The PivotTable toolbar

Unless you already popped it up and then got rid of it, creating a pivot table automatically brings up the PivotTable toolbar. There are handy buttons to outline, collapse, and expand the pivot table, change the calculation of the data fields, and call up the Wizard.

TIP **If the PivotTable toolbar doesn't appear, right-click either the** Standard or Formatting toolbar, and select PivotTable from the shortcut menu.

Fig. 16.13
This small table conveys a lot of information in compact form. We can see at a glance which customer ordered what part, what they paid for it, and how many they ordered.

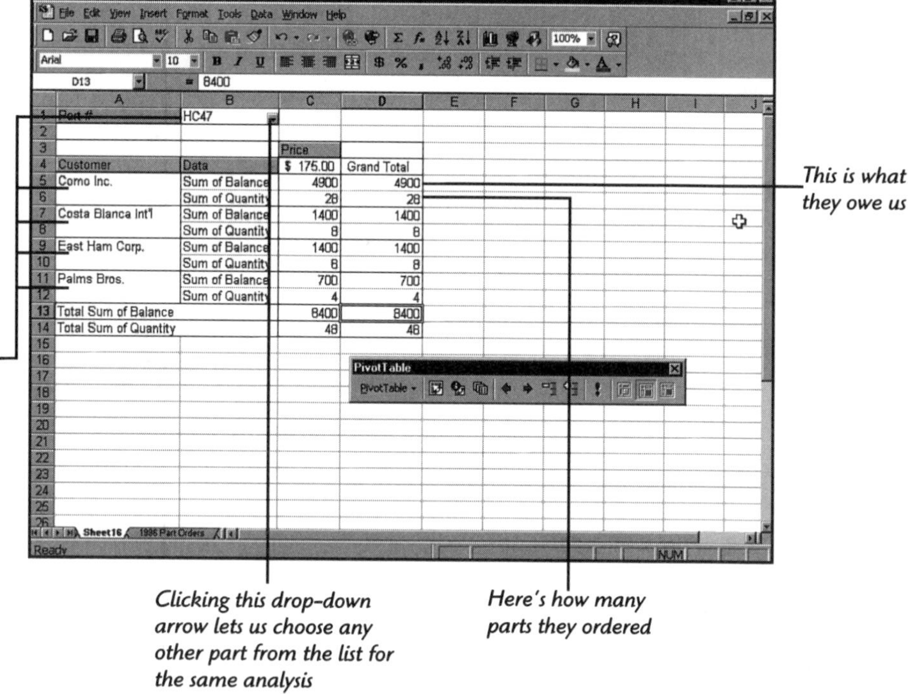

Clicking the Show Pages button pops up the Show Pages dialog box. Select a field from the Show All Pages Of list, click OK, and you get a pivot table analysis for each record in the list. Each analysis is on a separate worksheet, as shown in Figure 16.14.

That's a little like having your cake and eating it too. You get the analysis for each record, without drowning in a sea of numbers on one table.

Pivot tables let you see data from every angle

Pivot tables are so called because they can be reoriented to display different views of your data. To do that, you drag a field button on the table into a new position. That "pivots" your view of the data, as though you were spinning a globe to view the other side of the world.

Suppose you had a pivot table like the one in Figure 16.13, showing your customer's orders filtered by the different parts in your inventory. Now you want to see that information filtered by particular customers, not parts.

Fig. 16.14
Show Pages on the PivotTable toolbar automatically puts the pivot table analysis for each record on a separate worksheet.

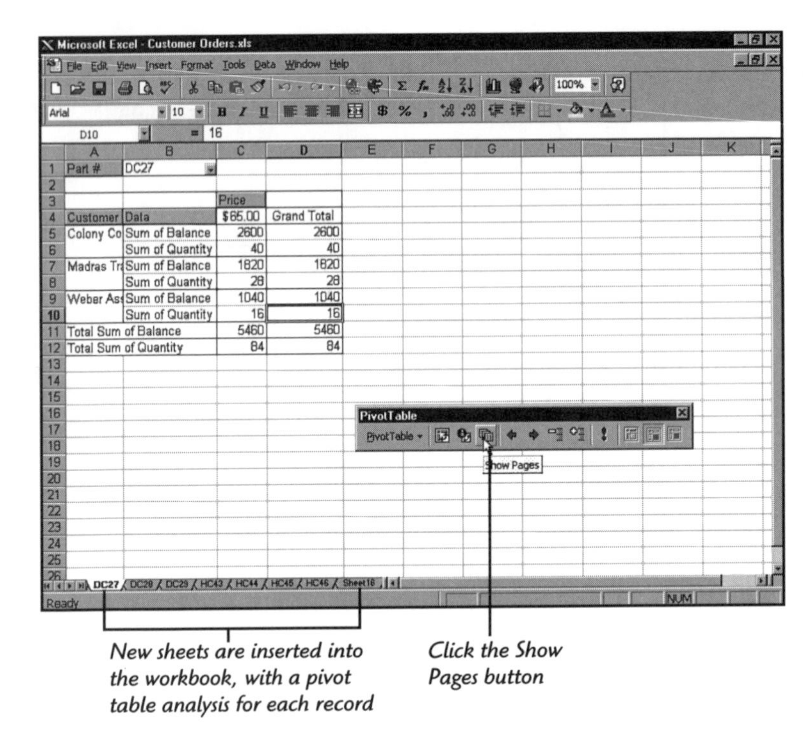

Just drag the Customer field button out of the Row area of the table, and into the Page area, as shown in Figure 16.15.

Fig. 16.15
By "pivoting" a pivot table, you can view your data from any perspective you choose.

The Page area of the table is like a built-in AutoFilter

As you drag a Row field button, the pointer is joined by an Insert marker

The gray I-beam lets you know where your dragged button will end up

Microsoft Excel - Customer Orders.xls

	A	B	C	D
1	Part #	HC47		
2				
3			Price	
4	Customer	Data	$ 175.00	Grand Total
5	Como Inc.	Sum of Balance	4900	4900
6		Sum of Quantity	28	28
7	Costa Blanca Int'l	Sum of Balance	1400	1400
8		Sum of Quantity	8	8
9	East Ham Corp.	Sum of Balance	1400	1400
10		Sum of Quantity	8	8
11	Palms Bros.	Sum of Balance	700	700
12		Sum of Quantity	4	4
13	Total Sum of Balance		8400	8400
14	Total Sum of Quantity		48	48

PivotTable

DC28 / DC29 / HC43 / HC44 / HC45 / HC46 / Sheet16 / 1996

Drop to place this field on the page axis

When you release a Row field button into the Page area of the pivot table, the button gets one of those AutoFilter-style drop-down arrows. Figure 16.16 shows all the Part #s selected, and the order information for a selected client on display.

Fig. 16.16
A simple drag-and-drop operation gives us an entirely new perspective on the data.

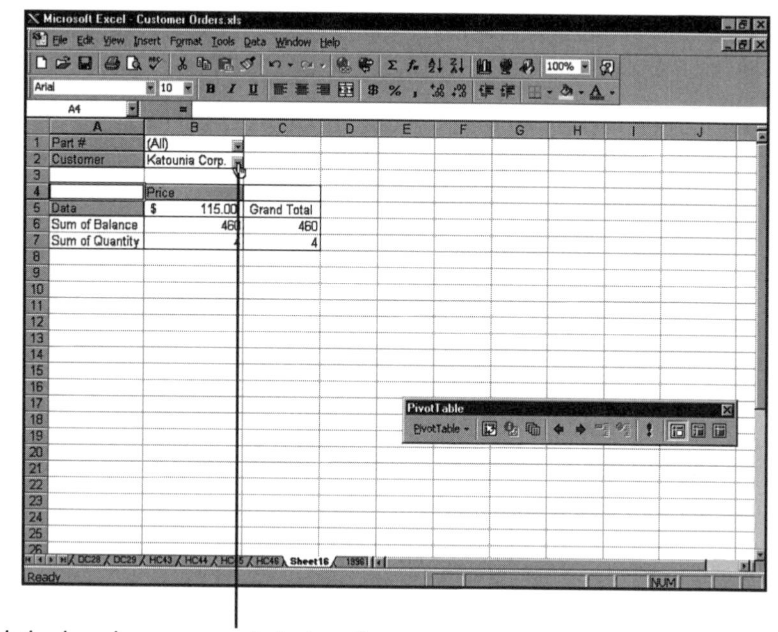

Click the drop-down arrow and select another customer

To restore the table's original orientation, drag the field button back to its original position.

Part VII: Beyond the Basics: Your Workbooks, the Office, and the World

17

Linking and Sharing Workbooks

In this chapter:

- **Why should I link workbooks?**
- **Can I link formulas?**
- **I need to grab a range and link it to another workbook**
- **We can ALL work on this list at the same time?**
- **How do I find a missing link?!**

Teamwork gets the job done faster, whether it's a team of colleagues working simultaneously on the same worksheet, or a team of workbooks linked together . . . .

When an amateur naturalist named Dawson found the "missing link" back in 1912, it led to a lot of trouble. His human skull with an ape's jaw, dug up at a place called Piltdown in England, seemed to be the remains of our lost ancestor. Forty years later, scientists discovered that "Piltdown Man," the missing link, was really just a link in a chain of fraud. Dawson's find was indeed a human skull and an ape's jaw—but from two different creatures.

Those scientists may have been guilty of wishful thinking. But aren't we always looking for ways to link things? Human evolution or your old snow chains, things run more smoothly when they're solidly linked.

Excel workbooks are no different. Linking one workbook to another creates an efficient system of workbooks, sharing data and formulas. If you're on a network, you can share lists among different computers, and even work on a shared list simultaneously with your colleagues.

It's easy to do. And if you go wrong, finding the missing link is no trouble at all.

Why do I need links?

Three different people, all working on the annual budget. One's doing income estimates. Another, taxes. A third, expenses. Income sends numbers to Taxes, who types them in and sends them on to Expenses, who types them in and sends them back to Taxes. Then a number changes and it all has to be done again.

What if you could set things up so that a change in one workbook automatically carries over to other workbooks? That's what linking cells does. Like the baton in a relay race, data gets passed from workbook to workbook on-the-fly.

Plain English, please!

Cell **links** are not to be confused with **hyperlinks**. Cell links are like wires connecting a wall switch to a lamp. Just as you flip a switch up or down to turn a light on or off, when you change one linked cell, the other cells it's linked to also change. Hyperlinks are more like doorways inserted into a worksheet. A hyperlink is a bit of text or an icon associated with the address of a document on the Internet, a local network, or your own hard drive. When you click the hyperlink, you go through the door and straight to the address associated with it. See Chapter 22 for more information about hyperlinks. ”

You have two ways to link cells across workbooks.

- Copying and pasting with the Edit, Paste Special command is the fast way to grab a range in one workbook and paste it in another workbook. The pasted cells are updated by any changes made in the original cells.
- Or start a formula in one workbook, then select cells in another workbook. The selected cells are added to your formula. Change a number in those cells, and it goes straight into the formula in the other workbook.

“ ***Plain English, please!***

Here's some linking jargon. The workbook you start in is called the **source** workbook. The workbook you link to it is called the **dependent** workbook, because the linked cells in it depend on the source workbook. A cell or range reference in one workbook that refers to another workbook is called an **external reference**. When would you use these terms? Mostly when you look in Excel's online help. ”

Linking workbooks by point and click

Universal Widgets has income estimates in a workbook called Income. Our estimated taxes are in a workbook called Tax. The tax expert has estimated our effective tax rate to be 15 percent.

We want to grab the income totals from the Income workbook and plug them into our Tax workbook. That way if the income estimates are changed, the changes will show up automatically in our tax calculations. Here's what we do:

1 Click the Open button and open both workbooks, Estimated Taxes and Estimated Income in the example. Figure 17.1 shows the holes in the worksheet where we'll plug in our numbers.

2 Select the cell where we want our link to show up. It's B2, 1st Quarter Income Tax. Click the Edit Formula button on the formula bar to start

the formula, then type **.15***. Any number that's plugged in now will be multiplied by .15, our effective tax rate.

3 Switch to the workbook where the value is stored, Estimated Income.xls in the example. Click the cell holding the value, B5 (see Figure 17.2).

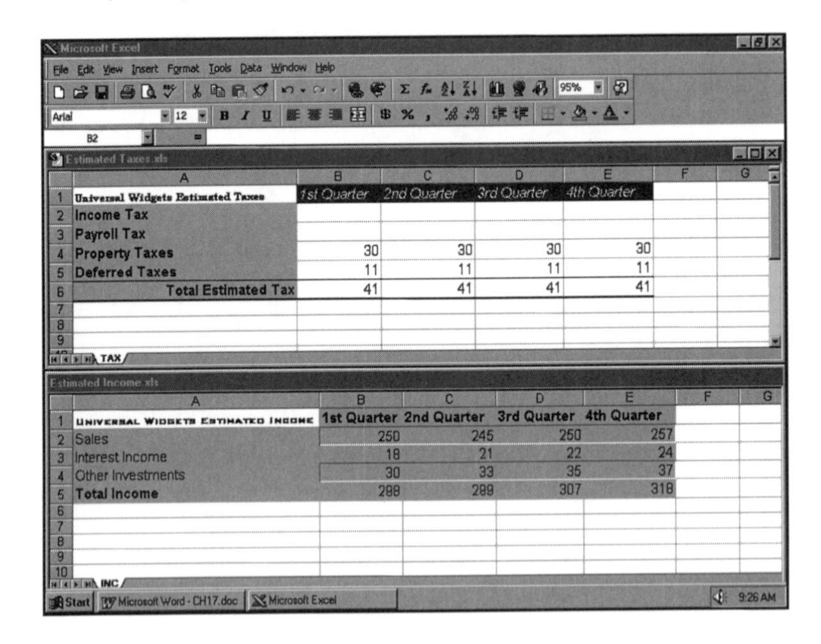

Fig. 17.1 Those gaps in the worksheet where our income and payroll taxes belong will be filled in from two other workbooks.

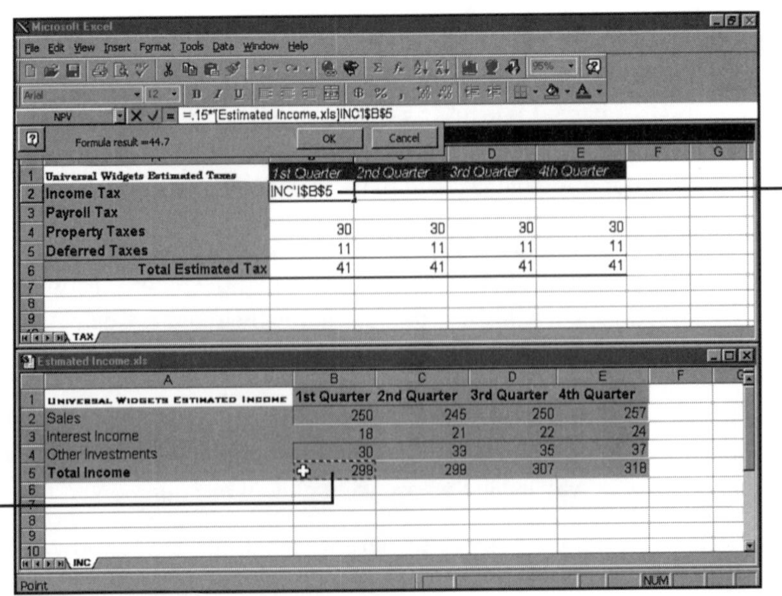

Fig. 17.2 Switching to the source workbook, Estimated Income, gets us to 1st Quarter Total Income. That's the value we want to link to the formula in the Estimated Tax workbook.

Start the formula in a cell in the dependent workbook

Flip to the source workbook and select the cell you want linked; it's dumped into the formula in the dependent workbook

You have a few choices for switching back and forth between workbooks. If you like to view the workbooks full-screen, click Window, then select the workbook you want from the menu. Or press Ctrl+Tab to cycle through the open workbooks one way; Shift+Ctrl+Tab to cycle back the other way. If you prefer, press Alt+W for the menu, then type the window number. Otherwise, click Window, Arrange and put them on the screen together, as I've done. Whichever suits you—they all work.

4 Press Enter, and the link is set up. Any changes to B5 in the Estimated Income workbook will show up in the Estimated Taxes workbook. Figure 17.3 shows the result.

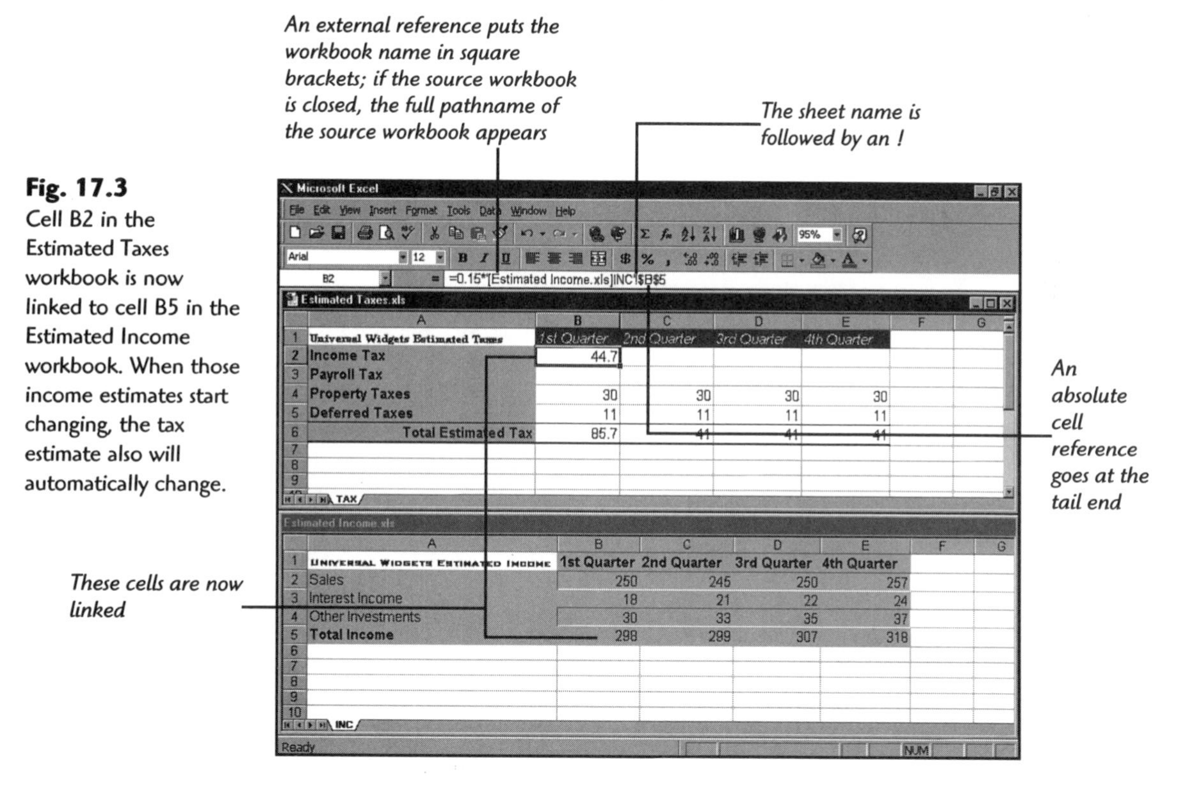

Fig. 17.3
Cell B2 in the Estimated Taxes workbook is now linked to cell B5 in the Estimated Income workbook. When those income estimates start changing, the tax estimate also will automatically change.

Cell B5 in the Estimated Income workbook is actually a SUM function, adding up the numbers in column B. Functions and formulas work fine in links. Any changes in the numbers in column B will show up in the sum, and show up in turn in the Estimated Taxes workbook.

I want to link the 2nd, 3rd, and 4th Quarters too, but dragging the fill handle doesn't work. What's wrong?

You have an absolute cell reference at the end of your external reference. You want to copy the formula when you drag the fill handle, but with the absolute reference in there, you're simply copying the value in the cell. Here's a quick fix: select the link you want to copy, then press F2, then F4 and Enter (repeating F4 cycles through the absolute/relative options). Pressing F4 once makes the column a relative reference. Now use the fill handle to copy across the range, and you'll copy your formula instead of the value in the cell.

If you make external references relative in order to copy them, use the F2, F4 combination to make the references absolute again when you're done. Otherwise, your links may get tangled if you move things around.

Want to see more worksheet, fewer gadgets?

If you're working on two or more workbooks at the same time, you might find it helpful to clear some of Excel's gadgets off the screen. That way you'll see more of your workbooks when they're crammed into windows. Click Tools, Options and click the View tab in the Options dialog box. Deselect whatever screen elements you can temporarily do without, like the sheet tabs, scroll bars, and status bar. Or choose the View menu to deselect and hide some of these items. If your eyesight is good, you can also set the screen magnification to a lower value. Click the Zoom Control drop-down arrow on the Standard toolbar and choose a setting lower than 100 percent. For a setting other than the choices in the Zoom Control menu, click View, Zoom. In the Zoom dialog box, type a new value in the Custom text box to set your own magnification level.

The Windows 95 taskbar is another screen hogger. To hide it, as I've done for the figures throughout *Using Excel 97*, right-click the taskbar background and choose Properties from the shortcut menu. Click the Taskbar Options tab in the Taskbar Properties dialog box that pops up, select Auto Hide, and click OK. That puts the taskbar out of sight. To pop it up again, just slide the pointer to the bottom of the screen; when you move the pointer again, the taskbar drops out of sight.

Linking with copy and paste

Universal Widgets is halfway home. With income linked to taxes, changes in our income estimates will update our tax figures automatically. Now we want our Expense workbook to reflect those tax estimates as they change.

We'll copy and paste them with the Paste Special command, and here's how to do that:

1. Open the Estimated Expenses workbook. With all three workbooks open, you have the same choice of putting them on the screen at the same time, or flipping back and forth between full-screen views. You can also click Window, Hide to hide workbooks you don't need, as we've done here with Estimated Income.

2. Select the range to be copied in the Estimated Taxes workbook, then click the Copy button. Here, we're copying B6:E6, our total estimated taxes.

TIP **To hide or display the Standard toolbar the quick way, press Ctrl+7.**

3. Now flip to the Estimated Expenses workbook. Select the cell at the beginning of the range you want to fill. There's no need to select the whole range.
4. Click Edit, Paste Special, as shown in Figure 17.4.
5. Click Paste Link. The tax estimates are filled in across the range, as shown in Figure 17.5.

Every change in the income estimates will automatically adjust the tax figures, which in turn get dumped into the Expense workbook. This will save us typing, time, and potential errors.

We have one missing link left to take care of. We want payroll taxes to reflect changes in payroll expense estimates, so we'll set up another link between the Estimated Taxes workbook and the Estimated Expenses workbook to cover that. Payroll tax is one percent, so this link will be along the lines of our first one, using point and click instead of copy and paste.

Figure 17.6 shows the completed workbook system.

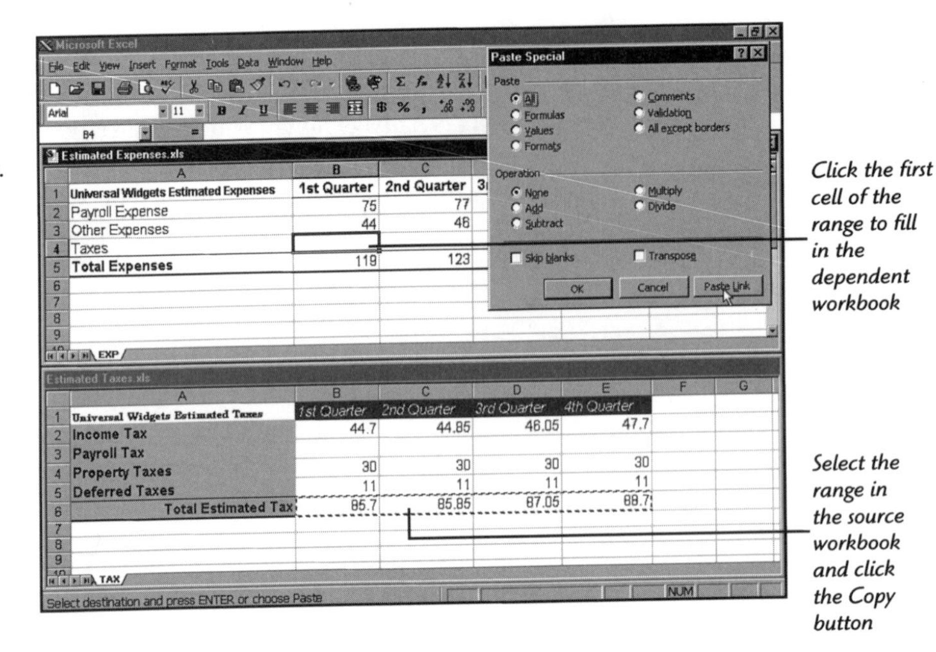

Fig. 17.4 The Paste Special dialog box gives you a lot of options. All we want here is Paste Link.

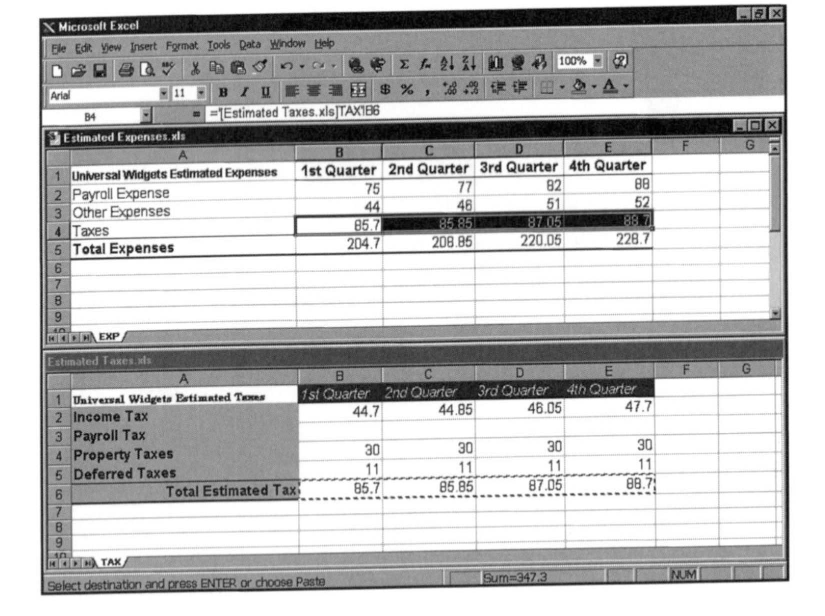

Fig. 17.5 Our link is established with a few clicks.

Fig. 17.6
With the last link in place, we have a fully automated update system.

Total Income cells are linked to Income Tax cells for each quarter

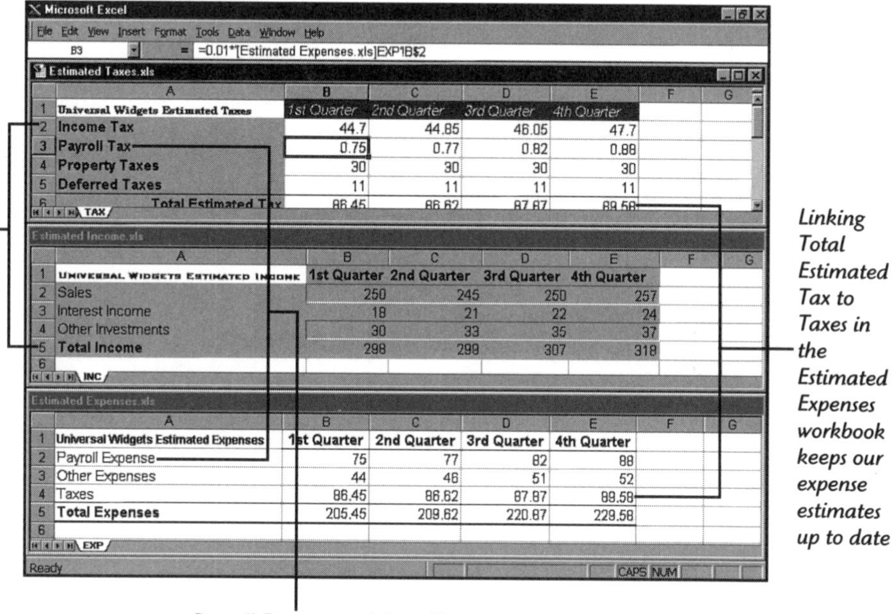

Payroll Expense and Payroll Tax are also linked

Managing linked workbook files

You can open and close linked workbooks just like ordinary files, but there are a few twists.

If you open a workbook with links to unopened workbooks, Excel asks if you want to reestablish the links. Click Yes to update, and Excel reads any changes in the other files. No keeps the workbook you opened as it was when you last saved it.

CAUTION **Changing sheet names in linked workbooks is no problem. The** links are updated to reflect the new names. If you change the name of the workbook, though, other workbooks in the linked system won't be able to find the data they're looking for. You'll have a missing link on your hands, but it can be found (see the following section on editing links). To avoid the problem entirely, always save the source workbooks before the dependent workbook.

Editing links

It's easyto lose track of what's linked to what when you start building linked workbook systems.

To display all the links in the worksheet, click Edit, Links. That pops up the Links dialog box, as shown in Figure 17.7.

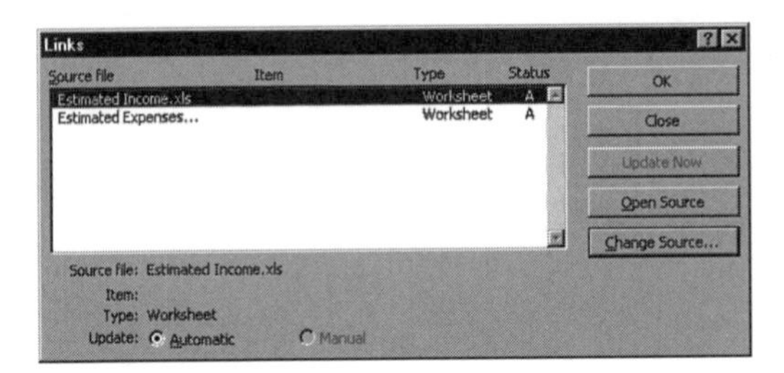

Fig. 17.7
The Links dialog box shows all your links for the active workbook, and gives you some file managing options.

TIP **Here's a quick way to open all your linked workbooks. Open the** dependent workbook, Estimated Taxes in our example. Click Edit, Links for the Links dialog box. Select all the linked workbooks on the Source File list by Ctrl+clicking each one. When they're all highlighted, click Open Source. They'll all open at once.

If you lose a link because of a changed file name, this is the place to find it. Click Change Source to get the Change Links dialog box, as shown in Figure 17.8.

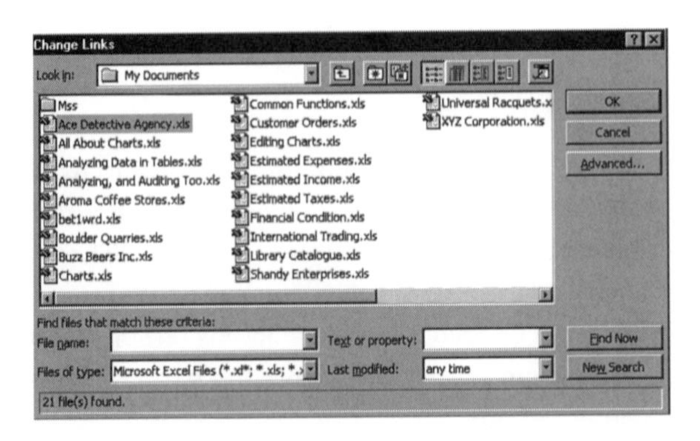

Fig. 17.8
Missing links? Pick a workbook file from the list and reestablish them.

Double-click the file you want from the list to restore the lost link.

On a network? Share your workbooks

Remember the sneaker net? The earliest type of PC network was so-called because you had to copy your latest file to floppy disk and run the disk over to your coworker's computer on foot. It worked, after a fashion.

Nowadays network hookups are a little more sophisticated. They're less exercise, but more efficient, at least when they're up and working. Excel 97 takes advantage of modern PC networks with its shared workbooks feature. If you put your workbook on the network, your colleagues can get at it from their own computers. You and your colleagues can even work on the same workbook simultaneously. That makes for a big saving in time, to say nothing of shoe rubber.

Setting up a shared list

To share your workbook with colleagues on a network, open the workbook and click Tools, Share Workbook. That pops up the Share Workbook dialog box shown in Figure 17.9.

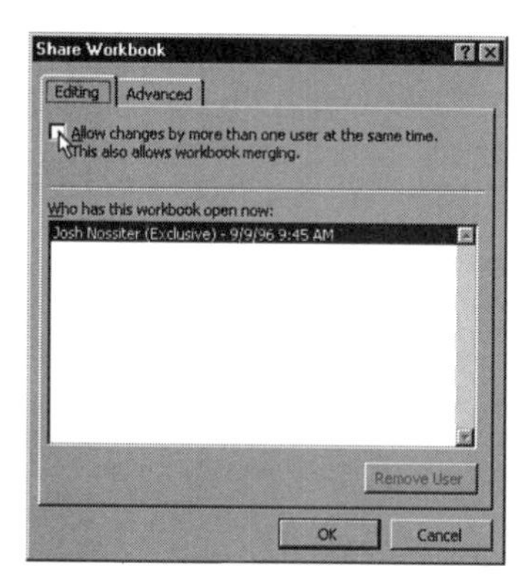

Fig. 17.9
Sharing it makes a workbook available to colleagues on a network.

Click the Allow Changes by More than One User at the Same Time check box to let others enter data and make changes to the workbook. If you leave it unchecked, others on the network can view a read-only file, but can't make any changes.

Click OK in the Share Workbook dialog box. You may be prompted to enter your name to identify yourself to others sharing the workbook.

When you save a shared workbook, you save your edits and all the changes made to the list by others as well. If any changes conflict—maybe someone entered a different spelling in the same record—you'll be prompted to choose which edits to retain. To view a worksheet with a list of such conflicts, click Tools, Share Workbook for the Share Workbook dialog box. Click the Advanced tab and select the Ask Me Which Changes Win option.

To see who else has the list opened, click the Editing tab in the Share Workbook dialog box for a listing of your fellow users.

18 Data Maps and Templates, for Data that Fits a Mold

In this chapter:

- Just what is a data map, anyway?
- Okay, I want to create a map
- How do I redraw the map?
- Pin maps, to pin down key locations
- Data not mappable? Use a template

Pour your data into Excel's maps and templates, and dull numbers turn into dramatic graphics and professional-looking forms . . . .

The ancient Egyptians had a unique problem. When the Nile river flooded its banks every year, property lines washed away. With fences and boundary markers disappearing with annoying regularity, how could the Egyptians tell where one property ended and another began? They drew maps. Property data in the form of maps let our 3,000-year-old ancestors laugh (or at least smile weakly) at the vagaries of nature.

Maps are like molds for data. They shape information—statistical, financial, geographical, you name it—in a way that makes it understandable at a glance. Excel **data maps** do exactly that for your worksheet numbers.

Not all data lends itself to map form. Mapping invoices, for example, wouldn't make much sense. For data like that, Excel has another kind of mold. Excel **templates** are prefabricated worksheets, complete with formatting and built-in functions, for budgets, invoices, and other practical items.

No matter what the data, Excel has a mold to whip it into shape.

What's a data map?

Old-fashioned map-making required intrepid expeditions into uncharted seas and unexplored continents. Nowadays, we use satellite photos. With Excel data maps, you need only your keyboard and trusty mouse.

All it takes to create an Excel map is a column of geographical data. Sales data by state, for example, or production figures from far-flung factories abroad; any data associated with geographical locations can be put on an Excel map.

Why would you want to make a data map in the first place?

- Like a chart, a data map is a graphical representation of your data. Instead of boring rows and columns of figures, you get a colorful picture.
- A data map can give you insights that the numbers on their own might not offer. Looking at 50 rows of sales data for each of the 50 states might not tell you much; put the data on a map, and you can see at a glance which states' sales teams need extra help. For example, Figure 18.1 shows a data map in which the states with the fewest sales are displayed in lighter shades.

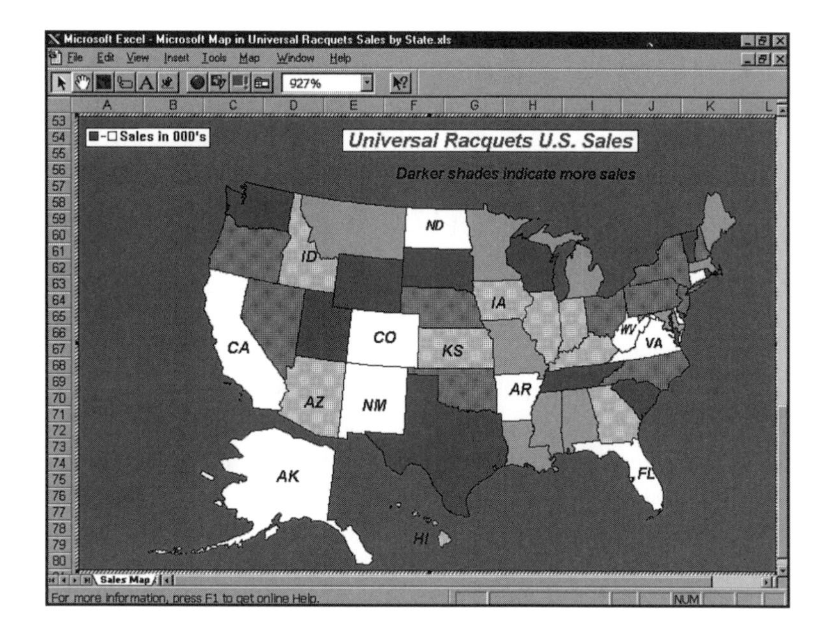

Fig. 18.1
The underlying data is 50 rows of sales by state; the map shows pretty clearly which states need sales help.

- For presentations and reports, maps make a dramatic departure from the usual dull tables. If you use Microsoft PowerPoint or a similar program, you can turn an Excel data map into a nifty slide with a few clicks.

How do I create a map?

It's easy to create a data map. Select a range, click the Map button on the toolbar, then drag the mouse pointer. After you release the mouse button and make a few dialog box choices, the map pops right onto the worksheet, complete with any data you included in the selected range.

But for this to work, one column of your data has to contain one of the following:

- The names of world countries, like France, England, China, and Zaire. You can even use Andorra, Liechtenstein, and San Marino if you tend to think small.
- Any or all Canadian provinces, from Alberta to the Yukon Territory.
- The Mexican states, like Baja California or the Yucatan, and including the *Distrito Federal*, the Federal District.

- Standard regions of the United Kingdom: Scotland, Wales, and Northern Ireland work; so does East Anglia. Cornwall does not.
- The Australian states and territories, such as New South Wales and Tasmania.
- U.S. Postal ZIP codes. Just make sure to enter ZIP codes as text, which you do by typing an apostrophe (') before the ZIP code itself: for example, **'46290**. Otherwise, Excel formats them as numbers, which could lead to dropped zeroes or added decimal places.
- Any or all of the 50 U.S. states, and the District of Columbia.

These place names have to be in a column, and spelling does matter. If you misspell the name of a state or country, Excel won't automatically map your data. You can use abbreviations for most places, however: NM for New Mexico, for example, or PL for Poland.

You can't use the names of cities or regions. Paris won't work, nor will Midwest.

The Mapstats worksheet holds the place names you need

If you have any doubts about your data, you'll make map-making a lot easier if you take a look at the database that Excel uses to create maps. You might want to do this before you try to map your data.

A workbook called **Mapstats** is included in Excel 97, and it's located in the Program Files\Common Files\Microsoft Shared\Datamap\Data folder. To view it, click the Open button on the toolbar. Keep clicking and scrolling until you get to the Program Files\Common Files\Microsoft Shared\Datamap\Data folder, then double-click the Mapstats workbook.

Each worksheet of the Mapstats workbook contains the place names and demographic data that you can include in Excel data maps. If you're not sure of your spelling, check the lists here first, as shown in Figure 18.2.

Place names with their correct abbreviations and spellings are in Columns A and B of each worksheet; the other columns hold population data for each state and country, broken down by gender, age, and location (urban or rural).

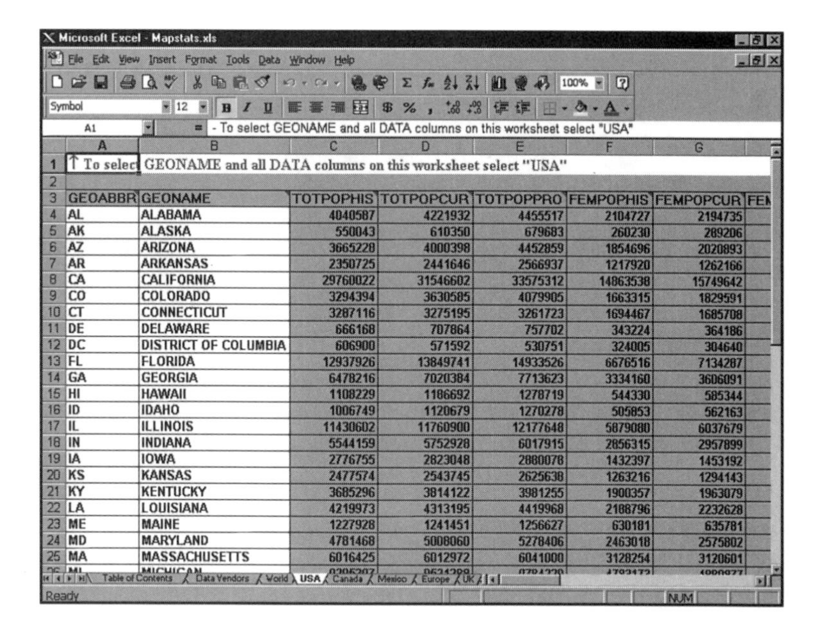

GEOABBR	GEONAME	TOTPOPHIS	TOTPOPCUR	TOTPOPPRO	FEMPOPHIS	FEMPOPCUR
AL	ALABAMA	4040587	4221932	4455517	2104727	2194735
AK	ALASKA	550043	610350	679683	260230	289206
AZ	ARIZONA	3665228	4000398	4452859	1854696	2020893
AR	ARKANSAS	2350725	2441646	2566937	1217920	1262166
CA	CALIFORNIA	29760022	31546602	33575312	14863538	15749642
CO	COLORADO	3294394	3630585	4079905	1663315	1829591
CT	CONNECTICUT	3287116	3275195	3261723	1694467	1685708
DE	DELAWARE	666168	707864	757702	343224	364186
DC	DISTRICT OF COLUMBIA	606900	571592	530751	324005	304640
FL	FLORIDA	12937926	13849741	14933526	6676516	7134287
GA	GEORGIA	6478216	7020384	7713623	3334160	3606091
HI	HAWAII	1108229	1186692	1278719	544330	585344
ID	IDAHO	1006749	1120679	1270278	505853	562163
IL	ILLINOIS	11430602	11760900	12177648	5879080	6037679
IN	INDIANA	5544159	5752928	6017915	2856315	2957899
IA	IOWA	2776755	2823048	2880078	1432397	1453192
KS	KANSAS	2477574	2543745	2625638	1263216	1294143
KY	KENTUCKY	3685296	3814122	3981255	1900357	1963079
LA	LOUISIANA	4219973	4313195	4419968	2188796	2232628
ME	MAINE	1227928	1241451	1256627	630181	635781
MD	MARYLAND	4781468	5008060	5278406	2463018	2575802
MA	MASSACHUSETTS	6016425	6012972	6041000	3128254	3120601

Fig. 18.2
Click the worksheet tabs of the Mapstats workbook to view the geographic and demographic data for each of Excel's maps.

Map-making is just a drag

When you have your data, geographic and otherwise, arranged in a table, you're all set. To create a data map:

1. Select the range containing the data you want to include in the map. The range has to include your place names in a column. Otherwise, include any other data you want displayed on the map. You can always add more data to the map after you create it.

2. Click the Map button on the Standard toolbar. Position the pointer crosshair at the upper-left corner of where you want your map to be, and drag to the lower-right corner, as shown in Figure 18.3.

TIP **Press Alt as you drag with the crosshair, and your inserted** object—map, drawing, or chart—aligns with the worksheet gridlines.

3. Release the mouse button. For some data, like the names of U.S. states in Figure 18.3, you get a choice of different maps in the Multiple Maps Available dialog box. Make your choice, then click OK (see Figure 18.4).

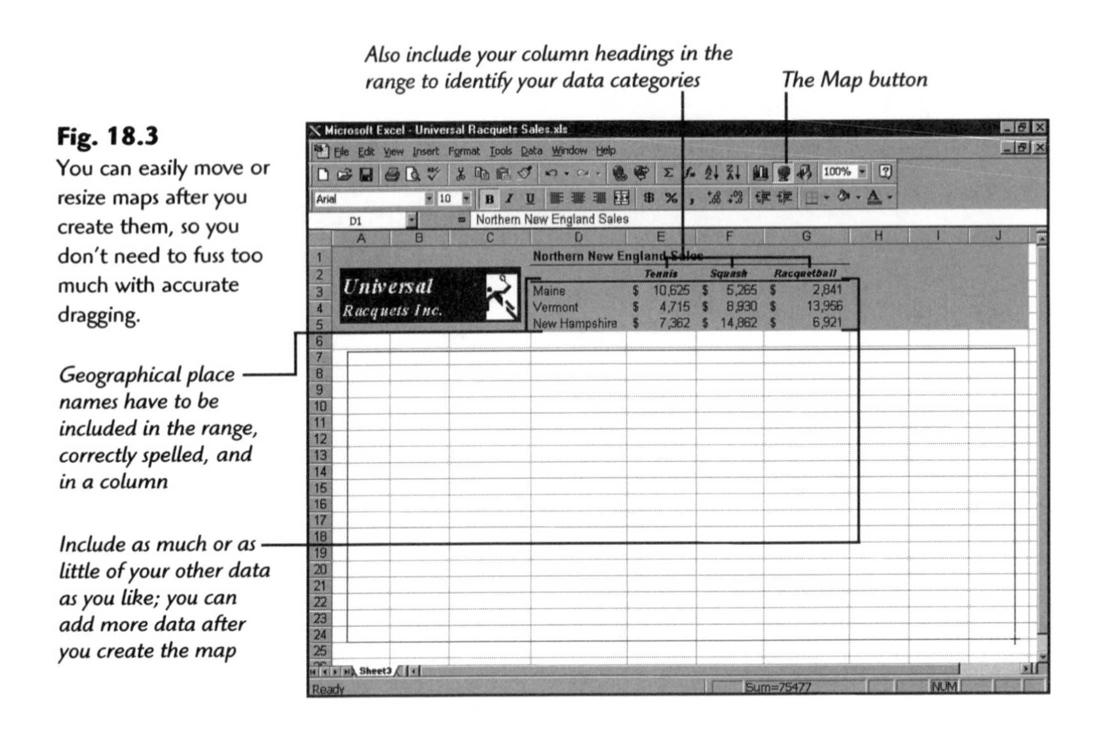

Fig. 18.3
You can easily move or resize maps after you create them, so you don't need to fuss too much with accurate dragging.

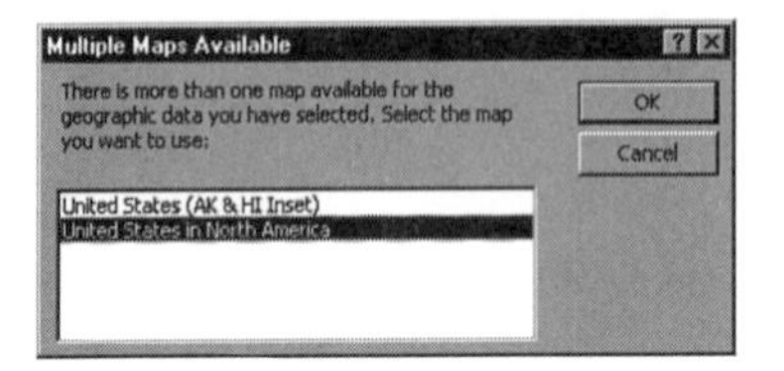

Fig. 18.4
Because this map is focused on Northern New England, we don't need the U.S. map with insets for Hawaii and Alaska.

Q&A Why did I get a dialog box that's telling me Unable to Create Map?

The Unable to Create Map dialog box pops up if you've either misspelled a place name within the selected range or if Excel doesn't recognize the place names in your data. You can go ahead and select a map from the list and proceed manually. Or click Cancel and check your spelling—and your geography!

4 Your map appears on the worksheet, and the Microsoft Map Control dialog box pops up. Here's where you decide what data to include in the map, and how you want the map formatted. Just drag your column titles, shown as buttons at the top of the dialog box, into the box and onto the Column labels. Excel automatically supplies formatting for each column category when you drag it into the box. Figure 18.5 shows the Microsoft Map Control dialog box.

Fig. 18.5
If your choices in the Microsoft Map Control dialog box don't turn out exactly the way you want, you can redisplay the dialog box and change things around.

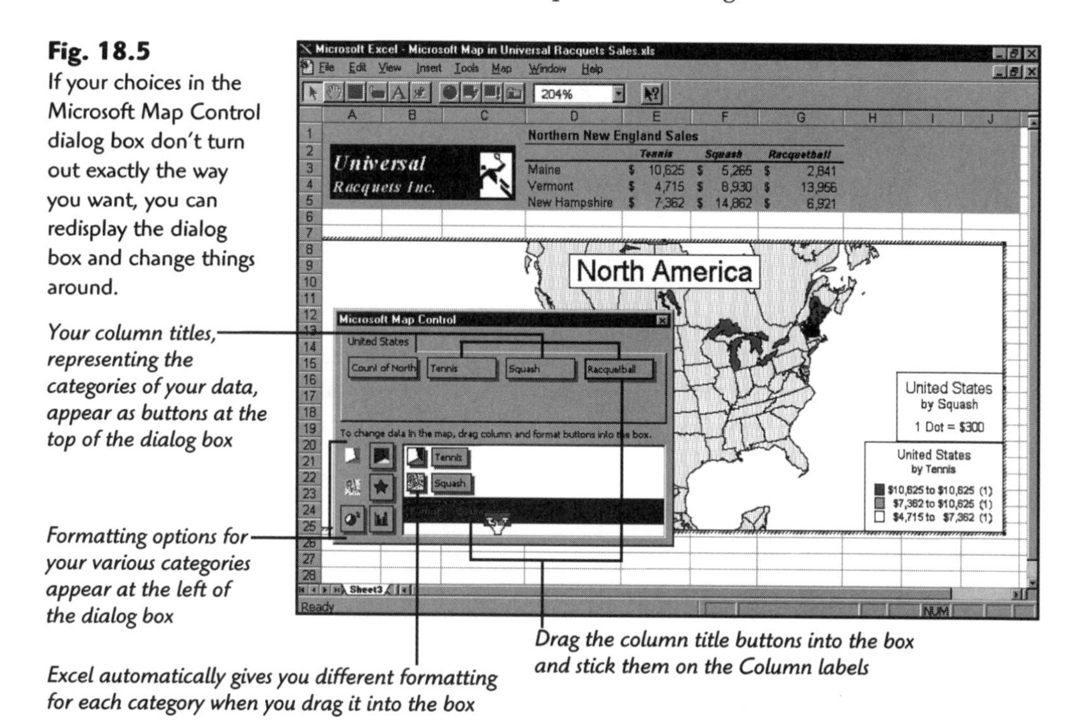

The icons in the Microsoft Map Control dialog box determine how your data is formatted on the map. Here's what they do:

This button	gives you	which
	Value Shading	Colors the map areas in shades representing the values in a category of your data. Darker shades are higher values.
	Category Shading	Colors the map areas in different shades representing the different categories of your data.
	Dot Density	Lays down a pattern of dots in the map areas, with each dot representing a specified number (which you can change) of items in a data category.
	Graduated Symbol	Puts a symbol representing a data category in each map area. The bigger the symbol, the higher the value in the category.
	Pie Chart and Column Chart	Displays your data categories as pie or column charts in each map area.

5 For now, we'll accept Excel's formatting choices. You can always return to the Microsoft Map Control dialog box and change things around after the map is created. After all of your column categories have been dragged onto the column labels in the Microsoft Map Control dialog box, click the Show/Hide Microsoft Map Control button on the Map toolbar to hide the dialog box.

6 You'll probably want to magnify the section of the map that displays your data. To do that, first center the map around your data. Click the Center Map button, and then click the section of the map you want to magnify.

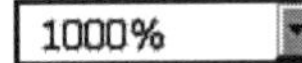

7 Now click the Zoom Percentage of Map arrow on the Map toolbar. Choose a higher magnification from the drop-down menu. If your map covers a small geographical area, try the highest zoom setting (see Figure 18.6).

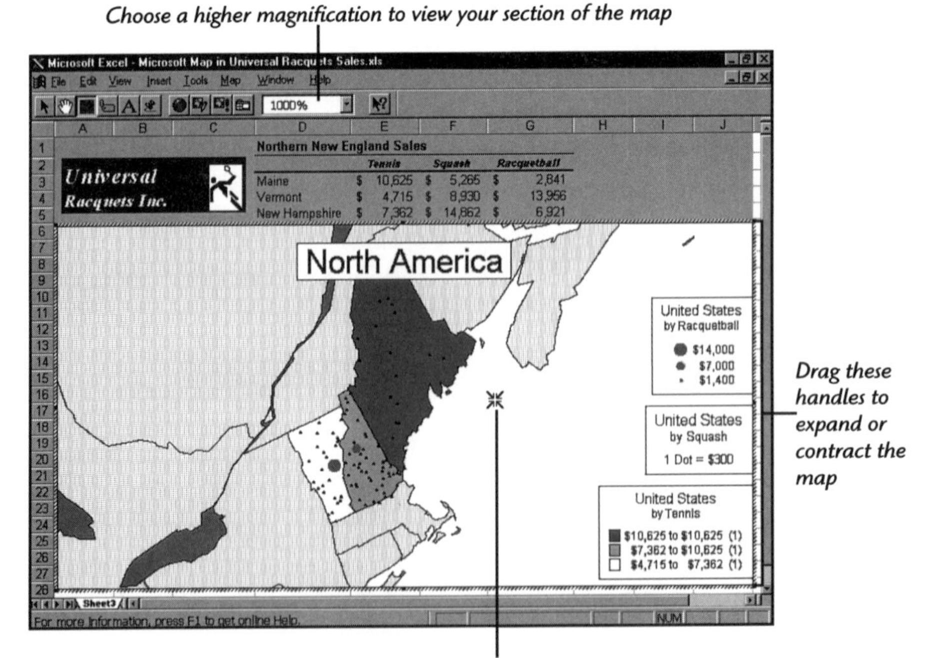

Choose a higher magnification to view your section of the map

Drag these handles to expand or contract the map

Click the section of the map that holds your data with the Center Map compass

Fig. 18.6
Clicking with the Center Map compass puts your area of the map front and center.

8 After you center and zoom the map, you may want to fine-tune the way the map is positioned inside its frame. No problem. Click the Grabber button, and the pointer turns into a grabby little hand. Drag inside the map until you have it correctly positioned. If you need to, drag the handles around the map frame to expand the map (refer to Figure 18.6).

9. When you're done centering, zooming, and grabbing, you'll have a magnified section of map displaying your data, as shown in Figure 18.7.

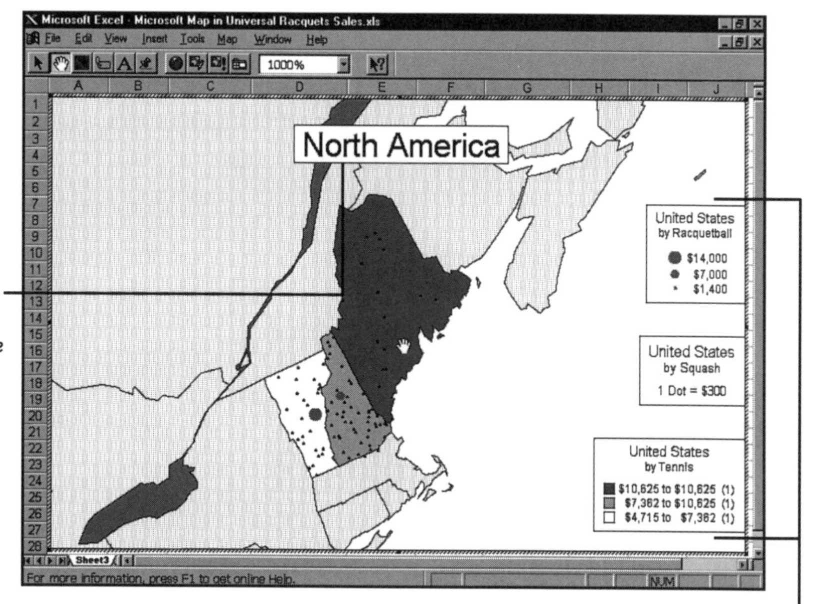

Fig. 18.7
Everything on the map—colors, symbols, formatting, titles, and legends—can be moved and reformatted.

This is the map title; double-click it to type in something different, or drag to move it anywhere you like

These are the legends; drag to move them, and double-click to format or hide them

Figure 18.7 displays a lot of information in a compact way. The different shades in the background of the states—value shading—indicate different levels of tennis racquet sales, with darker shades representing more sales. Those dots—dot density—represent squash racquet sales; the denser the clusters of dots, the higher the value the dots represent. By sheer coincidence, they even look like squash balls. The round blobs (graduated symbols, if you want to be technical, or racquetball balls as long as we're free-associating) show varying levels of racquetball racquet sales. The bigger the graduated symbol, the higher the value that it represents.

Still, this map is missing a few things. A more informative title, for example. We might want to label the states with their names. We can even display the locations of our distributors. Read on.

Move over, Napoleon: I'm redrawing the map

The map in Figure 18.7 is—charitably speaking—a work in progress. Some tinkering is needed, and your own maps will probably require the same treatment. Adding labels and changing fonts and formatting is easy to do.

You can alter everything on the map. You can also add or remove **map features**. Major cities are map features; so are airports and highways. To add or remove map features, right-click the map and select Features from the shortcut menu. (If your map isn't selected, double-click the map first to put that fuzzy border around it.)

That gets you the Map Features dialog box shown in Figure 18.8.

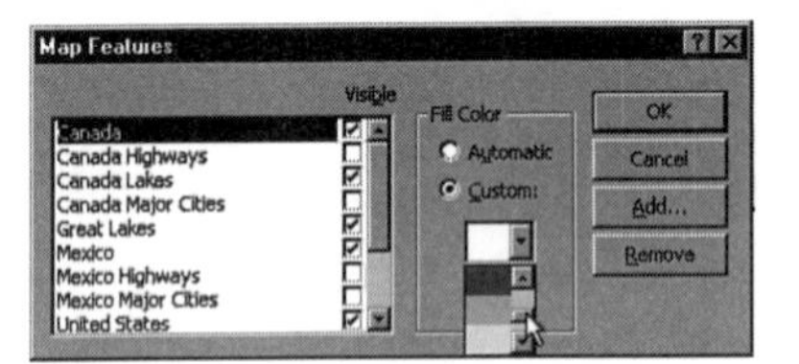

Fig. 18.8
To change the default fill color, select the Custom option and click the drop-down arrow.

To add or remove any of the features on the list, just click a check box, then click OK. For additional map features, click Add and take your pick from the list in the Add Map Features dialog box. Click OK to close each dialog box and add the selected features to the map.

Plain English, please!

If you investigate the Add Map Features dialog box, you might wonder about the **World Graticule** feature. That's the grid of longitudinal and latitudinal lines that you see on globes and in atlases.

This map needs labels

You'll surely want to label your map with the names of countries or states. You can even insert your data values as labels.

To insert map labels:

1 If it's not already selected, double-click the map, then click the Map Labels button on the Map toolbar.

2 That pops up the Map Labels dialog box (see Figure 18.9). If you want place names, select Map Feature Names. If you want your data to appear on the map, choose Values From and select a category from the drop-down list.

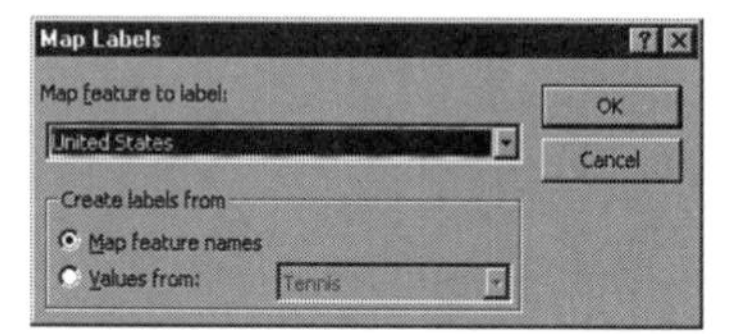

Fig. 18.9
To label a different map feature—Canada, for example—click the drop-down arrow and take your pick.

3 Click OK in the Map Labels dialog box, and the pointer turns into a crosshair. Position the pointer on areas of the map, and the corresponding place name or value appears.

4 Click, and the label is inserted in the map, as shown in Figure 18.10.

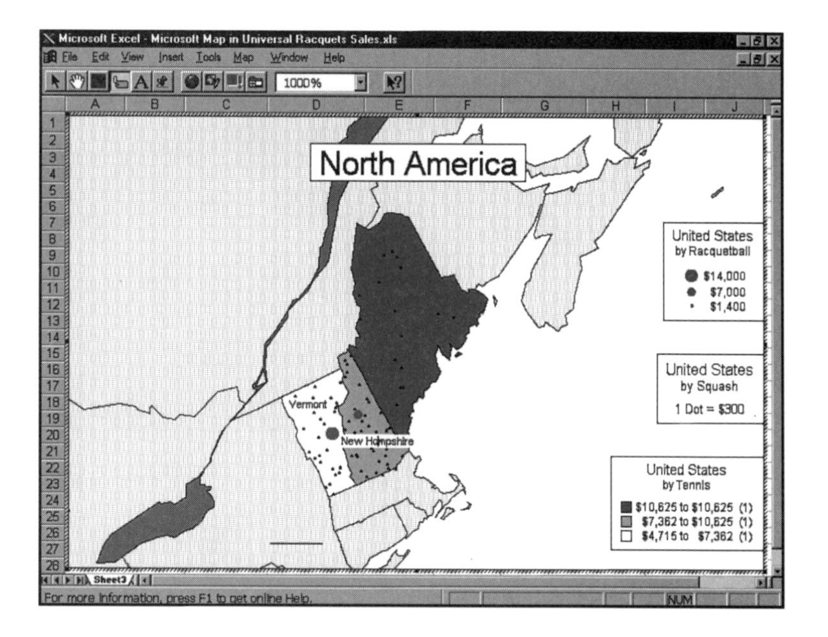

Fig. 18.10
To move a label after it's inserted, just click and drag it.

To change the label's font, right-click it and select Format Font from the shortcut menu. You'll need to do that if you insert labels on dark shaded areas. A small black font will be invisible. Make it big and white so it'll be clear.

To get rid of the crosshair when you're finished labeling, click the Select Objects button on the toolbar.

This map needs a makeover

Although the blobs you get by default worked out pretty well as a representation of racquetball racquet sales in our example, you may want something different in the way of a graduated symbol.

To change the formatting of the graduated symbol, double-click the map if it's not already selected. Then click Map, Graduated Symbol Options, as shown in Figure 18.11.

Fig. 18.11
Change the map's formatting on the Map menu.

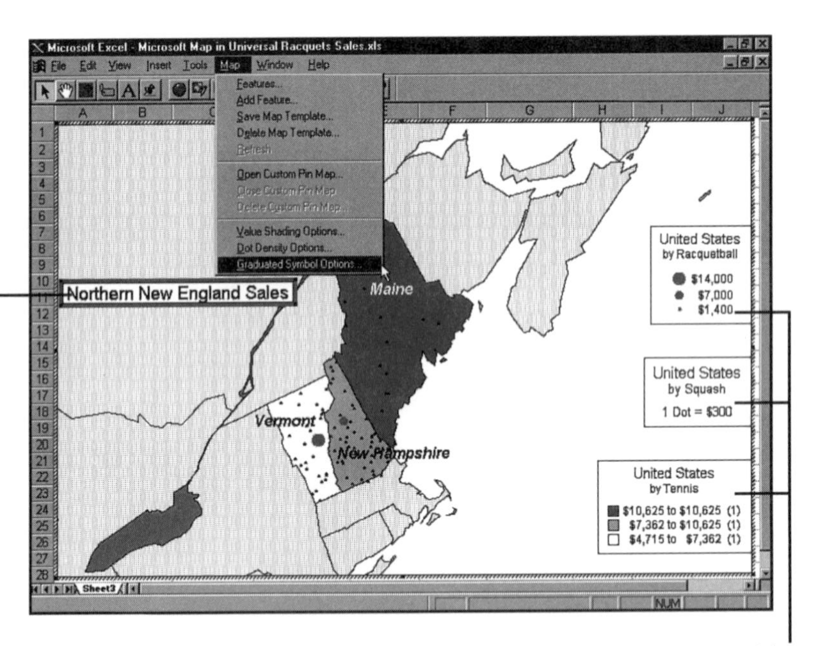

Right-click the map title to change fonts as I did here; double-click to change the text

Double-click the legends to change text and fonts

That pops up the Graduated Symbol Options tab of the Format Properties dialog box. Click Modify Symbol and choose something different from the Symbol dialog box that appears (see Figure 18.12). If you don't like any of the choices in the default Map Symbols font, click the Font button and select a different font.

TIP **If you've never had any use for Wingdings, here's your chance:** Wingdings make good graduated map symbols.

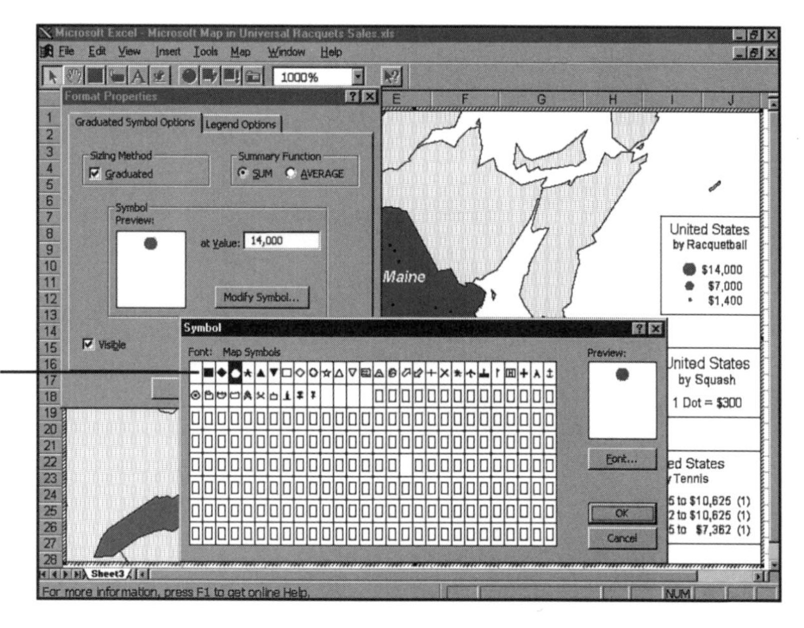

Fig. 18.12
The At Value figure in the Graduated Symbol Option tab is the highest value in the category, rounded up. Change it to alter the scale of the graduated symbols.

Double-click any of these symbols to replace the default blobs as graduated symbols

How about different dot densities and value shading?

Want a different color scheme in your map? Click Map, Value Shading Options to open the Format Properties dialog box with the Value Shading Options tab in view. Click the Color drop-down arrow and choose another color. Figure 18.13 shows the Value Shading Options tab.

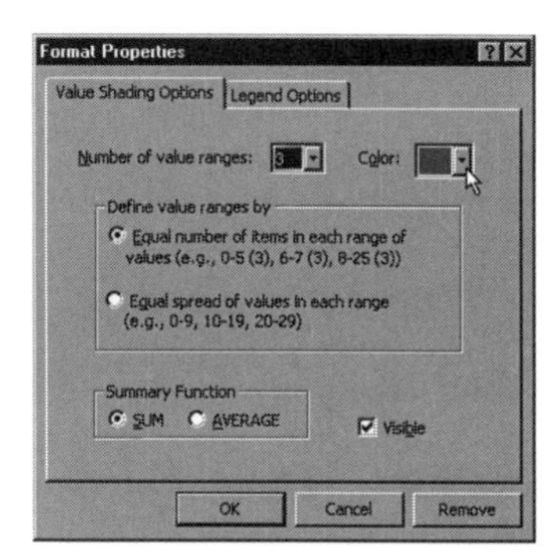

Fig. 18.13
You'll get graduated shades of any color you choose here.

If you want to see more, fewer, or smaller dots, click Map, Dot Density Options to open the Dot Density Options tab of the Format Properties dialog box (see Figure 18.14).

Enter a smaller number in the Units text box for more dots; select Small Dot Size if your dots look too blotchy.

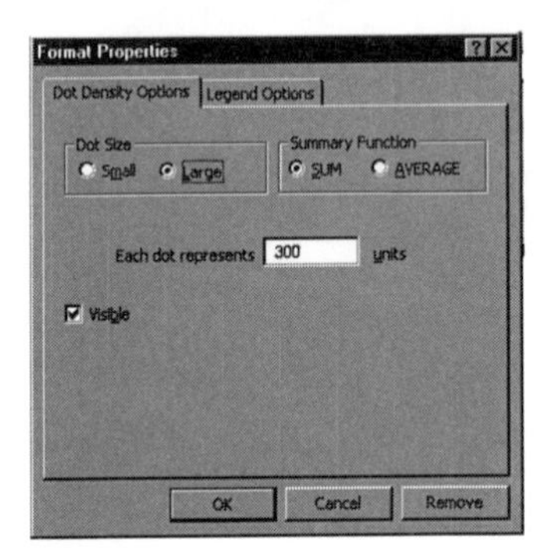

Fig. 18.14
Click the Average option if you want the dots to represent average instead of summary values.

What's a pin map?

There's a popular restaurant near my home, one of whose attractions is a map and a supply of pins. The idea is for diners to grab a pin and stick it on the map to show where they come from.

You can do the same thing with Excel data maps. If your map isn't already selected, double-click it. Then click the Custom Pin Map button on the toolbar and type a description of the map in the Custom Pin Map dialog box. Click OK, and the pointer turns into a menacing-looking pin.

Click anywhere on the map to insert a pin. Each time you click the map, a little pin appears where you click. Type the text you want at the flashing cursor alongside the pin, and press Enter.

Stick your map as full of pins as you like. To format the pin itself, right-click it and select Format from the shortcut menu. Choose a different symbol in the Symbol dialog box that pops up. To make the pin bigger or smaller, click the Font button in the Symbol dialog box and choose a different size.

To turn off pin-sticking, click the Select Objects button on the toolbar.

Right-click the pin legend to format it, or drag the text to move it to a different spot.

If you drag the pin, rather than the pin legend text, the text and the pin move together.

You might wind up with something that looks like Figure 18.15.

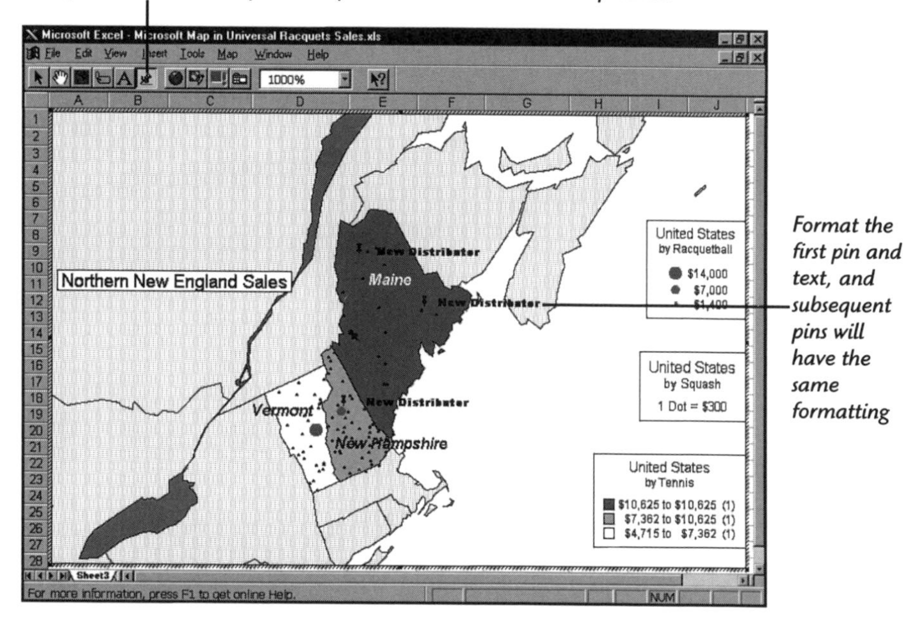

Fig. 18.15
Pin maps are useful for highlighting custom information, like the location of your new distributors in states with weak sales.

I forgot New York!

Adding more data to a map is a snap. Double-click the map, then select Insert, Data. That pops up the Data Map dialog box. Select the range containing the extra data, click OK in the Data Map dialog box, and the data appears in the map.

Just make sure that one column of the extra data contains geographical information. If, for example, you want to add the demographic data in the Mapstats workbook to an existing map, open the Mapstats workbook, click Insert, Data, and select the data you want on your map.

I want to put a chart on the map

If you want to represent your data with pie charts or column charts instead of value shading, graduated symbols, or dot density, use the Microsoft Map Control dialog box to reformat your map.

To put charts on the map:

1. Double-click the map if it's not already selected.

2. Click the Show/Hide Microsoft Map Control button on the toolbar. That pops up the Microsoft Map Control dialog box.

3. Drag your column titles out of the box; a little recycle bin appears, and the column titles vanish into it when you release the mouse button. Now drag either the Pie or Column Chart button onto the Format label in the box. Drag each of your column titles onto the Column labels next to the chart icon. It should look like Figure 18.16.

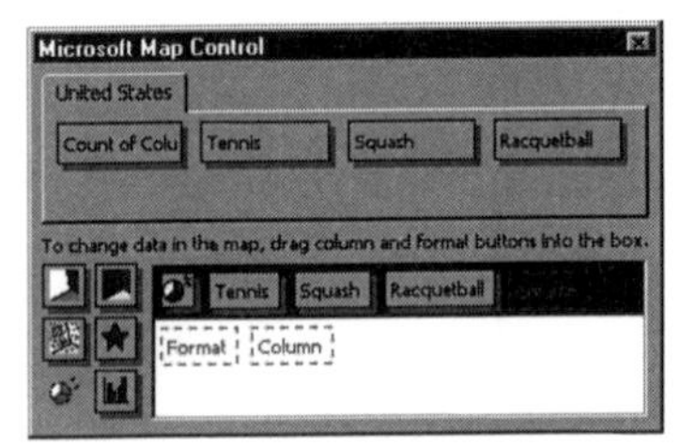

Fig. 18.16
Just as with the other map symbols, the map symbol on the left formats the data in the columns on the right.

4. Close the Microsoft Map Control dialog box, and the charts spring up on the map, as shown in Figure 18.17.

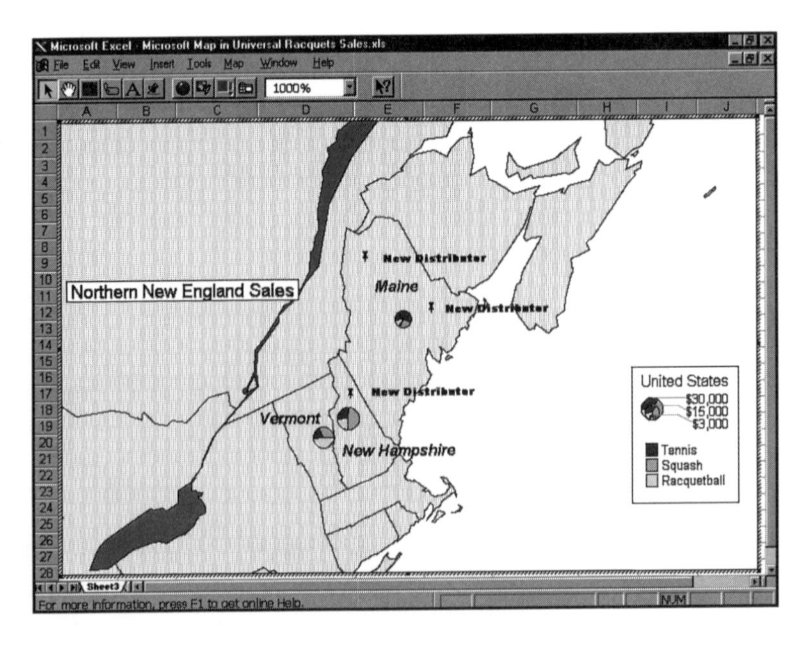

Fig. 18.17
You can put either pie or column charts on the map, but not both.

For data that doesn't fit the map, use a template

Templatesare like stencils for data: the template gives you a structure for your worksheet, and you fill it in with your own data.

To view Excel's collection of templates, click File, New to open the New dialog box. Click the Spreadsheet Solutions tab to see the selection of prefab workbooks (see Figure 18.18).

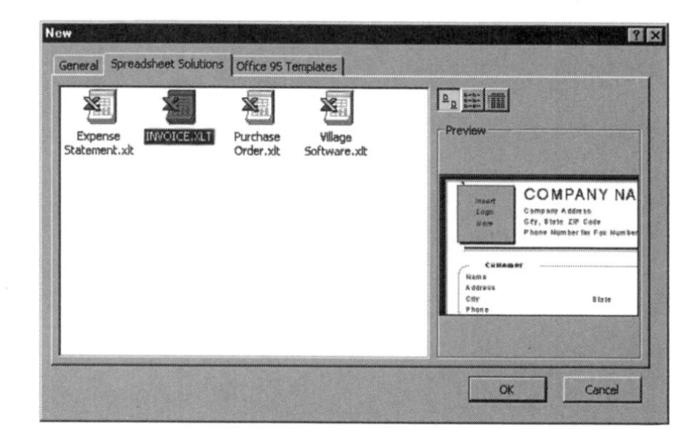

Fig. 18.18
Double-click any of these workbook templates, then fill in the blanks with data.

You might have a different selection of templates in your own New dialog box, depending on which ones you chose when you installed Excel. If you don't see some of these in your own New dialog box, run setup from your CD or program disks and install additional templates.

Bills to send? Try the Invoice template

Is there anything more aggravating than getting bills? Possibly preparing and sending them out. Excel can make the chore a little less burdensome. The Invoice template gives you a formatted, customizable invoice. Just fill in the blanks, click the Print button on the toolbar, and your invoice is ready for mailing.

Your invoice data is saved to a prefabricated Excel list, called Invdb, located in the Msoffice\Excel\Library folder. As with any Excel list, you can search, sort, and filter your data (see Chapters 15 and 16 for more on managing lists).

To get to the Invoice template, Click File, New, Spreadsheet Solutions, then double-click the Invoice template.

The template opens to the Invoice worksheet, and the handy Invoice toolbar pops up. Click the Customize Your Invoice worksheet tab, and enter your data at the top of the worksheet. You get a custom masthead (Excel calls it the Invoice Lettertype Boilerplate) at the bottom of the sheet, as shown in Figure 18.19.

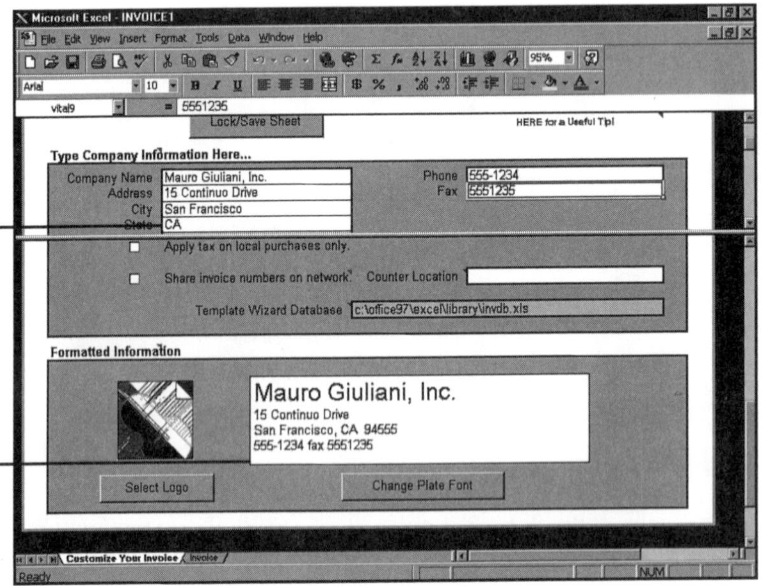

Text you enter up here...

...winds up as a masthead down here

Fig. 18.19
A split-screen view. Click the Select Logo button, then pluck a logo from any clip art file to add a custom logo.

TIP **Templates are peppered with helpful Cell Comments, marked** by little red triangles in the upper-right corner of a cell. Point at them for handy explanations and suggestions.

Put the Template Wizard to work on an invoice database

After you enter your company information on the Customize Your Invoice worksheet, click the Save button and save the workbook as a template. The next time you open the New dialog box, it'll show up on the General tab.

To create an invoice, click the Invoice worksheet tab and enter your data. To assign a unique number to the invoice, click the Assign a Number button on the Invoice toolbar.

Now you can put the Template Wizard to work. Use the Wizard to either update the Invdb list or to create a new list with data from the invoices you create with the Invoice template. To add the invoice data to the template database, Invdb:

1. Click the Capture Data in a Database button on the toolbar, and the Template Wizard springs to life, as shown in Figure 18.20.

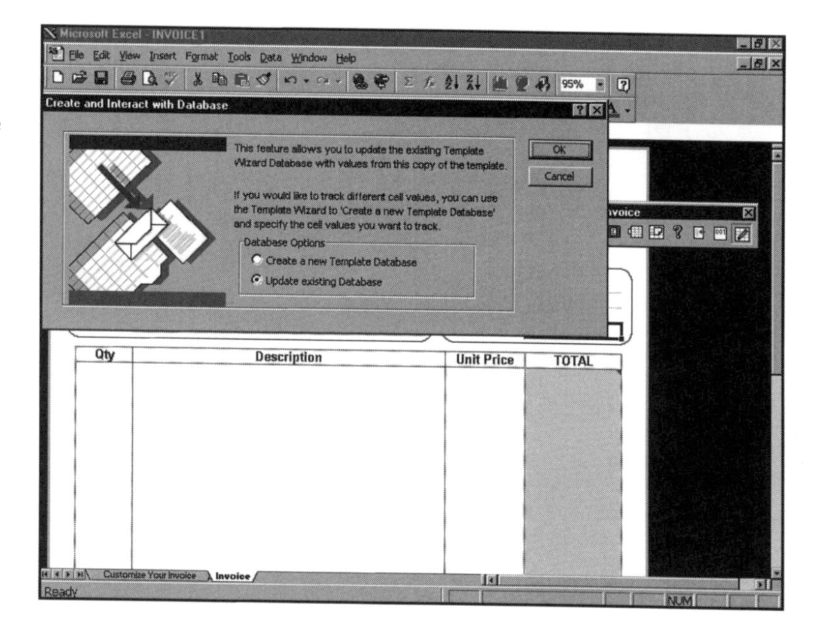

Fig. 18.20
The Update Existing Database option sticks the invoice data in the Invdb workbook.

2. Choose Update Existing Database and click OK. The Template File—Save to Database dialog box pops up. Choose Create a New Record, then click OK. The invoice data is added as a record in the Invdb workbook, as shown in Figure 18.21.

Use the Invoice template to create additional invoices. Each new invoice will be added as a record in the Invdb workbook. It's a painless way to create a billing database and generate invoices at the same time.

TIP **To print invoices created with the Invoice template, just click** the Print button on the toolbar. The margin setting and other page setup settings are already taken care of by the template.

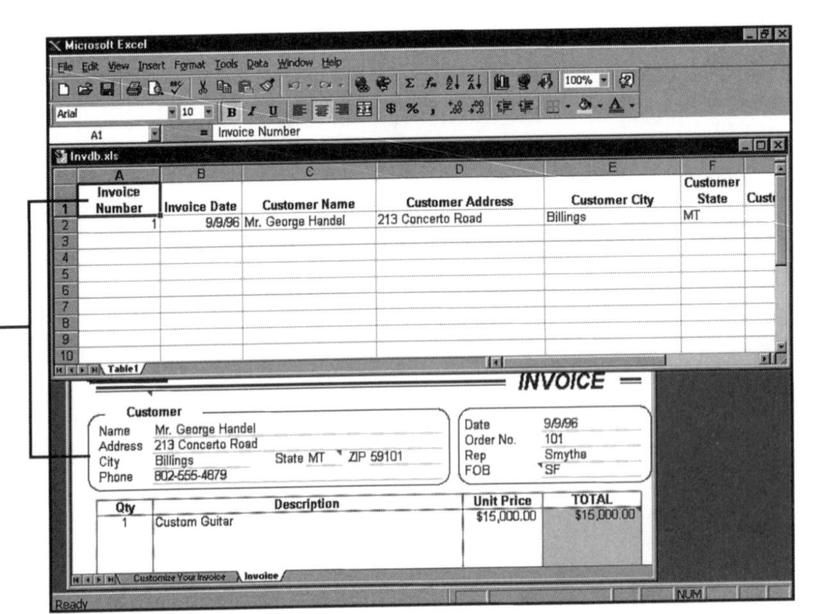

Fig. 18.21
Both workbooks are open at once, and arranged with the Window, Arrange, Horizontal command.

The invoice data entered in the Invoice template becomes a record in the Invdb list

19 Introduction to Macros

In this chapter:

- **What is a macro?**
- **When do I use macros?**
- **I need to change the way this macro works**
- **This macro isn't working!**

Tired of doing the same old worksheet chores, again and again? Instead of doing them yourself, teach Excel to do them for you. . . . .

Remember the argument that computers are going to replace people in the workplace? Doomsayers *still* cling to this fallacy. But a funny thing happened on the way to the water cooler. Most companies *add* people, just to look after their computers. Sure, computers automate a lot of tasks; but the smarter computers get, the more they need smart people to run them. Computers can't think. People can.

Macros can't think either. They just automate repetitive tasks. They can't duplicate your creativity, but they do duplicate your keystrokes. If you find yourself doing the same things all the time in Excel, create a macro to do them for you. It'll leave you more time for thinking.

What is a macro?

Macros are like the cruise control in your car. For dull jobs like maintaining speed on long stretches of empty freeway, they're great. But for anything that requires skill and judgment, like dodging traffic in city streets, do it the old-fashioned way.

When you record a macro, every keystroke and mouse click you make is being watched, noted, and stored by Excel. When you replay or **run** the macro, those keystrokes and mouse clicks are played back, exactly as you performed them.

Why is it called a macro?

Macro, the opposite of micro, comes from the Greek language. As a prefix, it means large or long: think of microeconomics and macroeconomics. (If your newly promoted colleague gets big-headed on you, call him macrocephalic, meaning big-headed. That'll take him down a peg or two.) A macro in computer lingo is a single command that executes a large, or macro, number of other commands.

And if an author is putting you to sleep, he's becoming macrostylous, or long-styled.

When should I use a macro?

Think about how you use Excel. Maybe you create new worksheets with identical formatting all the time. Or you write the same long formula over and over again. Perhaps you set up your print jobs with special margin settings and page alignments whenever you print. Those chores are all candidates for replacement with a macro.

You can do any time-consuming, repetitive job that requires several commands or clicks faster with a macro.

How do I create a macro?

Recording a macro is easy:

1 Turn on the macro recorder.

2 Do the chore you want recorded.

3 Turn off the macro recorder.

The next time you need to do that chore, run the macro and it'll be done for you.

You can throw in a few twists. Have your macro stop and prompt you for data input, for example, or have one macro launch another macro. You should also name the macro. Assign it a key combination or a menu command if you want to. Other than that, it's just a matter of recording whatever you're doing.

Setting up a worksheet with a macro

Here's one Excel chore I find tedious: setting up a worksheet. I do it the same way pretty often, so it's about time I created a macro to do it for me.

To record a macro:

1 Choose Tools, Macro, Record New Macro. If you can live with the name Macro1, and you don't care about where or how your macro is run, click OK in the Record Macro dialog box. Otherwise, type a new

name for the macro, but don't use spaces or punctuation in the name (see Figure 19.1). Consider these other options as well:

- Adding a description in the Description text box is a good idea. If you're like me, you'll forget what this macro does by next week. Even if your memory is better than that, you may not remember what it does a year from now.
- If you want your macro to run with a Ctrl+*key* combination, type a keyboard character in the Shortcut Key text box.
- Store Macro In Personal Macro Workbook creates a special hidden workbook that opens whenever you run Excel. Any macro stored there is available to all your workbooks. In Excel-speak, it's **global**. Storing a macro in This Workbook or a New Workbook means the macro can be run only when those workbooks are open.

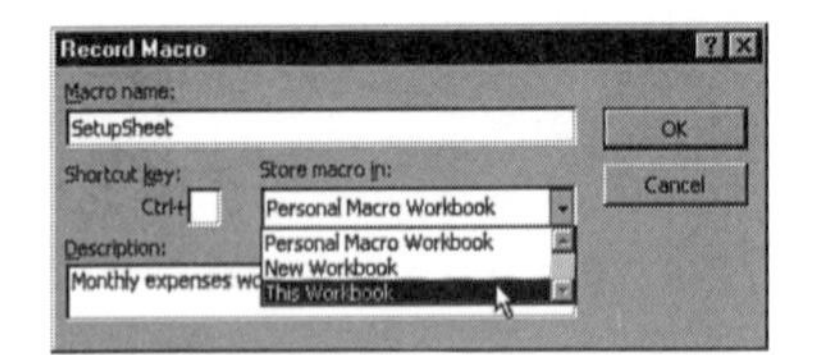

Fig. 19.1
Use the Description text box to remind you what the macro does. If you don't bother with a name, Excel gives it one for you: Macro1, Macro2, and so on. Not overly descriptive, are they?

2 Click OK, and you're off to the races. The Record Macro toolbar appears, and the macro records everything you do, including mistakes. Put in a title, row headings, and then format the whole thing. Add a TODAY function to insert today's date, and AutoSum the column. It might look like Figure 19.2.

TIP **By default, macros use absolute cell references. Whatever** actions you record will act on the same cells on the worksheet. If you want your macro to act on any cells on the worksheet (using the active cell as the upper-left border of the macro), click the Relative Reference button on the Record Macro toolbar *before* you perform the actions you want to record.

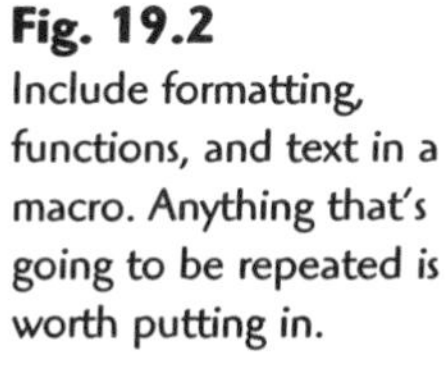

Fig. 19.2
Include formatting, functions, and text in a macro. Anything that's going to be repeated is worth putting in.

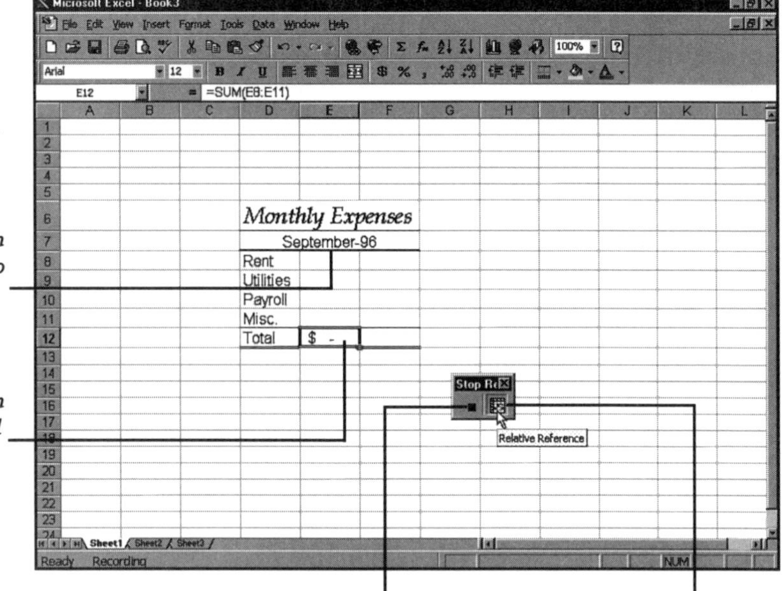

Click Paste Function on the Standard toolbar to insert a TODAY function here

Putting a SUM function here with AutoSum will total any numbers you stick in the column

The Stop Macro button; click it to stop recording

Click the Relative Reference button if you want your macro to act on any cells in the worksheet

TIP **Functions like TODAY, whose values are volatile, are useful in** macros. The values they return change automatically whenever you run the macro. TODAY will insert the correct date no matter when you run the macro.

3 Click the Stop Macro button and you're done. Whenever you want this sheet set up, you can run the macro instead of typing it all in.

Running a macro from the menu

Running macros is even easier than recording them. Press Alt+F8 to open the Macros dialog box (or choose Tools, Macro, Macros). Select the macro from the list, and click Run. That's all there is to it.

Editing a macro: background

The macro recorder is like a tireless secretary, standing by to take dictation at all times. Behind the scenes, some pretty amazing things were going on while you recorded that macro. Every keystroke and mouse click you made was being taken down in a kind of shorthand.

It's a special shorthand called Visual Basic. Some words are recognizable, though others might be a little obscure. The syntax may not be exactly what you're used to either.

Plain English, please!

Syntax means the systematic arrangement of the parts. We know syntax in English grammar as the rules that govern sentence construction. English isn't necessarily strict about syntax; writers break the rules all the time and call it poetic license. Visual Basic is more exacting, and requires correct syntax. It's as fussy about syntax as the functions we looked at in Chapters 9 and 10. Arguments in many functions have to be in the right order for the function to work properly; the syntax, in other words, has to be correct.

Figure 19.3 shows the macro we recorded as it appears in Excel's macro language, Visual Basic.

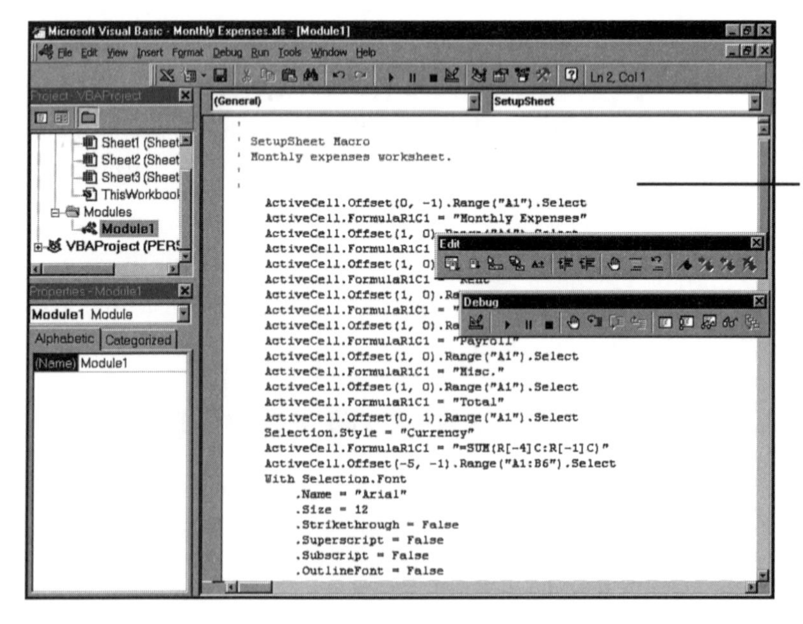

Fig. 19.3
Here's your macro, written in the macro shorthand called Visual Basic. You can edit it or write it from scratch, just like text.

What is Visual Basic?

Visual Basic is actually a lot more than shorthand. It's a language you can use to communicate directly with Excel. When you want Excel to do things like format a cell, you ordinarily use the menus or a toolbar button. Using Visual Basic, you bypass the menus and buttons and give the command directly. It's like going into a restaurant, ignoring the menu, and telling the chef what you want right to his face.

Why would you do that? Maybe you want your steak done just so, or maybe you don't like what's on the menu at all. You use Visual Basic the same way: to customize how Excel does things, or to tell it do something that's just not on a menu.

Learn VB with Excel's online language manual

Unlike a testy kitchen artiste, Excel won't pick up a cleaver when you start giving it orders. But this chef doesn't speak much English—to get through to Excel, you have to learn a little of its language.

There's extensive online Help for Visual Basic, though making sense of it will require a fair investment of time. Choose Help, Contents and Index to open the Help Topics dialog box. Click the Contents tab, and double-click Microsoft Excel Visual Basic Reference. You'll get the Visual Basic Reference topics shown in Figure 19.4.

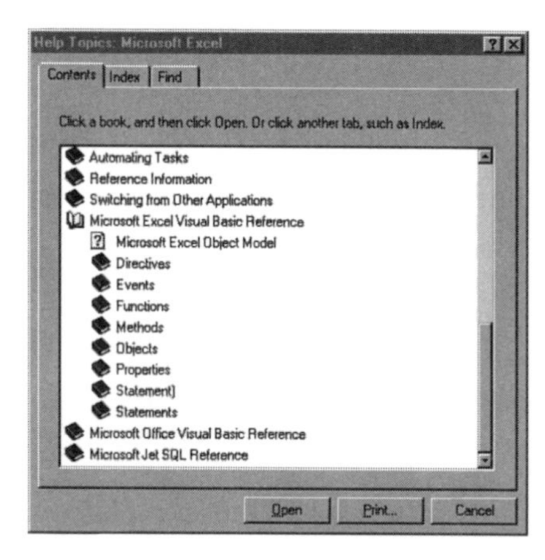

Fig. 19.4
Excel's online Visual Basic Reference is your guide to the language of macros.

I don't see any Microsoft Visual Basic help topics in the Help Topics dialog box!

Visual Basic help isn't installed in a Typical Excel installation. You'll have to dig out your Excel (or Office) CD and run Setup to install Visual Basic Help.

Do I have to learn Visual Basic to edit macros?

If a macro doesn't run correctly, there are several things you can do about it. You can replace it; just record the macro again and save it with the same name. You can also delete it: choose Tools, Macro, Macros (or press Alt+F8). Select the macro, click Delete, and start over.

If you stored your macro in the Personal Macro Worksheet, you'll have to unhide the worksheet before editing or deleting the macro. Click Window, Unhide to do that. Remember to hide the worksheet again when you're finished to get it out of the way.

But if you have a small change to make, you can edit the macro—even if you're not fluent in Visual Basic.

Editing a macro

Let's change "Rent" to "Lease" in our macro to see how editing a macro is done.

1 Choose Tools, Macro, Macros, select the macro, and click Edit.

2 That takes you to the Microsoft Visual Basic editor. If your macro appears as a minimized icon, just click the Maximize button on the icon. Click the Find button, and type in **rent** (see Figure 19.5). Click Find Next to go straight to the word you seek.

3 When you type text while recording a macro, Visual Basic puts the text in quotation marks. You want to leave those alone when you edit the macro, but otherwise it's just like editing ordinary text. Now that Find has highlighted `"Rent"`, just type **Lease** right over it. Don't add any extra spaces or move the quotes.

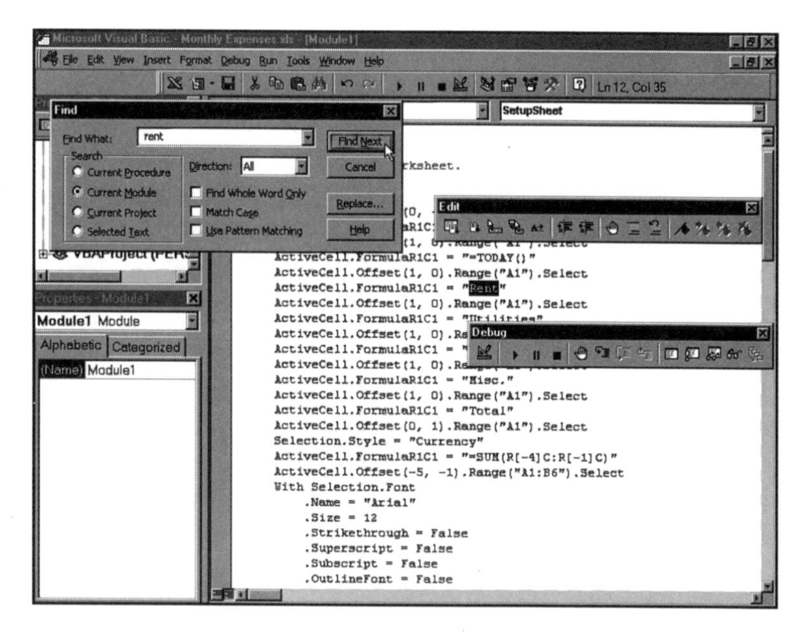

Fig. 19.5
Editing tools like Find and Replace are handy for fixing or changing macros. Think of Visual Basic as text in another language and it's not too intimidating.

4 Choose File, Close and return to Microsoft Excel. Any changes you make in the macro are saved along with the rest of the workbook. When you run the macro again, you get Lease instead of Rent.

TIP

Don't forget about Excel's handy automatic editing tool, Replace. Here's an alternative to editing macro text by hand: click the Replace button in the Find dialog box, type **rent** in the Find What text box, and **Lease** in the Replace With text box. Click Replace and your fix is made.

CAUTION

Macro text is stuffed with the terms and punctuation of Visual Basic, which Excel adds when the macro is being recorded. When you're tinkering with the text of your macro, be careful not to move or delete any of it by accident. One accidentally moved or deleted period can throw the whole macro out of whack. Find and Replace is safer for this kind of work. In the example, I just wanted to show that you can go in and tinker with macro text by hand.

Why isn't this macro working right, and how can I fix it?

It's easy to make a minor slip when you're recording a macro. Problem is, that minor slip might have major consequences when you try to run the macro. It might not do what you expect, and in certain frustrating instances, it might not do anything at all (except give you an error message).

Although fluency in Visual Basic is required to really get under the hood of a faulty macro, non-experts can at least see where their macro is going wrong. When you run a macro, all the commands you recorded are executed instantly. Text and numbers that you typed are retyped at superhuman speed. That makes it impossible to see the command, text, or number that's responsible for the problem. You'll find it more helpful to watch your macro run one step at a time, so you can pinpoint the trouble spot.

To see your macro run step-by-step:

1. Press Alt+F8 to open the Macro dialog box. Select your macro, and click Step Into.
2. The Visual Basic editing window opens. If your macro appears as a minimized icon in the Visual Basic window, click the icon's Maximize button to view the macro code. To see the worksheet and the macro code at the same time, right-click the Windows taskbar background and choose Tile Horizontally.
3. Click the Step Into button on the Debug toolbar. That highlights the first line of code in the Visual Basic window, and runs the first line of the macro in the workbook. Keep clicking the Step Into button to work your way through the macro code line by line, while you watch the macro unfold in the workbook, as shown in Figure 19.6.
4. When you reach the trouble spot in your macro, try editing the line (or lines) of code in the Visual Basic window. Click File, Close and return to Microsoft Excel when you're done.

The Step Into button is only one of the many gadgets in the Microsoft Visual Basic editor to fix—or **debug**—broken macros. Unlike the other gadgets, you don't need any Visual Basic expertise to operate it.

Fig. 19.6
When your macro takes a misstep, run it step-by-step to see where you went wrong.

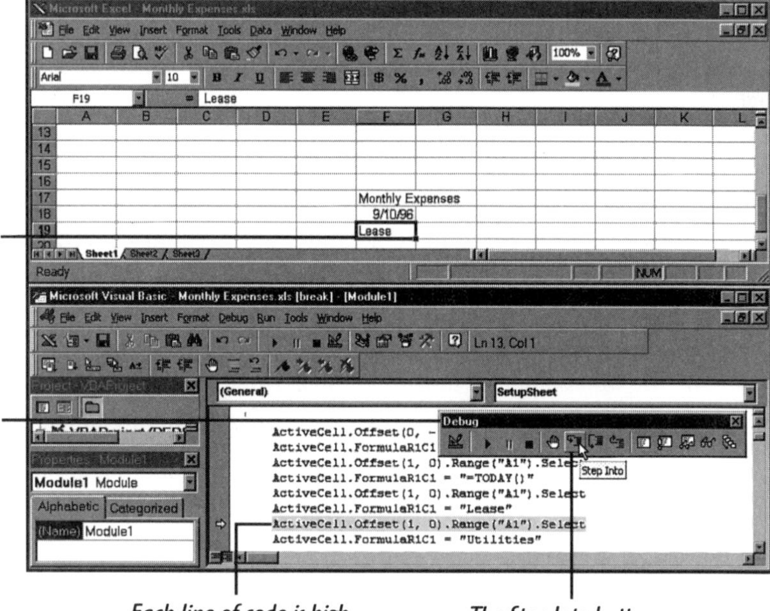

The corresponding part of the macro runs in the workbook after you click Step Into again

If a toolbar gets in the way, double-click the title bar to dock it at the top of the screen

Each line of code is highlighted in turn when you click the Step Into button

The Step Into button

I want to get at my macro quickly

You can run any macro from the Tools, Macro, Macros menu. For macros that you use all the time, consider assigning them to a key combination. You can do that in the Record Macro dialog box before you start recording (refer to Figure 19.1). Or, you can give a macro a shortcut key combination after it's been recorded.

TIP **You can also assign a macro to a custom toolbar button. See** Chapter 21 for details on how to do that.

Choose Tools, Macro, Macros. Select the macro, then click Options. Type any letter on the keyboard to assign a Ctrl+*key* shortcut key combination, as shown in Figure 19.7.

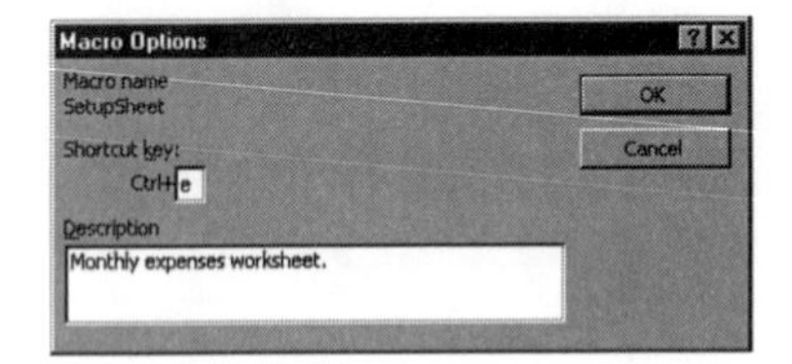

Fig. 19.7
Type a keyboard letter to assign your macro to a handy keyboard shortcut.

Only letters work; numbers and other keyboard characters won't be accepted. If you later forget your macro's keyboard shortcut, just press Alt+F8, select the macro in the Macro dialog box, and click Options to view the selected letter.

20 Exchanging Data with Other Programs

In this chapter:

- **How can I send data between Excel and my other programs?**
- **What is embedding?**
- **I want to put my Excel chart in a Word document**
- **How can I turn a chunk of text into an Excel list?**
- **This chart would look great in a PowerPoint slide**

Sharing data between Excel and the other programs you use is the efficient way to give your work more flexibility and flair . . . .

The young Republic of the United States tossed a few other ideas around before finally settling on a familiar motto to put on its new seal: *E Pluribus Unum*. "From the Many, One." So what if it was also the motto of a popular magazine? It had a nice ring. It fit neatly (and still does) on all the new money. And it conveyed a powerful truth: many colonies are a lot stronger as one nation.

The same is true of computer programs. Bring the power of many programs together in one document, and you have a stronger document. You do that by exchanging data between Excel and your other applications.

What do you mean by exchanging data?

You have a chart created in Excel, and you want to add it to your report in Word. Or maybe you wrote a long memo in Word (or another Windows word processor), and you want to include it in an Excel workbook. You have three ways of passing that data back and forth:

- Good old **copy** or **cut and paste**. Cutting (or copying) and pasting between Windows applications works pretty much the same way it does in them.
- **Linking** data between Windows programs is exactly like linking Excel workbooks. Set up the link, make changes in your Excel data, and a linked chart in Word gets the same changes. (See Chapter 17 for more information on linking.)
- **Embedding** an object from one program into another is a little different. You can grab a document from Word, embed it in Excel, and then make changes to the document right in Excel. No need to flip back to Word. Meanwhile, the original document in Word isn't affected by any changes you make to the clone in Excel. The Excel document is a copy of the Word document, but a live copy—one you can alter in all the ways you can alter a regular Word document.

Confusing? Think of it this way. Linking is like hooking up an intercom system between two offices. Whatever's said in one office is heard in the other office. Embedding is like pushing one of the offices through the wall so that part of it is actually inside the other office!

I use Excel with Microsoft Word and PowerPoint in this chapter for the sake of illustration, mostly because all three programs are part of Microsoft Office, which you might be using anyway. But you're not limited to Word and PowerPoint for exchanging data with Excel. You can cut and paste between any Windows application with a couple of mouse clicks.

I need to grab something from one program and stick it in another, fast!

You've just written a brilliant formula in Excel, and you're describing it to your colleagues in a Word document. Don't retype the whole thing—copy and paste instead.

1 Click the cell with the formula in it, then click the formula bar and highlight the formula by dragging.

2 Click the Copy button.

3 Switch to Word (press Alt+Tab or click the Word icon on the taskbar).

4 Put the cursor where you want the formula, and click the Paste button.

This works both ways. To grab something in Word and stick it in Excel, do the same thing in reverse. And it doesn't only apply to formulas. Copy or cut and paste charts, tables, or graphic objects—it's your choice.

No wonder they say "OLE!"

Embedding and linking are neat tricks. To perform them, the programs you use must have a special capability built in. It's called **OLE** (pronounced *oh-lay*) and it stands for **Object Linking and Embedding**. Most major applications for Windows support OLE. If you're not sure about a particular program, look for references to OLE in the documentation. If it isn't mentioned, chances are linking and embedding won't be possible for that program.

Microsoft Office programs like Word and Excel will try to paste the copied material in the format that makes it easiest to edit:

- Excel tables pasted into Word are automatically converted to Word tables. Word tables pasted into Excel preserve their column and row structure, and are given the identical layout in Excel columns and rows.
- Word text separated by tabs and hard returns automatically flows into separate columns and rows when you paste it into Excel.
- If the program you're pasting material into can't determine the best format, the material is pasted as an embedded object if both programs support OLE. You can double-click the embedded object, and edit it with the tools of the program used to create it. If your programs don't support OLE, material is pasted as a simple picture.

Why does the Paste button look like a clipboard?

Anything you cut or copy gets dumped in the Windows Clipboard, a temporary storage bin. You can see what's in it, which is helpful if you want to be sure of what you copied before pasting it somewhere else.

Click the Start button and select Programs, Accessories, Clipboard Viewer. Your last cut or copied selection will be on view in the Clipboard window. Use the Clipboard Viewer menu bar to clear or save the Clipboard contents. You can also ignore the Clipboard completely. It operates behind the scenes, and it works without you having to do a thing.

If you don't see the Clipboard Viewer on the Start, Programs, Accessories menu, you have to install it. Click Start, Settings, Control Panel. Double-click the Add/Remove Programs folder, then click the Windows Setup tab in the Add/Remove Properties dialog box. Double-click Accessories on the Components list, click the Clipboard Viewer check box, and click OK twice.

How do I put an Excel chart in my Word document?

Here's something you're likely to want to do: dress up a letter with a chart you created in Excel. You can paste a chart as an embedded object and use

Excel's charting features to edit the chart from within Word. Or link it, so that the pasted chart in Word is updated whenever you change your Excel data. We'll try it both ways.

Although copying and pasting charts, or any other objects, is a straightforward maneuver, there are a few things you can do at the outset to make it even easier:

- Excel chart sheets are too big for Word documents. Chart sheets are what you get when you select the Place Chart As New Sheet option in Step 4 of the Chart Wizard. Chart sheets are designed to fill the page, so they would be out of scale inserted in a page of text in Word. That doesn't mean you *can't* insert a chart sheet in Word. You just have to resize the chart in Excel before shipping it over to Word.
- Embedded charts are the kind you get when you choose the Place Chart As Object In option in the Chart Wizard's last step. You probably won't have to resize an embedded Excel chart as drastically as a chart sheet before inserting it in Word.
- Do your chart editing and resizing in Excel before you insert the chart in Word. You *can* tinker with Excel charts from within Word, but you'll find it easier to do your tinkering in Excel first.

Save your work before copying and pasting between applications. Windows 95 is much more stable than previous incarnations of Windows, especially for maneuvers like these. But unexpected things can still happen, and there's nothing worse than losing a morning's work because your application decides to go south on you.

Any objections?

Do you object to all this talk of objects? Aren't we talking about text, charts, and maybe pictures, too? We are, and they're all **objects**, at least in computer-speak. If you think of objects as things that you can hold in your hand, or at least touch, this may take a little getting used to. Windows' use of the word seems to go back to the way it was used by medieval philosophers. Their word *objectum* meant something thrown in front of the mind. And if you do a lot of complicated linking and embedding, you might consider the older English meaning of the word "object:" something that invites ridicule or pity.

Getting chart sheets from Excel to Word the easy way

Word's online Help advises you to use chart sheets (rather than charts embedded in worksheets) when you paste a chart in Word. One small problem: chart sheets take up most of the page in Word documents. The fix? Resize the chart first.

To resize an Excel chart sheet and paste it in a Word document:

1 With both Word and Excel running, switch to Excel. Click your chart sheet tab to display the chart.

2 Click File, Page Setup on the Excel menu bar to open Excel's Page Setup dialog box.

3 Click the Chart tab and select the Custom option (see Figure 20.1).

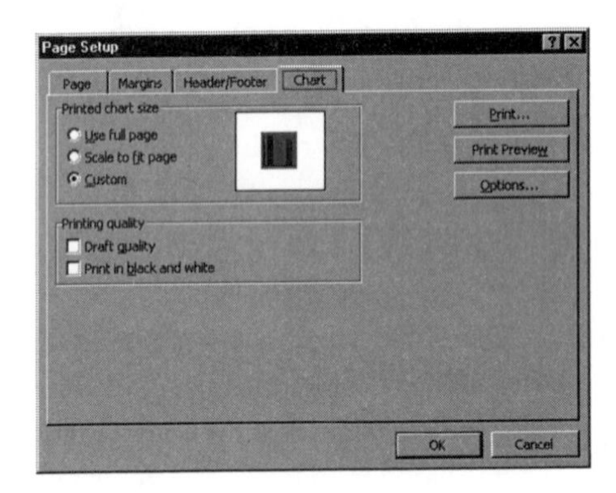

Fig. 20.1
Even though you're not printing the chart, you can only resize chart sheets with the Page Setup Custom option.

4 Click OK, and you'll see that your chart is surrounded with a broken-line border, labeled Chart Area, in the lower-right corner.

5 Click the broken-line border around the chart; the border changes from broken line to patterned, and handles pop up around it. Now drag any handle to resize the chart, as shown in Figure 20.2.

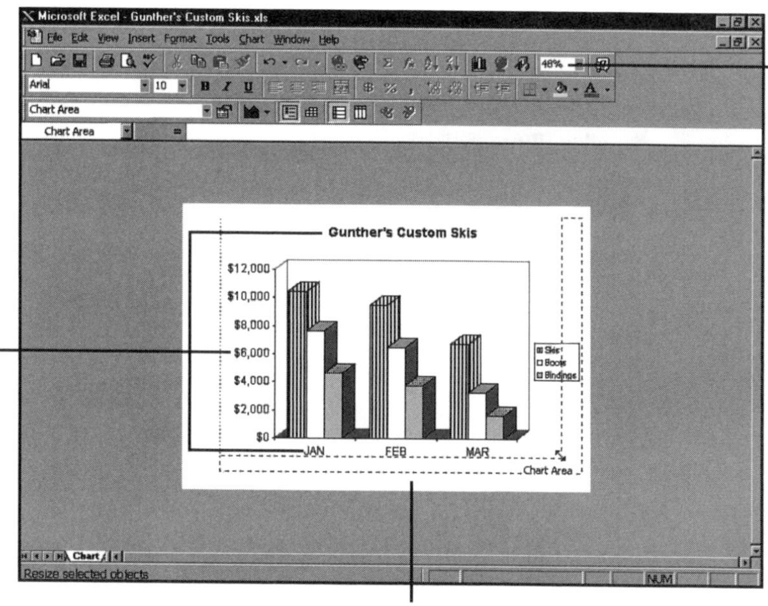

Fig. 20.2
As you drag a handle, the border changes back to a broken line. Quirky, but it works.

Remember that chart sheets aren't displayed at 100% magnification, so this chart looks smaller than it really is

You'll want smaller font sizes for the chart title and axis labels to get the chart to fit on the Word page

If resizing the Chart Area does odd things to your chart's appearance, click the Plot Area to select it, then drag to resize it

TIP **To keep the chart in proportion as you resize it, drag a corner** handle.

6 After you drag the chart down to size and select smaller font sizes for the chart title and axis labels, click the Zoom Control drop-down arrow on the toolbar (refer to Figure 20.2) and select 100% so you can see the chart's actual size. Drag to resize further if you have to; you'll want the chart small enough to fit in a page full of text.

7 Got your chart resized? The handles around the Chart Area should still be displayed; if they're not, click the chart to get them back. Then click the Copy button on the Excel toolbar. That copies the chart to the Windows Clipboard.

8 Now switch to Word. Put the insertion point where you want the chart and click the Paste button on the Word toolbar. The chart pops right into your document at the insertion point, as shown in Figure 20.3.

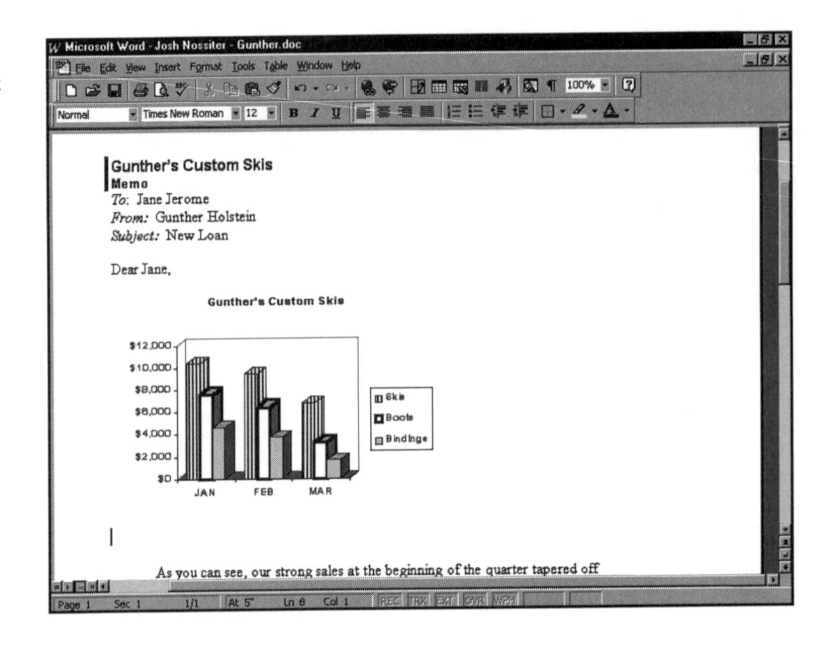

Fig. 20.3
Inserting a chart is just like inserting text; everything around it gets shoved aside to make room.

As you can see in Figure 20.3, just plopping a chart into the middle of a document may not give you exactly what you want. Existing text gets unceremoniously pushed aside by an inserted object. It's easily fixed, though.

I want text to flow around my chart

Charts look like they really belong in documents when text flows around them. Otherwise, a reader will think you just pasted in the chart any old way (which is exactly what we just did).

To wrap text around an inserted chart:

1. Right-click the inserted chart in your Word document and choose Format Object from the shortcut menu.
2. In the Format Object dialog box that appears, click the Wrapping tab.
3. Choose a Wrapping style and a side to wrap to, and click OK. Figure 20.4 shows text wrapped with the Tight and Left options.

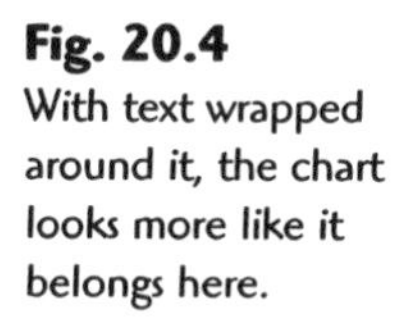

Fig. 20.4
With text wrapped around it, the chart looks more like it belongs here.

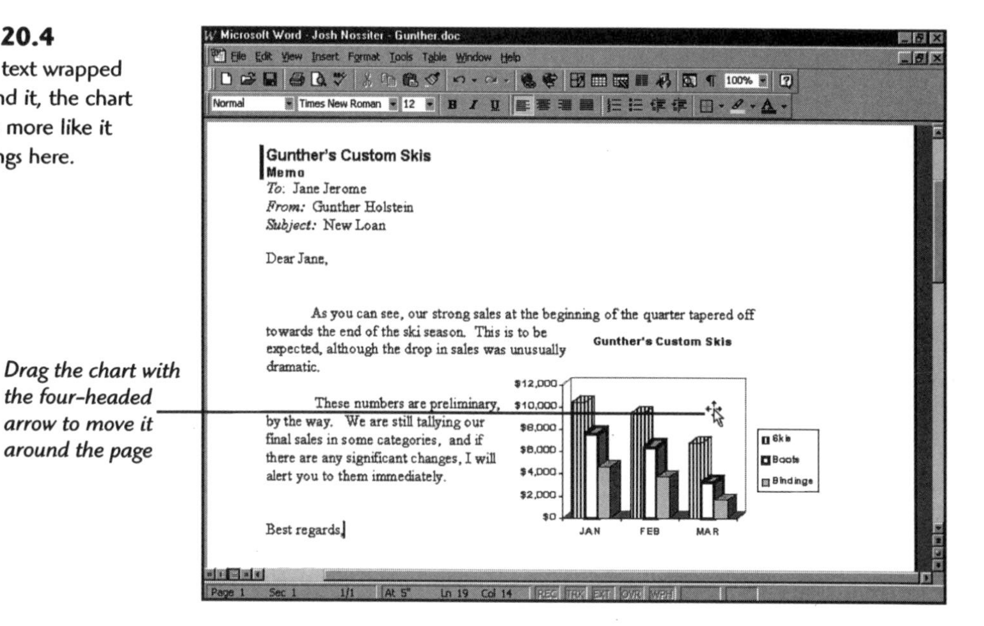

Drag the chart with the four-headed arrow to move it around the page

What if I want to insert an embedded Excel chart?

You can insert charts embedded in Excel worksheets into Word documents just as easily as chart sheets. Select the chart in Excel, click the Copy button on the Excel Standard toolbar, then paste the chart in Word.

Linking data to the Word chart

Pasting that chart into a Word document with the toolbar Paste button gives you a static object. That's fine if the data used to create the chart doesn't change. But when you do need to make changes in the data, you want the chart to reflect them.

Set up a link instead. Now when you change the data in Excel, the changes will show up in the chart in Word.

1. Copy the Excel chart, then flip to Word.
2. Position the cursor, then choose Edit, Paste Special.

3 Click Paste Link, as shown in Figure 20.5.

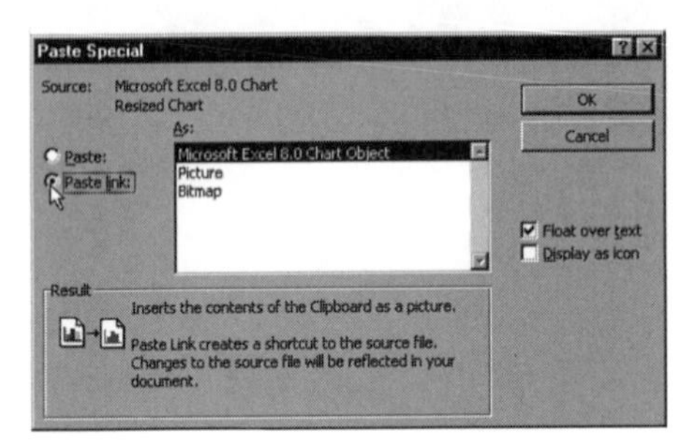

Fig. 20.5
Pasting as a link puts the chart in the document as an embedded object, just as we did before. The difference is that now when the data changes in Excel, the Word chart is also updated.

4 The Paste Special dialog box gives you a few other pasting options:

- Pasting as a Microsoft Excel Chart Object gives you an embedded object that you can edit with Excel's charting tools. That's just like the pasted chart we got with the Copy and Paste buttons earlier, with one big difference: pasted as a link, changes in the original chart update the embedded object copy. That doesn't work both ways, though. If you edit a linked, embedded object in Word, the Excel original is unaffected.

- Pasting as a Picture gets you a simple copy of the chart. A picture uses less memory than an embedded copy, but you can't use Excel's tools to edit the chart in Word. For Excel charts in Word, you can't paste a picture as a link.

- Pasting as a Bitmap gives you an exact duplicate of your original chart. This option uses a lot of memory and disk space, and it can make Word irritatingly slow to use. Chances are, you won't notice any difference in the appearance of a bitmap copy anyway.

- The Display As Icon option inserts the chart in Word, but it appears as an icon. That results in the fastest Word performance and uses the least memory, but you don't see the way the chart looks in your document. You can double-click the icon to edit the chart.

5 Make your choices in the Paste Special dialog box, then click OK.

If you paste the chart into Word as a link, it'll be updated automatically whenever you change the original chart or data in Excel.

Figure 20.6 shows both the pasted chart in Word and the original chart in Excel, linked together.

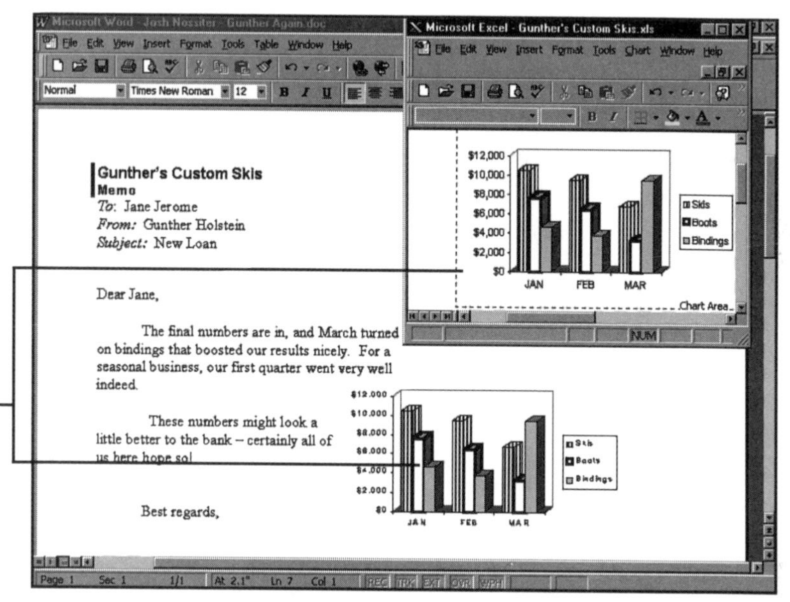

Fig. 20.6
Gunther had a run on bindings in March. When he added the extra sales to his Excel table, the chart in Word (and his request for a loan) got a lot of extra punch.

The two charts are now linked; any changes in the Excel data automatically change the chart in Word

I think I lost the link. What do I do?

Missing links happen, especially if you change the file name of a linked workbook. The Edit, Links command gives you the tools to fix it. Reestablishing links works the same way between programs as it does between workbooks.

I'm tired of flipping back and forth between applications

Embedding a Word document as an object in Excel lets you work on the document right from Excel. This option eats up a lot of memory, though. Not only the text, but also all the data needed to edit the document, is exchanged between the programs.

1. Copy the Word text you want to embed in the Excel worksheet.
2. Select the cell in Excel that's the upper-left corner of the embedded object. Then choose Edit, Paste Special from the Excel menu bar.

3 Click Paste, As Microsoft Word Document Object. The text you selected in Word pops into your Excel worksheet, as shown in Figure 20.7.

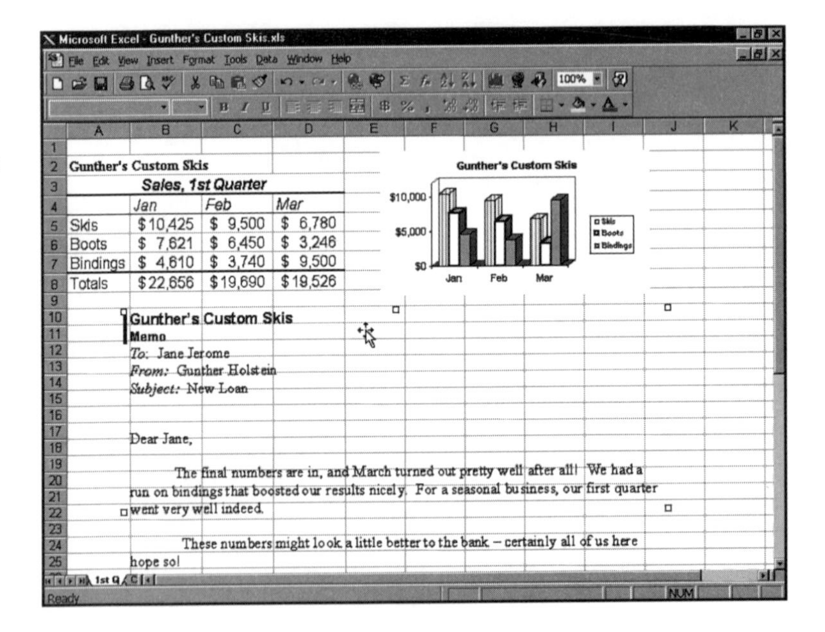

Fig. 20.7
Embedded objects look like any other kind of pasted object, until you double-click them.

The result is an actual chunk of Word, embedded right in the Excel worksheet. When you double-click the embedded Word document to edit it, the Word Standard and Formatting toolbars pop up right in Excel, as shown in Figure 20.8.

Always save your work before you try linking-and-embedding maneuvers, and keep saving as you go along. OLE works, most of the time. But it taxes your system resources and memory, and it can give you the occasional unpredictable result. If things lock up on you and you have to resort to Ctrl+Alt+Delete (as I've had to do a couple of times in the course of writing this chapter!), at least your work will be saved.

To return to your worksheet and restore the Excel toolbars, click anywhere in the worksheet outside the embedded Word document.

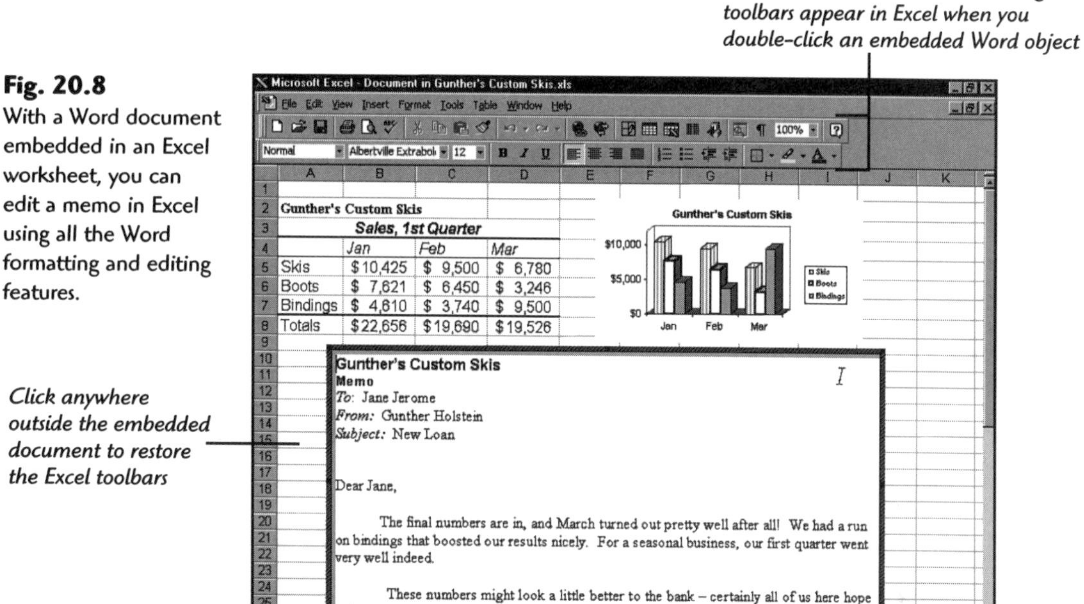

Fig. 20.8
With a Word document embedded in an Excel worksheet, you can edit a memo in Excel using all the Word formatting and editing features.

I need to stick text from another program into an Excel list

Excel can do all kinds of tricks with lists. Sorting, filtering, and subtotaling are all Excel tools for getting useful information out of long lists of text and numbers.

You might have a list like that in another program, a word processor maybe, or a computerized phone book. Wouldn't it be handy to turn that ordinary list into an Excel list? Then you can turn loose all the Excel database features.

And it's easy to do with the Excel Text Wizard:

1. Select the text you want and copy it.
2. Switch to Excel and paste it. You'll have a slight mess that looks like Figure 20.9.

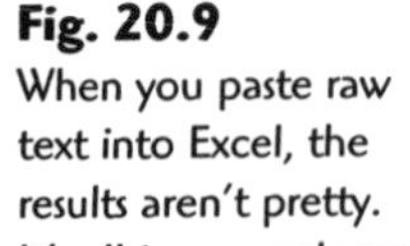

Fig. 20.9
When you paste raw text into Excel, the results aren't pretty. It's all in one column for now, but that's easy to fix.

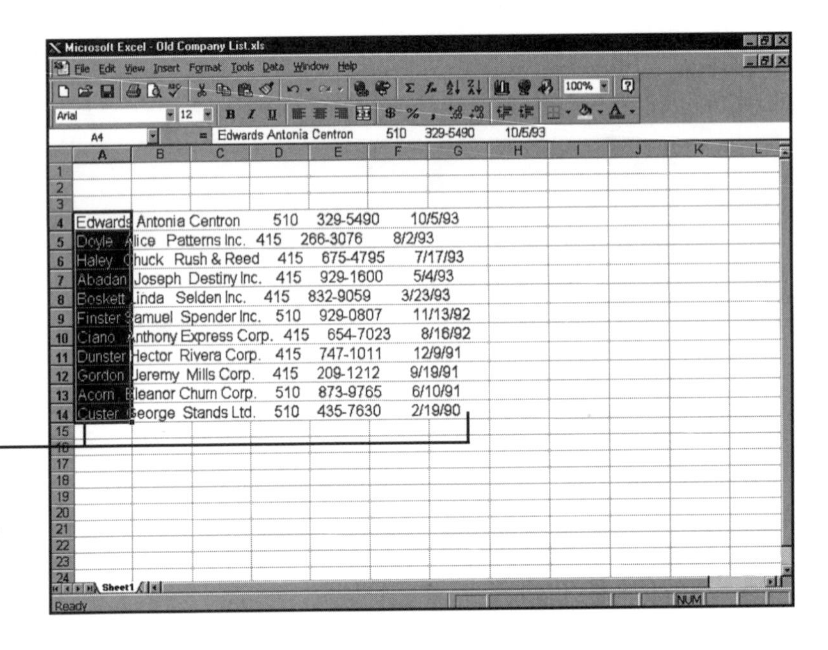

Text that might have been in several columns in another program winds up in one column when pasted in Excel; this text is all in column A

3 Even though it's spilling out all over the place, Excel has dumped all the text into column A. You want it divided neatly into separate columns. Select all of the occupied column, A in the example.

4 Choose Data, Text To Columns. The Text Wizard pops up, as shown in Figure 20.10.

Fig. 20.10
The Text Wizard guesses at the current formatting of your data and chooses between delimited and fixed width for you.

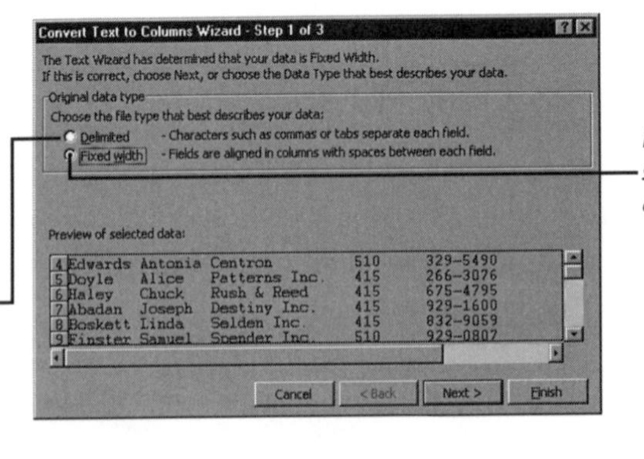

Delimited text is broken up into fields by punctuation marks

Fixed Width text has fields separated by spaces; tabs are delimiters masquerading as spaces

5 Click Next after you decide on your data type (or when Excel has decided for you). Step 2 of the Text Wizard lets you fix the column width for each field, or add or get rid of columns (see Figure 20.11).

Fig. 20.11
If the data's in the right columns, but the widths are off, don't worry about it here. You can make exact width adjustments after the list is set up.

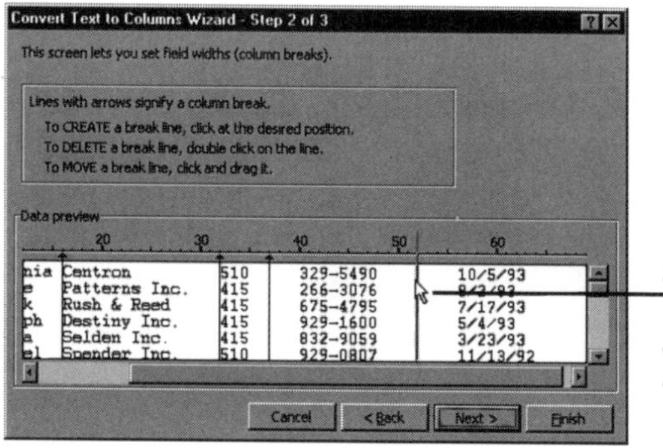

Drag a line to move it; click once wherever you want to add a line, or double-click a line to delete it

6 Step 3 is for fine-tuning. For Column Data Format, the best choice is General. That gives you numbers as numbers, dates as dates, and text as text—which is probably what you want. You can always go back in and change things if you need to. You can also decide to leave out a column here. Just click it, and select Do Not Import Column (Skip). If you do have a column of dates, selecting Date as a data format ensures that Excel won't convert them to text or numbers (see Figure 20.12).

Fig. 20.12
The choices you make here are for each column separately, so you have plenty of flexibility. Click the column and make your selection.

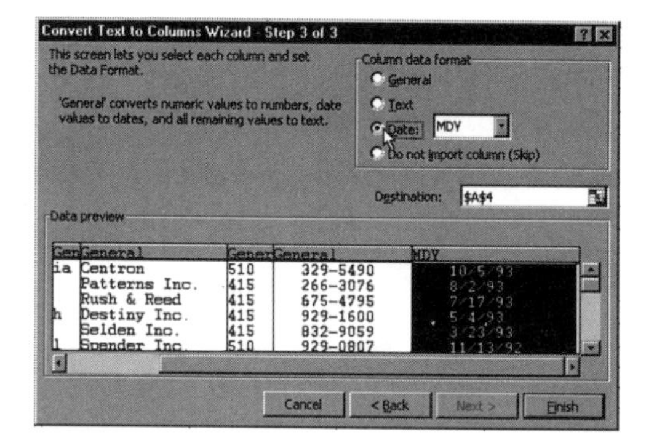

7 Click Finish, and you're done. Add a header row and formatting, and your raw text is an Excel list. Figure 20.13 shows the finished product.

Q&A ***I got the error message*** `No data selected to parse` ***instead of the Text Wizard. And what does "parse" mean, anyway?***

Remember that all your data's been dumped into one column, even though it might look like it's in several. You selected a blank cell. Just click a cell in the first column with data in it instead. **Parse** means to separate into its component parts.

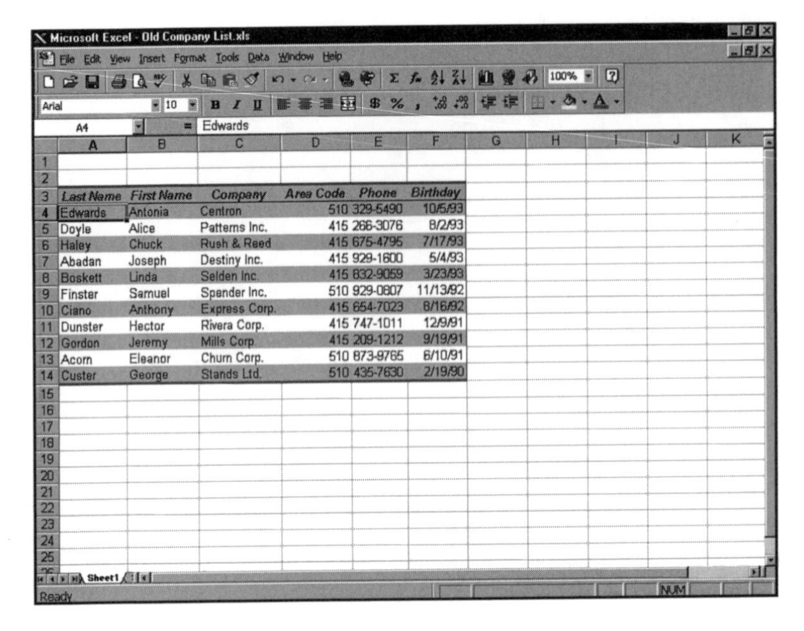

Last Name	First Name	Company	Area Code	Phone	Birthday
Edwards	Antonia	Centron	510	329-5490	10/5/93
Doyle	Alice	Patterns Inc.	415	266-3076	8/2/93
Haley	Chuck	Rush & Reed	415	675-4795	7/17/93
Abadan	Joseph	Destiny Inc.	415	929-1600	5/4/93
Boskett	Linda	Selden Inc.	415	832-9059	3/23/93
Finster	Samuel	Spender Inc.	510	929-0807	11/13/92
Ciano	Anthony	Express Corp.	415	654-7023	8/16/92
Dunster	Hector	Rivera Corp.	415	747-1011	12/9/91
Gordon	Jeremy	Mills Corp.	415	209-1212	9/19/91
Acorn	Eleanor	Churn Corp.	510	873-9765	6/10/91
Custer	George	Stands Ltd.	510	435-7630	2/19/90

Fig. 20.13
Now's the time to adjust column widths to get them exactly right, add formatting, and stick in the header row.

If you want to take text from a DOS program and stick it in an Excel list, here's how to do it: open the DOS program in Windows, then press Alt+spacebar to minimize it. Right-click the minimized DOS program icon on the taskbar and choose Properties. In the Properties dialog box, click the Screen tab and select Window and Display Toolbar. Click OK, and the program appears in a window, complete with toolbar buttons for marking and copying. Click the Mark button, drag through the text you want, then click the Copy button or press Enter to copy it to the Clipboard. Switch to Excel, paste it in a worksheet, and you're ready for the Text Wizard.

I want my chart in a PowerPoint slide

Microsoft Office includes a powerful graphics and presentations program called PowerPoint. PowerPoint includes a library of clip art and drawing tools, and the idea behind the program is to create slide shows.

PowerPoint has built-in charts, but why reinvent the wheel? You'll want to put your Excel charts into PowerPoint slides, and that's very easy to do:

1 Click the Excel chart to select it.

2 Click the Copy button on the toolbar.

3 Switch to PowerPoint. In Slide View, select Edit, Paste Special. The Paste Special dialog box gives you a few options, but your best choices are either As Microsoft Excel Chart Object (if you want to use Excel to edit the chart in PowerPoint) or As Picture (if you want to use the PowerPoint tools for editing).

4 Click Paste Link if you plan on updating the chart data; otherwise, a simple Paste works fine. Click OK, and the Excel chart becomes a PowerPoint slide. Figure 20.14 shows the start of a PowerPoint slide show built around an Excel chart.

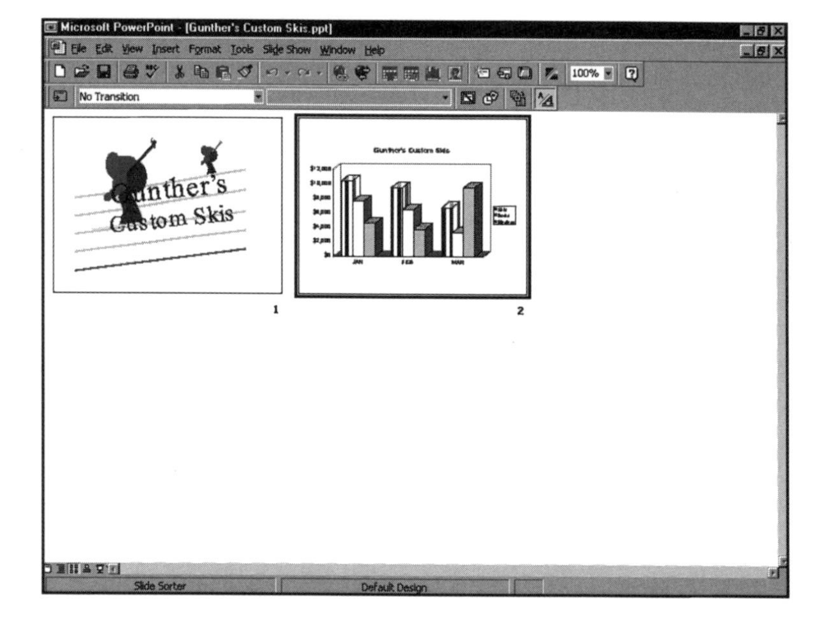

Fig. 20.14
PowerPoint has all kinds of graphics that you can customize to help a pitch succeed.

21 Having It Your Way: Customizing Excel, Customizing Worksheets

In this chapter:

- **I want all my tools where I can see them**
- **Can I make my own Excel tools?**
- **I need to build a form**
- **How can I get this worksheet some attention?**
- **I'm supposed to draw them the picture! Can Excel help?**

You like your office arranged just so. Phone here, stapler there, artwork of your choice on the wall. Here are some tricks to customize worksheets the same way . . . .

Sunny side up, or over easy? Brown shoes with that blue suit, or black? While it seems as though the world gets more standard-ized every day, there's still a little room for individuality. Big Macs might be available from Peoria to Peking, but that doesn't mean you can't get a bowl of bird's nest soup if you want it.

That putty-colored computer humming away in front of you looks just like mine. The familiar Excel grid on your screen is on mine too. It's on millions of other screens identical to ours.

But we all put Excel to different uses. And we can tailor Excel to the different ways we use it. There are all kinds of tricks to customize the program, and to add custom touches to your worksheets. Some are bound to make you more efficient; others may just suit your style.

And I'll take mine scrambled, please.

Customizing the way Excel starts

You're working on a weeks-long Excel project. You start Excel every day, click the File menu, click the workbook file name you're working on, and finally get to it.

Save yourself a few milliseconds. Put a shortcut to your workbook right on the Windows desktop. When you double-click the shortcut, you'll launch Excel and open the workbook at the same time.

To create a desktop shortcut to your workbook:

1. Click the Open button on the Standard toolbar. Right-click your workbook file name and choose Copy on the shortcut menu.
2. Close the Open dialog box, then right-click anywhere on the taskbar background and choose Minimize All Windows.
3. Right-click the Windows desktop background, and select Paste Shortcut. The icon for your workbook shortcut pops onto the desktop.

Now when you turn on your computer, you can get right to work. When the project's finished, drag the shortcut icon into the Recycle Bin (that doesn't delete the workbook, just the shortcut to the workbook).

When you save a file in Excel, by default it's saved to the My Documents folder. If you want to save your files to a different folder, you can. (You might want to keep all the workbooks for a particular project in their own folder, for example.) Click Tools, Options, General. Click the Default File Location text box, and type in the name of the new folder.

Do I have to see the same old thing every time I run Excel?

Maybe your desk is a spotless expanse of shiny, polished wood. All your work is in drawers and file cabinets. Or maybe you have piles of paper and books obscuring that battered old desktop. Excel accommodates itself to both styles. Crowd the screen with toolbars, formula bars, and status bars, or make it as austere as you like.

Keep your tools out, or put them away

Use the View menu to control what's on the screen. Click Toolbars for a list of the available toolbars. Click the ones you want, and they pop up on-screen after you click OK. Get rid of the formula bar or the status bar if you want to. Just click those options on the View menu; click them again to put them back. Or right-click any toolbar for the shortcut menu, and pick your toolbar there.

Once popped up, toolbars **float**. They appear at different spots on the screen. You can drag them out of the way by dragging their title bars. Or **dock** them against the top or sides of the screen by dragging them over to those locations. Figure 21.1 shows you what it's all about.

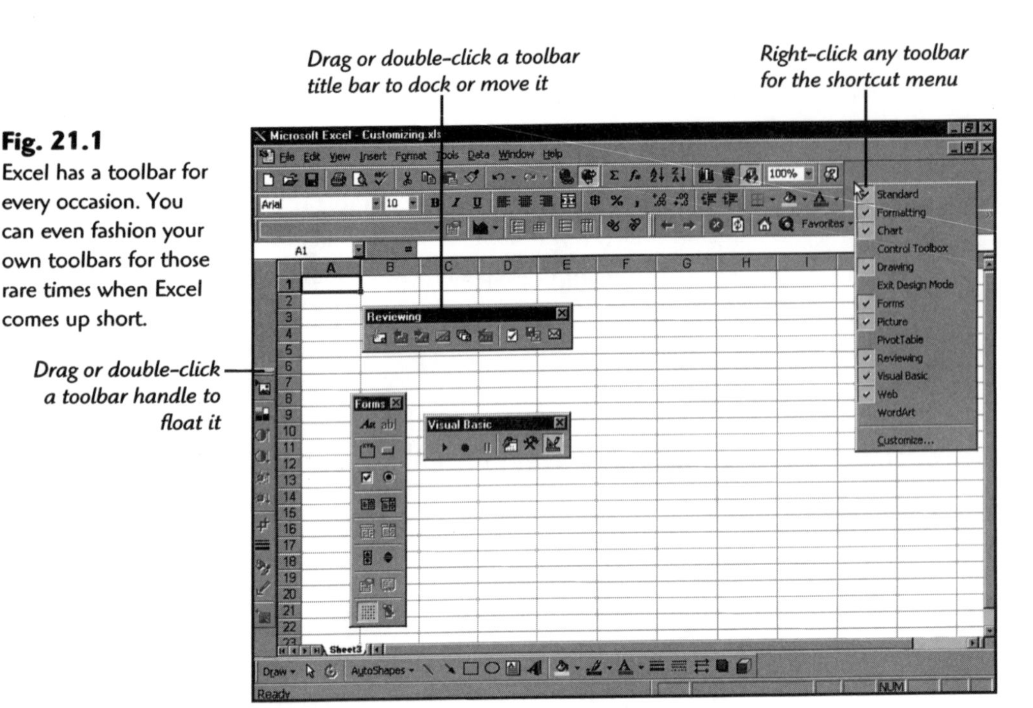

Fig. 21.1
Excel has a toolbar for every occasion. You can even fashion your own toolbars for those rare times when Excel comes up short.

For a more spare look, click View, Full Screen. That gets rid of all status, formula, and tool bars. Click View, Full Screen again to bring them back.

The quick way to dock a toolbar: double-click the title. To float it again, double-click the toolbar handle.

Each toolbar you display eats up a little more memory. If you load the screen with toolbars and things start to slow down, that's why. If you go overboard, you might get an `Out of Memory` message.

I want to make my own toolbar

Here's an occasional fantasy of mine—maybe you've had it too. Wouldn't it be great to rip those obscure little buttons off the VCR, rearrange them so they were usable instead of useless, even add a couple buttons to do things that are otherwise absurdly complex (like setting the timer)?

You can do something like this in Excel. The existing toolbars do most of the chores you need to accomplish, from creating macros to formatting text and numbers. But for more specialized jobs, there's a library of extra toolbar buttons that you can either add to existing toolbars, or use to make your own toolbar.

The Formulas toolbar is born

How useful is popping up and floating and docking toolbars? You can spend a lot of time playing around with this stuff and find hours gone by with nothing to show for it. But you can also save yourself a lot of time and trouble by building toolbars for specialized uses.

Find yourself writing a lot of formulas, for example? Build a Formulas toolbar. Instead of typing symbols like +,), or , click buttons instead. It'll be quicker, and you'll make fewer errors. Here's how to build your own Formula toolbar:

1. Select View, Toolbars, Customize and click New in the Customize dialog box that appears.

TIP **By my count there are three ways to open the Customize dialog** box: click Tools, Customize; click View, Toolbars, Customize; or right-click any toolbar and choose Customize. Take whichever route you find the most direct—they all lead to the same place.

2. The New Toolbar dialog box appears. Type a name in the Toolbar Name text box, and click OK. The embryonic new toolbar appears on the screen, and the new toolbar name shows up on the list of toolbars (see Figure 21.2.)
3. Click the Commands tab in the Customize dialog box. Scroll down the list of Categories and select Insert.
4. Scroll down the list of Commands in the Insert category, and you'll see a collection of useful buttons to help in formula writing (see Figure 21.3).
5. Drag any button you want over to the new toolbar. Release the mouse button, and it's added to the bar. Click Close when you're finished. Figure 21.4 shows the final result.

Fig. 21.2
All it takes to create a new toolbar is a name.

The new toolbar will expand as you add buttons to it

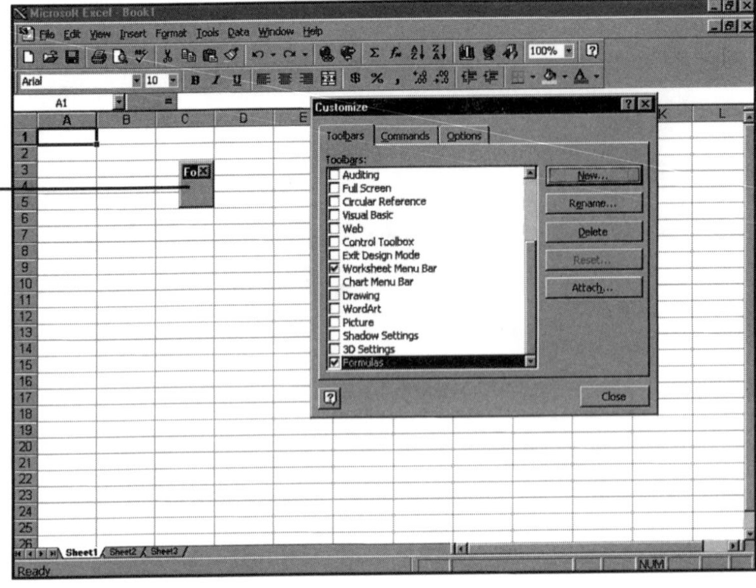

Fig. 21.3
Each of these buttons is fully functional when it's dragged onto a toolbar, just like the buttons you already use on the Standard or Formatting toolbar.

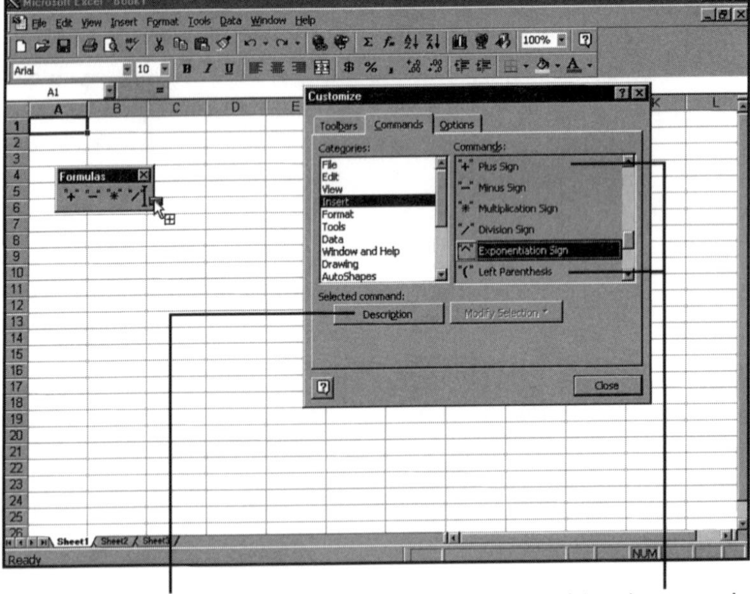

Select any of the commands, then click Description to see what it does

Drag any of these buttons to the baby toolbar and it grows to accommodate it

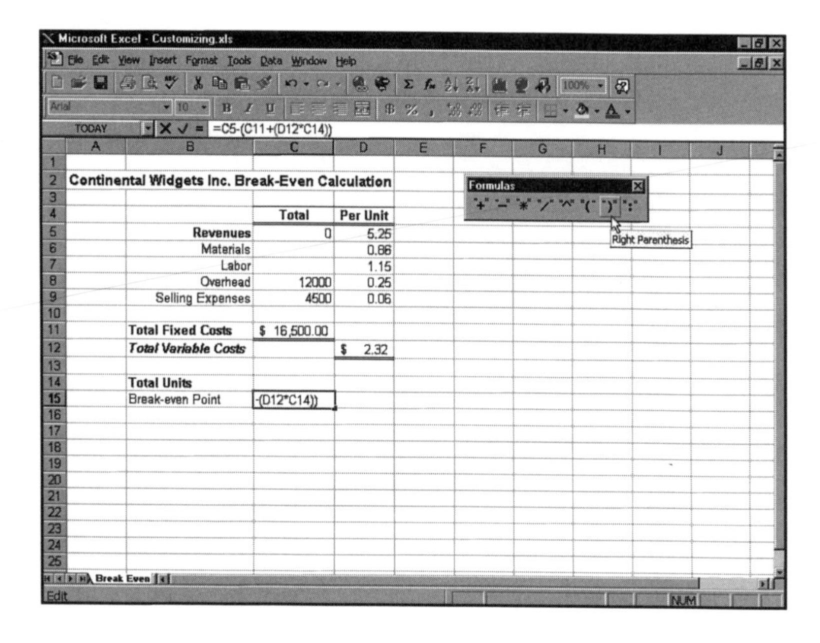

Fig. 21.4
A new toolbar is born. These buttons work like any other buttons, and they even have their own ScreenTips when you point at them.

Get rid of the toolbar by clicking the Close box. To get it back, click View, Toolbars and you'll see it on the Toolbars list. To delete a custom toolbar, click View, Toolbars, select the custom toolbar, and click Delete.

You can't delete Excel's built-in toolbars, so the Delete button doesn't appear in the Toolbars dialog box unless you select a custom toolbar.

Can I add a button or two to Excel's toolbars?

Maybe you want to add another choice or two to the Chart toolbar. To add buttons to an existing toolbar:

1. Click View, Toolbars, Customize, Toolbars. Click the Chart check box to pop up the Chart toolbar.
2. Click the Commands tab of the Customize dialog box and select Charting in the list of Categories.

3 Scroll down the list of Charting Commands, and drag your choice over to the Chart toolbar. It looks like Figure 21.5.

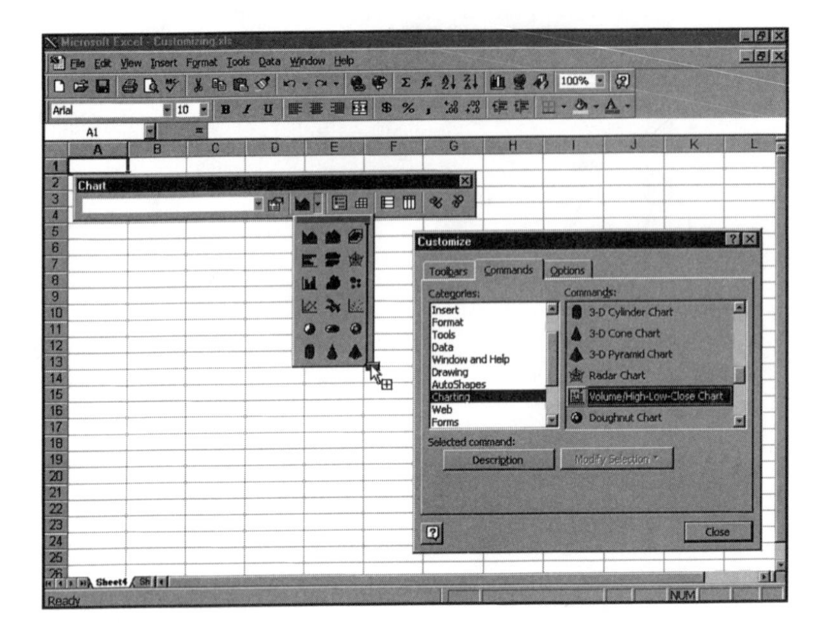

Fig. 21.5
Customizing Excel's existing toolbars is a drag-and-drop affair.

To return any customized toolbar to its original state, click View, Toolbars, Customize, Toolbars. Select the toolbar, and click Reset. When you close the Customize dialog box, any changes you made to the toolbar will be erased.

Assigning a macro to a button

With all the choices of buttons that Excel offers in the Customize dialog box, you might find that none of them do exactly what you want to do. That's okay too; just write a macro that does the job, then stick a button on it.

In Chapter 19, we wrote a macro that set up a monthly expenses worksheet. Let's assign it to a button and add it to the Forms toolbar.

1 Click View, Toolbars, Customize, Toolbars and select Forms to pop up the Forms toolbar.

2 Now click the Commands tab in the Customize dialog box, and select Macros in the Categories list. Drag the Custom button over to the Forms toolbar (see Figure 21.6).

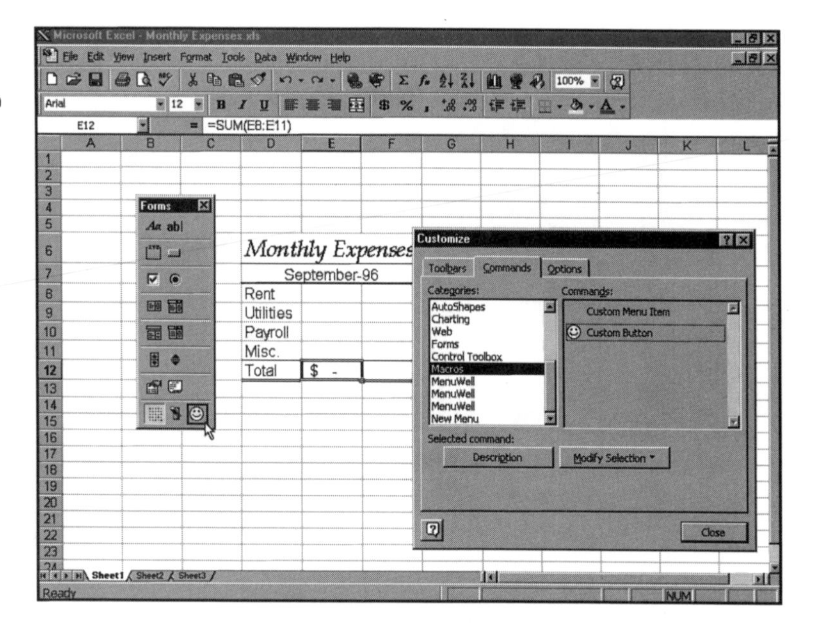

Fig. 21.6
This button doesn't do anything yet. But assign a macro to it, and it'll do anything you want.

3 Click the Modify Selection button and choose Assign Macro from the menu that pops up. The Assign Macro dialog box appears; select the macro you want to assign to the new button and click OK.

4 Click the Modify Selection button again, and choose Change Button Image. A menu of button choices appears; select any that seem appropriate (see Figure 21.7).

5 Your selection on the Change Button Image menu replaces the image on the toolbar as soon as you click it. If you want to draw your own button, or modify any of the stock images, choose Modify Selection, Edit Button Image. The Button Editor dialog box pops up (see Figure 21.8).

6 Click OK in the Button Editor dialog box, then close the Customize dialog box to save your changes. When you next want to run your macro, just click the button on the toolbar.

You can assign any macro to a button, and stick the button on any toolbar, including toolbars you create yourself.

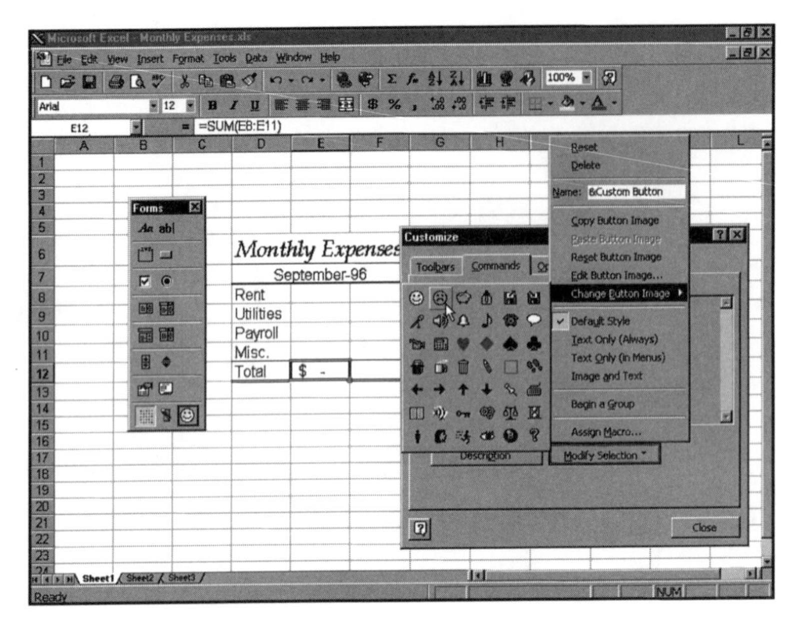

Fig. 21.7
Well, what button would you have chosen for the monthly expenses? Just drag any button off the menu and onto a toolbar.

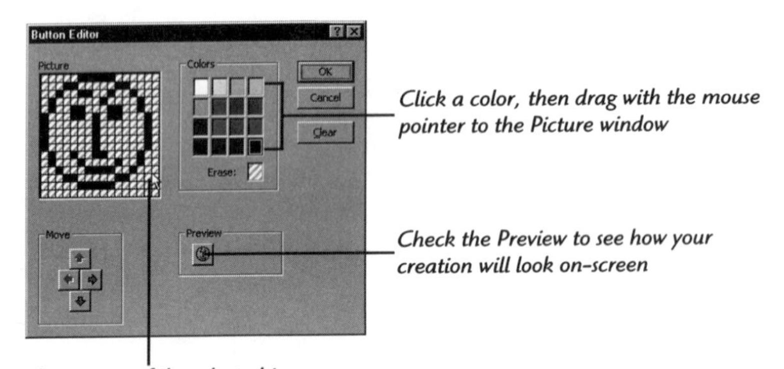

Fig. 21.8
Those with an artistic bent can create an original toolbar button.

What's the Forms toolbar for?

Those little gadgets on the Forms toolbar are called **controls**. They're check boxes, scroll bars, and buttons, just like the ones you see in Excel dialog boxes. You use them to create custom forms for data entry and calculation. Hooked up to Visual Basic routines, they create custom dialog boxes.

Using the Forms toolbar is like building your own radio from a kit. You start with a pile of buttons and switches and wire them all together (then you hope something happens when you turn on the juice). Click a control on the toolbar and the pointer turns into a crosshair. Position the pointer on the worksheet, and then drag to size the control.

When the control's in place, right-click for the shortcut menu to format the control and link it to worksheet cells containing formulas or values. Figure 21.9 gives you an idea of what it's all about.

This control is called a spinner because it spins through a series of values

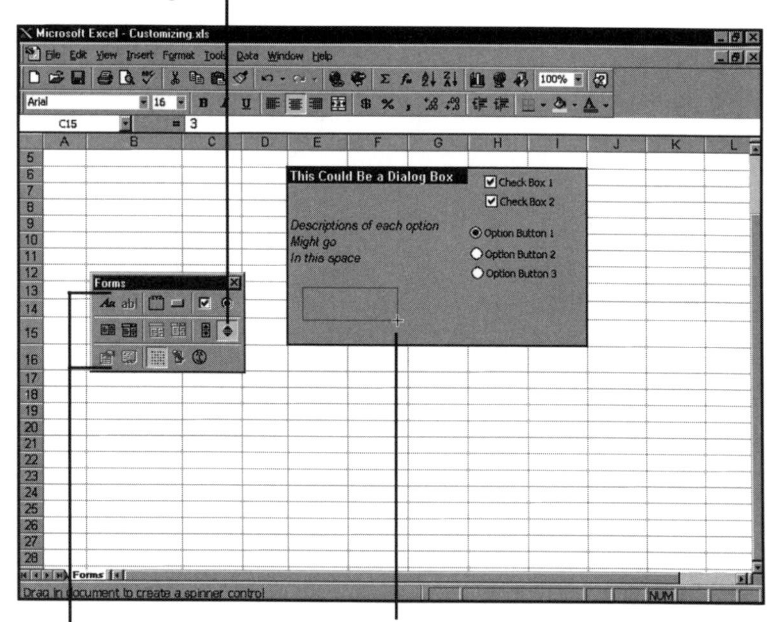

Click any of these controls and the pointer turns into a crosshair

Position the crosshair and drag to the lower-right corner of where you want the control

Fig. 21.9
Turn off the grid lines, add some shading, and when you pull controls from the Forms toolbar, you make a custom form. These controls look convincing, but they don't do anything yet.

The two-button control with opposing arrows is called a **spinner** (refer to Figure. 21.8). When it's in place, point at it and right-click for the shortcut menu. Select Format Control Object and click the Control tab in the Format Control dialog box (see Figure 21.10).

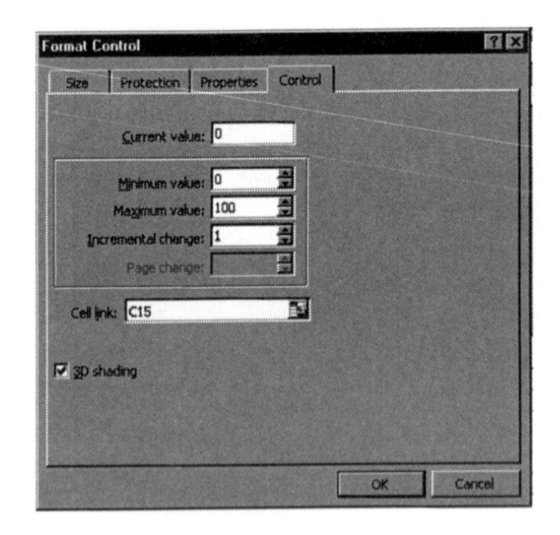

Fig. 21.10
Link a spinner to a cell on the worksheet, and give it a range of values in the Format Object dialog box.

When you click the spinner after linking it to cell C15, the values in cell C15 will increase or decrease by increments of whatever you set, to a maximum or minimum value that you also set (see Figure 21.11).

The check boxes are linked to C13 and C14—checked, they return a value of TRUE in the linked cell; unchecked, a value of FALSE

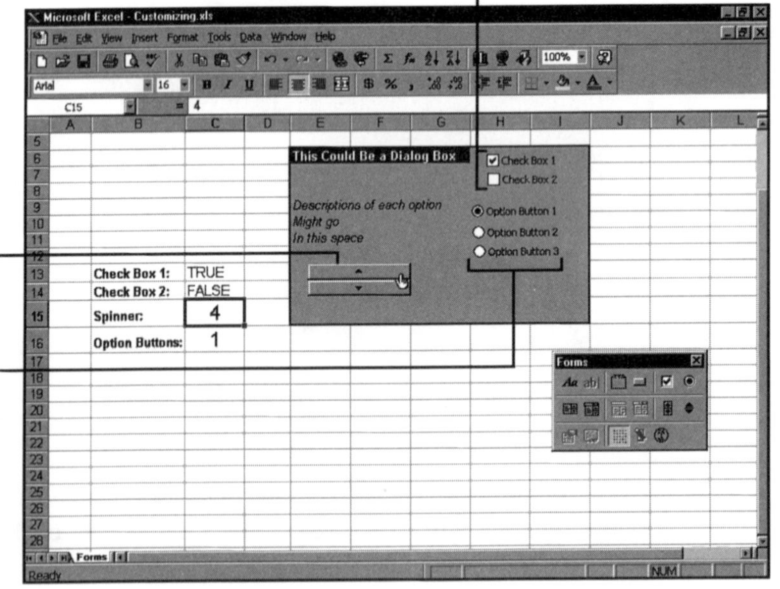

Fig. 21.11
Clicking the spinner arrows increases or decreases the value in cell C15.

The spinner is linked to C15—hold down one of the arrows and the values "spin" through their range

Option buttons are used in a group, where selecting one deselects the others—linked to cell C16 here, the three option buttons give you 1, 2, or 3

Can't draw a straight line? You can now

French painter Georges Braque once observed that "Art is meant to disturb." He must have been talking about my artwork. I have trouble drawing crooked lines, much less straight ones. It's very disturbing.

Fortunately, Excel provides tools that allow even the artistically challenged to draw. Click the Drawing button on the Standard toolbar to pop up the Drawing toolbar.

You can jazz up a worksheet with arrows, shapes, and patterns. This works like the Forms toolbar—click a button (tool to be precise) and the pointer turns into a crosshair. Position the crosshair and drag to the lower-right corner of where you want the object. Figures 21.12 and 21.13 give you the idea.

You don't need a perfectly steady hand to draw exact horizontal, vertical, or diagonal lines and arrows. Just select your line or arrow from the toolbar and hold down the Shift key as you drag the crosshair. For perfect circles or squares, just Shift+drag the oval or rectangle tools.

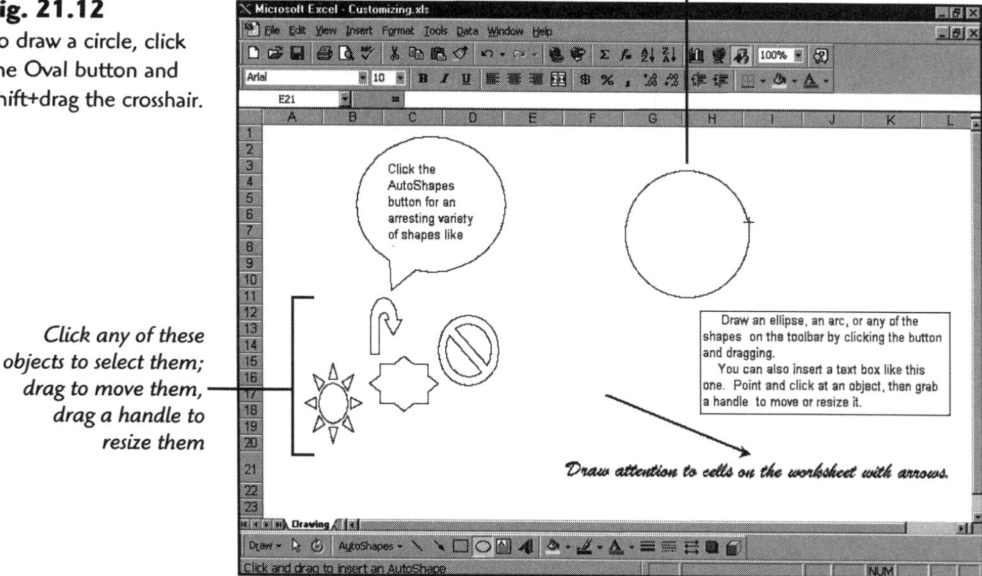

Fig. 21.12
To draw a circle, click the Oval button and Shift+drag the crosshair.

To add an arrow or two to your charts, click the Arrow button on the Drawing toolbar, position the crosshair where you want the arrow shaft to begin, and drag to where you want the arrowhead. If your arrow shaft looks shaky, try holding down the Shift key as you drag for a straighter arrow (see Figure 21.13).

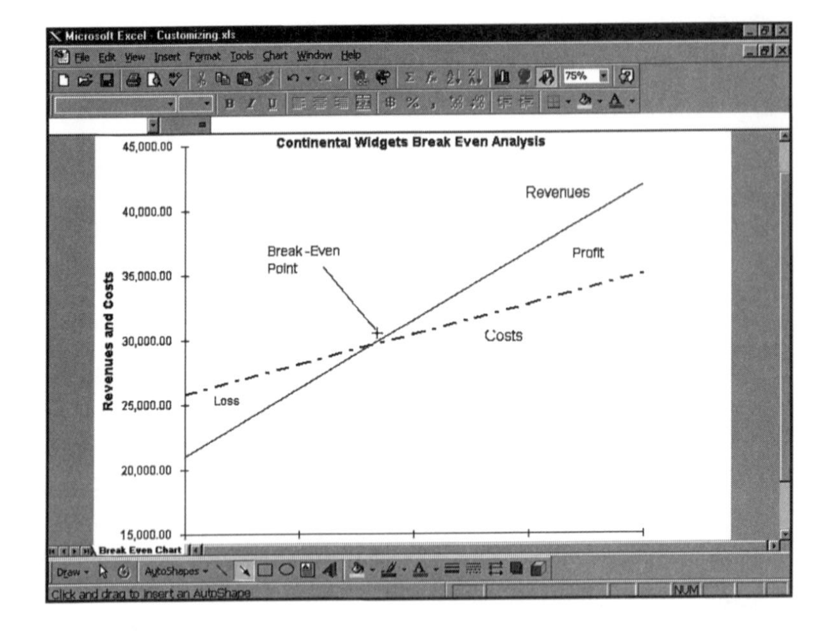

Fig. 21.13 When you release the mouse button, the arrowhead will snap into place at the end of the shaft.

To move an object, drag it with the four-headed arrow. To resize an object, click to select it, then drag a handle. To change colors or patterns, right-click an object and choose Format from the shortcut menu.

For shapelier shapes, click an AutoShape

You'll find a wide selection of arrows and other shapes on the Drawing toolbar's AutoShapes menu. Because the shapes are preformatted, they need a minimum of fussing to get them right.

For a perfectly straight double-headed arrow, for example, click AutoShapes, Lines, and choose the double-headed arrow. Drag with the crosshair, and when you release the mouse button the arrow appears, as shown in Figure 21.14.

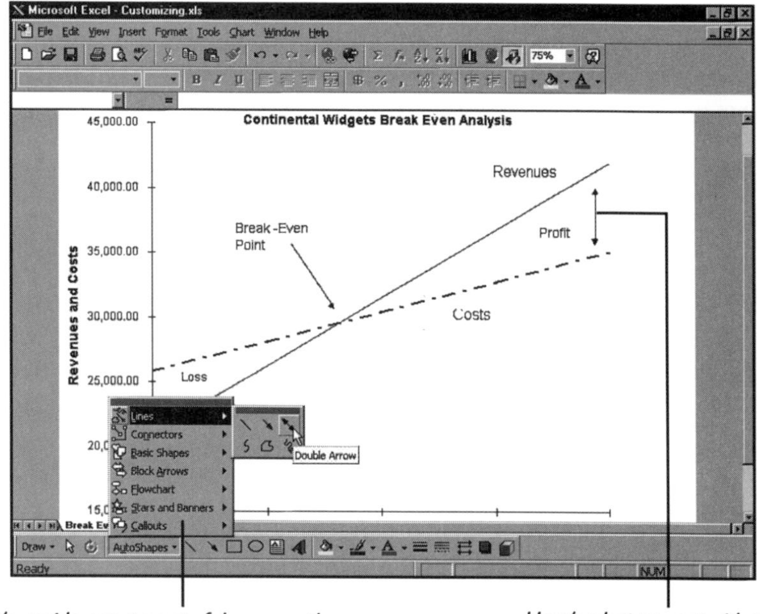

Fig. 21.14 Preformatted AutoShapes can save you a lot of time if you're customizing a chart.

There's a wide assortment of shapes on the menu; choose one, then drag with the crosshair to draw it

Here's what you get with the double-headed arrow AutoShape

Worksheet needs attention? Try a little WordArt, Clip Art

Worksheets tend to be sober affairs. Numbers have to be accurate, after all, calculated with exactitude and presented with clarity. Which doesn't mean that worksheets have to look boring. And the speedy way to add interest to a worksheet is with Excel's new WordArt feature. WordArt gives you startling effects for worksheet titles, or any other brief bit of text.

To jazz up a worksheet with WordArt:

1. Click the WordArt button on the Drawing toolbar. The WordArt Gallery appears (see Figure 21.15).

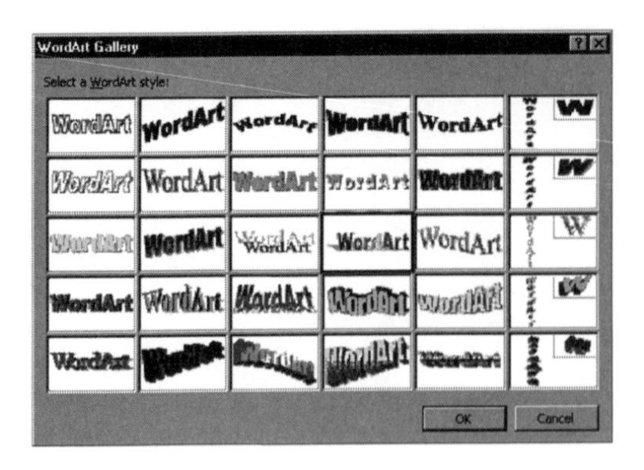

Fig. 21.15
When you type your own text, it'll take the color and shape of any WordArt style you choose here.

2 Your own text will replace the word `WordArt` in any of the shapes and colors on view in the WordArt Gallery. Double-click any WordArt style that strikes your fancy.

3 The Edit WordArt Text dialog box pops up. Type your own text in the Text box, and select a new font and font size if you want them (see Figure 21.16.)

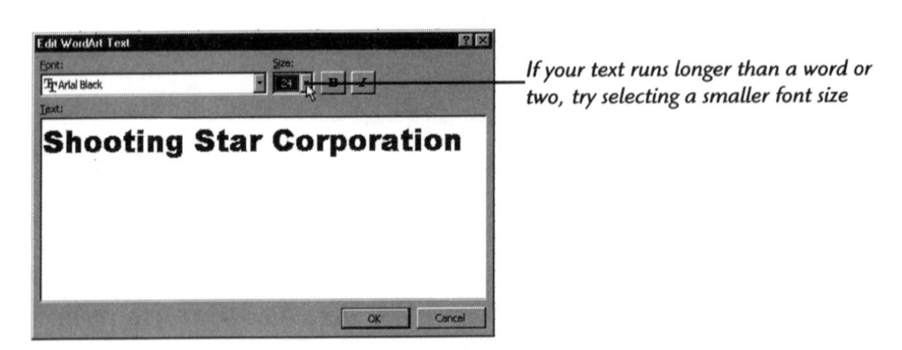

Fig. 21.16
You can type any text you like in here, but try to keep it short; longer text distorts the WordArt characters.

4 Click OK in the Edit WordArt Text dialog box when you're finished typing and formatting your text. The WordArt object is inserted into the active worksheet, and the WordArt toolbar pops up. Like any Excel graphic object, WordArt can be resized and moved around the sheet. Drag a handle to resize, and drag the object with the four-headed arrow to move it (see Figure 21.17).

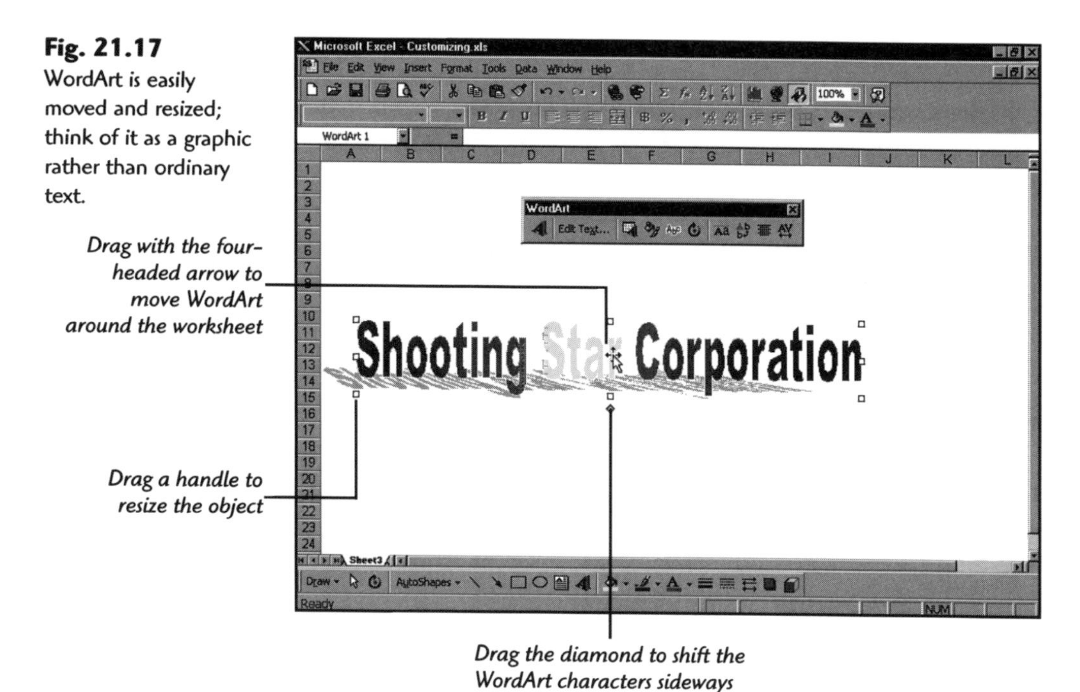

Fig. 21.17
WordArt is easily moved and resized; think of it as a graphic rather than ordinary text.

After you insert, move, and resize your WordArt, you might be completely satisfied with what you have. If you're not satisfied, you can alter WordArt to suit in almost any way you can think of. To do that, read on.

My WordArt needs some work

Between the Drawing and WordArt toolbars, you have all the tools you need to transform one of the stock WordArt styles into a custom creation. Change the shape, the colors, add shadow and 3-D effects—the possibilities are limited only by the amount of time you have for playing around with this.

The WordArt Toolbar

What do the buttons on this toolbar do? Well, it's like this:

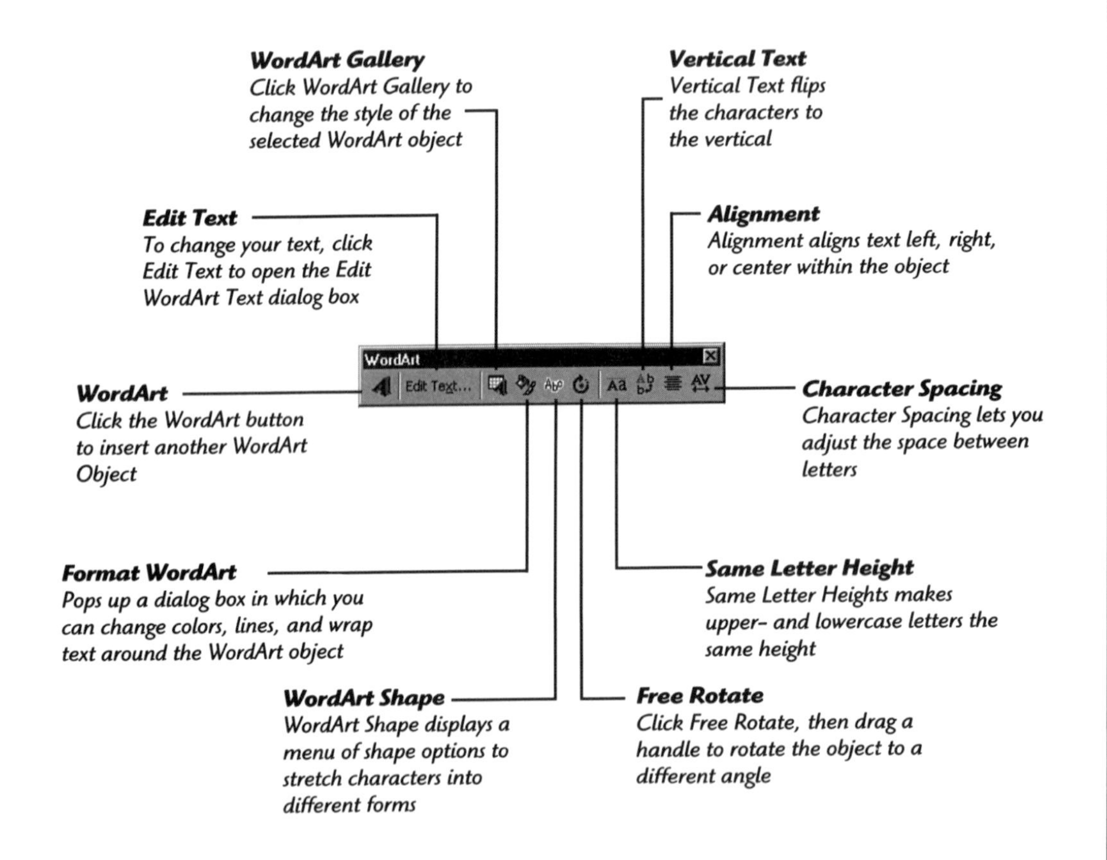

To customize an inserted WordArt object:

1. WordArt is inserted into a worksheet with the sizing handles and WordArt toolbar displayed. If you lose the handles and the toolbar, just click the WordArt object to get them back.
2. Want to stretch and bend those WordArt characters into a different shape? Click the WordArt Shape button on the WordArt toolbar and choose a new shape from the menu (see Figure 21.18).

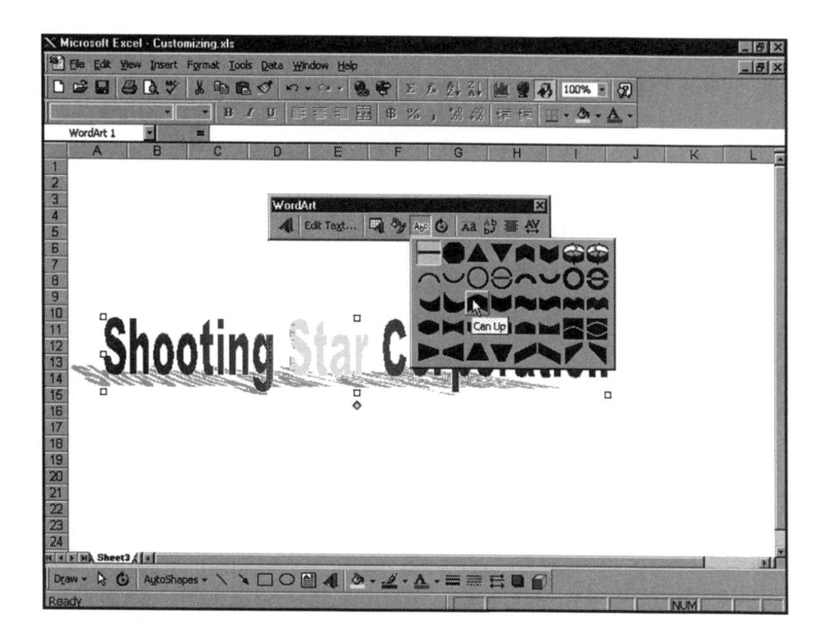

Fig. 21.18
Some of these shapes may not be exactly shapely, but they're certainly startling.

If you change the WordArt shape and you don't like the results, click the Undo button on the Standard toolbar to restore the WordArt object to its original shape. Then try a different option on the WordArt Shape menu.

3. If horizontal text seems a tad conventional, click the Vertical Text button on the WordArt toolbar to flip the characters to the vertical.

4. Don't leave your WordArt object in the shade; click the Shadow button on the Drawing toolbar and select a shadow style from the menu.

5 Or click the 3-D button on the Drawing toolbar and take your pick of effects from the menu. Click the 3-D button again and choose 3-D Settings to pop up the 3-D Settings toolbar. Click the Lighting button and choose the direction from which your 3-D effect is lit (see Figure 21.19).

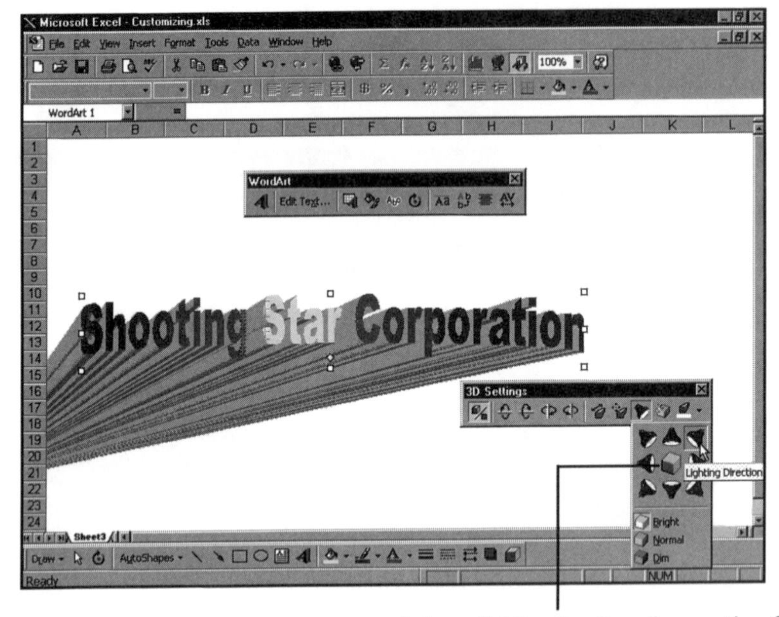

Fig. 21.19
Of all the nifty new Excel features, this one stands out—even the menu is interesting.

Select a lighting direction, then see the effect on the cube in the middle of the menu

CAUTION **Not all WordArt's shapes and styles lend themselves to 3-D** effects. Some will be illegible if you add 3-D. Trial and error is the way to go here; you just have to tinker until you're satisfied.

At the end of the day, you'll wind up with a worksheet title that's sure to get a little attention. Excel's new gadgets are so much fun to play with, that it may well be the end of the day before you're finished!

When words and numbers fail, insert a picture

It's one of the more annoying business clichés, and we've all heard it: "draw me the picture." What is meant, of course, is "explain this in terms so absurdly simple that even I can understand it." With Excel, you can save your breath. When a worksheet point has to be made with cartoonish simplicity, just insert a cartoon. The Microsoft Clip Gallery 3.0 has a simple picture for every occasion, and any of them can be inserted into your worksheet.

To view Excel's artwork, choose Insert, Picture, Clip Art. That pops up the Microsoft Clip Gallery 3.0 shown in Figure 21.20.

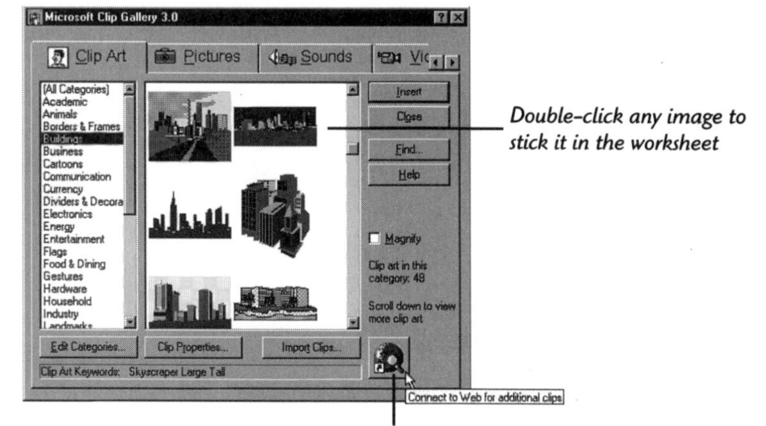

Fig. 21.20
Excel makes it easy to fill up worksheets with graphics of all kinds; just make sure you save some room for the numbers.

Once inserted in the worksheet, you can move, resize, and modify clip art just like any other object.

22 There's a World of Data on the World Wide Web

In this chapter:

- **Cyberspace? URL? Hyperlinks? Explain, please!**
- **Where do I find financial news and data on the Web?**
- **I want to stick stock quotes in my worksheet**
- **How do I publish my worksheet on the Net?**
- **I'm missing a few hyperlinks**

Looking up data used to mean peering at tables in dusty volumes or faded newspapers. On the World Wide Web, you can scour the whole world for information without leaving your chair. . . . .

The business library, whether it's the local public branch or your own company's private affair, is a great institution. Those shelves of volumes and periodicals hold the data you need—somewhere. The library's quiet and dusty precincts are a refuge from the office hurly-burly, and time spent in the hushed stacks is always a pleasure.

The trouble is, who has the time? Even if the library is just down the hall, a visit means dropping whatever you're doing, possibly for hours that simply can't be spared. And however delightful browsing might be, libraries invariably pose the problem that American writer and doctor Oliver Wendell Holmes, Sr., complained about more than a hundred years ago: "...the first volume of the book I inquire for is out, unless I happen to want the second volume, when *that* is out."

Excel users have a built-in library, one that covers every conceivable topic, that doesn't require stirring from the desk, and whose material is never "out." The World Wide Web (or Web) has something about pretty much everything, from stock quotes to Etruscan art. There's no dust, but there's also no excuse to get out of the office.

Excel is your Web connection

Even the best-intentioned writing about the great international network of computers that makes up the Internet slips into a sea of references to **URLs**, **browsers**, and **cyberspace** (see the sidebar for definitions). The murky tangle of Internet terms obscures the fact that the Internet, and especially its user-friendly graphical face, the **World Wide Web**, can be practical and fun. For research, technical support, news, and entertainment, the Internet is an unparalleled resource.

Why do I get an `Unable to open http://...` *message when I try to connect to the Internet?*

Have you installed the Internet Explorer yet? Excel's (or Office's) installation program put a Setup for Microsoft Explorer 3.0 icon on your Windows desktop. Double-click the icon and follow the directions for installing the Explorer on your system. If you *have* installed the Explorer and you're getting this error, save any open documents, close Excel, and restart the program. Try the connection again, and it should work.

What's on the Web, and how do I find it?

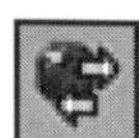

The Web is a generalist's paradise; there's something for just about everyone. There's also plenty of scope for special interests, and Excel users who follow the financial markets will find dozens of sources for financial data on the Web. Some of that data is a couple of mouse clicks away. Use the following steps to view financial news and read stock quotes.

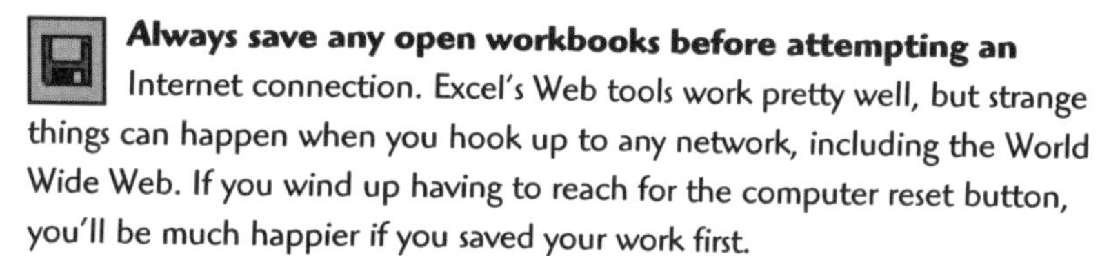

Always save any open workbooks before attempting an Internet connection. Excel's Web tools work pretty well, but strange things can happen when you hook up to any network, including the World Wide Web. If you wind up having to reach for the computer reset button, you'll be much happier if you saved your work first.

1. Click the Web Toolbar button on the Standard toolbar; on the Web toolbar that pops up, type **http://www.dbc.com** in the Address text box (see Figure 22.1).

I'm Lost in Cyberspace

Like any other subculture, the Internet has its own language and customs. Take the language. Please. Words like "hot" and "cool," "zine" and "cyberspace," and the many variants of "to surf," are seen at every turn. The jargon of the Internet is a strange brew of California beach town and science fiction, which isn't surprising. Although the Web was invented in Europe (at CERN, the European particle physics lab), many of its devotees hail from our own left coast. Science fiction being the reading of choice among computer adepts, the mingling of sci-fi and Beach Boys was inevitable. **Cyberspace** is a word invented by William Gibson, author of a science fiction yarn called *Neuromancer*. It's usually taken to mean the whole realm of computers linked together on the global Internet network. To **surf** the Web means to browse, more or less aimlessly, among the millions of documents posted on the Web. A **zine** is an electronic magazine, along with its variants **e-zine** and **web-zine**. If you're drawing a blank at any of the terms in common use on the Web, visit one of the many glossaries or **FAQs** (acronym for frequently asked questions). The Microsoft Web page has both a good FAQ and a glossary. The **URL** (uniform resource locator, or address) for the Microsoft Web site is **http://www.msn.com**. Click Help, Microsoft on the Web, Frequently Asked Questions to go straight there. You can also enjoy and profit from the Web without knowing anything about its arcana; it's pretty user-friendly, which is why it was invented in the first place.

Fig. 22.1
Navigating the Web is easy from Excel; type an address, press Enter, and you're on your way.

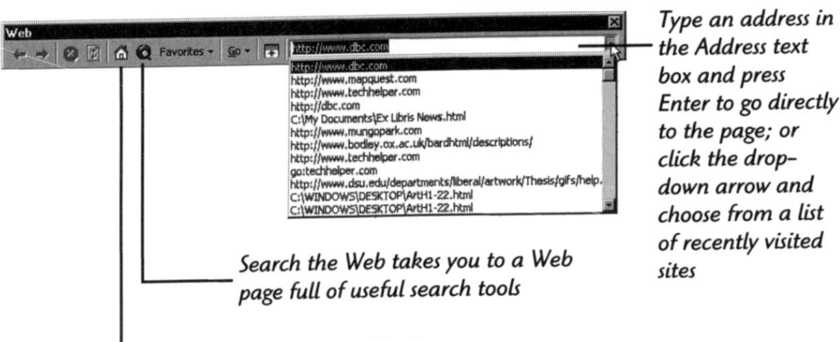

Start Page takes you directly to Microsoft's Start Page, a good jumping off point for Web explorations

Plain English, please!

What's in an **URL** (pronounced "earl" by some)? Addresses on the Web, or uniform resource locators in the jargon, have some things in common. All share the http://www. prefix, and though the other elements of the URL vary, they give you clues as to what a Web site might be about. The bit that follows the www. in the prefix is called the **domain name.** In the URL *http://www.mcp.com,* for example, *mcp.com* is the domain name. The domain name is the giveaway: the .com in mcp.com stands for commercial organization (that happens to be Macmillan Computer Publishing's Web site). If the domain name has an .edu suffix, it's an academic institution, like a college. Non-profits like National Public Radio have an .org suffix, and government sites have domain names that end in .gov. **99**

2 Choose Connect in your Internet service provider's Connect To dialog box. After the usual modem wailing and whistling noises, your Web browser pops up. You're wafted straight to the Data Broadcasting Corporation's Web site, DBC Online.

3 There's a mass of market data and news available; click any of the links shown in Figure 22.2.

TIP **When you visit a Web page that you plan to revisit, add the page** to your list of favorites. Click the Favorites button on the browser toolbar and select Add to Favorites. For your next visit, click the Favorites button and select the added site from the list.

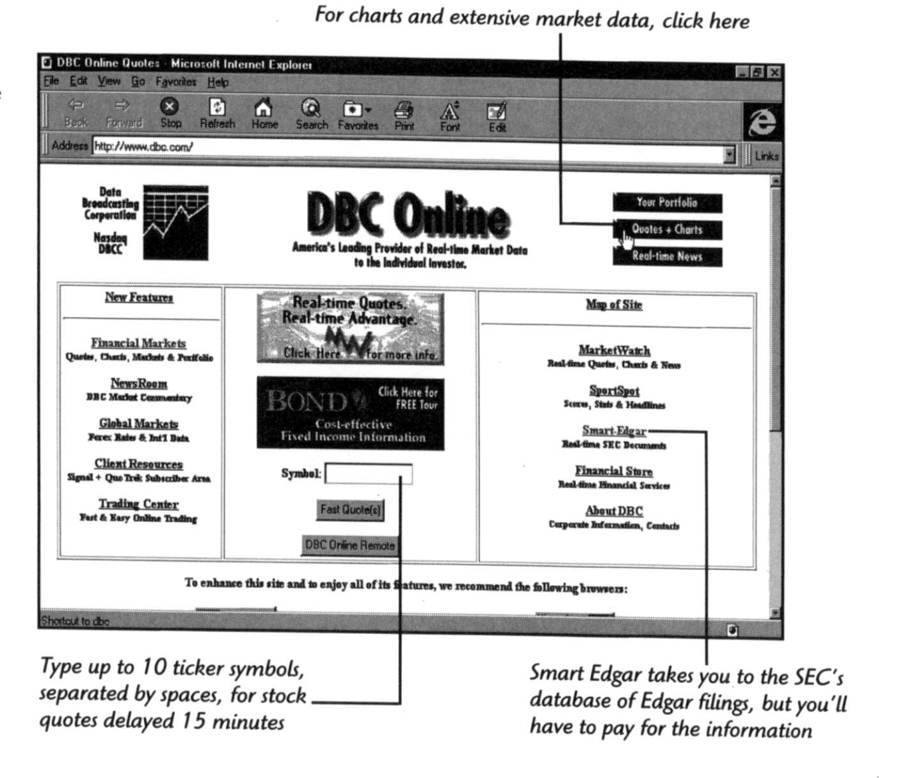

Fig. 22.2
DBC Online is just one of many sources for financial data on the Web.

Although much of what DBC online has to offer is free, some of the content, like real-time stock quotes and SEC Edgar documents, carries a charge. Two other sources of mostly free financial (and other) news to consider:

- *The Wall Street Journal*'s online edition (**http://www.wsj.com**) has practically all the text of the daily print edition. There's also a searchable archive of the past two weeks' editions, stock quotes, company and industry data, and a facility for setting up a customized online *Journal* that'll follow only the news and companies you select. The online *Journal* was free for Microsoft Explorer 3.0 users at the time of this writing.
- The Pointcast Network (**http://www.pointcast.com**) has one of the more remarkable gadgets on the Web. If you visit the site, be sure to download the free Pointcast software. Although it's a minor nuisance to do so, the reward is this: your computer monitor turns into a personal news service, a little like having your own private Headline News

Network. Feed the Pointcast software the ticker symbols for the companies you follow, and Pointcast will scour the Web for you, scooping up news and stock prices whenever you click Update. After it collects the news and data you want, it disconnects and displays its findings for you. Figure 22.3 shows the Pointcast software after it's set up.

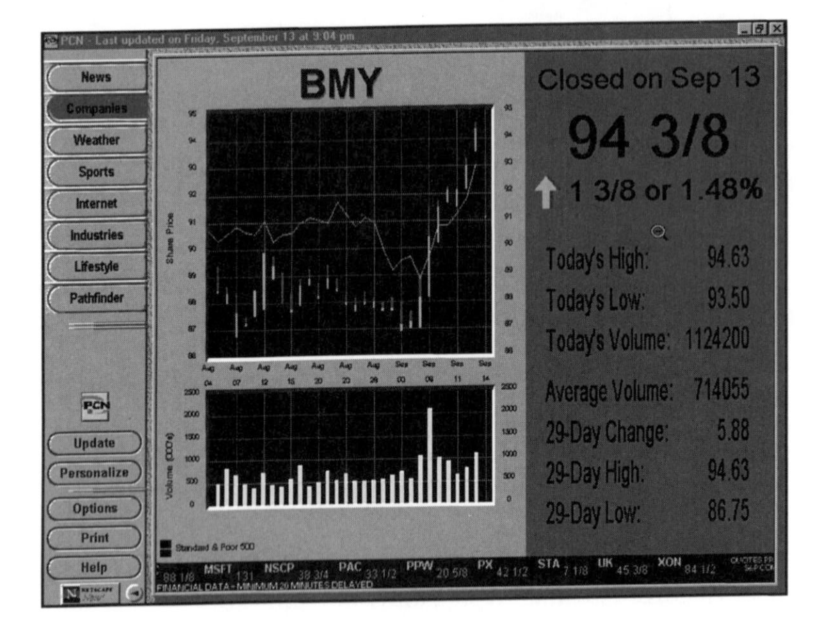

Fig. 22.3
Pointcast after an update. The program turns into a screen saver when your computer is idle, flashing news and stock quotes across the screen.

Pointcast establishes itself as your screen saver in a pushy fashion, without so much as a by your leave. If you don't want Pointcast as a screen saver after you install the software, right-click the Windows desktop background and choose Properties. Click the Screen Saver tab in the Display Properties dialog box, click the Screen Saver drop-down arrow, and choose another screen saver from the list—or None.

Had enough news and financial data? There's much more to the Web

You could spend a lifetime browsing through the millions of documents on the Web. Only a fraction of them are devoted to news and finance, so you'll find plenty of general interest matter as well. Try the Search button on the browser's toolbar; if you're using Microsoft Explorer 3.0 as a browser, that takes you to the invaluable Find It Fast page. Type a few words that describe what you're looking for, and click Search, as shown in Figure 22.4.

Fig. 22.4
Microsoft's Find It Fast page puts all the top Web search services, and more, in one place.

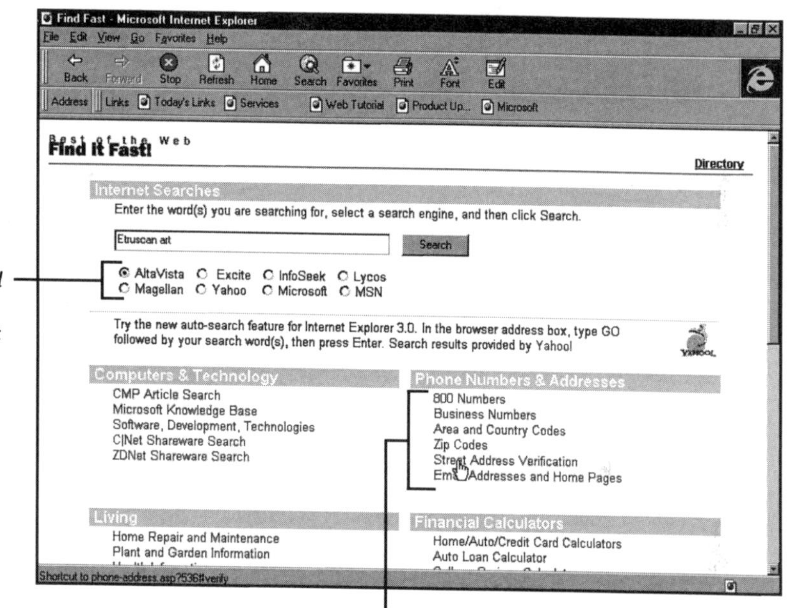

Search engines are search services provided by various Internet companies; experiment with them to see which suits you best

Although they're not underlined, these are all links (you know you've hit a link when the pointer turns into a hand); click any that look interesting

In your rambles on the Web, you'll soon find that getting around is easy—just click a link. Finding what you want is more challenging. For standard fare, such as the news, sports, and stock quotes, there are hundreds of sources, DBC and the *Journal* among them. For reference information, such as ZIP codes, Bartlett's, and Roget's, the links on Microsoft's Find It Fast page are more than adequate.

Use search engines, such as Yahoo, InfoSeek, and AltaVista for more esoteric matter. You can access all of them from the Find It Fast page, and each one works in a different way. Yahoo organizes the Web by category, which narrows the choices and makes it easy to use. AltaVista is broader. AltaVista searches typically return many (many!) documents, most of which will be completely irrelevant, though you'll strike the occasional vein of gold as well.

Here are a few general interest Web sites you might want to visit:

- MapQuest (**http://www.mapquest.com**) is one of the handier sites on the Web. It's an interactive street atlas for the entire world. Click the Interactive Atlas link on the MapQuest home page, choose Find, enter the country, city, and even street you're looking for, and click Search. A detailed street map for the location appears, which you can zoom and pan (see Figure 22.5).

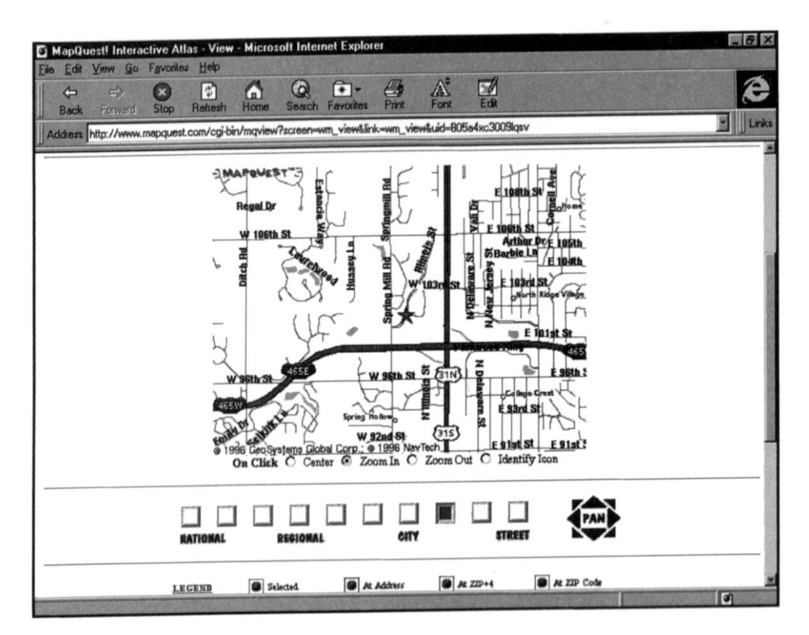

Fig. 22.5
MapQuest can also display points of interest on its maps—features like businesses, museums, and restaurants.

- Research-It (**http://www.itools.com/research-it/research-it.html**) is another good place for the information hungry. Want to look up a word in Italian, Japanese, German, or Spanish? Maybe you need to conjugate French verbs, or find some English rhymes. Here's the Web page for all those things.

- There are hundreds of magazines on the Web, both online versions of print magazines and journals that you won't find on any conventional newsstand. There's a thorough listing at the Dominis eZines Database Web page (**http://www.dominis.com/Zines**).

How do I pull data off the Web and into my worksheet?

Excel's Web toolbar gives you a direct link to the world of information on the Web. And while you can print or save documents that you find on your travels around the Web, actually using the information in a work-sheet involves some extra labor. It's like the difference between simply reading a library book and studying and taking notes on the book. Fortunately, the extra labor involved is very slight. Excel, at least for some data, takes notes for you automatically.

Here's the way to grab stock quotes from the Web and stick them in an Excel worksheet:

1 In a new worksheet, choose Data, Get External Data, Run Web Query.

2 In the Run Query dialog box that pops up, double-click Multiple Stock Quotes by PC Quote, Inc.iqy (see Figure 22.6).

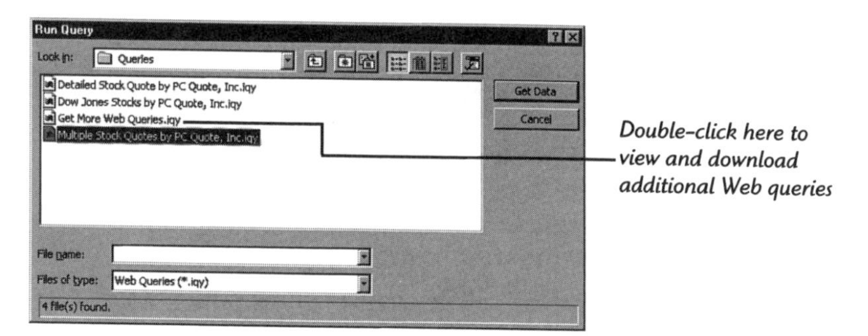

Fig. 22.6
These built-in queries are designed to call up a database and grab the data you specify.

3 The Returning Data to Excel dialog box appears. If you want the data in the current worksheet, click OK. Otherwise, choose New Worksheet and click OK.

4 In the Enter Parameter Value dialog box that pops up, type up to 20 stock symbols, separated by spaces. Click the Use this Value/Reference for Future Refreshes check box so you won't have to reenter the stock symbols when you update prices (see Figure 22.7).

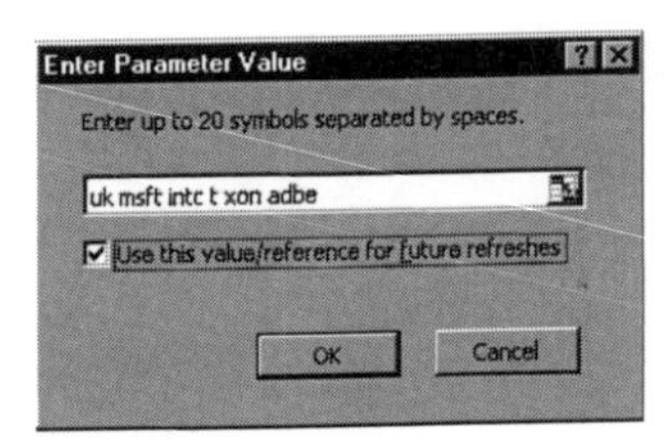

Fig. 22.7
Save your worksheet after you run the query, and you won't have to enter the ticker symbols again.

5. Click OK in the Enter Parameter Value dialog box.
6. In the Connect To dialog box that appears, click Connect. Excel hooks up to the Internet database of stock quotes and the worksheet fills in with the current quotes (delayed at least 15 minutes), as shown in Figure 22.8.

These are links to the PCQUOTE database on the Web; click them to get current news on the selected company

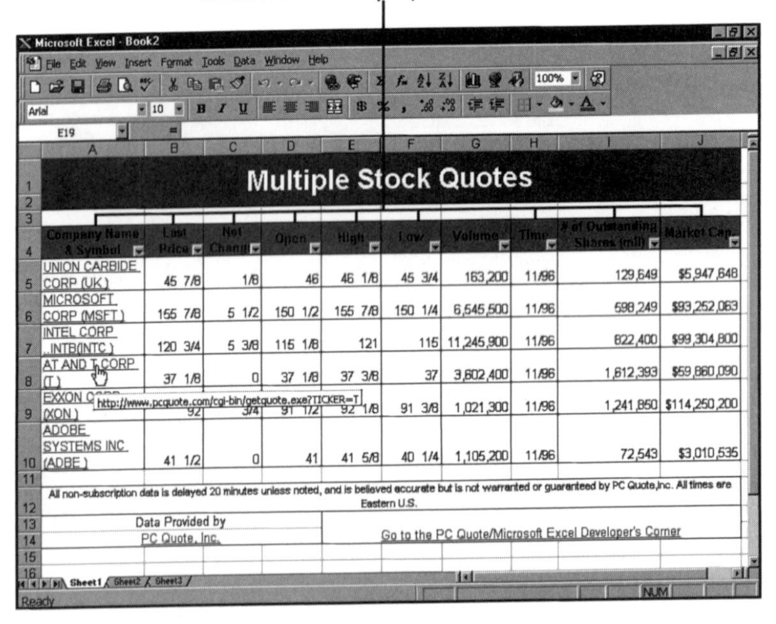

Fig. 22.8
When you have your quotes in a table, you can analyze and chart them any way you like.

To update your stock prices, connect to the Web and click the Refresh Current Page button on the Web toolbar.

This worksheet deserves an audience

Many companies these days run local computer networks modeled on the Web. **Intranets,** Web-like local networks, can take advantage of the quality that makes the Web so popular: the easy shunting of text, data, and graphics from one computer to another. Intranets are often set up to blend seamlessly with the Web itself, so that surfers can flip between the local network and the global network without being aware of it.

HTML is what makes all this possible. Excel uses its own special codes and conventions to format workbooks. Intranets and the Web share an entirely different set of codes and conventions called HTML—hypertext markup language. Excel's Internet publishing tools convert workbooks to the Web format, and Excel converts HTML documents into Excel format. Excel's Internet Assistant lets you publish your worksheets to the world, or to the local network, with ease.

Plain English, please!

Hypertext markup language, or HTML, is what makes the Web tick. It's a formatting language that allows the insertion of special codes to link documents together. Hypertext links are like cross-references in an encyclopedia—they direct you to another page with related information. Hypertext links are automatic though: click the links in a hypertext document (they're usually underlined words), and you travel automatically to other documents. Those document addresses are embedded in the link. Excel lets you insert the hypertext links of your choice in any Web documents you create. **99**

How do I convert my worksheet into a Web page?

It's a snap to convert an Excel worksheet into an HTML document, but a few things get lost in the translation. Some of your formatting, for one thing, won't make the conversion. The resulting HTML document will be clear enough, but it may not look much like your original. And make sure to give the work-sheet a meaningful name. Double-click the sheet tab, type a name, and press Enter if you haven't already done it. Excel's HTML converter uses the worksheet name as the header of your Web page-to-be, so you'll want something informative on the worksheet tab.

You can't create a fancy Web page with Excel. The HTML converter produces a table containing your data, including charts, but that's about it. Don't waste your time on elaborate formatting and graphics; they won't convert to HTML. Chart sheets are good candidates for Web pages; Excel does preserve chart formatting. If you include your data table on a chart sheet (click the Data Table button on the Chart toolbar to do that), the data table will be included on the Web page.

TIP **Before you convert a chart sheet to HTML, shrink the plot area.** To do that, click the plot area and drag a corner handle toward the center of the chart. If you don't shrink the plot area, the converted chart will more than fill a Web browser viewing window.

When your worksheet is ready for posting on the local intranet or the Web, call on Excel's Internet Assistant:

1 Save your workbook in regular XLS format with a click of the Save button.

2 Click anywhere in a data table, or click the sheet tab of your chart sheet. If you're converting a worksheet with a table and an embedded chart, select the range holding both the table and the chart. Click File, Save As HTML. Step 1 of the Internet Assistant Wizard pops up, and quides you through the process of turning a worksheet into a Web page (see Figure 22.9).

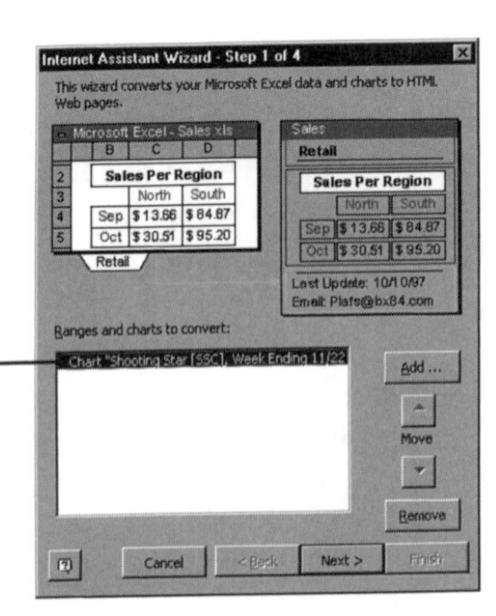

Fig. 22.9
If you already selected a range, you don't need to do anything in Step 1 of the Internet Assistant Wizard.

Chart sheets displaying the underlying data are good candidates for HTML conversion

How come I don't see a Save As HTML option on the File menu?

The Internet Assistant is an add-in, a component of the program that's bundled with Excel, but that's not necessarily installed with Excel. If you chose a Typical installation, the Internet Assistant might not have been included with the rest of your Excel setup, and you won't see the Save As HTML option on the File menu. There's an easy fix. Choose Tools, Add-Ins. In the Add-Ins dialog box that appears, click the Internet Assistant Wizard check box and click OK. That installs the Internet Assistant Wizard for you.

If you don't see the Internet Assistant Wizard listed in the Add-Ins dialog box, get out your original Office or Excel CD and run a maintenance installation to add the Internet Assistant Wizard. It's a bit of a nuisance, but at least you don't have to reinstall the whole program—you're just modifying your current installation with the addition of the Internet Assistant.

3. Click Next in Step 1 of the Internet Assistant Wizard. In Step 2, choose between creating a new HTML document or adding the selected range to an existing HTML document. Because we're producing a new document, select Create and click Next.
4. Step 3 of the Internet Assistant Wizard gives us some options for altering the appearance of the finished Web page. The Title will appear in the browser title bar, so type a new one if you want. The document Header appears at the top of the Web page. By default, it's the worksheet name that appears on the sheet tab. Change it if you want a different header for your page. The Description is a good place to type a brief introduction to your page. You also can add horizontal lines and append your e-mail address, as shown in Figure 22.10.
5. Click Next in Step 3 of the Internet Assistant Wizard, and we're at the finish line. Unless your network administrator or Internet service provider tells you something different, accept the default for the Which Code Page option in Step 4. Microsoft FrontPage users can add an Excel page right to their FrontPage Web. If you don't use FrontPage, choose Save the Result as an HTML File. Type a file name and the path of the folder where you want the file stored; or click Browse and choose the folder (see Figure 22.11).

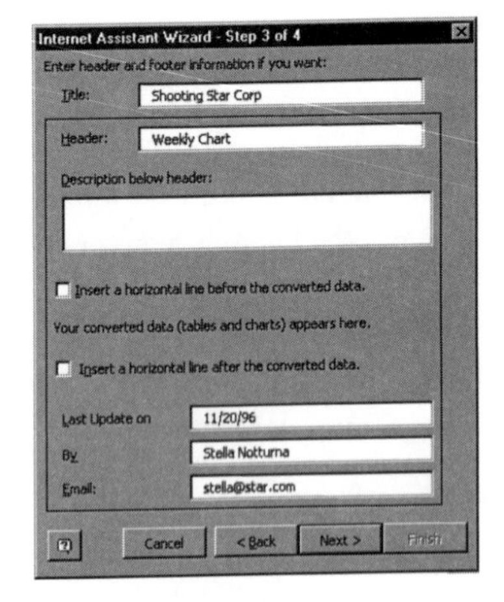

Fig. 22.10
Add custom touches like horizontal lines and a description to your Web page in the Internet Assistant Wizard Step 3.

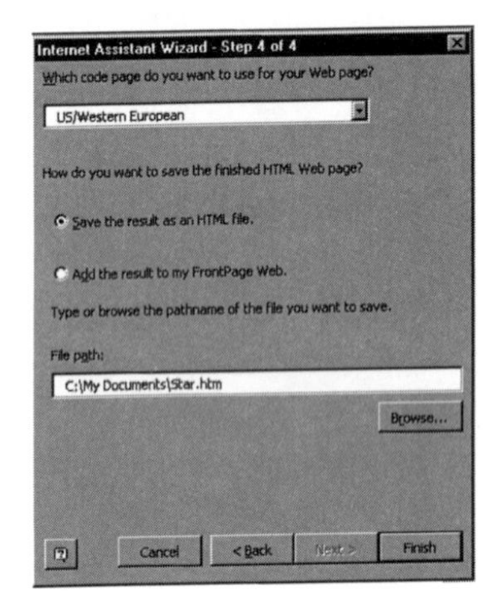

Fig. 22.11
In Step 4, choose where to save your Web page: either to a file folder, or directly to a FrontPage web.

6 Click Finish in Step 4 of the Internet Assistant Wizard to save your Excel Web page.

It's the finish, but there's not much of a grand finale. You find yourself back where you started, staring at your original Excel worksheet. You can open and edit your Web page in Excel—just click the Open button on the Standard toolbar, choose HTML Documents from the Files of Type drop-down list, and double-click your file.

Can I see what my page looks like on the Web?

A Web page opened in Excel won't look exactly like a page viewed in a Web browser, such as the Internet Explorer. Different browsers display HTML documents differently, and no browser displays a document as it appears in Excel. For a sneak preview, you can open the HTML document in your own browser. That will at least give you a notion of how Web or network surfers see your work.

To open an HTML document in the Microsoft Internet Explorer:

1. Click Start, Programs, Microsoft Internet Explorer.
2. In the Connect To dialog box, click Cancel. That runs the Internet Explorer without connecting to the Web. You'll get several `Invalid Data` error message boxes—just click OK in each box to get rid of them.
3. Choose File, Open from the Internet Explorer menu bar. In the Open dialog box, click Browse.
4. Double-click your way to the HTML file you just created, then double-click the file to open it in the Internet Explorer (see Figure 22.12).

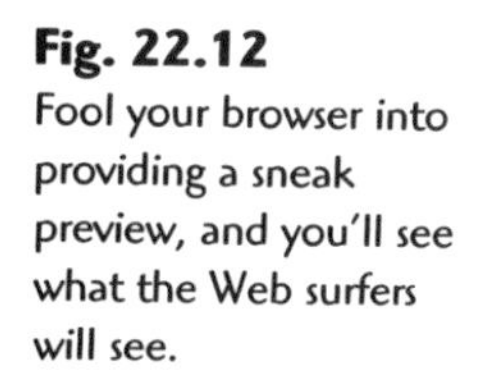

Fig. 22.12
Fool your browser into providing a sneak preview, and you'll see what the Web surfers will see.

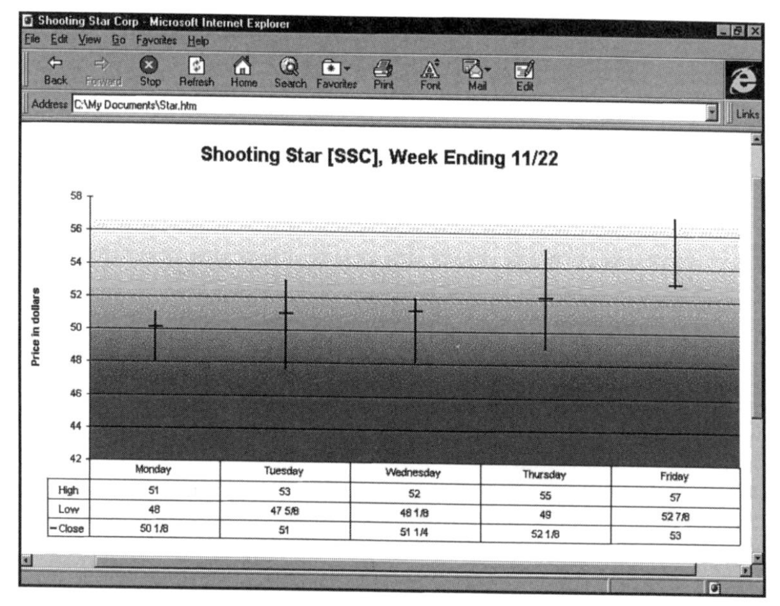

Missing hyperlinks? Add some

Hyperlinks are those underlined bits of text that you click to get from place to place on the Web. They put the Web in the World Wide Web, linking the documents on the network together in a great global daisy chain. You'll want to add your own links to other Web pages, and to other pages on the intranet. You can also link cells within a worksheet. That's especially handy for worksheets on the Web or the intranet, because the link can take readers on quick trips to sections of the worksheet that aren't immediately in view in their browser's window.

To add hyperlinks to other documents and Web pages:

1. Select the link cell. If there's text in the cell, the text will be displayed in blue, underlined, boldface when you establish the link. If the cell is blank, the address you're linking the cell to will be displayed.

2. Click the Insert Hyperlink button on the Standard toolbar. The Insert Hyperlink dialog box pops up (see Figure 22.13).

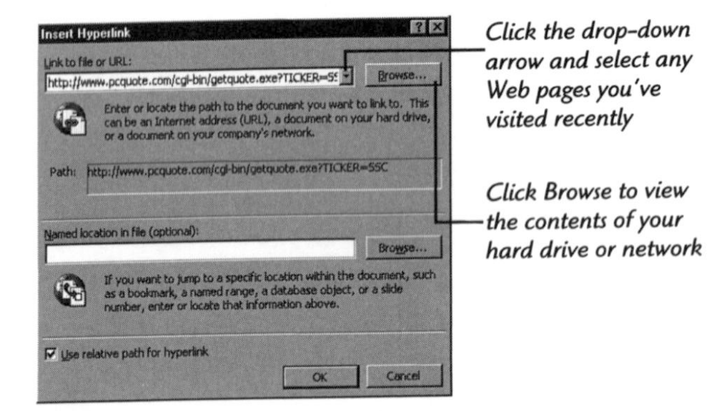

Fig. 22.13
Hyperlinks take readers on quick trips across a document, or around the world.

If you're prompted to save your worksheet before inserting a hyperlink, do so. Even if the prompt doesn't appear, save your worksheet. Hyperlinks work—most of the time. The occasional lock-up they cause is a minor irritant. If you haven't saved your work, it's a major disaster.

3. Click inside the Link to file or URL text box, and type the address or path of the document you want to link. Click the Browse button to see the contents of your hard drive or network, then double-click a file to pop its address or path into the text box. Or click the drop-down arrow

and select a Web site from a list taken from your Web browser's history file, or from a recently opened HTML document.

The first item on the drop-down list is a blank http:// address. Select it, then type the rest of the address. That saves you from typing and retyping that annoying Web prefix.

4. Click OK, and the link is established.

5. Point at the link, and the pointer turns into a little hand. Click the link, and you go straight to the linked document (see Figure 22.14).

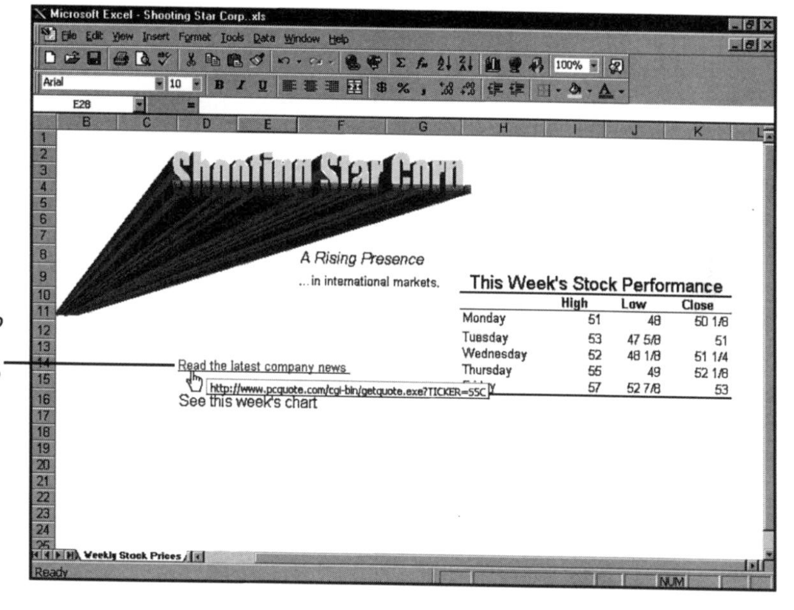

	High	Low	Close
Monday	51	48	50 1/8
Tuesday	53	47 5/8	51
Wednesday	52	48 1/8	51 1/4
Thursday	56	49	52 1/8
Friday	57	52 7/8	53

Fig. 22.14
When you point at a link, you even get a reminder of where the link will take you.

To edit the link text, use the arrow keys to make it the active cell, then press F2 to move the insertion point into the link

I can't click a link without traveling to the document it's linked to. So how do I edit link text!?

Because you can't click the link without activating it, use the arrow keys to make the link the active cell. Press F2, and the insertion point appears inside the cell. Edit the text, and press Enter to save your changes.

To edit the hyperlink, right-click the link and choose Hyperlink, Edit Hyperlink. To delete the link, select it with the arrow keys and press Delete.

I need links within this long worksheet

The great drawback to reading anything on a computer monitor is that we can see so little of it at any one time. Reading long Web pages requires a lot of scrolling. You can relieve your reader's scrolling blues with links within the page itself. For example, link cells at the top of the worksheet with cells out of the monitor window at the bottom of the page.

To link cells within a worksheet:

1. Select the cell or range you want readers to go to when they click the link (a range, for example, at the bottom of the worksheet).
2. Click the Name text box on the formula bar. Type a name for the range and press Enter.
3. Select the cell you want for the link. This cell will contain the underlined hyperlink text that readers will click to go to the named range we just created.

4. Click the Insert Hyperlink button. In the Insert Hyperlink dialog box, click the Browse button next to the Named Location in File text box.
5. That pops up the Browse Excel Workbook dialog box. If the link is within the worksheet, like this one, choose Defined Name and select the named range on the list.
6. Click OK in the Browse Excel Workbook dialog box, and OK in the Insert Hyperlink dialog box. The link is established, and when readers click it, the window will jump straight to the named range or cell. The split screen view in Figure 22.15 gives you the idea.

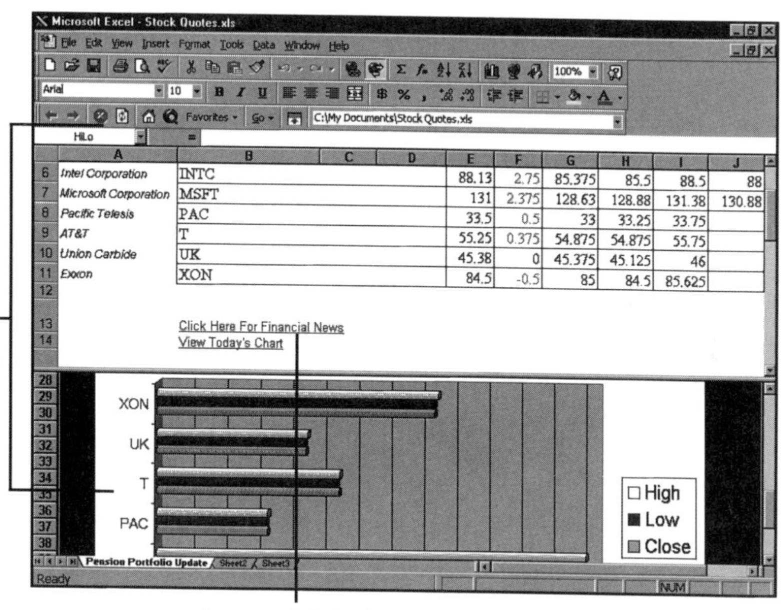

Fig. 22.15
Named range links make handy automated cross-references in long Web pages.

The window scrolls automatically to this named range farther down the worksheet...

...when you click this link at the top of the worksheet

Parting shots

Here we are at the end of the book. I hope you've found reading *Using Excel 97* as enjoyable as I found writing it. We've covered a lot of ground, but with a program as capable (and as immense) as Excel, we couldn't cover absolutely everything.

That's probably inevitable, and okay. As you use the program, you'll uncover plenty of nooks and crannies on your own. I learn new things about Excel all the time, even though I've logged more than a few hours with it.

Investigate and experiment. If you don't like the results you get, just try again. Virtually everything you do in Excel is reversible, and experimentation costs nothing, except maybe a few minutes of your time.

http://www.mcp.com/que

Index

Symbols

A

B

C

G

P

Q-R

T

U-V

X-Y-Z

QUE® has the right choice for every computer user

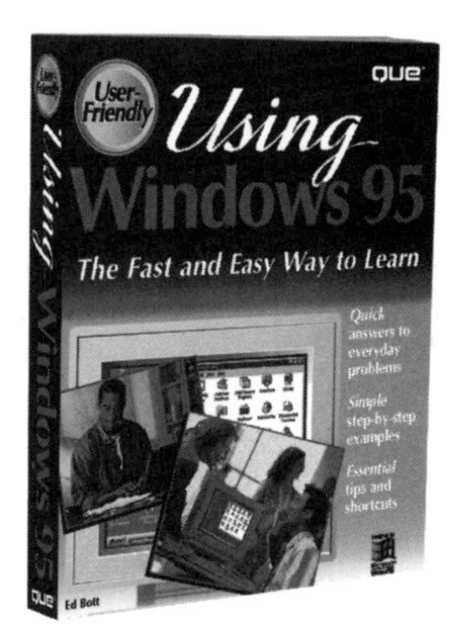

From the new computer user to the advanced programmer, we've got the right computer book for you. Our user-friendly *Using* series offers just the information you need to perform specific tasks quickly and move onto other things. And, for computer users ready to advance to new levels, QUE *Special Edition Using* books, the perfect all-in-one resource—and recognized authority on detailed reference information.

The *Using* series for casual users

Who should use this book?

Everyday users who:

- Work with computers in the office or at home
- Are familiar with computers but not in love with technology
- Just want to "get the job done"
- Don't want to read a lot of material

The user-friendly reference

- The fastest access to the one best way to get things done
- Bite-sized information for quick and easy reference
- Nontechnical approach in plain English
- Real-world analogies to explain new concepts
- Troubleshooting tips to help solve problems
- Visual elements and screen pictures that reinforce topics
- Expert authors who are experienced in training and instruction

Special Edition Using for accomplished users

Who should use this book?

Proficient computer users who:

- Have a more technical understanding of computers
- Are interested in technological trends
- Want in-depth reference information
- Prefer more detailed explanations and examples

The most complete reference

- Thorough explanations of various ways to perform tasks
- In-depth coverage of all topics
- Technical information cross-referenced for easy access
- Professional tips, tricks, and shortcuts for experienced users
- Advanced troubleshooting information with alternative approaches
- Visual elements and screen pictures that reinforce topics
- Technically qualified authors who are experts in their fields
- "Techniques from the Pros" sections with advice from well-known computer professionals

Complete and Return this Card for a *FREE* Computer Book Catalog

Thank you for purchasing this book! You have purchased a superior computer book written expressly for your needs. To continue to provide the kind of up-to-date, pertinent coverage you've come to expect from us, we need to hear from you. Please take a minute to complete and return this self-addressed, postage-paid form. In return, we'll send you a free catalog of all our computer books on topics ranging from word processing to programming and the internet.

Mr. ☐ Mrs. ☐ Ms. ☐ Dr. ☐

Name (first) ☐☐☐☐☐☐☐☐☐☐☐ (M.I.) ☐ (last) ☐☐☐☐☐☐☐☐☐☐☐☐☐☐☐

Address ☐☐☐☐☐☐☐☐☐☐☐☐☐☐☐☐☐☐☐☐☐☐☐☐☐☐☐☐☐☐☐☐☐☐☐

City ☐☐☐☐☐☐☐☐☐☐☐☐☐☐☐ State ☐☐ Zip ☐☐☐☐☐ ☐☐☐☐

Phone ☐☐☐ ☐☐☐ ☐☐☐☐ Fax ☐☐☐ ☐☐☐ ☐☐☐☐

Company Name ☐☐☐☐☐☐☐☐☐☐☐☐☐☐☐☐☐☐☐☐☐☐☐☐☐☐☐☐☐☐☐☐☐

E-mail address ☐☐☐☐☐☐☐☐☐☐☐☐☐☐☐☐☐☐☐☐☐☐☐☐☐☐☐☐☐☐☐☐☐

1. Please check at least (3) influencing factors for purchasing this book.

- Front or back cover information on book ☐
- Special approach to the content ☐
- Completeness of content ☐
- Author's reputation ☐
- Publisher's reputation ☐
- Book cover design or layout ☐
- Index or table of contents of book ☐
- Price of book ☐
- Special effects, graphics, illustrations ☐
- Other (Please specify): ____________ ☐

2. How did you first learn about this book?

- Saw in Macmillan Computer Publishing catalog ☐
- Recommended by store personnel ☐
- Saw the book on bookshelf at store ☐
- Recommended by a friend ☐
- Received advertisement in the mail ☐
- Saw an advertisement in: ____________ ☐
- Read book review in: ____________ ☐
- Other (Please specify): ____________ ☐

3. How many computer books have you purchased in the last six months?

- This book only ☐
- 2 books ☐
- 3 to 5 books ☐
- More than 5 ☐

4. Where did you purchase this book?

- Bookstore ☐
- Computer Store ☐
- Consumer Electronics Store ☐
- Department Store ☐
- Office Club ☐
- Warehouse Club ☐
- Mail Order ☐
- Direct from Publisher ☐
- Internet site ☐
- Other (Please specify): ____________ ☐

5. How long have you been using a computer?

- ☐ Less than 6 months
- ☐ 6 months to a year
- ☐ 1 to 3 years
- ☐ More than 3 years

6. What is your level of experience with personal computers and with the subject of this book?

	With PCs	With subject of book
New	☐	☐
Casual	☐	☐
Accomplished	☐	☐
Expert	☐	☐

Source Code ISBN: 0-7897-0955-4

7. Which of the following best describes your job title?

- Administrative Assistant ☐
- Coordinator ☐
- Manager/Supervisor ☐
- Director ☐
- Vice President ☐
- President/CEO/COO ☐
- Lawyer/Doctor/Medical Professional ☐
- Teacher/Educator/Trainer ☐
- Engineer/Technician ☐
- Consultant ☐
- Not employed/Student/Retired ☐
- Other (Please specify): ____________ ☐

8. Which of the following best describes the area of the company your job title falls under?

- Accounting ☐
- Engineering ☐
- Manufacturing ☐
- Operations ☐
- Marketing ☐
- Sales ☐
- Other (Please specify): ____________ ☐

9. What is your age?

- Under 20 ☐
- 21-29 ☐
- 30-39 ☐
- 40-49 ☐
- 50-59 ☐
- 60-over ☐

10. Are you:

- Male ☐
- Female ☐

11. Which computer publications do you read regularly? (Please list)

____

____

____

____

____

____

____

____

Comments: ____________________

____

____

Fold here and scotch-tape to mail.

NO POSTAGE NECESSARY IF MAILED IN THE UNITED STATES

BUSINESS REPLY MAIL

FIRST-CLASS MAIL PERMIT NO. 9918 INDIANAPOLIS IN

POSTAGE WILL BE PAID BY THE ADDRESSEE

ATTN MARKETING
MACMILLAN COMPUTER PUBLISHING
MACMILLAN PUBLISHING USA
201 W 103RD ST
INDIANAPOLIS IN 46290-9042